A Colorado History

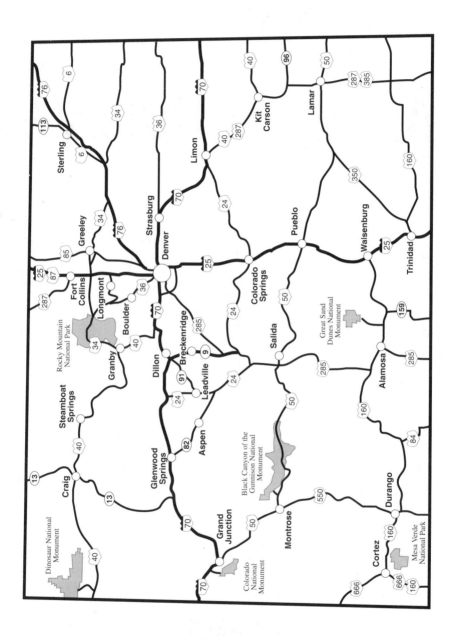

A Colorado History

Carl Ubbelohde

Maxine Benson

Duane A. Smith

E i g h t h   E d i t i o n

PRUETT

PRUETT PUBLISHING COMPANY
BOULDER, COLORADO

First edition published in 1965. Eighth edition published in 2001.
All rights reserved. No part of this book may be reproduced without written
permission from the publisher, except in the case of brief excerpts in critical
reviews and articles. Address all inquiries to: Pruett Publishing Company,
7464 Arapahoe Road, Suite A9, Boulder, CO 80303; www.pruettpublishing.com.

Library of Congress Cataloging in Publication Data

Ubbelohde, Carl
    A Colorado history / Carl Ubbelohde, Maxine Benson, Duane A. Smith.—8th ed.
      p. cm.
    Includes bibliographical references and index.
    ISBN 0-87108-923-8 (alk. paper)
     1. Colorado—History. I. Benson, Maxine. II. Smith, Duane A. III. Title.

F776.U195 2001
978.8—dc21   2001041894

Eighth Edition

10 09 08 07 06 05 04 03 02   5 4 3 2

Printed in the United States of America

Contents

Preface

Thirty-five years ago, when the first edition of this history was published, Lyndon B. Johnson was president of the United States, there was no Internet, and CNN had not been created. The population of the state of Colorado was less than half of what it is today. John A. Love was nearing the end of his first term as governor and people were cleaning up after the disastrous South Platte River flood. There was a twenty-five-cent toll on the turnpike between Boulder and Denver. Prospectors overran the Western Slope in the continuing uranium rush.

Obviously, Colorado has changed. As historians we have attempted to record and explain those changes. But we also know that some things do not change. Therefore we have attempted to record and explain the continuities in the history of Colorado throughout this book and especially in the new final chapter we have crafted for this edition. In addition, the suggested reading section has been brought up to date and some illustrations have been added.

Historians always owe a special obligation to the librarians and archivists who are the custodians of the records of the past. Over the years we have used the treasures of many institutions and have been helped in our work by many librarians and archivists. We particularly want to acknowledge our debt to the librarians of the Western History Department of the Denver Public Library, the Colorado Historical Society, and the Center of Southwest Studies in Durango. As well we thank our first publisher, Fred Pruett, our present publisher, Jim Pruett, and our editor, Alice Levine. They all have helped us as we have worked on this book. Errors in fact and interpretation, of course, are ours alone.

Carl Ubbelohde
Henry Eldridge Bourke Professor of History Emeritus
Case Western Reserve University
Cleveland, Ohio

Maxine Benson
Denver, Colorado

Duane A. Smith
Professor of History
Fort Lewis College
Durango, Colorado

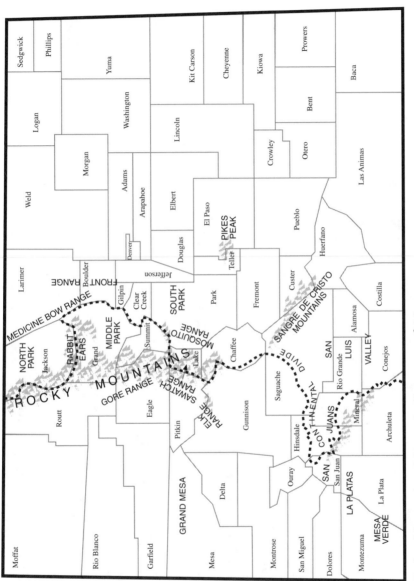

Parks, Mountains, Mountain Ranges, and Mesas

Prologue: The Land

In 1893 young Wellesley College English professor Katharine Lee Bates was one of the tourists who reached the 14,110-foot summit of Pike's Peak. Like others before and since, she was inspired in an entirely unexpected manner by the grandeur surrounding her. "I was looking out over the sea-like expanse of fertile country," she wrote later "[when the opening lines] floated into my mind":

O beautiful for spacious skies,
For amber waves of grain
For purple mountain majesties
Above the fruited plain!

She impressively put into words what many have felt when viewing the land we know as Colorado.

In Colorado's history, the land weaves a constant theme; for the Anasazi of Mesa Verde to the American of today, the land has played a major role. It has been both a blessing and a curse. Colorado has been blessed with some of the greatest varieties of scenery, climate, and land forms to be found anywhere in one limited geographical area. Yet those who misjudged or underestimated it found the land unforgiving.

The salient facts that impress visitor and resident alike are extraordinary: 56 "named summits over 14,000 feet," according to the U.S. Geological Survey—79 percent of the nation's fourteeners outside of Alaska; over one thousand peaks higher than 10,000 feet; an approximate mean elevation of 6,800 feet, which makes Colorado "the crest of the continent"; striking contrasts in altitude, from the state's lowest, 3,350 near Holly, to the highest, Mount Elbert at 14,433. Five major rivers head in the Colorado Rockies and two of these, the Rio Grande and the Colorado, are famous in American history. A crisp, dry climate sets the stage for enjoyable viewing of these wonders.

Found within Colorado's 104,247 square miles (it is the eighth largest state) are major geographical features—plains, mountains, plateaus, and deserts. Within these units lie myriad small land forms, such as the four treeless parks—North, Middle, and South parks and the San Luis Valley—cradled behind the first range of mountains. Altogether, all of these have shaped Colorado history and the life within the rectangular boundaries decreed by the government in 1861.

Colorado is not entirely mountainous, popular belief to the contrary, although since settlement, the mountains have attracted the greatest attention. Explorers, fur trappers, and settlers journeying into Colorado from the East first encountered the plains (slightly over 40 percent of the state). They rushed through to get somewhere else, and by giving the plains the name "Great American Desert" and by describing them as "flatter than a pancake," they created an image, which, unfortunately, has retained its hold for well over a century. Eastern Colorado started and remained a poor relation to the more glamorous part of the state.

The plains, nevertheless, offer a natural beauty amid what the non-discerning might picture as monotonous and uninspiring vistas. Nutritious grasses once covered these prairies, attracting the buffalo, their Indian hunters, and finally the rancher. Later came the farmers to the river bottom; then with irrigation and dry land farming methods, they moved out onto the drier uplands. Living on the prairie has always been a constant struggle with the land and its limitations. The land, more often than not, has won.

Nestled at the western end of the plains, along the foothills, are the counties and cities that today dominate Colorado. Settlements grew there for very good geographical reasons. Many started near the canyon routes into the mountains or along the rivers, which provided water for agriculture and industry. The climate is less severe in the foothills than in the mountains or on the prairies, and residents could enjoy the benefits of both within a few miles' drive.

Colorado's mountains, part of the lengthy Rocky Mountain chain, are backboned by the Continental Divide (at its highest elevations within the state). The Divide separates Colorado's river systems into those that eventually flow to the east to the Gulf of Mexico and, those that flow down the Western Slope, to the Gulf of California. As the traveler quickly found out, these mountains did not present one monolithic barrier but rather two series of ranges, with several smaller picket-lines to the west.

"The high country is distinct: bold, rocky, rugged, and dotted with lakes," wrote Kenneth Erickson and Albert W. Smith in their *Atlas of Colorado*. It is also blessed with natural resources from precious metals to snow, and scenery that has thrilled generations of tourists. This region symbolizes the Colorado of promotion and poster.

Notwithstanding such attributes, plus the minerals dug from the mountainsides and creek valleys, water is Colorado's most valuable natural resource. Rainfall remains scant; the annual state average, 16.6 inches, is not evenly distributed, creating semiarid and arid regions to exasperate settlers. Rivers radiate like spokes from the mountains (precipitation increases with elevation); where their basins stretch, settlement took root, and where there was little water, people tried to compensate with dams and irrigation ditches.

Snow has evolved into one of Colorado's most important natural resources. After World War II, skiing emerged as a major tourist attraction and an economic blessing for mountain communities; more significant, the high country serves as the watershed for much of the mountain west.

Part of the Western Slope is located in the mountains, but to the west stand the plateaus amid a touch of deserts. Isolated by the mountainous barrier, the plateaus were not settled until late, except in places where gold and silver beckoned the adventuresome; the isolation shaped development and attitudes. The Colorado River Valley dominates the heartland, while the northwest, with scant rainfall and a maze of canyons and plateaus, lingered as a beautiful and often inhospitable frontier until relatively recent discoveries of mineral fuels.

These most rugged of Colorado mountains, the San Juans, separate the southwestern corner from the rest of the Western Slope. Throughout this region, as on the plains, Coloradans have had to come to grips with a varied environment and climate. Not all the accommodations have succeeded.

Coloradans cannot guarantee it, they cannot touch it, but they can feel it—Colorado's coquettish climate is as famous an asset as are the mountains. This intangible element has been an attraction since the 1860s, appreciated best, perhaps, by traveling elsewhere to sample weather other people have to endure.

The climate varies tremendously and an old Colorado saying advises, "If you don't like the weather, stick around for a half hour or so."

Several seasons seem to pass in review some days. A lack of humidity, cool summer nights, and the complex nature of the mountain climates quickly attract attention. So does the harshness that often edges wind, rain, and snowstorms. No neat seasonal divisions fit into the maverick Colorado almanac; spring spends little time in the high country.

Always the prologue to its history, Colorado's land has often been rashly exploited, as David Lavender so aptly described in his *Colorado*. "It's a vast land and it has been a hard-used one. The Anasazi overstrained their part of it. So did the miners who recklessly slashed down the forest around their workings and who spewed such great quantities of waste into the streams that they became rivers of gray sludge. Stockmen overgrazed the mesas. Dam builders drowned the canyons and are still drowning them." Past, present, future—the land dominates Colorado. As they look to the future, Coloradans have to weigh carefully their plans against their individual and collective impact on this land and act according to that realization. In no other manner will this priceless heritage be preserved.

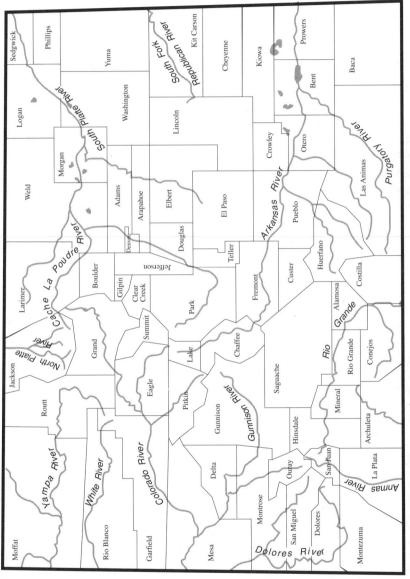

Colorado's Major Rivers and Counties

ONE

A Prehistoric Prelude:
The Dwellers in the Cliffs

High above the valley floor stands the flat tableland. In later years the Spaniards called the river the Rio de los Mancos—the River of the Cripples; they termed the tableland Mesa Verde. Still later, Americans came, ran survey lines, and found that the tableland fell within the borders of what became Colorado. But that was centuries after the original mesa dwellers had vanished from the land.

The modern tourist, driving from Durango to Cortez on U.S. 160, sees the mesa looming large to the left, rising 2,000 feet straight up from the floor of the valley. Twenty miles wide, it slopes backward fifteen miles to the south from the startling promontory. This flat tableland is cruelly severed by rugged canyons cut by eroding river water. On the mesa, and in its canyon walls, stands evidence of a civilization that had died long before any white person had climbed to the top of the tableland. No real knowledge or tradition passed from the cliff dwellers to their successors on the mesa; there is no historical link between the two civilizations. But in the remnants of the cliff dwellers we find much to ponder in casting up accounts of our own civilization.

Sometime in the unrecorded past, according to educated guesses, Homo sapiens crossed a land bridge that is now known as the Bering Strait and pushed down through the continents. The exact date of these migrations may never be known. Perhaps 15,000, perhaps 20,000 or more years ago, early humans found themselves in the New World. Nomadic, depending upon wild animals and natural foods for sustenance, the Paleo-Indians battled the elements and the terrain for their very existence. Some of them slowly changed their nomadic life and became agricultural people with fixed abodes.

The arrival of home-seeking Paleo-Indians in the Mesa Verde region probably coincided with the beginning of the Christian Era in the Old World. From that time on, for the next thirteen centuries, they occupied the area. These farmers passed through four more-or-less defined periods of advancement until, before they left the mesa, they would boast of a complex civilization.

The first era, called the Basketmaker Period, extended from approximately the year A.D. 1 to 450. As long as these people retained their undomiciled lives, they left little evidence for the archeologist to use in reconstructing the patterns of their society. With the advent of fixed abodes arose the opportunity for the accumulation of artifacts that could later be unearthed and studied; long unused tools, household utensils, and weapons give us a picture of this culture. Thus the earliest mesa dwellers of whom we have knowledge date from the era when they shed their nomadic habits and began to take up farming.

These black-haired, brown-skinned hunters learned the techniques of cultivating corn and squash, beginning the march from wanderers to stay-at-homes, with new leisure to develop arts and crafts. Of course that march was slow. Most of these early people probably never lived in houses, but sought shelter when it was needed in natural caves. Nor did they know how to make pottery. Their name, Basketmakers, comes from their substitute for pottery—skillfully constructed, often decorated baskets. They designed baskets as containers for food and supplies; they wove baskets so tightly they could hold water and by dropping heated stones into them, they could use them for cooking food.

Without houses, without pottery, the Basketmakers were handicapped in comparison with later mesa dwellers. Probably their most serious deficiency was the lack of a good weapon. The bow and arrow had not yet made its appearance, and the first Basketmakers used, instead, the atlatl. This arm-extender, or spear-thrower, was a flattened, slender stick used to extend the reach of the arm and provide greater thrust in throwing a dart or a spear.

Although the warm summer months on the mesa provided a climate in which clothing was not needed, the winter weather was severe enough to make clothes essential for comfort. The Basketmakers depended upon animal skins and woven fur strips fashioned into robes for protection against the cold. They wove sandals from yucca fibers. The only other article of clothing was a string apron worn by the women. Obviously, the Basketmakers limited their wardrobes to essentials. Nevertheless, they were fond of jewelry and trinkets, and they fashioned bones, seeds, and stones into ornaments for their necks and ears.

The Basketmakers' implements and tools ranged from wooden planting sticks to knives and scrapers, pipes and whistles. They used a *metate*, or grinding stone, to make flour of their corn. Their children were cradled in flexible reed boards with soft padding under the head, allowing the infants' skulls to develop naturally without abnormal flattening.

What elements of religion these Basketmakers professed and practiced is not easily deduced. They buried tools and jewelry with the dead, perhaps for the use of the departed in an afterlife. Burials were usually made in floors of caves or crevices in rocks; often more than one body was placed in the same grave.

Such was the culture at the end of the first developmental period. These early people had made tremendous strides from their nomadic life, conquering the secrets of planting and cultivating, harvesting and storing crops. Now modifications of those improvements slowly began to appear. The culture evolved into something so different from what it had been that a new term is needed to describe it.

The term Modified Basketmaker Period identifies the second developmental era, from A.D. 450 to 750. The changes were not simultaneous, but gradually three new elements made the Basketmakers' lives more complex. To the amazing improvements their ancestors had perfected, the Basketmakers added pottery, houses, and the bow and arrow.

The clay pottery that replaced the baskets probably was an invention borrowed from other tribes rather than indigenously developed. Even so, the mesa dwellers learned the new art slowly. Their first clumsy vessels were constructed of pure clay; the pots had little strength and less beauty. But the creators gradually added refinements: straw mixed with the clay, sand added for temper. The pots provided a startling change from the basket days. New foods were added to the diet, and new methods of water storage eased the struggle for existence against the hazards of nature.

For housing, the Modified Basketmakers developed the pithouse. They dug a hole several feet deep and from ten to twenty feet in diameter. Then, using logs as a framework for the portion above the ground, they covered the framework with interwoven reeds and grass and placed a layer of earth over this "lath" to form combination sidewalls and roof. A small opening in the center of the roof provided both a smokehole for the firepit and an entrance; they went in and out by ladder. A ventilating tunnel furnished air for the fire in the pit. They built some of their pit-houses—probably the early ones—in caves, but gradually they abandoned those inaccessible sites for more expansive locations on the top of the mesa and in the valley floors. The new sites were relatively unprotected and suggest that the Modified Basketmakers lived without particular fear of their neighbors.

During these same years the bow and arrow replaced the atlatl. The mesa people probably borrowed the bow and arrow, like pottery, from others. With characteristics peculiarly attractive to the game hunter, the new weapon offered greater accuracy at longer ranges than the atlatl.

Pottery, pithouses, and the bow and arrow were the radical advances of the era, but there were others. Beans were brought into the area as a new crop, and previously unknown varieties of corn appeared. The people domesticated the turkey, perhaps not for meat but certainly for the string-cloth fashioned from feathers to be woven into robes.

Then about A.D. 750 another demarcation line was crossed: the Developmental Pueblo Period lasted until A.D. 1100. The world *pueblo* (Spanish for village or town) has been applied to the most significant change during the eighth and following centuries. The Basketmakers had constructed most of their pithouses as single family structures. They had grouped their dwellings into villages, and some ruins indicate long rows of flat-roofed houses. In the Developmental Pueblo Period, the people experimented with more complex multiple units, with walls of various materials, suggesting a pragmatic approach to an ancient housing problem. They erected these new apartment houses all over the top of Mesa Verde. Ruins of similar structures exist in an extended area of the Four Corners region, into Utah, Arizona, and New Mexico. Population expansion seems obvious, while the unprotected nature of the mesa-top dwellings suggests a period of tribal peace.

The first pueblos were rather crudely constructed of posts and adobe. By the end of the period, however, adobe had given way to masonry, increasingly well set. Some walls were now two stories high. And the kiva (a Hopi word used by archeologists to describe the rooms that resemble the modern Pueblo ceremonial chamber) now began to resemble the standard Mesa Verde kiva. Circular, subterranean, some twelve to fourteen feet in diameter, seven or eight feet deep, with walls of dressed stone, the kiva was located in front of the living rooms. Masonry pillars supported the roof of logs and adobe. Like the earlier pithouses, the kiva's only door was a small opening in the center of the roof, which also served as a smokehole. A vertical shaft brought air for the ceremonial fire on the floor. The *sipapu*, or small opening into the ground, a symbolic entrance to the underworld or Mother Earth, indicates religious purposes for the kiva, although it probably was used for recreation as well. The resemblance between these kivas and the modern Pueblo ceremonial chambers affords an important clue to possible relationships between the prehistoric mesa dwellers and modern Pueblo tribes.

Thus the Developmental Pueblo society moved in architecture from the pithouse to the pueblo; from relatively crude to quite advanced construction. And there were other changes. The dull, natural hues of the pottery were abandoned for clear white, which showed designs more advantageously. Flat metates, as contrasted with the earlier trough-shaped stones, provided improvement in grinding corn.

The most novel change was the introduction of the wooden cradle board replacing the Basketmakers' pliable, pillowed reed-and-grass cradle. When archeologists unearth Pueblo skeletons they find the skulls deformed, with an exaggerated flattening of the back. For a time scholars believed that the Basketmakers and the Pueblos were two distinct, unrelated groups because of this radical difference in head shapes. More recently, with added study of physical characteristics, many authorities have come to believe that the skull differences resulted largely from the type of cradle board. The hard wooden board of the Pueblos was probably borrowed from some other group and became a popular fad.

The last two centuries of life on the mesa saw the climax of the long advance from simple agriculture to a complex culture: the Great, or Classic, Pueblo Period of A.D. 1100 to 1300. During these two hundred years the Pueblos achieved their finest architecture. They carefully cut and laid up masonry walls; they plastered and decorated some of those walls with designs. Their villages became larger, containing many rooms; some rose to heights of three and four floors. The ruins of Far

View House provide an interesting example. Here the people built an integrated complex of living and storage rooms, kivas, a walled court, and a tower.

Farming also reached new heights. Most crops were cultivated on the mesa top, but some small, terrace-like patches at the heads of the canyons were also used. In the floors of the canyons, the Pueblo people constructed dams for water storage—the earliest irrigation works in Colorado. Corn, beans, squash, and gourds were the main crops. For some items the people probably were dependent on trading expeditions outside the region, perhaps to the south. Cotton probably was not grown in any quantity on Mesa Verde, so the presence of woven cotton cloth among the ruins suggests trade with others. Salt, seashells, and turquoise also were acquired through trade.

This commerce with other people is one of the fascinating imponderables of these mysterious people. Just one old bill-of-lading would tell us much about them. But the Pueblo people never developed a system of writing. And that was only one of their limitations. They had no horses or livestock. They never developed the wheel. They used no metals.

Despite these limitations, the Classic Pueblo Period was a time of greatness. Some archeologists also believe it was a period of regimentation, with previously developed patterns used over and over again. The kivas became highly standardized, suggesting more rigid ceremonial practices. There also appears to have been a drawing together of the population and possibly a decline in total numbers. The pueblo dwellings became much larger, and tall round towers were built. Since the towers were usually connected by an underground tunnel with the kivas, they may have been used in ceremonies. But their strategic location, and possible use as watch towers, also suggests the need for vigilant defense.

And then the most startling innovation occurred. The people deserted the mesa top and built their pueblos in the caves in the walls of the canyons. Many families were involved in this descent to the caves; estimates of 600 to 800 separate cliff dwellings demonstrate the magnitude of the migration. Paradoxically, it was here, within the confined caves, that the pueblo builders produced their architectural masterpieces: Spruce Tree House, Square Tower House, and, most marvelous of all, Cliff Palace.

Cliff Palace contained more than 200 rooms, forming a city in itself. It was built in terraces, rising three and four stories in places, with twenty-three kivas and housing adequate for more than 200 people. The

Long House, Mesa Verde, photographed by Swedish archeologist Gustaf Nordenskiöld in 1891.

quality of the masonry construction and the interior plastering and painting of the walls in red and white represent refinements beyond anything known before.

Again the suggestion seems obvious: Defensible sites for homes had become a necessity. Certainly the cliff dwellings in the almost inaccessible canyon walls provided an uncommon measure of security. Apparently some great danger, not present earlier, had come to threaten the mesa dwellers. But who or what that danger might have been can only be guessed at. Raids by nomadic tribes might have provided the impetus to drive the people from the mesa into the caves of the canyons. Or they may have fled a civil war. Most of the Anasazi, as they became known, continued to live in valleys and mesas throughout the region. Only a small minority lived at Mesa Verde.

Whatever caused the concentration, it marked the beginning of the end of the Pueblo people in the Mesa Verde area. For a few more generations the cliff dwellers lived in their apartment houses in the caves. Then, at the end of the thirteenth century, they withdrew. They probably drifted southward; at least, tribal traditions of the Tewa, Hopi, and Zuni Indians tell of earlier migrations from the north.

The fact that the last quarter of the century—the years from 1272 to 1299—were years of extended drought may partly explain the withdrawal. They may have thought their gods had abandoned them and they may have decided to seek other lands with better, more reliable water supplies. But they had survived earlier long droughts, so there had to be another reason for their departure.

Perhaps it was a combination of overpopulation and environmental changes. They had farmed the same land for centuries, decreasing its fertility, and they had hunted and cut timber in the same region, reducing these resources. At the same time greater numbers of Anasazi lived in the area; population pressures, decreasing natural resources, and a changing environment may have been too much to overcome. For the first, but not the last time in Colorado, humans and the environment had clashed.

By the end of the thirteenth century, the pueblos had become ghost towns, the fields overrun with sagebrush. With their human inhabitants gone, the sophisticated structures suffered the usual ravages of wind and rain and began to decay and crumble. Before the processes of ruin had entirely erased the traces of these people, people of the modern world stumbled into the area. In time we would act to preserve what remained as a monument to a civilization that had vanished—a prehistoric civilization of Colorado.

TWO

A Spanish Borderland

About two centuries after the cliff dwellers left Mesa Verde one of the great divides of human history was crossed. In 1492 three small vessels flying the Spanish flag and commanded by Christopher Columbus made their landfall in the Caribbean Sea. The Old World and the New World had met, and a new era had begun.

The frontiers of the Western Hemisphere now beckoned the leading nations of western Europe. Exploration, exploitation, and colonization became the great international games. The prizes—power, prestige, glorification of God through conversion of the heathen, and riches of gold and silver for royal treasuries—were enticing lures. For more than three centuries the game continued as the continents of America became pawns of the kings of Europe.

The Spanish nation was clearly in the lead during the sixteenth century. The Court of Madrid had financed Columbus and with the help of the papacy, it gained a demarcation between its lands and those of its then most dangerous rival, neighboring Portugal. Spain hurried preparations for additional voyages of discovery and conquest.

From its original toehold in the Caribbean islands, Spain pushed its fledgling empire in all directions. By 1521 Hernán Cortés had reduced

Mexico to a Spanish province, starting the flow of riches from its gold and silver mines eastward across the Atlantic. Reaching out in search of further riches and souls for conversion, the conquerors continued their march.

Gold was the great lure that led all onward; beyond the horizon might be a second Mexico. The expedition led by Don Pánfilo de Narváez from Florida westward in 1528 was perhaps typical of many. In some ways, however, it was unusual. Only four men escaped death from a shipwreck on the shores of the Texas Gulf coast. One of the survivors was Cabeza de Vaca, the treasurer of the expedition. With his three comrades, he wandered the wilds of the interior regions of present-day Texas for six years. When these four "ghosts of the past" finally found their way to Mexico, they brought with them hair-raising tales of their exploits and rumors about seven cities of great wealth, situated somewhere to the north.

The rumors were similar to a European legend of seven bishops who had built seven cities on an island called Antillia in the Atlantic Ocean. That similarity should have made de Vaca's stories suspect, but in a new day of new worlds anything could be believed. To test the tale Antonio de Mendoza, the viceroy of New Spain, proposed a small scouting expedition to explore the northern frontier. He commissioned a Franciscan, Fray Marcos de Niza, to conduct the test. Estevan, an Arab Moor who had been with de Vaca, accompanied the friar. In 1539 Marcos and Estevan hurried northward from Mexico. They crossed the barren wastes of Sonora and eventually arrived in the Zuni country of what is now western New Mexico. Marcos sent Estevan on ahead; he never saw him again, for the Zuni killed the Moor. The friar, learning of Estevan's fate, dared not go directly to the pueblo. But he climbed a ridge overlooking the buildings and viewed them from a distance. He seems to have assumed that he had found the fabulous Seven Cities.

Marcos hurried back to Mexico with his report corroborating de Vaca's rumor. The viceroy decided to mount a full-scale expedition. He selected his personal friend, thirty-year-old Don Francisco Vásquez de Coronado, to lead the great enterprise. Together they gathered a remarkably strong force to search for the Seven Cities, now called Cibola. Young Spanish noblemen eagerly volunteered for adventure and a chance at the gold. Some 200 horsemen, 70 foot soldiers, and almost 1,000 Indians joined the command. Livestock were driven along as a self-propelled food supply. The assembled expedition made a magnificent display as it rendezvoused at Compostella on the Pacific side of New Spain in the spring of 1540.

Once the march began, the glamour and the splendor wilted quickly. Northward from Compostella the caravan moved through desert country, finally reaching Hawikuh, the first of the Zuni pueblos. Cibola turned out to be no towering city of gold but only an unimposing village of Indian farmers. Fray Marcos's examination had been too hasty; his reports appeared fraudulent.

From Zuni, Coronado turned his forces eastward. Passing the Sky City of Acoma Pueblo, they traveled to the villages in the upper Rio Grande Valley. They spent the winter (1540-1541) near present-day Albuquerque. There they heard reports that the gold they were seeking was somewhere northeastward, at Gran Quivira. The Pueblo Indians probably hoped to lure the Spanish away from their villages with these rumors. When spring came, Coronado set out to discover Quivira. He and his men journeyed into what is now the Texas Panhandle and then turned north into the Arkansas River Valley in what is now Kansas. There they discovered that the villages of the Wichita Indians were even less imposing, even less like Cibola, than the pueblos of New Mexico.

Coronado turned his forces back again to the Rio Grande Valley, where they spent another winter. When warm weather returned they retraced their long pathway to Mexico. So ended the Coronado expedition—without silver or gold.

Of course, knowledge of the country had been gained and later colonizers could profit from that. And substantial foundations had been added to Spain's claim to the northern regions. But prospecting had turned sour. For decades thereafter, the Spaniards diverted their eyes from the north. More than a half-century passed before interest in the Rio Grande Valley revived.

When Spain again looked toward pueblo-land, it was for a different reason. England's bold sea dog, Francis Drake, had sailed his *Golden Hind* into the Pacific; Spain was certain he had found the Northwest Passage. To secure its claims against rival England, Spain decided to settle its northern frontier. In 1598, Juan de Oñate started for the valley of the pueblos, under contract from the Crown, with 130 soldier-settler families, a band of Franciscan friars, 270 Indian and black slaves, and 7,000 head of stock. The "kingdom and provinces of New Mexico" were born that year. By 1609 Spain had founded the Royal City of Santa Fe, for many years to be the capital of the northern outposts of the empire, 1,500 miles from the seat of the viceroyalty at Mexico City.

Cross and Crown played dual roles in New Mexico as they had earlier in New Spain. The missionary friars were as eager to save the souls of Pueblo Indians as soldiers were to stretch the boundaries of the empire. Together priest and captain established an uneasy ascendancy over the Pueblo tribes as far north as Taos. The Spanish tried to protect the Pueblo people against the nomadic tribes of the plains. In the seventeenth century, the Apaches, and their kinsmen the Navajos, kept up a perpetual pressure on the fringes of the New Mexican outpost.

The widespread Apache family, an Athapascan tribe of unexact origins, was divided into many subgroups. Together they encircled the pueblo region. Not all of the Indians were unfriendly; those roaming the regions to the northeast—called by the Spaniards the Palomas, Quartelejos, Carlaneas, and Jicarillas—tended to keep the peace. But the Faraon Apaches on the east and the Gila Apaches and Navajos on the west seemed to be constantly hostile.

Farther north, in the mountains whose streams fed the Rio Grande, lived the then-friendly Utes. These Indians probably were originally from the northwest, for they were allied in language with the Shoshone family. They never practiced agriculture, living instead by the spoils of their hunts and wars. The Utes were the most permanent residents of the Colorado region. They were in possession of the mountain passes at the time of the earliest Spanish penetration and would remain there far into the future.

It was not easy for Spain to devise a consistent policy toward the nomadic tribes. The friars attempted to spread the gospel among them, but the lack of fixed abodes and the hostility of most of the tribes made conversions difficult. White settlers and their pueblo converts traded with the plains hunters, especially at the Taos fairs where the Indians exchanged deerskins, buffalo hides, and captive slaves for knives, horses, beads, and trinkets. But when raids endangered the mission villages, warfare ensued. And when runaway slaves from the pueblos sought sanctuary among the nomads, the Spaniards used force, if necessary, to win them back.

Gradually, through expeditions against Indians and journeys to retrieve fugitives, the Spaniards pushed northward from Santa Fe, acquainting themselves with the area of present-day Colorado. Although it may not have been the first such expedition, sometime in the years between 1664 and 1680 Juan de Archuleta led a search party north from Taos to find and recapture Pueblo Indians who had escaped to a place called El Quartelejo. The exact location of El Quartelejo has never been determined, but it was probably in southeastern Colorado, fifty or sixty miles east of the present city of Pueblo. From Archuleta's expedition, the Spaniards learned about the valley of the Arkansas River, known to them as the Nepesta, or Nepestle, River.

Toward the end of the seventeenth century, Spanish control of New Mexico was almost nonexistent. In 1680 the Pueblos revolted against the Europeans. The white colonists who escaped being killed fled southward to the Franciscan mission near El Paso where they remained for twelve years, waiting for a day of return. In 1692, under the leadership of Don Diego de Vargas, Spain reestablished supremacy over the pueblo villages.

During these same years significant changes occurred in the regions north of Santa Fe. The Comanches, an offshoot of the Shoshone tribe of Wyoming, moved their customary hunting grounds south to escape the pressures of the Sioux. Their linguistic kinsfolk, the Utes, joined them in wars against the Apaches and the Pueblos.

And there were other newcomers. Following La Salle's trip down the Mississippi River in 1682, French traders and explorers traveled up the rivers that fed the Father of Waters. France soon claimed the drainage basins of the many tributaries to the west, stretching all the way to the crest of the Rocky Mountains. As French traders advanced up the Red and Arkansas Rivers from Louisiana, their trade with the plains Indians in arms and horses flourished.

Pueblo revolts, Comanche and Ute raids, and French aggression each played a part in opening the northern regions to the Spaniards. The return to Santa Fe in 1692 under Vargas did not immediately end Pueblo efforts to rid themselves of the Spanish. In 1696 revolt flared again. The Picuris Pueblos fled northeastward to El Quartelejo. In 1706 Juan de Ulibarri, in command of 40 troops and 100 Indian allies, marched out to bring them back. Ulibarri traversed the region from Taos to the site of the present city of Pueblo and then turned east to Quartelejo. Here, in a formal ceremony, he claimed the area for his Spanish sovereign, Philip V.

Ulibarri brought unwelcome news to the officials in Santa Fe. French traders had successfully penetrated the western plains. The

Quartelejo Apaches reported frequent raids on their people by the powerful Pawnee tribe from the Platte River region to the north. The Pawnee were friends of the French; French arms and tools captured in skirmishes were exhibited to prove it.

Similar disquieting evidence was uncovered thirteen years later, in 1719. Don Antonio Valverde, the governor of New Mexico, set forth that year on an extensive expedition to punish the Utes and Comanches. Valverde led his men through the country of friendly Jicarilla Apaches in northeastern New Mexico to the headwaters of the Purgatory River (then the Rio de las Animas Perdidas en Purgatorio—the River of the Souls Lost in Purgatory), to the Arkansas River, and then east to the vicinity of present-day Las Animas. Here they were met by Quartelejo Apaches who substantiated the rumors of French activity and impressed upon them the problems they faced from raiding Comanches, Utes, and Pawnees.

The viceroyalty at Mexico City seemed to fear the French menace much more than the Indians. A Council of War in January 1720 ordered Governor Valverde to conduct reconnaissance against the intruding French. In response, Valverde sent an expedition led by Don Pedro de Villasur northeast to seek out the French. Villasur followed the now traditional route to El Quartelejo and from there continued north until he reached the Platte River. He then turned his force to follow the Platte downstream. Somewhere near the forks of the Platte, the Pawnees ambushed the Spanish, killing thirty-two of the forty-two soldiers, including the leader, Villasur.

The authorities at Mexico City now urged the establishment of a presidio, or military garrison, at El Quartelejo as a buffer against the French. The New Mexican officials, however, argued against it. They claimed the location was too distant and too exposed to be safe, and proposed the site called La Jicarilla, closer to the New Mexican settlements, as an alternative. In the end, no outpost was established at all. Rather, the Spanish invited the friendly Apaches to resettle in the Taos Valley.

Actually, the French intrusion was temporarily halted. The Comanches had no desire to allow their Apache enemies to receive French arms and had created a buffer zone through which French traders did not pass. But farther north the French investigated other routes. Etienne Veniard de Bourgmont, in 1724, moved as far west as present central Kansas, presumably searching for a trade route from the Mississippi Valley to Santa Fe. And after him, in 1739, such a route actually was opened by two French brothers, Pierre and Paul Mallet, who traveled from

Kaskaskia, in Illinois, up to the Missouri and Platte Rivers and then southward to the Arkansas River. From there an Indian guide led them to Santa Fe. An embryonic trade route now connected French and Spanish New World settlements.

Mid-eighteenth century witnessed remarkable changes on the northern New Mexican frontier. The Comanches had driven the northern Apaches from their homelands. Some of the Apaches sought sanctuary near the pueblos in the Rio Grande Valley. Others fled farther south. With French arms readily available, Comanche raids on the New Mexican settlements increased.

In addition, the Ute-Comanche alliance came to an end. The reasons for the break between the former allies are unclear, but the effect for the Spanish was beneficial. Now the Utes made peace at Taos and in a "diplomatic revolution," joined the Apaches and Spanish in their wars against the Comanches.

The rivalry between France and Spain also began to abate. In Europe, Spain and France were now allied in wars against Great Britain. This, of itself, did not bring a sudden end to their rivalry in America. Spain still viewed French control of Louisiana with sufferance and continued its determined policy of keeping the French from extending their province farther toward the southwest. But in 1762, France ceded to Spain all of Louisiana west of the Mississippi River. The northern frontier was again Spanish land and would remain so for the next forty years.

Spain's interest now shifted to the regions northwest of Santa Fe. Three years after the cession of Louisiana, in 1765, Don Juan Maria de Rivera led an exploring party from Santa Fe along the San Juan Mountains to the Gunnison River in search of precious metals. Rivera's party returned with ore samples, although they were not rich enough to generate great excitement. Even so, other prospectors probably followed Rivera into the La Plata region. At least, by the next decade the principal rivers there were designated by Spanish names.

New dangers now began to appear in the Far West, where Russia and Great Britain were threatening Spain's Pacific coast claims. The authorities of New Spain began to consider the feasibility of an overland route to connect the California settlements with those of the Rio Grande Valley and northern Mexico. This consideration led to what some historians have called the greatest Spanish exploring adventure in the Southwest.

In 1776, year of independence for some far-off British colonies along the Atlantic coast, two Spanish priests started northwestward from Santa

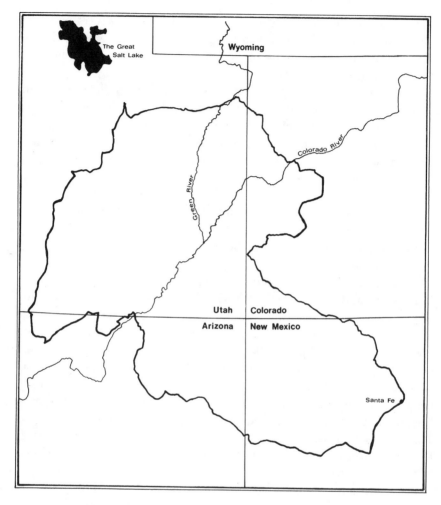

Route of Dominguez and Escalante in 1776.

Fe. Fathers Francisco Atanasio Domínguez and Silvestre Vélez de Escalante, with eight other men (several of whom had been with Rivera earlier and thus knew something of the country they now traversed) worked their way along the San Juan Mountains to the Dolores River. From there the expedition traveled to the Gunnison and then north to the White River. Turning west, they headed toward the Great Salt Lake. The heavy snows and winter storms forced them to return to Santa Fe without reaching California, but the two Franciscan friars had led the first white expedition through some of the most treacherous terrain in all North America.

Meanwhile, encounters with the Indians continued. Since the Comanches were particularly dangerous, the Spanish believed that crushing them would have excellent effects in dealing later with other tribes. In 1779 Governor Don Juan Bautista de Anza, with 573 men, later to be joined by Apache and Ute allies, traveled northward from Santa Fe into the San Luis Valley. They crossed Poncha Pass and a segment of South Park. Instead of Comanches they found only a large herd of grazing buffalo. Climbing the Front Range, they dropped down onto the eastern foothills. There were the Comanches, led by Cuerno Verde—Greenhorn—their great chief. Anza's men delivered a resounding defeat to the Indians. Cuerno Verde, his eldest son, and some of his most renowned warriors died from wounds inflicted at the final encounter on Greenhorn Creek near the base of Greenhorn Mountain.

The Comanches were ready to make peace with the Spaniards, but an obstacle stood in the way. The friendly Utes, now sworn enemies of the Comanches, feared the effect such a peace might have on their own relations with the Spanish. Consequently, the first step was to ally the Utes and Comanches again. This Governor Anza accomplished in 1786, after which peace with the Comanches was possible. After suitable ceremonies the Comanches agreed to treaty terms with the Spanish, promising to give up their nomadic life and settle in villages after the manner of the Pueblos. Spain agreed to help them in the transition. Governor Anza selected a site in the Arkansas Valley, probably near the present city of Pueblo. He sent laborers and supplies to build houses, seeds for planting fields, sheep, and cattle.

The Spanish called the intended settlement San Carlos. Begun in 1787, it failed early. The first year a Comanche woman died at the village. The Indians considered this a divine sign of the disapproval of their gods. They hurried away and the Spanish could not lure them back. So ended the first and last attempt by the Spanish to settle a village within the boundaries of present-day Colorado.

From Coronado in 1540 to short-lived San Carlos in 1787, Spain failed to push its settlements north of Santa Fe. To the east colonies were established in Texas; on the Pacific coast Spain's missions in California flourished. But the stretches north of New Mexico were never settled. In its search for precious metals, Spain failed to uncover the riches of the

Rocky Mountains. The "northern mystery" eluded Spain. Utes and Comanches retained their hunting grounds, unspoiled by adobe pueblo,
mission, or presidio. In the coming century, other men would dig the
gold and silver the Spanish sought, but failed to find, in the northern
borderland.

THREE

EXPLORING LOUISIANA

With the closing of the eighteenth century, European domination of North America neared an end. On the Atlantic seaboard, thirteen British colonies waged a war for independence and established a new republic. The United States of America stood as a model for others who pursued revolution and independence.

Europe was soon rocked by the wars of the French Revolution and the Napoleonic struggles that followed. Out of those upheavals came a large severance of territory from the empire called New Spain. In 1800 Napoleon Bonaparte secured for France its old colony of Louisiana, giving to Spain in return a kingdom in Italy. At the same time of this retrocession, France agreed that it would neither sell nor trade Louisiana to any other country.

But Napoleon's dreams of a revived French empire in North America vanished with his failure to control Hispaniola in the Caribbean. He offered Louisiana to the United States, and the young republic quickly grabbed the bargain. In 1803, in the most advantageous real estate transaction in its history, the United States doubled its size. Through the purchase, the eastern stretches of the former Spanish frontier became the territory of the United States.

The American people could not fully appreciate the bargain they had made, for the land beyond the Mississippi River was almost completely unknown to them. But official expeditions, financed by the federal government, soon started westward to gather information about the new territories. The famed Lewis and Clark Expedition, planned before the territory was purchased, traversed the northern regions to the Pacific coast. And at the time that Lewis and Clark headed homeward, another exploring expedition was dispatched toward the southwest, led by a young lieutenant of the U.S. Army, Zebulon Montgomery Pike.

Lieutenant Pike was born in New Jersey in 1779. He had entered the army at an early age and had risen to the rank of lieutenant by 1805. In that year the army gave him his first opportunity at exploring. He headed an investigation of the upper Mississippi basin, visiting trading posts and taking official possession of the area for the United States.

The next year, on July 15, 1806, twenty-seven-year-old Pike set out from Fort Belle Fontaine, above St. Louis, on his southwestern expedition. Most of the twenty-two men with him were veterans from the Mississippi expedition. Their instructions were to return a party of Osage Indians who had been captured by the Potawatomis to their native villages; to arrive, if possible, at some "understanding" with the Comanches; to observe the geography, natural history, and topography; and to collect mineral and botanical specimens. When they reached the Arkansas River they were to split into two groups. Some of the men would descend the river to its mouth; the others would follow the river to its source, locate the headwaters of the Red River, and then descend that stream.

Pike's group traveled by boat to the Osage Indian villages near the present boundary between Kansas and Missouri. There they obtained horses and crossed the prairies to the Republican River where they met the old allies of the French, the Pawnees. An expedition of 600 mounted Spanish troops from Santa Fe, led by Lieutenant Don Facundo Malgares, had recently visited the Pawnees. In some way the New Mexican officials had heard of Pike's expedition and had sent Lieutenant Malgares to find him.

The Spaniards appeared formidable to the Pawnees, especially compared with the small American force. The Indians advised Pike to turn east and forget about exploring, explaining that they had promised the Spanish they would warn Americans against advancing farther west. Although somewhat apprehensive that the Pawnees might try to detain him, Pike determined to move on to the Arkansas River.

At the Big Bend of that river, Pike divided his party as directed. Six men descended the river in canoes while Pike led the rest of the company upstream. In mid-November they sighted the Rocky Mountains, giving "with one accord . . . three *cheers* to the *Mexican Mountains.*" By the end of the month they had reached the present site of Pueblo where they built a breastwork of logs for defense against hostile Indians or Spaniards.

North of the breastwork was a high peak that Pike had earlier described as a "small blue cloud" when he first saw it from the prairies. He now decided to try to reach its summit. Two and one-half days of climbing brought Pike and his companions near the top of Mount Miller (or possibly Blue Mountain), from which they could see the high peak they had set out to climb, still miles away. Pike decided that "no human being could have ascended to its pinical [*sic*]" in the condition he and his men were in; they wore only light cotton overalls. Snow lay waist-deep on the ground. So Pike failed to reach the summit, but he was the first American to describe the mountain, and men who came after him called it Pike's Peak.

Moving west from the breastwork, the explorers camped one night near the present site of Florence; the next night found them at the mouth of the Royal Gorge. Pike believed he was now near the headwaters of the Arkansas, convinced that the narrow canyon indicated the main body of the river was below and not above him. He detoured to the north, moved into South Park—the Bayou Salado of the Spanish—and examined the regions of the upper Arkansas, mistaking the river for the Red. It was now late in December. Supplies were running low. For two days before Christmas the men were practically without food. Then they found buffalo on which they feasted to celebrate the holiday, deep in the ranges of the Rockies.

By the fifth of January they had followed the Arkansas downstream through its gorge, discovering to their intense disappointment that they were back again where they had started. They had not found the Red River; their situation grew more and more desperate. Their horses were unfit for riding and their supplies were almost entirely expended. Pike built a blockhouse and left two men there; still determined to find the Red River, he led the rest of his company southward.

They endured incredible hardships. But despite frozen feet and near starvation, they crossed the Sangre de Cristo range into the San Luis Valley. When they reached the Conejos River, Pike and his men built a fort

Pike's Stockade, as reconstructed by the Colorado Historical Society.

of cottonwood logs. There the Stars and Stripes fluttered for the first time in the breezes of the San Luis Valley.

Pike thought he was on the Red River; actually, the Conejos is a tributary of the Rio Grande. Since they were west of the Rio Grande, the Americans were interlopers on presumed Spanish soil. In February, scouts from New Mexico found them and invited them to go to Santa Fe. Although politely phrased, the request was obviously a command, not a casual suggestion. Knowing that he had not force to fight the Spanish, Pike agreed to go.

In Santa Fe, Governor Joaquín del Real Alencaster confiscated Pike's papers and interrogated him at length. The governor seemed convinced that the Americans were spies and decided to send them to Chihuahua, 550 miles to the south. Alencaster assigned Lieutenant Malgares the duty of escorting Pike's party on most of the long journey. So the Spanish officer who had ridden out to intercept Pike on the Kansas plains the year before now guarded the American prisoners.

At Chihuahua, Governor Nemesio Salcedo, after examining both the men and their papers, decided to keep the papers and send the men home. Again under guard, Pike and his companions were marched to the Louisiana-Texas border, where in July 1807 the Spanish released them.

Pike had been promoted to captain during the expedition and other promotions followed. During the War of 1812, the thirty-four-year-old Pike, then a brigadier general, was fatally wounded leading the American attack on York (Toronto), Canada.

In some respects, Pike's expedition proved disappointing; he failed to find the source of the Arkansas and Red Rivers. But he gathered valuable information about the geography and natural resources of the Southwest. Even though the Spanish confiscated many of his papers, Pike published his observations and impressions of what he had done and seen. His report, printed in 1810, was eagerly read in the United States. Europeans seemed no less interested as editions of Pike's journal appeared in England, France, Germany, and Holland. Zebulon Montgomery Pike was the first American—the first writer in English—to describe the mountain of his name and other such landmarks as South Park, the Royal Gorge, the Sangre de Cristo Mountains, and the San Luis Valley. Add to that his descriptions of the Spanish borderlands, from Taos to Chihuahua, and it is understandable why an expansion-minded America delighted in his report.

When Pike made his exploratory journey into the Southwest, a definitive boundary had not been negotiated to divide American Louisiana from the provinces of New Spain. At the time of the purchase, Talleyrand, the French foreign minister, is reported to have answered questions by the Americans about the limits of Louisiana: "You have made a noble bargain and I presume you will make the best of it." "Making the best of it" was exactly what the Americans proceeded to do. The northern boundary was established in negotiations with Great Britain in 1818 at the forty-ninth parallel, from the Lake of the Woods on the east to the Stony (Rocky) Mountains on the west. The following year John Quincy Adams, the American secretary of state, negotiated a treaty with Spain delineating the southern and western boundaries. The two nations agreed on a line drawn westward along the Red River, north on the one hundredth meridian, west again on the Arkansas River, north from its source to the forty-second parallel, and from there straight west to the Pacific Ocean. Everything north and east of the line was American; everything south and west was Spanish.

In the area now definitely established as U.S. territory lived Indians who were not consulted about their preference of white man's rule. The boundary line was drawn and agreed to at Washington and Madrid without regard for the inhabitants of the region. Yet while white men argued the fine points of their dividing line, the Indians were engaged in determining their own possession of the region.

The high country of the Central Rockies was still in the hands of the Utes. The Weeminuche, Mouache, and Capote (Southern Utes) lived in the southwestern corner of future Colorado; the Tabeguache, or Uncompahgre, band in the central Western Slope area; and the Grand River, Yampa, and Uintah bands formed the Northern Utes. They kept a watchful eye on the plains to the east, where another transition in tribal occupancy was developing. In much the same fashion as the Comanches had moved south, pushing the Apaches from the Eastern Slope, new tribes from the north now were filling up the land between the Arkansas and Platte Rivers. Among the newcomers were the Kiowas, drifting south from the headwaters of the Yellowstone and Missouri Rivers. In time the Kiowas became friends of the Comanches and joined them in their hunting grounds, south of the Arkansas River.

At about the same time, or possibly a little later, two other new tribes took up a roving residence on the Eastern Slope plains. Both of these tribes were from the great Algonquian linguistic stock of the northeast: the Arapahoes and the Cheyennes. The Arapahoes originally had come from the Great Lakes region. Pressure, presumably by the Sioux (beyond which undoubtedly was similar pressure from advancing white people), caused the Arapahoes to move south and west. As they took up temporary hunting grounds in the Black Hills, they were joined by their linguistic kinsfolk, the Cheyennes.

White men first encountered the Cheyenne tribes in the middle of the eighteenth century in northern Minnesota. When they left the upper Mississippi Valley, like the Arapahoes, they turned from a somewhat sedentary people to nomads on the plains. Moving first to the Missouri River, they found homes near the junction of that waterway and the Cheyenne River. From there, with the pressure of the Sioux still upon them, they wandered into the Black Hills and friendship with the Arapahoes.

Together the two tribes then moved along the eastern base of the Rockies, forcing the Kiowas to join the Comanches south of the Arkansas River. Perhaps by 1815, that river divided the tribes as an uneasy, unstable boundary. Sometime around the year 1840, the Arapahoes and Cheyennes would effect a peace settlement with the Kiowas and Comanches. Meanwhile, the undying friendship and alliance between the Arapahoes and the Cheyennes continued. The relationship begun in the Black Hills would remain even after the Cheyenne tribe had divided into two groups, with a southern segment clustered in the reaches of the Arkansas River and a northern group living in the area of the North Platte and Yellowstone headwaters.

These, then, were the tribes of the Rocky Mountain frontier at the time Spain and the United States arranged their international boundary: the Utes in the mountains, the Cheyennes and Arapahoes on the plains from the Arkansas to the Platte Rivers, and the Kiowas and Comanches south of the Arkansas River. Toward the east, the Pawnee tribe chased buffalo in the Republican River area; in the North Platte region, the Sioux sometimes hunted in the outskirts of the Cheyenne and Arapahoe lands.

All of the tribes were nomadic, except the Pawnee, who built earth lodges. The others lived in tepees or lodges made of buffalo skins stretched over a framework of light poles; these abodes were easy to dismantle and transport. The Indians' basic diet was buffalo meat, but they also enjoyed meals of antelope, deer, rabbit, and dog. Buffalo and deer skins (often elaborately decorated) provided clothing. The bow and arrow gave the tribes an excellent weapon for both hunt and war. With portable lodges, horses for transportation, and a buffalo culture that made use of every item of the shaggy beast, the plains Indians wandered as game and weather directed. Although their areas of hunting and "home" were more or less well delineated, the tribes did not live completely isolated from each other. The plains Indians sometimes sought pines for lodge poles in the mountains; when buffalo became scarce in the mountain parks, the Utes would descend to the plains for some killing. Between the Arapahoe and Cheyenne tribes on the plains and the Utes in the mountains, hostility was ever present.

One of the first reports that the Arapahoes and Cheyennes had come to live in the Eastern Slope area was brought back to the eastern states in 1820 by the members of the Long Expedition to the mountains. For thirteen years after the return of Pike and his men, the western region had received scant attention from official Washington. Other events took the limelight—the continuing maritime problems with Great Britain and France; the actual war with Great Britain; the settlement of the Indian problems in the Old Northwest and in the Florida region; the expansion of population, industry, and agriculture in the burst of prosperity immediately following the war.

Then, with the settlement of the boundaries of Louisiana, official attention again was directed toward the West. Initial plans for a new reconnaissance of the western reaches were much more ambitious and extensive than the blueprint for Pike's journey had been. The Yellowstone Expedition, as the public liked to call the new survey, envisioned a force of men moving up the Missouri River, searching the area for scientific information and establishing a federal fort at the Mandan Indian villages or at the mouth of the Yellowstone River. The troops would keep the peace between whites and Indians, negate the influence of British traders, and open a route to Oregon and, perhaps, even to China beyond. The army commissioned Colonel Henry Atkinson to lead the military phase of the expedition; Major Stephen H. Long was put in charge of the scientific phase.

Stephen H. Long, like his fellow officer Pike, was eastern-born, a native of New Hampshire and a graduate of Dartmouth College. He had taught school and, on entering the Army Engineer Corps, had become a mathematics instructor at West Point. His exploring career started in 1817 when he was sent to investigate the portage of the Wisconsin and Fox Rivers and the upper Mississippi. He had also been commissioned to select sites for defensive forts in Arkansas and Minnesota.

In July 1819, the much-heralded Yellowstone Expedition got under way. A steamboat, with bow decorations in the form of a dragon spitting smoke, designed to awe the Indians, started up the Missouri River. It progressed no farther than Council Bluffs and there, as autumn descended, the expedition halted, largely because of the difficulties of steamboating on the shallow Missouri. The men built Fort Atkinson for winter quarters, and there an unfortunate outbreak of scurvy in the garrison resulted in many deaths. A curious American public, expecting significant reports from the expedition, was severely disappointed. Congress began to withdraw its support from the scheme.

Despite the trouble, however, the army did decide to conduct a different sort of expedition. Major Long, after a winter in the East, was sent back to Council Bluffs with directions to conduct a short, quick trip out to the western mountains to search for the source of the Platte River. He was to return by way of the Arkansas and Red Rivers. Thus, while the federal government wrote off the military phase as a failure, it allowed the scientific phase something of a second chance.

"View of the Rocky Mountains on the Platte 50 miles from their base," as depicted by Long expedition artist Samuel Seymour.

Major Long organized an exploring party of nineteen men, including topographers, a map maker, a zoologist, a physician-botanist-geologist, a naturalist, and a landscape painter. The men were mounted on horses and, because the summer weather favored rapid travel, they made extraordinarily good time crossing the prairies. By the end of June 1820, they were in view of the Rockies. Riding up the Platte Valley they viewed the mountain that later trappers and traders would call Long's Peak, mistaking it at first for Pike's "great peak." The party continued past the present sites of Greeley and Denver, celebrating the Fourth of July in the river valley where "imagination only" had "travelled before . . . where civilization never existed—and yet . . . within the limits" of the United States. Each man got a gill of whiskey from the rations to celebrate the day.

Long guided his men over the divide separating the Platte and Arkansas Valleys, following Monument Creek to the site of present-day Colorado Springs. Here Edwin James, the young scientist who would later write the history of the expedition, decided to try to climb Pike's Peak. With six companions, he started out early one morning. Four of the men remained at the base of the mountain to make measurements; they would miscalculate the height of the peak by 3,000 feet because they assumed they were much lower in elevation themselves than they really were. Dr. James and two of the men, each equipped with a blanket, a few pounds of buffalo meat, and a pound of cornmeal, climbed from noon on, camping that night on the mountain side. The next morning they started upward again and by mid-afternoon they had reached the summit. They were the first white men on record to climb America's most famous mountain, and James was the first botanist in North America to collect specimens of the brilliant alpine flora above timberline. Major Long, in honor of their feat, labeled the mountain James' Peak in his reports. To the public, however, the mountain still belonged to Pike.

From the peak, Long's party continued southward to the Arkansas River. They examined the valley westward to the Royal Gorge and then moved downstream for a distance. Following plans, Long now split the men into two parties. Each group was to make its way back east to Fort Smith by a different route. Captain John R. Bell, with eleven men, descended the Arkansas River, while Major Long and the rest of the party turned south to search for the Red River. They crossed the Purgatoire and the Cimarron, and came to a large river they assumed to be the Red. On this stream they turned eastward, only to discover after a time that the river emptied into the Arkansas and that they had been on the Canadian, not the Red River.

By the middle of September the two groups again were together at Fort Smith, both having traveled downstream on the same river. The expedition had accomplished nothing as far as determining the sources of the Platte, Arkansas, or Red Rivers. When compared with Pike's earlier journey, which had actually pierced the ranges of the Rockies, the Long exploration looks like a summer's outing in the mountains. Long and his men seem to have acted more like soldiers, less like explorers; they performed perfunctorily, without particular enterprise or imagination. They did collect quantities of important information about the Indian tribes of the plains and scientific information about the flora and fauna of the regions they traversed. But they had failed to identify the river heads they were commissioned to find, and the source of that elusive stream, the Red River of the South, was still unmapped.

Major Long later made other exploratory trips to the regions of Minnesota and the Red River of the North. Later still he became a railroad engineer, surveying part of the original route of the Baltimore and Ohio Railroad, inventing a new type of railroad bridge, and writing the first textbook on railroading published in the United States. He died in 1864.

From the time of his western expedition until long after his death, the effects of the reports from his trip to the mountains would live on. Those reports had been particularly discouraging about the country east of the Rocky Mountains. Long labeled the region the Great American Desert on his maps, and his reports expanded on Pike's earlier pessimistic predictions that the "vast plains . . . may become in time equally celebrated as the sandy desarts [sic] of Africa; for I saw in my route, in various places, tracts of many leagues, where the wind had thrown up the sand, in all the fanciful forms of the ocean's rolling wave, and on which not a speck of vegetable matter existed."

Major Long's reports claimed the whole region to be "uninhabitable by a people depending on agriculture" for a livelihood; the area would much better "remain the unmolested haunt of the native hunter, the bison, and the jackall." The concept of the Great American Desert proved long lived: for generations, maps in school texts continued the label and description, and American children grew up believing the high plains did indeed resemble the sandy Sahara.

Almost two decades of exploring by official expeditions had accomplished little more than slight scratchings on the surface of the Louisiana Purchase. A few of the rivers had been charted, but many more remained unmapped. It was left to the mountain men, following the beaver trails, to become the true explorers of the Rocky Mountain frontier.

FOUR

THE FUR FRONTIER

Major Long's Great American Desert looked to some like a gift from the gods. An inhospitable desert frontier would ensure the purity of republican America against dangerous contacts with Old World monarchical institutions. What better defense against Spanish intrigues could there be than a wide buffer zone separating the United States and Spanish New Mexico? But to other Americans the desert was a challenge. In land miles, Santa Fe was only half as far from the Missouri River as it was from the Mexican capital. All trade goods had to be brought into New Mexico from the south, across hundreds of miles of difficult terrain. But if the western prairies could be crossed, and Santa Fe reached from the American river towns, a splendid commerce might be built, bridging the international boundary.

The idea was not new; the French had pursued the same scheme in the eighteenth century. Now, as then, obstacles stood in the way. Not the least of these was the age-old Spanish hostility toward alien interference in their imperial trade. But if Spanish rule in Mexico should end, that obstacle might be removed.

When the news of the abortive Hidalgo Revolt reached the United States in 1812, a group of nine or ten men, including Robert McKnight,

James Baird, and Samuel Chambers, started overland from the Missouri Valley with trade goods for New Mexico. They expected a friendly welcome and large profits in a province no longer a part of the Spanish Empire. But by the time they reached Santa Fe the revolt had been crushed. Instead of welcoming the Americans, the New Mexican officials imprisoned them in the *calabozos*. There they spent almost a decade. The unlucky prairie traders were not released until the Iturbide revolution brought actual independence to Mexico in 1821.

Once the ties of empire had been broken, Mexican officials were indeed willing to expand their sources of supply. William Becknell was one of the first to discover the change in policy. Becknell was a merchant in the town of Franklin, Missouri. In September 1821, with twenty men, he traveled along the Arkansas River and crossed Raton Pass into New Mexico. By the end of January 1822, he was back in Franklin, reportedly emptying moneybags of big silver dollars on the streets and spreading the good word that the Mexicans wanted American trade. Becknell hurried to return with more goods. This time he used three wagons on a new route that cut across the Cimarron Desert. In so doing he justly earned his nickname, The Father of the Santa Fe Trade, for he demonstrated that wagons could be used to cross the prairies. His route became the main trail of the westering merchants.

Trailing down to Santa Fe gradually became a more-or-less organized enterprise. The trail started at Independence, Missouri, a town connected by river boats with St. Louis, the emporium of all western trade. From Independence, the wagoners crossed well-watered prairies 150 miles to the tall timbers of Council Grove. There they halted and organized "trains," electing a captain who was charged with maintaining order and defense. Leaving Council Grove, the wagon trains lumbered southwest to the Arkansas River where the route divided. The main approach crossed the Cimarron Desert, the most frightful stretch of the journey. For fifty miles not a single water hole could be found. This main trail led directly southwest into Santa Fe.

The alternate route from the Arkansas crossing continued upstream along the river. This was the Mountain Branch section of the trail, leading to the vicinity of present-day La Junta and then cutting off across Raton Pass into Taos or Santa Fe.

The wagon men found prairie travel slow and full of danger. The distance covered each day was determined as much by water courses and springs as by the speed of the oxen or mules pulling the wagons. At best

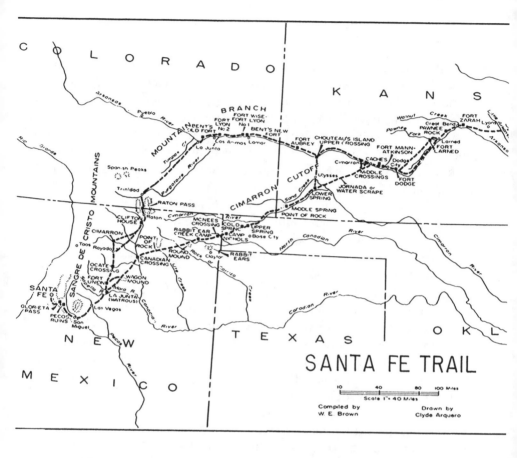

the men could anticipate fifteen miles a day. And along most of the route defenses could never be relaxed. Kiowa and Comanche tribesmen often contested the wagon trains' passage through their hunting lands. But despite the hardships and dangers the trade was lucrative—and romantic. For Anglo-Americans raised on a puritan morality, exotic Santa Fe offered girls who danced fandangoes, smoked cigarettes, and openly flirted.

Romance aside, Santa Fe was also a place where hard cash—gold and silver—could be won in exchange for goods from the States. The caravaners brought assortments of hardware and dry goods, especially brightly colored textiles. They leisurely bartered these American goods for furs, skins, gold, and silver. The profits of the trade varied greatly from year to year, for the whim of the provincial governor seemed to determine the customs duties. He might vary the tax on wagons from $10 to $750. Under such circumstances, bribery became a fine art and smuggling seemed a necessity.

The wagon traders took the gold and silver back to the Missouri River towns to pay off their creditors or to purchase new merchandise for the next season. The furs and skins—mostly beaver pelts and buffalo robes—could be sent for sale to St. Louis where they brought handsome profits. Santa Fe became a gathering place for furs from a wide area, including the mountain regions to the north.

The fur trappers and traders were another group of men who refused to be intimidated by the Great American Desert. Beaver fur was one of the most precious commodities on the continent. Nature had given it to man for the taking. The beaver pelt provided a high-priced product in a small package: a single pelt sold in eastern markets for $6 to $8, yet it was small and light enough in weight to be brought out of the interior regions where the trapping took place.

Trapping and trading for furs in the Rocky Mountains had begun even before the Santa Fe Trail was opened. When the Spanish dragoons escorted Pike to Santa Fe in 1807, he found there a James Purcell who had been trading with the Indians on the South Platte and in South Park. And Manuel Lisa, whose Missouri Fur Company had earlier penetrated the beaver lands of the upper Missouri River Valley, sent men south along the mountains to trade with the Indians in 1810 and the following year dispatched a party to the Arkansas Valley.

Ezekiel Williams, one of the leaders of that party, had taken nineteen trappers to the headwaters of both the Arkansas and South Platte Rivers. Trapping and trading as they went, the men met a variety of fates. Some wandered south to Santa Fe; some were killed by Indians. Williams and two companions were captured by the Arapahoes. After two years, Williams escaped and made his way back to Missouri. The next year he went west to the mountains again, this time with a party of trappers led by Joseph Philibert. He found the furs that he had cached on his earlier venture; these and the harvest of pelts gathered by the rest of the party were brought back to the States.

The situation looked promising for fur-gathering in the mountains. Two St. Louis merchants, Auguste Chouteau and Julius de Munn, bought out Joseph Philibert and went west with forty-five trappers in 1815. But after two successful seasons, the company was captured by the Spaniards despite earlier encouragement the Americans had received from New Mexican officials. In Santa Fe, the trappers were tried by court martial. They were set free but their furs and trade goods, worth an estimated $30,000, were confiscated. That acted like a brake on others who had intended to follow Chouteau and de Munn to the Southwest for furs. But, as in the case of the trade on the Santa Fe Trail, once the Mexicans had achieved their independence they reversed the policy toward American traders.

One of the first outfits to discover the changed attitude at Santa Fe was the Glenn-Fowler Company. Hugh Glenn and Jacob Fowler, with eighteen men, left Fort Smith, Arkansas, in September 1821 on an expedition to the Arkansas River Valley. Early the following year they built a "House nine loggs High" on the future site of Pueblo. From there they trapped and traded in the surrounding area and sent expeditions to Taos and Santa Fe. Their success was soon duplicated by others.

The techniques of the fur business of the central Rockies varied. Some white men gathered furs themselves; others remained traders, dependent on Indian and white trappers to bring in the pelts and exchange them for such trade goods as flour, cloth, tobacco, and trinkets. Although proscribed by federal licensing regulations, whiskey was often a commodity in this commerce.

However the trade was conducted, it was cannibalistic in nature. The trappers were always consuming their source of supply, and they continually had to move farther into the interior. There were advantages from this constant movement: if the traders contacted Indians who had not been well educated in the business, they could expect to pay lower prices for the beaver pelts, and, like the Spaniards searching for gold and silver, they always dreamed of the bonanza beaver pond, just over the horizon.

Taos, New Mexico, provided all that was needed as a base of operations for the trappers of the Arkansas and San Luis Valleys, and most of the Western Slope area as well. Here men could dispose of their furs to the merchants of the Santa Fe trade. Here, where New Mexican officials were less numerous than in Santa Fe, the fur men might hope to evade trapping and trading regulations. Here too they could find relaxation with a species of liquor dubbed "Taos Lightning" and other questionable comforts of a frontier adobe village.

The trappers and traders were a conglomerate lot: French-Canadians who brought with them extensive knowledge of fur gathering, Mexicans who moved north to try their hand at the game, Americans who wandered up the river courses into the mountains. Nationality faded as the fur men adopted as common garb the utilitarian fringed-buckskin suit. Uneducated but wise to the ways of rivers and trails, this "reckless breed of men" needed little capital to embark on the enterprise. A rifle, some traps, and a horse or two provided the minimum investment for fur gathering. It was a lonesome, often perilous, always difficult life. But when the season ended with a goodly crop of pelts, the trapper could return to Taos and home.

Taos provided a center for the individual trappers of the southern and Western Slope streams. Farther north, the fur merchants inaugurated another type of operation. With the great Missouri River complex as a natural highway, the northern area had attracted the attention of large fur companies even before Lewis and Clark reported the region excellent for trapping. The trading companies working the area were merciless in their competition for furs; each tried to monopolize the choicest trapping lands and squeeze its competitors from the region.

Operating out of the Pacific Northwest was the far-flung, British-owned Hudson's Bay Company, with its base at Astoria (later Fort Vancouver) and a regional post at Fort Hall in present Idaho. John Jacob Astor's American Fur Company settled the headquarters of its Western Department at St. Louis and operated out of Fort Union at the mouth of the Yellowstone River. Groups of trappers led by Nathaniel J. Wyeth and Captain B. L. E. Bonneville increased the competition. But the man who introduced the most novel feature of the trade was General William Ashley.

Ashley's initial enterprises in the upper Missouri basin were unspectacular, despite the later luster of the names of some of his employees: Jim Bridger, Thomas Fitzpatrick, Jedediah Smith, Louis Vasquez. What brought Ashley fame and fortune was a new technique of pelt gathering. Instead of depending on the trappers to come to a permanent trading post, Ashley devised the most romantic feature of the fur frontier—the summer rendezvous. This "fair in the wilderness" convened in ever-changing locations. Pierre's Hole in eastern Idaho might be chosen for the rendezvous one year; Cache Valley on Bear River north of the Great Salt Lake or Brown's Hole on the Green River might be chosen the following season.

The site was known in advance by the mountain men and company brigades, and when the agents arrived with wagons of trade goods, trappers from all over the Rockies appeared for the event. The rendezvous was more than a trading experience. It offered the otherwise solitary trappers gaiety, gambling, contests of skill, whiskey to drink—a combination bazaar, carnival, and reckless spree.

For the fur merchant, the rendezvous held other attractions. Since no permanent trading post was involved, Indian fears of encroachment on their hunting lands were reduced. The traders could move the site from season to season, to take advantage of the best trapping conditions. And since the pelts were all gathered at one time, the merchant could arrange more easily for their transportation out of the mountains to the markets in the East.

The rendezvous brought instant success in the form of a personal fortune to General Ashley. In 1826 he sold the business to three of his ablest employees: Jedediah Smith, David E. Jackson, and William Sublette. They managed the enterprise for four years and then sold it to a larger group of mountain men (Thomas Fitzpatrick, James Bridger, Milton Sublette, Henry Fraeb, and Baptiste Gervais), organized as the Rocky Mountain Fur Company. It took that company three seasons to pay off the debt and it operated one year after that—a year full of competition from the acquisitive American Fur Company, a better financed organization with superior marketing facilities. In 1834, the Rocky Mountain Fur Company gave up the struggle, selling its assets to the American Fur Company.

The rendezvous system attracted attention, but some traders preferred to use permanent trading posts. On the Gunnison River, near the present site of Delta, Antoine Robidoux built Fort Uncompahgre (sometimes known as Fort Robidoux). Robidoux had found his way into the Green River country in the mid-1820s. By 1833 he had a score or more men trapping for him in the valleys of the Western Slope and had built a reputation for himself as the "kingpin" trader of the region. In Brown's Hole, in the extreme northwestern corner of present Colorado, Fort Davy Crockett provided a base for beaver trappers. This post was short-lived and so restricted in attractions that the mountain men called it Fort Misery.

The building of forts and trading posts on the Eastern Slope was delayed until after the best years of beaver trapping. During the decade from 1830 to 1840 both the supply and the price of beaver skins declined. The animals became scarcer and the fashions in Paris and London changed as the silk top hat replaced the beaver hat. Pelts dropped in price until they brought little more than $1 each. Many traders then turned from beaver pelts to buffalo robes, and permanent posts became more necessary.

White men did not hunt the buffalo during these years. They left the work to the Indians. The division of labor in the tribes dictated that the men conduct the hunt while the women stretched and dried the robes. A buffalo robe could be bought for $3 or $4 unless it was a "silk" robe—fine-haired, of slightly lighter color—and then the price might be double that amount.

The robe merchant kept his trading goods at a post to which the Indians could bring their robes—a simpler process than bartering on the prairies. The robes were bulky and needed protected storage. The trading posts along the Eastern Slope answered those needs. From them the robes could be shipped on wagon caravans along the Santa Fe Trail to the south or the new Oregon Trail to the north.

The activities of Bent, St. Vrain and Company dominated the buffalo robe trade in the region for years. The four Bent brothers—Charles, William, Robert, and George—had followed the western trade to Santa Fe from their home in St. Louis. Their partnership with Ceran St. Vrain proved to be extremely successful. Bent's Fort—or Williams's Fort, as the company termed it—was built in 1833 on the north (American) bank of the Arkansas River, between present-day La Junta and Las Animas. The location was excellent: the post could be utilized by the Indian robe hunters of the prairies and by the remaining fur trappers in the mountains. At the same time, the fort sat astride the mountain branch of the Santa Fe Trail.

The Bents constructed their fort of thick adobe, with walls fifteen feet high and towers at two corners. A gateway in one of the walls provided the entrance to the *placita*, or courtyard. Inside the walls, low-roofed warehouses, living rooms, kitchen, and storage sheds were backed up against the outside walls. There was a corral for horses at the rear of the fort. And on the river bank, an adobe ice house provided facilities for keeping meat as well as the necessary ingredient for iced drinks during the hot summer weather.

For almost two decades the company and its fort on the Arkansas dominated the robe trade of the valley and extended regions beyond. The fort was also a welcome haven for travelers on the Santa Fe Trail and provided a quasi-military base in the midst of the Arapahoe and Cheyenne Indians. Colonel Henry Dodge counseled there with the plains Indians in 1835 during a summer march with his First Dragoon companies of United States troops. More usual visitors were the veteran mountain men. A group of them was usually in attendance at the fort—men like Thomas Fitzpatrick and Jim Bridger, Dick Wootton and Jim Beckwourth, Kit Carson, and Jim Baker.

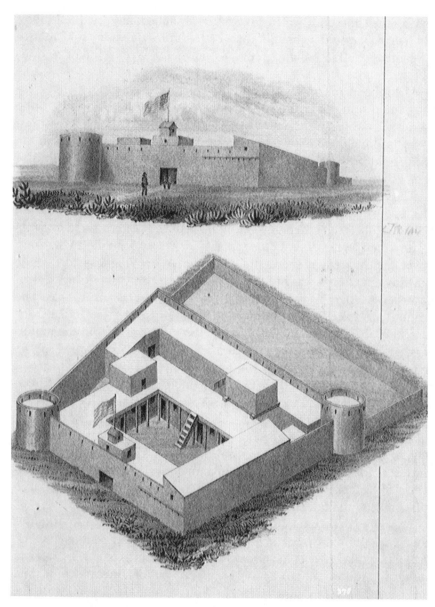

Bent's Fort, as depicted by Lt. James W. Abert in 1845.

Bent's Fort dominated but did not control the territory. Farther up-stream on the Arkansas River, John Gantt and Jefferson Blackwell built a trading post in 1832. It proved to be as short-lived as a similar struc-ture Maurice Le Doux built near the site of present-day Florence. When the trade in buffalo robes replaced the commerce in beaver pelts, the South Platte Valley to the north became dotted with adobe trading posts.

The first of these valley forts was operated by two experienced mountain men, Louis Vasquez and Andrew Sublette. In the autumn of 1835, these partners located Fort Vasquez on the river near the present town of Platteville. For a few years they seem to have conducted a brisk business. In 1840 or 1841, Vasquez and Sublette sold their facilities to another partnership, which soon became bankrupt and quit the post in 1842.

A second trading post was erected in the valley shortly after Fort Vasquez was built. Lancaster P. Lupton, a West Point graduate who came west with the Dodge excursion in 1835, was intrigued with trading pos-sibilities in the area and resigned his army commission to return and build Fort Lupton in 1836. For nine years he traded with the Indians. When trade slackened, he tried planting crops and grazing livestock near his fort.

Two other mountain men, Henry Fraeb and Peter A. Sarpy, financed in part by the Western Department of the American Fur Company, built Fort Jackson in 1837 near present-day Ione. Like the beaver trade, the robe commerce was competitive. Sarpy once informed his partner: "My object is to do all the harm possible to the opposition and yet without harming ourselves." Such competition often introduced liquor into the trading, with ruinous effect on both Indians and the honest traders.

The potential threats of Fort Lupton and Jackson stirred Bent, St. Vrain and Company to build a post farther north on the Platte, about six miles northwest of the present town of Platteville. This "branch" enter-prise they called Fort Lookout, later changing the name to Fort George and finally to Fort St. Vrain. The company also bought Fort Jackson from Fraeb and Sarpy in 1838; however, they probably never used that post since it was only ten miles from their own Fort St. Vrain.

By 1840, the best days of the trade were ended. The beaver trade was gone; the buffalo trade could not support so many trading posts. In time all of the forts were deserted. Yet despite their failure to mature into per-manent settlements, certain advances had been made. The valleys and passes of the mountain ranges were now known to the mountain men who later would guide "official" explorers through them. The Indian tribes had been met and traded with. The legend of the Great American Desert had been banished from the minds of at least a few. All these things would seem more significant later, when greater numbers invaded the Rocky Mountain frontier.

FIVE

THE FRONTIER IN TRANSITION

The decline of the fur and robe trade in the Rocky Mountain region ushered in an era of transition. For two decades trappers and traders had tramped the trails and passes until most of the area had been seen, although little of it had been mapped. But except for the trading posts along the Arkansas and Platte Rivers, nothing resembling permanent settlements had yet taken root. The arid plains were uninviting to agriculturalists and the Indian trade could support a limited population at best. Both Mexican and American governments may have looked upon the region as a desirable buffer zone, desolate and inhospitable enough to keep their citizens apart.

By 1840, however, many Americans were no longer interested in isolation from Mexico's northern provinces. Expansion was in the air. The Texans' successful revolt against Mexican rule had projected the question of annexation of that province into domestic politics. Beyond Texas was California, increasingly desirable to expansionists, and north of that was the Oregon country, still in dispute between its joint landlords, Great Britain and the United States.

The long Oregon Trail, leading up the Platte River, across South Pass, along the Green and Snake Rivers, with a final plunge from Fort

Boise to the valley of the Columbia, provided the entrance to the rich agricultural paradise of the Pacific Northwest. The trail to Oregon was not only long; some of the stretches, particularly the mountain crossings, taxed the immigrants' strength and determination. As the number of travelers to Oregon increased, western expansionists demanded surveys of the trail to find better crossings of the Divide and to locate sites for military posts to protect the travelers. This was to be done at government expense in the public interest. No one was more insistent that the government hurry such aid—to help the frontier-seeking farmer and to ensure American title to the Oregon country—than a senator from Missouri, Thomas Hart Benton.

Benton, the acknowledged spokesman for the trans-Mississippi West, sponsored a $30,000 federal appropriation for preliminary mapping of the major trails over the mountains in 1842. Perhaps it was not surprising that the man chosen to lead the surveying party was Benton's son-in-law, twenty-nine-year-old John Charles Frémont.

Frémont was born in Savannah, Georgia, in 1813. In true Horatio Alger fashion he had overcome the obstacles of illegitimate birth, the early death of his father, and extreme poverty as a youth. Educated at Charleston College, he taught mathematics in the Navy and assisted in surveys for the U.S. Topographical Corps. His patron, Joel Poinsett, secured a commission as second lieutenant for him in the corps in 1838. For three years Frémont worked on surveys between the Missouri River and the northern frontier. Then, in 1841, he provided social Washington with a choice scandal by eloping with Jessie Benton, the daughter of the Missouri senator. Family peace restored, the senator managed to secure the assignment of surveying the Oregon Trail for his handsome son-in-law.

The expedition was to be a modest affair. With twenty-eight men, Frémont was to survey the country between the Missouri River and South Pass. This most easily traveled segment of the trail ran through country already familiar to many mountain men. But from the surveys accurate maps would result, sites for military posts could be suggested, and the virtues of the Oregon country would be advertised at a time when the joint British-American occupation annoyed disciples of Manifest Destiny.

Lieutenant Frémont was fortunate in employing Kit Carson as his guide, for few men knew more about the trails and passes of the West. Carson had been born in Kentucky in 1809 but had grown up in frontier

Missouri. In his teens he had joined a Bent, St. Vrain and Company wagon train on a journey to Santa Fe. For almost a decade he had trapped and traded out of Taos, seeking employment as a hunter at Bent's Fort when the fur trade declined. He had come back to civilization in 1842 but found it far from satisfying and was pleased to join Frémont in the expedition along the Oregon Trail.

The Frémont party traveled up the Platte River to Fort St. Vrain. From there the young leader headed for the American Fur Company post at Fort Laramie and then through the valley of the Sweetwater to South Pass. After a short excursion into the Wind River Mountains, Frémont and his men completed their relatively uneventful trip by journeying eastward to home. The expedition lasted only three and one-half months. Frémont spent the winter in Washington, D.C., compiling a report of his journey to serve as a trail guide for future immigrants.

In the spring of 1843, Frémont returned to the Rockies. From Fort St. Vrain, he and his guides, Kit Carson and Thomas Fitzpatrick, searched the front ranges for a useful pass over the Divide. In this search, Frémont was disappointed, as others had been before him and many would be later. Splitting his party, Frémont sent Fitzpatrick with some of the men on to Fort Laramie with the supplies. Carson and Frémont led the rest of the men up the sixty-mile canyon of the Cache la Poudre River, up and along the eastern base of the Medicine Bow Range, until they struck the Oregon Trail.

Moving westward, the survey explored the basin of Great Salt Lake and swung up into the valley of the Columbia, reaching Fort Vancouver. Then, instead of moving down the trail to home, Frémont took his men south and west, crossing the Sierra Nevada Mountains in a difficult climb (mid-winter 1844), and settled down for rest and refitting near Sutter's Fort in the Sacramento Valley in California.

On his way home, Frémont traversed the central Rockies, from Brown's Hole on the Green River, through North, Middle, and South Parks, and on through Bent's Fort. If he had been looking only for a suitable wagon route he had found one somewhat shorter than any surveyed earlier, although still impracticable for heavy vehicles. But by this time, Frémont probably had other objectives in mind. American interest in California was surging; knowledge of the passes leading into the province soon might become valuable military information.

In fact, the country was about to elect James K. Polk to the presidency on a platform featuring territorial expansion. Frémont's father-in-law was now the chairman of the Senate Military Committee, and the young surveyor had no difficulty in gaining War Department approval for a third expedition. The actual objectives of this third trip to the West are unclear. Probably both Benton and Frémont believed that by the time the expedition reached California the United States and Mexico would be at war. The scouts and scientists then could be converted into a small fighting corps to help wrest California from the Mexicans.

Frémont traveled the Santa Fe Trail to Bent's Fort. Again the trusted Carson served as guide, helping to move the expedition up the Arkansas River, over the Continental Divide, northwestward to the White River, across the Great Basin and the Sierras, and into the Sacramento Valley. There Frémont would find for himself and his men a place in the history of the Mexican War.

In the year of Frémont's third expedition (1845), Colonel Stephen Watts Kearny led a military reconnaissance from Fort Leavenworth to Fort Laramie, then to South Pass, back to Fort Laramie, south to Bent's Fort, and from there again to Leavenworth. His objectives included gathering information about the region, protecting travelers on the Oregon and Santa Fe Trails, and persuading the Indian tribes to be peaceful by demonstrating the military might of the army and by holding councils with them.

With officers like Frémont and Kearny, and fur traders and travelers crisscrossing the central Rockies, sooner or later someone was going to settle down and start raising vegetables on some river bank. In time it happened. As the fur trade waned and trappers found the old trail life less profitable, some of them forsook the roving life to attempt a little farming. When that happened, several short-lived, semiagricultural settlements were begun.

One of the first was called El Pueblo, also known as Milk Fort, because the inhabitants kept some goats at the place. It was located about five miles above Bent's Fort on the Arkansas River. Visitors described its inhabitants as Mexican and American mountain men, weary from their lives of trapping, who settled there to grow foodstuffs, which they sold to trading posts in the region. It was soon abandoned.

Others settled "the Pueblo," or Fort Pueblo, at the confluence of Fountain Creek and the Arkansas River, in 1842 or earlier. Frémont visited this village in 1843, noting in his journal that the residents were "mountaineers" and their wives came from "the valley of Taos." They farmed a little and conducted trade with the Indians. Three years later historian Francis Parkman stopped at the place during his western travels and commented on its primitive construction—"nothing more than a large square enclosure, surrounded by a wall of mud, miserably cracked and dilapidated."

In 1846 forty-three Mormons, trekking westward on the Oregon Trail, learned at Fort Laramie that they were ahead of rather than behind the main group of emigrants. Discovering that the rest of the party would winter near Council Bluffs, this small group moved southward to winter near Fort Pueblo. They were joined there by soldiers from the "Mormon battalion" who had enlisted in the U.S. Army during the Mexican War and now, sick or disabled, were sent to the Arkansas Valley to recuperate. In the spring of 1847 the Mormons continued their journey to the valley of the Great Salt Lake.

Agricultural settlements such as Hardscrabble west of Pueblo and Greenhorn to the south existed briefly in the 1840s and 1850s. Situated on the edge of the Mexican frontier beyond the reach of established law and religion, like Pueblo they were occupied by ex-trappers and their wives who fused American, Mexican, and Indian elements into lively multicultural communities. All, however, were deserted before the gold rush, victims of bad weather, conflicts with Indians, and the lure of California gold.

Although such settlements did not flourish, title to the area was worth contesting. In 1836, when the Texans revolted from Mexican rule, the defeated Mexican general, Santa Anna, promised the Rio Grande as the southern and western boundary for Texas. He soon claimed that the promise had been given under duress and refused to honor it. Thus both Mexico and Texas claimed the land between the Arkansas and the Rio Grande.

The Texas threats, coupled with certain signs of interest in the Texas claims by the United States, led Mexico to promote settlement there. Early in the years after 1840, Mexico granted lands north of Santa Fe in the areas south of the Arkansas Valley and in the San Luis Valley. Two grants in the San Luis Valley, the Tierra Amarilla and the Conejos Grants, had originally been given in the previous decade. Now the Conejos Grant was reaffirmed, and others were made. Carlos Beaubien and Guadalupe Miranda successfully petitioned for the later-named Maxwell Grant—more than 1,500,000 acres, stretching northeastward from Taos. To the north of the Maxwell Grant, reaching as far as the Arkansas River and encompassing almost 4 million acres of land, was the Las Animas

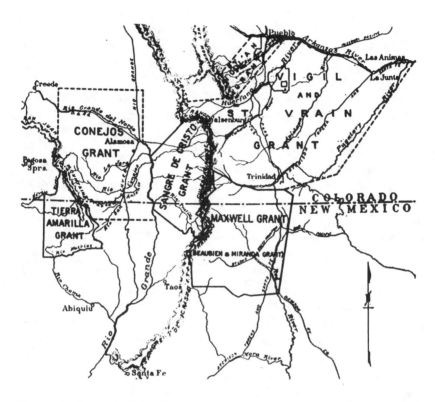

Mexican land grants in Colorado.

Grant, given to Cornelio Vigil and Ceran St. Vrain. Bordering these grants on the west were the Sangre de Cristo Grant, extending westward to the Rio Grande, given to Luis Lee and Narciso Beaubien in 1843, and the smaller Nolan Grant, south of the Arkansas River, received by Gervacio Nolan in 1843.

Mexico expected these men to colonize settlers on their grants, securing them against Texan or American claims. But the grants were made too late and the attempts of the owners to settle them were too feeble. Before the policy served its purpose, the United States annexed the Texas Republic (March 1845) and made the Texas claims to the Rio Grande boundary its own. The long anticipated war between the United States and Mexico began in May 1846. Before that summer ended, the land grants and much larger stretches of Mexico's domain would be taken.

In June 1846, the American Army of the West, commanded by Colonel Stephen W. Kearny, moved southwestward from Fort Leavenworth. After a month's march, 1,700 troops and the massive supply train reached Bent's Fort on the Arkansas River. From there, after rest and reorganization, the army started for its first objective—Santa Fe.

There was no Mexican resistance, as more than one traveler on the trail had predicted. On August 18 the American flag was raised over the Royal City. Kearny remained in Santa Fe for a month. Then, after appointing Charles Bent the governor of the province, the recently promoted General Kearny started for California. The conquest of New Mexico turned out to be less than completely bloodless. The following winter (1847) an uprising in New Mexico was crushed by the American forces in a battle at Taos Pueblo; but not before Charles Bent and others had lost their lives.

In February 1848, the Mexican War ended with the Treaty of Guadalupe Hidalgo. Mexico ceded to the United States the entire southwestern region, from Texas to the Pacific Ocean, from the Rio Grande to the forty-second parallel. All of what was to become Colorado was now American territory.

With the Mexican War ended, many Americans turned their attention to an idea frequently discussed before the fighting began: a transcontinental railroad to ease transportation to the Oregon country (American now, to the forty-ninth parallel, by virtue of a settlement with Great Britain in 1846) and to California. The war had demonstrated dramatically the difficulties of the long overland route and the longer sea voyage, either around Cape Horn or by way of the Isthmus. Most Americans assumed that the federal government would pay all or part of the costs for such a railroad. But there was little agreement as to the best route for the road. Every town in the Missouri and Mississippi Valleys viewed itself as a likely eastern terminus of the railroad.

St. Louis, in particular, was interested in the project. In 1848 businesses from that city hired John C. Frémont to find a suitable railroad route from St. Louis to the Pacific. Frémont had reached California at the end of his third expedition; he and his men aided in the American occupation of the province. He had become involved in a struggle there between Commodore Stockton and General Kearny, and after a much-publicized court martial, Frémont resigned his army commission. Now, under the St. Louis auspices, he conducted his fourth, near-fatal expedition to the West.

With thirty-three men he traveled the familiar path to Bent's Fort and Fort Pueblo. He had hoped to engage Kit Carson as guide, but Carson was not available. Another veteran mountain man, "Parson" Bill Williams, agreed to take the assignment. There were warnings of disaster from the veterans of the mountains and the forts, but Frémont was undisturbed by prophecies of doom. He was determined to make the journey in wintertime in order to prove completely the practicability of the railroad route.

The crossing of the Sangre de Cristo Mountains was accomplished despite the winter weather. Frémont moved his men across the San Luis Valley and heading into the San Juan Mountains, he attempted to cross the Continental Divide in the upper Rio Grande Valley. The snowdrifts deepened and the temperatures slid downward as the men climbed toward 12,000-foot elevations. They never crossed the Divide; the expedition bogged down completely in the extreme winter weather. The only hope for escape was rescue from the south, so Frémont sent four men to New Mexico. When sixteen days passed without word from them, he took four others and started south, leaving the rest of the party to follow as best they could. On his way down, Frémont found three of the four men he had sent out earlier; the fourth man had died. Pushing on into Taos on horses procured from Indians, Frémont started a relief party to rescue what remained of his group.

Most of his equipment was lost; all the mules were gone. Eleven of the thirty-three men perished in the winter wilderness. No other party exploring the Central Rockies paid such a price for failure. Historians still argue about who was to blame for the debacle. Frémont's admirers claim that Bill Williams was an unreliable guide, unfamiliar with the passes out of the San Luis Valley. Others insist that Frémont disregarded the advice of his hired scout and alone was responsible for electing the difficult crossing.

Frémont's failure to find a suitable railroad route for the businesses of St. Louis by no means ended the planning for a transcontinental line. In fact, the discovery of gold in California now emphasized the need anew. But the northern and southern sectional interests so bitterly contended the advantages of their own sections that no single route could be agreed upon. In 1853 Congress appropriated $150,000 for four separate surveys of possible routes to the Pacific. One of these would study the land between the thirty-eighth and thirty-ninth parallels.

Captain John Gunnison of the Topographical Corps was assigned this survey through the central Rockies. His command was rather extensive—thirty members of the scientific team and a military escort of thirty dragoons commanded by two officers. Using eighteen six-mule

Artist Richard H. Kern, a member of John C. Frémont's ill-fated fourth expedition, painted this watercolor entitled "Pike's Peak, 1848—'Mon Songe' [My Dream]" in 1853.

wagons, in addition to an instrument wagon and an ambulance, they hoped that the route could be thoroughly tested.

Gunnison's surveying party moved up the Santa Fe Trail, over La Veta Pass, into the San Luis Valley. Gunnison's way out of this mountain park was a distinct improvement over Frémont's attempted route five years earlier. The survey climbed up and over Cochetopa Pass and then down to the Gunnison River to the Grand (Colorado) River, for a distance following Escalante's route of three-quarters of a century earlier. The way was far from smooth; chopping trees and moving rocks to get the wagons through was hard work. In fact, Gunnison and his men concluded that the elevations they had traversed were so rugged that a railroad could be operated only after extensive, expensive tunneling.

When they reached the Grand River, the party turned to the west. In the Utah desert, Paiute Indians attacked the party, killing Captain Gunnison and seven of his men. Lieutenant E. G. Beckwith, the second-in-command, led the way into Salt Lake City and the party returned from there to the states the following year.

Richard H. Kern visited Fort Massachusetts with John W. Gunnison's surveying party in August 1853. Shortly after he drew the sketch on which this lithograph is based, Kern, Gunnison, and six other expedition members were killed by Indians in Utah.

When it was announced that John Gunnison would survey areas that Frémont had already traversed, the "Pathfinder of the West" was in Europe. Frémont now returned to the United States. With the help of his father-in-law, he financed his fifth and last expedition—a rival survey to Gunnison's. He followed almost exactly the route that Gunnison had marked; he contributed almost nothing to the general information about the area. He did, however, complete his survey during the winter months, thus demonstrating the feasibility of an all-weather route through the mountains.

The surveys for the Pacific railroad were completed in 1854, but the strife between North and South would delay the project for more than a decade. By the year 1854 the whole sectional issue was about to explode again. Four years earlier the forces of compromise had put together agreements designed to dispose of the thorny question of the status of slavery in the new lands acquired from Mexico. The creation of Utah and New Mexico territories as part of the Compromise of 1850 left an unorganized expanse of federal domain lying east of the Rockies. In 1854 that territory was divided at the fortieth parallel into the Kansas and Nebraska

Territories. Thus, from 1850 to 1854, future Colorado was politically divided into three parts: Utah Territory in the west, New Mexico Territory in the south, and the unorganized part of the Louisiana Purchase in the east, north of the Arkansas River. After 1854 the area of future Colorado was divided among four territories: Utah, New Mexico, Kansas, and Nebraska.

In the areas east of the mountains, the Indians showed increasing resentment of the trail (Oregon and Santa Fe) traffic through their hunting lands. In 1846 the federal government had created the Upper Platte and Arkansas Indian Agency and appointed Thomas Fitzpatrick as agent. Fitzpatrick, known in the West as Broken Hand, was an excellent choice for the position. He represented the best of the traditions of the veterans of the mountains, including acquaintance with the regional Indians. He centered his activities at Bent, St. Vrain and Company's fort on the Arkansas River. Here he met the Cheyennes and Arapahoes in council in August 1847. Two years after that, Bent's Fort was no more. Tradition relates that William Bent, disgusted at the federal government's refusal to agree to his purchase price, moved out his supplies and blew up the place. Bent then moved down the river, constructing a new, much less imposing Fort Bent, which the army eventually took over in 1860, renaming it Fort Wise.

Actually Bent's old fort had been quite far south for the agency's activities. The American Fur Company's post at Fort Laramie proved a more central location and, after the federal government bought it in 1849, the Indian agents used it in their work. Fort Laramie is particularly memorable as the site of the great plains Indian council of 1851. September was set for the largest gathering of the tribes ever held in the West. More than 10,000 Indians were there, some tribes "en masse" and others represented by delegations. Not all the tribes were friends, but they did not mar the occasion with conflict. Cheyenne, Arapahoe, Snake, Sioux, Assiniboin, Gros Ventres, Aricara, and Crow listened and replied solemnly to the harangues of Superintendent David Mitchell, head of the Central Superintendency at St. Louis, and Agent Fitzpatrick. Between the speeches and the pipe smoking there was time for military maneuvers, dances, and dog feasts during the fifteen-day session.

In the treaty that resulted the plains tribes agreed to live in peace and to hunt within tribal boundaries marked off for them. The Cheyennes and Arapahoes were assigned the area north of the Arkansas River and east of the mountains. The Indians agreed to allow white people to

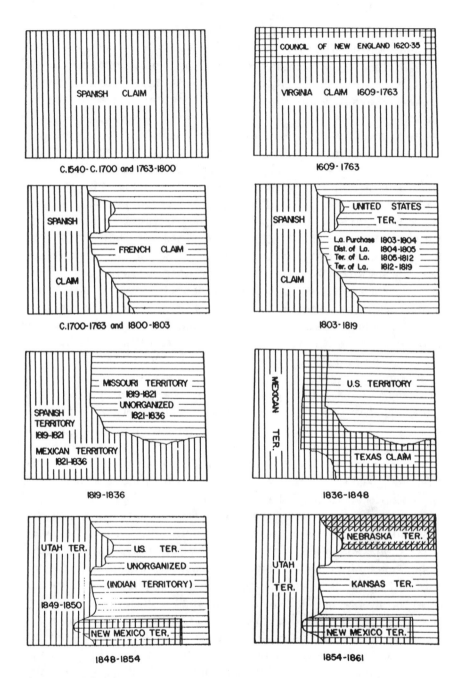

Claims over Colorado prior to 1861.

move through their tribal lands and to build forts for the protection of travelers on the overland trails. In return, the agents promised to bring out and distribute $50,000 worth of trade goods annually for the next fifteen years. (Congress reduced the trade goods provision to $15,000 when the treaty was ratified.) The terms agreed upon, the agents then distributed presents from twenty-seven bulging wagons. Along with a treaty made with the Comanches, Apaches, and Kiowas at Fort Atkinson two years later, the Fort Laramie Treaty awaited the test of time that alone would determine its effectiveness.

While government agents treated with the plains Indians, relations with the Utes also required attention, for the first permanent white settlements within present Colorado were being developed on lands Ute hunters traditionally controlled. The Treaty of Guadalupe Hidalgo that ended the Mexican War stipulated that all private property in the areas ceded to the United States would be respected. In this way the federal government became an interested party in the land grants the Mexican government had made earlier. The surveyor general of New Mexico Territory investigated the validity of the grants; Congress might then accept, modify, or reject his findings. And, in time, the federal courts were also involved, when conflicting claims resulted in litigation. Some of the claims were rather quickly disposed of: The Sangre de Cristo, the Maxwell, and the Tierra Amarilla Grants were confirmed in full. Congress reduced the Nolan and Vigil and St. Vrain Grants. The Conejos claim remained in litigation for decades and finally was rejected by the courts.

Although these lands had been granted to encourage settlement on Mexico's northern frontier, none of them contained a single village when the Mexican War ended. Three years after the peace treaty, in 1851, the first permanent white settlement in Colorado was planted: San Luis on the Culebra River. In the next few years, it was followed by San Pedro, San Acacio, and Guadalupe. The settlers, moving north from New Mexico, brought with them experience in irrigating arid lands and soon had dug ditches to water their fields of wheat, corn, and beans. Their cattle and sheep grazed in the San Luis Valley. The settlers reproduced their familiar adobe-constructed homes and by 1858, at Conejos, had erected Our Lady of Guadalupe Church—the first church structure within the boundaries of the future state of Colorado.

Life in the valley was slow-paced and always difficult. Clashes between whites and Indians helped to make it so. During the war the army had sent units from Santa Fe, commanded by Major William Gilpin, to check tribes in the north and west. The objective was tranquility, and efforts were made to persuade the Utes to remain peaceful. By 1849 success was reaped in the first formal treaty concluded between the United States and the Utes. The Indians agreed to peace and to settle on agricultural lands.

But the peace was not kept. When hunting became difficult for lack of game, the sheep and cattle of the settlers proved too desirable for the Utes to ignore. In 1852, in an effort to check the Indian raids, the United States built Fort Massachusetts to the north of the villages. Located on Ute Creek, at the foot of Mount Blanca, the fort housed a small garrison of soldiers and provided headquarters for the Indian agents. The fort alone, however, did not awe the Indians. Difficulties continued and an organized campaign against the Utes and Jicarilla Apaches seemed necessary.

In 1854 minor conflicts between whites and Indians reached a climax in the episode known as the Fort Pueblo Massacre. On Christmas Day, a celebration at the fort turned into a bloody fight in which fifteen white men were killed and a woman and two boys were carried away by the Indians. General John Garland, commanding at Fort Union, New Mexico, decided to march against the tribes. He added volunteers to his regular troops and sent them north to Fort Massachusetts. An encounter with a war party in the Saguache Valley in March 1855 resulted only in the flight of the outnumbered tribesmen. The following month Colonel Thomas Fauntleroy surprised a group of Indians across Poncha Pass. His men killed forty warriors and captured their supplies. Through the summer, minor fighting continued, but by autumn the Indians were ready for peace-making.

Near Abiquiu on the Chama River, New Mexico Governor David Meriwether and Agent Kit Carson concluded a treaty with the Mouache Utes and another with the Jicarilla Apaches. The U.S. Senate never ratified the treaties, probably because the lands to be reserved for the tribes were thought to encompass lands already settled by whites. But even without ratification, the treaties did improve the relationship between the settlers and the Indians for some years.

That relationship may have been helped by the relocation of Fort Massachusetts. Critics had earlier pointed out that the military post was too distant from the villages to protect the settlers. In 1858 the army moved the post six miles to the south where, although nearer the villages, it still commanded the approach from the east over the Sangre de Cristo Mountains. The post was now renamed Fort Garland. For almost three decades garrisons there would provide security for the San Luis settlers.

As the decade of the 1850s drew to a close, the Rocky Mountain frontier was a fairly quiet place. The Laramie and Atkinson Treaties provided a measure of safety for travelers on the overland routes to Oregon and California. The treaties with the Utes and Jicarilla Apaches and the garrison at Fort Garland had stabilized the San Luis frontier and protected the little agricultural villages in the valley. Except for those villagers and a few trappers and traders who remained to work the remnants of the fur frontier, the region was devoid of white population. With the main trails to the West running north and south of the mountain barrier, and the agricultural frontier still located back on the Missouri River line, it would have been safe to wager that many years would pass before many people would come to make their homes and their fortunes in the Rocky Mountain frontier.

SIX

GOLD RUSH

The high mountains had kept their secret well. No Spaniard ever found the key that would unlock the gold and silver treasures of the Rocky Mountains. Juan Rivera had traveled northward in 1765, looking for the precious metals. He had returned to Santa Fe with ore samples, but evidently the Spanish did not see in them the token of an El Dorado. As later trappers, traders, and explorers crossed and recrossed the mountain trails and passes, they sometimes found small quantities of gold in the streambeds. James Purcell, an American whom Zebulon Montgomery Pike met in New Mexico in 1807, told the explorer about finding gold in the northern ranges, but the inclusion of the story in Pike's report created no great interest. William Gilpin, traveler with Frémont and campaigner against the Indians, recounted tales of gold in the Rockies, but no one paid much attention to him, either. Then, in 1848-1849, the nation reeled under the excitement of the gold discoveries in the recently won province of California. After that, anything could be believed. The way was opened for El Dorados everywhere and anywhere. Some of the Forty-niners made their way to California by cross-country routes, over the Great American Desert and the Rocky Mountains. A few who stopped to prospect along the way found "color" on tributaries of the South Platte River, but not enough to detain them on their trek to California. However, some of those miners, after returning from the California camps, remembered the streams of the central Rockies.

One such man was William Green Russell of Georgia. He had accumulated considerable mining experience, both in his home state and in the California fields. After his return to Georgia, he decided to organize a prospecting party to survey the Rocky Mountains seriously. His brothers Oliver and Levi shared his hopes and dreams of a mining empire in the mountains. William was related by marriage to the Cherokee Indians, and much of the planning was based on correspondence with Cherokees in present-day Oklahoma, some of whom had actually found gold in the foothills of the Rockies on their way to California.

In February 1858, the three Russell brothers, with six companions, set out from Georgia for the West. On the Arkansas River they met the Cherokees as planned, and as they moved along the Santa Fe Trail other fortune seekers joined them. Eventually the party would number 104. When they reached Bent's Fort, they turned northwest and by May 23 were at the site where Cherry Creek flows into the South Platte River. There they stopped, got out their pans and gear, and started prospecting the riverbeds. They did not find anything promising on Cherry Creek, on Ralston Creek, or on any of the other streams rushing from the mountains. After twenty days some of the men decided to forgo the further pleasure of standing in the streambeds, washing out gravel with ice-cold water, and returned home.

The Russell brothers and ten other men stayed on, and during the first days of July 1858, they found "good diggings" at the mouth of Dry Creek. They panned out several hundred dollars' worth of gold dust before they exhausted the small pocket. The quantity was insignificant, but it was, perhaps, the most important discovery ever made within the region, for from this meager showing the great Pike's Peak gold rush developed.

The Russell group now was convinced of the ultimate success of their venture. They spread out along the ranges, seeking to duplicate their discovery on Dry Creek. While they were gone from the site of their first find, others joined them in the quest for gold. An entirely distinct and separate group of men had come west from Kansas Territory because of a rather unlikely story that an Indian named Fall Leaf had brought back from the mountains the previous year.

In 1857 the army had sent Colonel Edwin V. Sumner and a troop of soldiers to the Cheyenne country to chastise the Indians for raiding traffic on the Platte River Trail. Fall Leaf, a Delaware Indian guide on that expedition, brought back a "bunch of gold nuggets tied up in a rag." He claimed that he had bent over a mountain stream to drink and saw the nuggets lying on the rocks. John Easter, a butcher in Lawrence, Kansas, heard Fall Leaf's story and decided that such an indication of gold warranted a prospecting expedition. When the weather cleared in the spring, Easter had his group ready to move west, but by then Fall Leaf had decided not to go along. Promises of provisions for his family did not persuade him to guide the group to his magic stream. Perhaps he considered the party too small for safe travel; some say he was unable to go because of injuries; perhaps he was afraid he would not be able to find the same stream again.

The would-be argonauts were in a quandary, but they decided to go ahead with their plans. As they moved along the Santa Fe Trail they were joined by others until, like the Russells before them, their numbers were considerably increased. As they came up the Arkansas Valley, they strained their eyes for the first sight of Pike's Peak. They did their first prospecting in the shadow of that mountain. But they found no gold there or in South Park. They had decided to dig near Fort Garland when they heard the news that the Russells had found gold on Cherry Creek, and quickly changing plans, they hastened toward the north.

When the Russell group returned to Cherry Creek from their prospecting tour, they found the men from Lawrence, as well as some Indian traders who had joined them, delighted at the unusual prospect of companionship. And within a few weeks, gold seekers from the East began to arrive, explaining that the news was abroad in the land that there was gold at Pike's Peak. It had happened that in July, while the Russells were enjoying their first success at Dry Creek, John Cantrell and other mountain traders from Fort Laramie had visited them. These veterans of the Rockies had stayed a few days, digging in the sands a little themselves. Then they had gone to Kansas City for the winter. From them the first news confirming the rumors of Pike's Peak gold discoveries reached the rest of the world.

Those acquainted with prairie winters realized that the time for safe travel to the diggings had already passed, but there were some who decided to risk the chance of early blizzards in order to reach the goldfields ahead of the others. Most of these Fifty-eighters headed for the mouth of Cherry Creek where the Russell discovery had been reported. They found a group fixing up winter quarters, talking about the panning for gold they would do in the spring, and already engaged in manufacturing "cities."

The Lawrence party had been disappointed to find, on their arrival at Cherry Creek, that the Russells' gold pocket had already been cleaned out. But they decided they could capitalize on the situation anyway. They staked out a town—Montana City—a little to the north of Dry Creek. This venture died an early death, for the promoters soon recognized the superior advantages of another site and organized a second town—St. Charles—on the east side of Cherry Creek. Leaving one man to defend their embryo metropolis, the Lawrence group hurried back to Kansas Territory. There they would attempt to gain a charter for their town from the territorial legislature and advertise and promote their undertaking.

The St. Charles Town Company was strictly a business venture, with closed stock, requiring settlers to buy shares in the organization. Many of the gold seekers saw little necessity for purchasing cabin sites when so much land was available, free for the taking. Yet the advantages of organization for the protection of property and person could not be completely ignored. As the numbers on Cherry Creek increased, late in October, a public meeting was called and a new town company was established in rivalry to the St. Charles venture. On the opposite (west) side of Cherry Creek, the new Auraria Town Company, named after a town in the gold region of Georgia, staked out its site and advertised free entry to all settlers.

This was the situation when, in mid-November, General William Larimer led a group of men from Leavenworth, Lecompton, and Oskaloosa into the area. The general, his son Will, and their friend Dick Whitsitt were also experienced town promoters and, in addition, they had joined forces with a group of men from Lecompton commanded by "Colonel" Ed Wynkoop. These Lecompton men carried with them actual commissions as officers of Arapahoe County, signed by the governor of Kansas Territory. Arapahoe County included in its boundaries all of Kansas Territory west of the 103rd meridian. The territorial legislature had created it on paper in 1855, but it had never actually been organized. Many of Larimer's group, including these officials of Arapahoe County, seem to have come to the diggings mainly for the purpose of town-promotion and office-holding; gold mining was something they were content to leave to others.

Larimer and his allies surveyed the scene and decided to acquire the St. Charles site on the theory that it had been abandoned. The one St.

Charles man who had been left to guard the property later charged that the Larimer group won his consent to "jumping the claim" by serving him whiskey until he was inebriated. However gained, Larimer and his men were now in control of the real estate. With a hopeful eye toward the east, they renamed the town Denver City, after the governor of Kansas Territory, General James W. Denver.

Cherry Creek provided a boundary between Auraria and Denver City, separating the rival communities. But the promoters of those towns were not alone in their pretensions; other settlements with hopes for future greatness were soon initiated in the Pike's Peak region. North of the Cherry Creek settlements, gold seekers from Nebraska City camped at Red Rocks near the mouth of Boulder Canyon to begin Boulder City. Farther north, on the Cache la Poudre, fur trader Antoine Janise called a cluster of cabins Colona that was later renamed La Porte. West of Denver City and Auraria, in the valley of Clear Creek, Arapahoe City and Golden Gate were platted in the last weeks of 1858. And to the south, at the mouth of Fountain Creek, near the ruins of old Fort Pueblo, gold seekers laid out the town of Fountain City. Others staked the site of El Paso near Pike's Peak.

During the fall and winter the men in the new towns built their cabins and talked about their plans for prospecting when warm weather returned. The basis for their hopes was weak enough—only small pockets of gold dust like the one the Russells had found on Dry Creek in July. But those men who reached the area in the fall of 1858 at least could take comfort in the fact that they had completed the trip across the plains and would have a decided advantage over the argonauts who were certain to crowd the region when warm weather arrived.

In the valley of the Missouri River, self-appointed experts on the Pike's Peak diggings were already at work promoting the spring rush. D. C. Oakes, who had been in California during the rush days there, had come out to the Pike's Peak country with a group from Iowa. After a quick look around he had gone back to Pacific City, Iowa, and there he published a guidebook to the region. Oakes's creation was only one of many such "bestsellers" that flooded the country during the winter of 1859. In their enthusiasm, the authors of these Pike's Peak guidebooks often allowed themselves to be carried from reality into a golden, glistening dream world. They boldly announced that the gold was as common in the Pike's Peak region as the waters of the mountain streams or the sands along their banks. Intentionally or not, they led their readers to believe that the most useful equipment to carry to the diggings was containers to hold the gold nuggets picked up like pebbles from the streambeds. Small wonder that these literary products found ready readers.

Another group, almost as quick to take advantage of the news from Pike's Peak, were the merchants and shopkeepers in the towns along the Missouri River. Times were difficult for them: The panic of 1857 had plunged the country into a depression and the Midwest had been particularly hard hit. Many merchants believed that their salvation had appeared in the guise of the gold news, for if large numbers of argonauts could be enticed into equipping themselves at their particular establishments, the depression might be rocketed into prosperity. Every town in the valley proclaimed itself the best, the logical, the only good outfitting point for prospecting parties. Kansas City, Leavenworth, Atchison, Omaha, even St. Louis—each proclaimed itself the natural gateway to the Pike's Peak goldfields.

The cities situated on the already proven trails westward were in the best position to make good those claims. Towns astride the Oregon Trail (Platte River route) to the north or the Santa Fe Trail (Arkansas River route) to the south had an advantage over the others. Of all the crossings, the Platte River route probably was the most heavily traveled. But between the two well-established trails, two alternative routes came into prominence. Both the Smoky Hill Trail and the Republican River route had sponsors claiming them the most direct, the shortest, or the safest for travel.

As the winter of 1859 came to a close, the valley towns braced themselves for the anticipated horde of gold seekers. They were not disappointed. Their own advertising, coupled with that of the guidebook publishers, had churned up enormous interest in the mines. But these alone could not have created the tremendous excitement, based as it was on so flimsy a foundation as the small quantity of gold actually uncovered. The same economic conditions that had whipped the merchants in the valley towns to such labors also motivated many a gold seeker. Times were hard, cash was scarce; those who would never have left their homes in prosperous times decided to find their own panacea for the depression in Pike's Peak goldfields. Some who would certainly have been intimidated by the long journey to California blithely began the shorter, but still hazardous, trip to the Rocky Mountains.

No census taker stood and counted the argonauts who left the states for the goldfields that spring of 1859. Historians have estimated that

An 1859 emigrant train near St. Joseph, Missouri, bound for the goldfields.

number at somewhere around 100,000 people. Perhaps one-half that many actually reached the Rocky Mountains; the rest either changed their minds along the way or, unfortunately, met their deaths on the trails. Of the 50,000 who may have reached the diggings, probably one-half or more became discouraged at the hard work and small returns, and started homeward after only a few days or weeks at Cherry Creek. Those who did not join the "go backs" stayed to dig and wash and search for gold; many stayed to plant towns, open stores, provide services, and make their living "mining the miners."

Some of the Fifty-niners crossed the prairies on horseback. Others traveled by mule train. Probably most of them rode in wagons pulled by oxen, reportedly the best animal for the trip. Some of the emigrants who lacked the money to procure better transportation tramped westward on foot with packs on their backs, even though the attempt to cross the prairies this way was described by contemporaries as "madness—suicide—murder." A few of the gold seekers pushed wheelbarrows and handcarts. One dreamer tried a fantastic device: a Wind Wagon, with wheels underneath and sails above for the winds to propel. This prairie ship was scheduled to "sail" between Westport and Pike's Peak camps on a twelve-day, round-trip routine. The ship and its passengers would travel over 100 miles each day. Unfortunately, the romantic contraption came to anchor in a gulch not far from its port of clearance.

However the trip to the goldfields was made, it was an arduous undertaking. Seven hundred miles or more, the trails ran westward, "crossing countless unbridged water courses, always steep-banked and often miry, and at times so swollen by rains as to be utterly impassable by wagons. Part of this distance . . . [was] a desert, yielding grass, wood, and water only at intervals of several miles, and then very scantily . . . To cross it with teams in midsummer, when the water courses . . . [were] mainly dry, and the grass eaten up . . . [was] possible only to those who . . . [knew] where to look for grass and water."

There had been doubters of the story of Pike's Peak gold all through the late summer and fall of 1858—those who would have applauded Mark Twain's definition of a mine as a "hole in the ground owned by a liar." There were enough "humbug" criers to keep the uncertainty alive all winter. The editor of the *Chicago Press and Tribune* was such a critic. He cautioned his readers that "more cherries will be found at home than at Cherry Creek, and we believe there is more gold to be dug out of every Illinois farm than the owners will ever produce by quitting the home diggings for those on the headwaters of the Arkansas and Platte."

He had a point. If all the gold at Pike's Peak turned out to be only small deposits of gold dust like those found by the Russells and their immediate followers, mass disappointment was in the cards for thousands. Such a cruel fate would have brought horrible repercussions and a disastrous situation for the optimistic townmakers already at work on their plans. For a time it appeared that the cynical critics were right: Gold in paying quantity did not exist at Pike's Peak. As many of the early arrivals became discouraged, the contingents of "go backs" seemed to equal the westbound travelers on the trails. The chants of discontent threatened to swell into a chorus of "humbug."

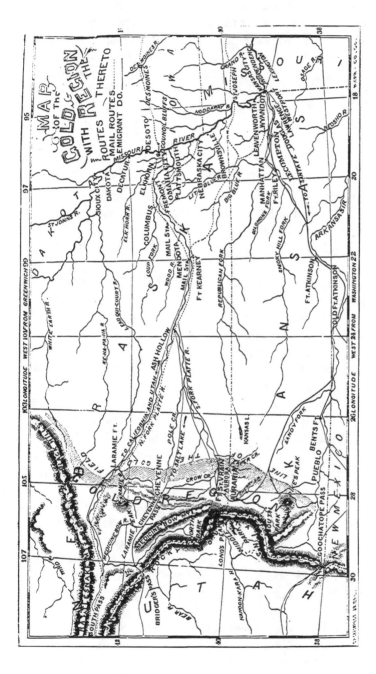

Routes to the goldfields, from a guidebook issued by William N. Byers and John H. Kellom in 1859.

Luckily for the future of the place, a few had kept searching during the winter months for the likely looking gulches. And before the spring of 1859 was very old, good news greeted the newcomers. Three independent discoveries of more than ordinary gold sites established beyond doubt the existence of Pike's Peak gold. Each of the finds was adventure in itself; together they provided the opening wedge into three gold camps that would dominate the region for some time.

George A. Jackson was a man of considerable mining experience, not unlike William Green Russell. He had been in California from 1853 to 1857, and in those years he had gained a practical education in prospecting for gold. In January 1859, he went hunting in the hills above Arapahoe City with some companions. Leaving them, he pushed his way alone up Clear Creek Canyon. Near the place where Chicago Creek joins Clear Creek, in the severest of difficulties, he made his find. Thawing the hard, frozen ground by building fires and melting snow in a tin cup to wash the debris, Jackson panned out about a half ounce of gold. He wore out his belt knife with the digging and he realized that he must wait until spring to exploit his discovery. He marked the spot and recorded in his diary: "Feel good tonight." Back in Arapahoe City he related his discovery only to Tom Golden, a man whose mouth was "as tight as a No. 4 Beaver trap" and who could be trusted to keep the secret.

A second streak of luck occurred the same month of January 1859. Six men from the settlement at the mouth of Boulder Canyon decided to try their fortunes at prospecting during an interval of warm winter weather. They found gold, in quantity, at the foot of Gold Hill.

Finally, in April, John H. Gregory, from Georgia, who had been panning on the north fork of Clear Creek, not too far from the Jackson discovery, retrieved gold that told his experienced eye that somewhere nearby a rich lode of gold in rock must have decomposed enough to allow nuggets to wash into the streambed. He was certain he had found the site of a paying lode mine, but a spring snowstorm ended his prospecting, and he returned to the settlements, keeping his secret to himself.

By that time the Boulder Canyon news was common property. Soon Jackson would meet with some argonauts from Chicago and together they would organize the Chicago Mining Company to exploit the Clear Creek placer. Then Gregory fell in with a group of Indiana gold seekers, led by Wilkes Defrees. In return for a grubstake, Gregory led them to his promising site and there, on May 6, the first lode mine was uncovered.

Placer mining in Gregory Gulch between Central City and Black Hawk in the early 1860s.

Now the news spread everywhere: three rich finds, exciting enough to empty the valley towns of their population as everyone rushed to the gulches to claim an early share of the diggings.

Denver, Auraria, and Boulder—and the other valley settlements—might be convinced, but there were still some doubters back East crying "humbug." In fact, so much controversy raged that three journalists from well-established newspapers decided to investigate the claims and report the honest facts to their readers. Henry Villard of the *Cincinnati Commercial*, Albert D. Richardson of the Boston *Journal*, and the national favorite, Editor Horace Greeley of the New York *Tribune*, surveyed the scene in June. Rumor still reports that the mine Greeley washed gold from was salted, but perhaps this was unnecessary. All three of the journalists seem to have caught something of the contagion of the place and even though their report cautioned against unwarranted enthusiasm, their generally favorable verdict undoubtedly helped to swell the tide of argonauts in the summer of 1859.

Certainly the Pike's Peak region experienced a phenomenal metamorphosis during those months. The area of greatest attraction was the region surrounding the original Gregory claim in Gregory Gulch. The Russell brothers, with a company of newly recruited Georgia prospectors and equipment enough to engage in full-scale mining, opened up placers in Russell Gulch, about two miles from Gregory's lode. In no time the valley claimed several towns—Black Hawk, Gregory Point, Mountain City, Central City, Nevadaville—all strung out up the steep incline.

Not everyone was satisfied with conditions at those camps. Some preferred Idaho, the leading town in the vicinity of Jackson's find. Others crossed the mountain passes into South Park, initiating such pick-and-shovel camps as Tarryall, Hamilton, Fairplay, and Buckskin Joe. By late summer, the prospectors had reached the Blue River on the other side of the divide.

When the snows of winter fell, the Pike's Peak area was a far different place from what it had been twelve months before. Mountain camps had drained population from the valley towns, although many miners probably climbed down from the high hills to spend the winter in the supply towns. Denver and Auraria no longer rested easy in their claims as the central points for supplying the mines to the west, for in June 1859, W. A. H. Loveland, and others, had opened the town called Golden City. And along the mountain base, others had platted settlements like Canon City and Colorado City. Obviously, a new day had dawned in the Rocky Mountain frontier.

SEVEN

MINERS AND MERCHANTS

When William Green Russell's party of gold seekers dug their first gold dust from the bed of Dry Creek, they found exactly the type of gold for which they had been looking. They had come to the Rocky Mountains to prospect for "free" gold. Gold in its free form exists in a variety of shapes: nuggets, scale, shot, wire, grains, flour, dust. It is usually found in streambeds or along the banks of creeks in sites called placers. The miner who worked the placer mine was, in many ways, the trailblazer for all other mining activities. Taking gold out of the gravel of a streambed is the simplest operation of mining. The gold needs no smelting or refining; it is not bulky and can be transported easily from frontier areas.

Every experienced prospector knew that gold in such a placer could well indicate proximity to another type of free gold deposit—a lode. Lodes are free gold in rock formation. The vein or streak of ore in the rock, usually quartz, might run for great distances into the earth, requiring more complex procedures for removing it from the surrounding rock, moving it to the surface, and separating the free gold from its matte of quartz or other rock.

Early gold mining in the central Rockies was either placer or lode mining, and almost every method used in the extraction process had been known in California during the rush days there. Many of the techniques, in fact, had their origins much earlier, for they were part of the European knowledge of mining, transferred to the New World through the Spanish experience in Mexico and California. Many of those who came to Pike's Peak had participated in the California rush and they introduced their accumulation of mining wisdom into the new fields. Through them, newcomers and amateurs mastered the arts.

Placer mining was the simplest of all mining operations, for the process of extraction involved only the separation of the free gold from the dirt, mud, or gravel with which it was mixed. In working a placer, the miner relied on his pan for washing the debris. Although many kinds of household utensils—from washpans to saucepans to frying pans—temporarily filled the requirement, a well-designed mining pan was made of sheet iron, with sloping sides and, perhaps, a copper bottom. The miner filled the pan with debris and water and, holding it just below the surface of the stream, dissolved the dirt and washed out the pebbles by agitating the pan. Because gold is a heavy metal, it sank to the bottom of the pan where it could be recovered with forceps or, more efficiently, by using mercury. The gold and the mercury formed an amalgam. By heating this amalgam, the miner could drive off the mercury, condense it, and use it again. The free gold remained as a residue.

Panning for gold was hard work. An experienced miner could work through only one-half cubic yard of dirt a day. To speed up the washing process "mass production" methods were introduced into the gulches almost from the beginning. The implements used—the rocker, the long tom, the sluice-box—all were variations on the gold pan theme. They all provided a means of agitating the debris, either by movement, in the case of the rocker, or by rushing water through a trough, as in the long tom and the sluice-box. Two people operating a rocker, one carrying the dirt and the other rocking, could clean out three to five cubic yards of dirt a day. But these methods were of value only for washing the coarser debris; a final panning of the residue garnered the fine gold.

These processes required a constant use of water. Without that precious liquid no pan, no rocker, no sluice could be operated. Thus, the mining season sometimes was limited to the warmer months of the year when the water in the creeks and streams was not frozen. And if the water was not immediately accessible to the gulch it had to be brought by ditches from the nearest source—or the dirt had to be dragged to the water. It was much easier to move water through ditches than to move the dirt to the streams, so the water channels were begun very early. Ditch digging in the mountains was also hard work. Some of the ditches had to carry water ten or twelve miles through rugged mountain terrain.

More ornate water works sometimes were constructed for the placer mines. Boom dams were used in some locations where the flow of the stream was not large enough to operate a sluice. Here the water was collected behind a dam and then let loose with a velocity great enough to wash the debris. Hydraulic mining was even more complex. In this process the water was dammed at elevations higher than the gulch and shot through hoses and nozzles, with pressure great enough to wash the gold-bearing gravel down stream banks or gulch walls.

Placer, or gulch, mining was "poor man's mining"; an individual could embark upon a career with a gold pan at very little expense. But placer mining was also likely to be rather limited in its returns. The big strikes were lode finds, and for those considerably more labor and equipment were required to redeem the precious metal. Near the surface the rocks might have decomposed enough for easy extraction. But the vein of ore soon lured the lode miner deeper into the earth. Shafts and tunnels would have to be dug to follow the vein. When pick-and-shovel work no longer loosened the pay-rock, the miner drilled holes to fill with powder and blasted the rock to bits. When the shaft had been dug quite deep, whims and windlasses were used to raise the ore to the surface. Deeper holes could be worked better with horizontal tunnels. The miners then could remove the ore much more easily and the tunnel also provided a drain for water that collected at the bottom of the shaft.

After the ore was worked loose from the rock and brought to the surface, the gold still had to be recovered from the quartz surrounding it. This required crushing. The early pulverizing implements were primitive, crude stone mortars, and Spanish *arrastres*. The *arrastre* consisted of two large rocks, the bottom one flat and the top one attached to a pole so that oxen or other animals could revolve it. After crushing, the gold still had to be separated from the debris by washing in pans. The *arrastre* was a slow, cumbersome mill. If the ore was high-grade and returned a proportionately large quantity of gold in each ton of ore, those operating it made reasonable profits from their labor. But for most ores, what was needed was a more rapid crushing method—an instrument capable of pulverizing more ore at less cost. That need was answered by the early introduction of stamp mills.

A stamp, or quartz, mill, in its elementary form, consists of heavy weights that are raised by mechanical means and then dropped on the ore. The first stamp mills in the Pike's Peak area were operated with water or horse power; when steam engines were introduced the efficiency of the mills increased remarkably. In 1859 only one stamp mill was in operation, near Nevada City. By the following season, however, more than 150 mills had been brought across the prairies and set up in the gulches. Ball mills were also used. These were iron spheres, into which the ore was placed, along with hard metal pellets. The sphere revolved on a shaft; the force of the hard pellets flying against the ore pulverized the rock. However crushed, the ore needed washing and treatment with mercury; thus water was as much a necessity for operation of the mills as it was for placer mining. Some dug wells in order to obtain clean water to use in milling rather than depend on muddy stream water. Obviously, mills were considerably more expensive than simple gold panning, but lode mining could more than pay the expense of freighting the machinery from the states, setting it up, and keeping it in repair for operation.

Those who came to the fields with some money, or at least some provisions, were the most fortunate of the argonauts. They could prospect for a time on their own capital, hoping to strike it rich before their reserves ran out. Those who had nothing were compelled to work as common laborers for others. They might expect to make from $1 to $3 a day in addition to their board. If they were frugal, they might accumulate enough money to start prospecting for themselves.

Although it is probable that almost everyone who came to the Pike's Peak goldfields in the early rush, at one time or another, tried the mining pan, there were many who found the work too hard, the returns too meager. Others came with no intention of mining for a daily occupation. Some had decided even before they crossed the plains that their own particular trade or talent would be in demand in the gold towns. The necessity of providing goods, supplies, and services for those in the diggings gave many a chance to make a living—and a few to make fortunes—from the miners' trade.

It has been estimated that the mining frontier required a population at least five times more numerous than the number actually working the mines. Thus, the variety of small business establishments that characterized any American town of the mid-nineteenth century was soon duplicated in the supply towns at the base of the mountains and, to a lesser extent, in the mining camps themselves. Blacksmiths, bakers and saloon keepers, butchers, hotel and boardinghouse proprietors, druggists, livery stable owners and dance hall managers, bankers, barbers, and retailers of general merchandise, jewelers, gunsmiths, and brewers—and scores of other merchants opened their shops on either side of the wide, dirt main streets of the towns.

Meat was usually the only commodity, except for wood, that the miners in the mountains provided for themselves. Even then, some of the gold seekers preferred to spend their waking hours digging and washing rather than hunting wild animals or chopping down trees. A few fresh vegetables were grown in the area. Within the first full season, the summer of 1859, some enterprising, perhaps disappointed gold seekers turned to onions and radishes instead of the glittering metal and began to irrigate small plots of ground in the valley of the South Platte River. Some corn was available from Charley Autobees's—and other— pioneer farms in the Huerfano Valley south of the diggings. But almost every other item of supply needed by the miners had to be brought into the camps from hundreds of miles away.

In no time at all a feud broke out over who was dependent upon whom in the supply business. The miners complained that they were held at the mercy of the merchants in the valley towns for the goods they needed; they were forced to pay discriminately high prices. The retailers and suppliers, however, insisted that they were making extremely small profits, despite the high prices. They pointed out that the great cost and radical fluctuations in prices were beyond their control; that they were dependent on an irregular and frightfully expensive transportation system for the goods carried across the prairies. The merchants tried to obtain their supplies from all directions: east from the Missouri Valley towns, south from New Mexican villages, west from the Mormon settlements in Utah. But regardless of the sources, prices were always high, partly because the demand for goods remained greater than the supply. The situation was bad enough during the summer months, but when winter weather increased the difficulties of transportation, prices went even higher.

Clashes between miners and merchants were inevitable, not only because of the prices charged for goods by the merchants but also because the tradesmen in town set the price for much of the miners' gold. Whatever barter took place during the early months of the gold rush soon gave way to a new standard circulating medium—gold dust. It was acknowledged a difficult medium to use. A pinch between thumb and forefinger was supposed to represent 25¢; larger amounts were determined by using a scale. The dust was elusive stuff, sticking to scales, pouches, and hands. One pioneer woman later recalled that in the post office, "once a week we would sweep the office floor and wash the sweepings and get quite a little gold dust." Moreover, the dust could be easily mixed with brass filings and other baser metals by amateur counterfeiters. In order to convert the dust to coins, it had to be shipped to the federal mint at Philadelphia or to one of the branch mints (San Francisco, New Orleans, Charlotte, N.C., or Dahlonega, Ga.). Costs of transportation on such precious cargoes were high, and fear of losses was always great, for renegades on the prairies might rob the stages. In addition, the delays in transactions between the Pike's Peak country and the eastern cities were frustrating, for they increased the difficulties of completing business transactions.

Clark, Gruber and Company, a Leavenworth banking house that had opened branch operations in Denver City, was one of the six banks in the town in 1860. After obtaining dies and machinery, Clark, Gruber and Company began to cast $10 gold pieces in July 1860. Private mints were not then illegal in the United States, but to make certain that its coins would be favorably received, this banking house used a little more gold in each coin than the federal coins contained. In time the company would also fabricate $2.50, $5, and $20 pieces, continuing their operations until the federal government bought their mint in 1863. (It was assumed that the United States would continue minting operations. Actually, the establishment became an assay office only, until 1906 when the Denver Mint was established. Clark, Gruber and Company, reorganized in 1865, became the First National Bank of Denver.) Two other private mints were in operation in the Pike's Peak country for a time, and some people experimented with scrip, or shinplasters, which were printed paper notes of small denomination. In these ways the problems of gold dust currency were partly overcome.

All this was helpful for the merchants in the valley towns, but the miners coming in to buy supplies had gold dust—not Clark, Gruber coins—in their jeans pockets. The price of gold remained in contention between miners and merchants. In the spring of 1861 the Central City merchants joined to establish a schedule of prices they would allow for gold, including such classifications as Clear Creek gold priced at $17 an ounce, Russell Gulch gold at $16 an ounce, the best average quality of retorted gold at $15 an ounce, and common, badly retorted, or dirty gold

at $12 an ounce. The Central City traders sent their schedule of prices to a newly formed Chamber of Commerce in Denver. That group added to the list and then attempted to make it effective among its members. In practical terms, the new prices meant reduced prices for some of the gold that was traded in Central City or Denver. Howls of protest went up from miners and mill owners, adding to the already smoldering hostility between mountain gulches and valley towns. That hostility had earlier been expressed by a speaker at a mass meeting of miners in Gregory Diggings: "The valleys were dependent upon the mountains but the mountains were not dependent upon Denver and Auraria. If we can purchase our goods at the same prices in Golden City, and they will receive our gold at the usual price, we had better patronize them, or if we should send a train of thirty or forty wagons to the States through Denver and Auraria, to supply our wants, they may be soon convinced as to whether the mountains were dependent upon the valleys." The Russell District miners put the case more bluntly: "Merchants furnishing us goods have no right whatever after making their profit on their goods to speculate upon our dust."

Although one can sympathize with the miners in their problems, the merchants also had difficulties of impressive dimensions in trying to bring supplies into the Pike's Peak region. The barrier of the Rocky Mountains deflected the main overland routes to the north (Oregon Trail) and south (Santa Fe Trail). At the same time, the mining districts were 600 miles from the sources of supply on the Missouri River. Most freighters used teams of oxen to pull the heavy merchandise wagons over the prairies. The beasts traveled very slowly; water and feed were scarce on the plains; attacks by Indians, robberies by renegades, and bad weather all added hazards to the commerce.

Moving supplies from the valley towns like Denver or Boulder or Golden City up the grades to the diggings was also difficult. There were no roads into the mountains worthy of the name until toll companies began to construct them after 1860. When they were finished, these roads added toll costs to the already high charges of freighting, even though many of the roads were so poorly designed and constructed that they were little better than trails. Each new season of mining brought added demands for extension of the roads, for each new season saw the opening of new gold camps, farther from the supply towns. These new camps also offered inducements for further town building: California Gulch, for example, with its rich placers at the headwaters of the Arkansas River, provided the impetus for the creation of Pueblo in July 1860, near the earlier settlement called Fountain City.

As for passenger travel to the gold frontier, Russell, Majors and Waddell of St. Joseph, Missouri, had a decided advantage over rival staging companies when the rush began, for they were already operating in the region. The federal government had recently granted them a contract to haul supplies to army units in Utah Territory. These men now created the Leavenworth and Pike's Peak Express Company to provide daily coach service between Kansas and the Cherry Creek settlements. With some forty coaches, each capable of carrying eight passengers, the Leavenworth and Pike's Peak Company charged a fare of $100 to $125 for a one-way trip, including meals. The journey took about twelve days at the beginning, but when the company substituted the South Platte route for the Republican River trail, it cut the time to about one week.

The coaches traveled continuously, day and night. Short stops were made along the way at stage or relay stations that would be distinctive features of prairie travel until the lines no longer operated. The stations always provided a source of amusement to foreign visitors. A French traveler described them: "At the relay stations you will find waiting a hand basin and a pitcher of water, with soap and a towel that turns endlessly around a roller. You will find mirrors, combs, and brushes, and even tooth brushes, all fastened by a long string, so that everyone may help himself and no one will carry them off. You might laugh in Paris at these democratic customs; here they are accepted by all and are even welcome, except perhaps the tooth brush, which is regarded with a suspicious eye."

Despite its original advantage over competitors, the Leavenworth and Pike's Peak Express was a short-lived company. In 1860 it was reorganized as the Central Overland, California and Pike's Peak Express

Company—a name so long that the initials COC&PP (Clean Out of Cash and Poor Pay) were inevitably substituted. This was the organization that ran the romantic but also short-lived Pony Express across western America. The Pony Express used a relay station at Julesburg, but never provided direct service to the Cherry Creek towns. Then, in 1861, the COC&PP sold out to Ben Holladay's Overland Mail and Express Company. Five years later, Holladay's line was taken over by the rival Wells, Fargo & Company.

At the beginning, the private stage companies carried letters, for high fees, to and from the mining camps. The Pike's Peakers, however, wanted direct, daily mail service. In March 1861, Congress offered a $1 million subsidy to the company that would undertake a daily transcontinental mail, with Denver and Salt Lake City serviced either by the main line or by extension routes. Denver now stirred itself to convince everyone of its claims for a location on the direct east-west route. What was needed was a usable pass through the mountains west of the city. Captain Edward L. Berthoud, hired to seek out such a pass, and his guide, Jim Bridger, found the crossing known today as Berthoud Pass. But despite their enthusiasm, further investigation revealed that the grade up Clear Creek Canyon would be difficult, while the high pass with its winter snows would require extensive tunneling for all-weather operations. Another decade and more would pass before the first wagon road would be built over Berthoud Pass.

So the daily mail service used the Oregon Trail, with the gold camps serviced by a tri-weekly branch from Julesburg. But in 1862, when Indian raids disrupted traffic on the main trail, the mail company did send its stages down the South Platte route to Denver and then north on the old Cherokee Trail. In this way, the Cherry Creek towns achieved their desire of a daily mail service that tied them to the rest of the country. Shortly after that, in 1863, a branch telegraph line crossed the sage hills from Julesburg to Denver, and in time other extensions would connect Central City and Pueblo to the main telegraph circuit. Thus the problems of communication were lessened considerably. Transportation difficulties, however, were not as easily ended. It was 1870 before the iron horse chugged along its rails into Denver to bring the benefits and the problems of railroading to the Pike's Peak country.

EIGHT

CULTURE COMES
TO THE GOLD TOWNS

The glorious Fourth of July in the election year of 1860 seemed like a good time for the fledgling communities of the Pike's Peak area to celebrate. In Denver an appointed committee of civic leaders worked out the arrangements for the patriotic occasion. A thirty-two gun salute greeted the sun rising over the eastern plains on the morning of the holiday to usher in the festivities. A parade through the main streets provided the first exciting attraction. Participating groups included the ladies of the Temple of Liberty, the Freemasons, the Odd Fellows, the Sons of Malta, the Pioneer Club, the Sabbath schools, and the Turnvereins. Such a list of organizations alone was enough to dispel any doubts about the civilization of the town that was less than two years old. Then, in traditional style, the orators reminded the Pike's Peakers of the glorious heritage of the Republic. The horse races at Reynolds Course, some three miles below Denver, probably provided the high point of the day. When another thirty-two gun salute marked the sunset, the citizens knew that, although separated by miles of prairie land from the rest of the nation, and still unacknowledged by the federal government, Denver had celebrated the Fourth of July in fitting fashion.

There was need for only one celebration in the Cherry Creek towns that year, for Denver City and Auraria had merged their interests and buried their antagonisms several months earlier. On the moonlit night of April 5, on the wooden bridge spanning Cherry Creek, the leaders of the rival communities had celebrated the union of their enterprises. Competition was a luxury these towns could no longer afford. Up the canyon of Clear Creek, Golden City was proving a dangerous rival. And to the north and the south other competitors threatened. The time had come to join hands. So the town of Auraria had died, and the combined city called Denver had been born.

It was to Denver that most of the newcomers headed. Here the stage lines and the freight routes from the east converged; here was the major supply center for the mountains to the west; here a ferry operated across the Platte River until bridges were built. From the very beginning, the confluence of Cherry Creek with the South Platte River acted like a magnet in drawing the immigrants to it. Despite the lack of trees and the somewhat barren aspects of the infant town, it was a welcome sight to the traveler, weary from the long and tiring stage ride across the plains. Miners deserting the high hills during the winter months found it equally attractive. Every year the place grew more civilized. What might be lacking one year was more than compensated for by the grandiose hopes and prophecies of what was to come the next.

The amazement at the speed with which Denver took on the aspects of an older, more established town was not confined to the local "boosters." Visitors to the region reacted with almost as much pride in the accomplishments. Travelers constantly registered surprise at what they termed Denver's "solid progress" despite all the discouraging circumstances of isolation, lack of authorized government, Indian scares, and the fluctuating prophecies about the future of the mining camps.

What was true of Denver was true to only a lesser degree of other towns in the valleys and in the mining districts. On the Upper Arkansas in California Gulch in July 1860, for example, Webster D. Anthony found a log cabin store, which boasted "the first Glass windows" in the settlement of Sacramento City, a thriving town where "only a few weeks ago not a house was seen." And in that same month, a visitor to New Tarryall in South Park wrote: "How long since this town was built? Two months. How many houses does it contain at present? About two hundred. What is the name of this principal street? Broadway."

The weather vanes of society were various, but one of the most obvious was the type of building that lined the streets of the towns. Construction seemed to follow a similar pattern of growth in all the centers.

The rude log cabins and tents of the first years were replaced by frame houses and shop buildings as soon as a saw mill had been brought into the area to afford the luxury of siding and boards. After frame buildings with shingled roofs came brick structures. The final step was the creation of stone and masonry buildings. In the early years, frame buildings dominated the frontier towns. If buildings were used for public purposes, fashion dictated a false front, with a painted sign to advertise the shop or service.

The towns were generally laid out, as much as possible, on the approved rectangular grid. In the gulch towns in the mountains it was sometimes impossible to plan any cross streets, for the canyon walls were so close together there was room for only one long main street. Everywhere the streets were unlighted and unpaved, becoming dusty in summer and turning into quagmires throughout much of the rest of the year.

The pride of every community—valley or gulch—was the church building or buildings, once erected. Nothing else seemed to indicate quite so surely the permanence of the town and its success in duplicating society back in the states. In the first years in the mining towns, the population was overwhelmingly male, for many men had come to the diggings planning to go home again as soon as they had found their gold or had exhausted their money. The town promoters realized that a stable, permanent population could not be assured until families became residents. A church building, with tower or steeple, and perhaps even a bell, openly advertised that a town was a fit place for women and children to live.

The emotional response to a completed church on the frontier was intensified by the ever-present awareness of the region's isolation from the rest of the country. As one of the early settlers recalled: "When for the first time the old bell pealed out in clear tones its call to worship—tones which were strange, indeed, to the ears of these isolated westerners—tears came to the eyes of more than one person whose soul was stirred by the memory of a little church back in the 'states.'"

The earliest religious services in the goldfields were presided over by men who had been lay leaders in their congregations back home. By the spring of 1859 such temporary and spontaneous services began to be replaced with more regularly framed organizations. In April the Methodist Episcopal Church established its Pike's Peak and Cherry Creek Mission within the Kansas-Nebraska Conference, sending out Messrs. William

Central City in the 1860s.

H. Goode and Jacob Adriance as missionaries to organize congregations. By August they had established what later became the Trinity Church in Denver.

The Methodists were followed on the scene by the Episcopalians, led by the Reverend Mr. H. J. Kehler, who established the Church of St. Johns in the Wilderness in Denver in 1860. Presbyterian services were also conducted in Denver that summer and a small Jewish society established the Temple Emanuel congregation the same year. The Baptists and Congregationalists followed shortly thereafter.

In the spring of 1860, Catholic Bishop John B. Miege traveled from Leavenworth, in Kansas, to Denver. Viewing the new settlements as too remote from his home cathedral for supervision, he recommended transferring the area to the jurisdiction of the bishop at Santa Fe. Thus Bishop John Lamy at the New Mexican capital sent his vicarate apostolic, Father Joseph P. Machebeuf, with Father John Raverdy, to Denver in October

1860. These priests managed, through hard labors, to finish a church building in time for celebration of the mass on Christmas Day 1860.

All these early religious establishments were of mission nature and provided a real test to the trained clergy who staffed them. The congregations in the settlements like Denver and Central City needed organization; buildings demanded financing and construction; small settlements, particularly in the mining gulches, needed ministering, too. Itinerant preaching was more the rule than the exception, as clergy of many faiths carried the gospel to miners in isolated gold camps. Most of the clergymen found affairs to their liking and proceeded to make their work a testament to their faith. Sometimes their first impressions were less than they had expected: when the Reverend Mr. William Crawford of the American Home Missionary Society arrived in Denver in 1863, he was tempted, he said, when preaching "to give out the hymn of Watts: 'Lord, what a wretched land is this, which yields us no supply, no cheering fruits, no wholesome trees, no streams of living joy.'" Yet, said Crawford, "some of the Denverites think they have found the best spot on earth. Poor, deluded mortals." But whatever their first thoughts, the clergy generally spared neither themselves nor their followers in their mission activities.

The companion civilizers of the churches were the schools. Although the initial population of the Pike's Peak gold towns tended to be predominantly male, it was not long before families who had settled in the region recognized the need for instruction for their children. By October 1859, Denver could boast its first classroom. This was a private establishment, headed by "Professor" O. J. Goldrick. The schoolmaster had come to Denver like a fugitive from the theatre—his contemporaries recalled later his arrival "as a bullwacker, driving his ox team, yet dressed in broadcloth suit, 'stovepipe' hat, and kid gloves"—a schoolmaster who, tradition boasts, cursed his oxen in learned Latin! Irishborn, with reputed study both at the University of Dublin and Columbia College in New York, Goldrick had taught school and worked for book publishers in Cincinnati before coming to the gold country. His Union-Day School cost each pupil $3 a month. On the first day thirteen children appeared in the classroom—"2 Indians, 2 Mexican, the rest white and from Missouri."

Following Goldrick's example, other schools were soon in operation. Some of these, like the first, were privately operated, although they probably were poor paying propositions since even the earliest of the "professors" found it necessary to become a casual newspaper correspondent to augment his income. Catholic and Episcopalian congregations sponsored other schools. By 1860, classes were being conducted also at Mount Vernon and Golden and at Boulder, where a frame building was erected especially for the purpose—Colorado's first schoolhouse. The Pike's Peak gold camps were much more comfortable places to which a man might bring his family once educational facilities, no matter how limited, were available for the children.

Since the mere mention of schools was likely to dispel doubts about life in the wilderness West in the minds of potential immigrants, town promoters saw the excellent advertising potential of such institutions. Perhaps for that reason, great excitement was generated over the possibilities of an institution of higher education. By May 1863, plans had been drawn and the Denver Seminary was begun, largely under the auspices of the Methodist Church, although its founders attempted to keep it from becoming too closely identified with any one denomination. They changed the name the following year to the Colorado Seminary and soon had managed the construction of a building and had secured a charter. Thus the institution that would later become the University of Denver was a going concern, almost before the public school movement was initiated.

Schools and universities were not the only institutions used by the publicists to attract attention to the area. Realizing that unless the instability of the mining population could be overcome by attracting more permanent residents than the "here today—gone tomorrow" prospectors, the early newspapers of the Pike's Peak region all succumbed to varying degrees of "boosterism." More sane in his approach than some, yet still unwilling to sell his adopted city short, William N. Byers and his *Rocky Mountain News* established an early ascendancy over the rest of the news sheets in the gold towns. Byers, a one-time surveyor, left his home in Omaha, Nebraska, in March 1859, in the vanguard of the argonauts moving west. With Dr. George Monell and Thomas Gibson, he set out for the diggings with a printing press and supplies for a newspaper in his wagon. On April 23 the infant *News* was born, beating out by minutes John Merrick's *Cherry Creek Pioneer* as the first Pike's Peak newspaper.

The competition proved brief, for Merrick sold his *Pioneer* to Thomas Gibson after he had run the first issue, taking his grubstake to the hills to finance some prospecting. Gibson would stay with the weekly *News* until the spring of 1860 when he started the daily *Rocky Mountain Herald*. Such competition forced Byers to convert the *News* to a daily too. And soon the area was full of rival enterprises: the *Register* at Gregory Gulch, the *Western Mountaineer* at Golden City, the Black Hawk *Journal*, the *Gold Reporter* at Mountain City, the *Boulder Valley News*. No self-respecting community in either valley or gulch could afford to ignore the possibilities of enticing an editor and a press to set up shop. As soon as a town was started, its founders and merchants needed a newspaper to demonstrate the success of their venture and to advertise the "city's" advantages. As the editor of the Canon City *Times* pointed out, "A city is as much indebted to its public journal for its progress and prosperity as to its avenues of trade." By 1867 five daily, eight weekly, and two monthly papers bore Colorado imprints. In the pages of those newspapers are the telling indications of the society they served. Here professionals—the lawyers, the doctors, the dentists—advertised their services. From the newspaper columns another aspect of the steady transition from wilderness to civilization can be traced, as professional associations are recorded. For example, by June 1860, enough physicians had arrived in the Cherry Creek area to create the Jefferson Medical Society. It lasted long enough to adopt a code of ethics and a uniform fee of $3 a visit. A city hospital had also been organized by that year.

The professional people were not the only ones who saw potential advantages from collective action. In the summer of 1863 the carpenters in Denver organized an association, through which they adopted a minimum wage resolution calling for payment of $4 a day for their work. And the typesetters in Denver had organized Typographical Union No. 49 even earlier.

Social, rather than economic forces, motivated the organization of other groups. Lodges and clubs seemed as easy to transport westward as stamp mills or flour barrels. The Masons, the Templars, the Odd Fellows, the Turnvereins, and many other organizations were soon well established in Denver, Central City, and many of the other towns. By 1866 Denver assumed it was aged enough to rate a Pioneer's Association, which, in exclusive fashion, restricted its membership to 1858-1859 immigrants—the pioneers of a mere seven or eight years earlier.

Much of the recreation of the pioneers was more casual, less formal, than that provided by clubs and lodges. Nature had created a splendid playground for the settlers, with trout streams, wild animals, and scenic wonders everywhere. The central Rockies had seen big hunts before the gold rush. In 1854 Irish Baronet Sir St. George Gore, with numerous re-tainers, dogs, horses, and wagons, had hunted through North, Middle, and South Parks, with the reported killing of several thousand buffalo, forty grizzly bears, and unnumbered antelope and deer. Now, with grow-ing enthusiasm, this sportsmen's paradise was openly advertised as the finest on the continent, and excursions from the valley towns as well as from the states—and even the Old World—racked up hunting records that often indicate something more like slaughter than sport.

Along with trout and grizzly bears, the mountains also provided hot springs, which were quickly converted into sites for health seekers, fur-thering an infant Colorado industry called tourism. For example, only a few years after the opening of the goldfields, the soda springs near Idaho Springs were in use as a water cure and bathing establishment.

In the gold towns, sporting events were a conspicuous and exciting part of life. Baseball arrived early; certainly by 1862 Denver fielded teams, and other towns followed suit, creating rivalries. Wrestling and boxing matches were natural accompaniments to the predominantly male society of the early years; a wrestling match highlighted the first Christmas celebration at Cherry Creek. Horse racing was another fa-vorite, perhaps the most widely enjoyed of all recreational occasions. Participants and spectators alike found the races, and the wagering on them, exciting avenues of escape from the drudgery and routine of fron-tier life. Guns, blankets, horses, gold dust, town lots, and mining claims could be and were wagered on the races.

And when the race was over, the place to retire and talk about it, or to plan the next event, was the town saloon. These poor men's social clubs played so conspicuous a part of the main-street life of western towns that, a century later, the image is still vivid. These liquor-dis-pensing establishments often were operated as adjuncts to gambling halls, billiard parlors, or bawdy houses. Tradition accords them a promi-nent place in the town life, and no stories are more often repeated than the incongruous tales of early religious services conducted in the bar room, with gambling tables quieted long enough to allow the "parson" a chance to preach.

Although it spoils the picture of the frontier as a place that was al-ways wild and always rough and always wide open, truth intrudes the qualification that temperance sentiment also was a positive force in most of the towns. Restrictions to regulate saloons appeared almost as soon as the saloons themselves. Some mining districts contented themselves by

Musicians pose on the balcony of Concert Hall, a noted Central City gambling establishment, about 1865.

declaring that "all Gambling houses and Drinking saloons that are open for the carrying on of their business on Sunday be considered . . . a nuisance." Others went further; the miners of Nevada District, for example, resolved "that there shall be no Bawdy Houses Grog shops or Gamboling Saloons within the Limits of this District."

More refined, but still well-patronized features of town life were the music halls and theatres. Offerings might be limited in the early years, but to sweat-stained miners or tired merchants seeking diversion from their laboring hours, the quality was less important than the opportunity for relaxation. Entertainers found appreciative, applauding patrons eager to view their offerings. And the gap between musical variety shows and genuine drama was quickly bridged. Home talent soon gave way to traveling companies of professional players.

With theatres and saloons, schools and churches, the towns matured. Sometimes, however, the pattern of progress was rather rudely jolted. On the wintry morning of April 19, 1863, a fire burned out of control in Denver, and before the volunteer fire companies managed to stop its advance, the flames had destroyed the heart of the city. The

The great Cherry Creek flood of 1864.

seventy buildings and estimated $197,200 worth of supplies consumed by the fire were a serious loss. But the city bounced back with enthusiasm as it contemplated the new construction that would replace the old, congratulating itself that the new buildings would be largely of brick and stone, instead of wood—"that fragile and combustible material" that identified the buildings of a pioneer town.

The Denver fire of 1863 was bad enough, but the next year the town suffered another and worse disaster. On the night of May 20, 1864, the waters of Cherry Creek rose and a "wall of water" swept down the valley, carrying with it the Methodist Church, the *Rocky Mountain News* office (which Editor Byers had diplomatically placed between the once-rival towns of Denver City and Auraria), the City Hall and all the records stored there. Denver counted eight known flood victims; several more died in outlying areas. The lesson could hardly be ignored, and a healthy respect for the character of the mountain streams was learned. But again, instead of grieving over the losses, the young town plunged forward with renewed determination.

With such enthusiasm and such energy the towns of the Pike's Peak region were built. Within little more than a decade of their births they seemed no longer strange, primitive objects to be considered pretentious in all their claims to greatness. Englishman James Thomson summed it up neatly when he described his impressions of Central City in 1872: "We have churches, chapels, schools, and a new large hotel, in which a very polite dancing party assembled the other evening. . . . We have a theatre, in which we now and then have actors. The rough old days with their perils and excitements, are quite over; the 'City' is civilised enough to be dull and commonplace, while not yet civilised enough to be sociable and pleasant." The birthing times were over. The Pike's Peak towns had entered their awkward adolescence.

NINE

LEGAL BEGINNINGS

"Pike's Peak or Bust" read the signs on the canvas wagon coverings. "Pike's Peak country" was the closest thing to a name the new diggings had. Actually, most of the area of the earliest gold strikes was legally a part of the Territory of Kansas. Since 1854, the fortieth parallel had separated that territory from Nebraska Territory to the north. South of the Arkansas River the New Mexican officials ruled, while the Western Slope was within the boundaries of the Utah Territory. These were the political boundaries. However, much of the land had been expressly reserved by treaty for various Indian tribes. Thus the Pike's Peak argonauts moved onto lands belonging to Indians, lands hundreds of miles away from the capitals of the four federal territories. Too distant for effective control from any one of them, the gold seekers were left to provide their own devices for law and order in the diggings.

If the immigrants settled in the valley towns, they found themselves provided with a type of organization formed mainly for purposes of town-booming and lot-selling. The town company leaders were interested in protecting property and developed instruments known as "people's courts"—mass meetings to try, and sometimes execute, criminals who violated the community's peace. It was government self-manufactured and, in many respects, quite democratic.

The miners in the gulches and hills followed the example of the town promoters and created their own governments, called "mining districts." These were more formally organized than the people's courts, for the miners wrote constitutions providing names, boundaries, and officers for their districts. They also regulated the size and method of proving claims and established procedures for settling disputes. The officers were few in number: a president; a recorder or secretary to enter the claims in the record books; a constable or sheriff to serve writs and summonses. Since miners did not want to lose unnecessary time at work, the officers were elected for short terms. They were not paid salaries but, rather, were allowed stipulated fees for their work. For example, the recorder in some districts collected $1 for each claim entered on the district records and corresponding amounts for other official duties.

The most important function of the district officers was to see that the claim system worked properly. Actually, all claims were of doubtful legality since the Indians still held title to much of the land. But acting on the assumption that the federal government would soon extinguish the Indian claims, the settlers proceeded to arrange a system of their own, based on the preemption laws. These federal statutes provided that actual settlers would have the first chance to purchase their holdings when their land was surveyed and offered for sale.

There were many types of claims arranged, each designed for a particular purpose or to suit certain conditions. The mountain, lode, or quartz claim gave the right to work a lode or vein of ore. Although the dimensions of all claims varied from district to district, and from time to time, the usual size of the lode claim was 100 feet in length and 50 feet in width. In most districts, prospectors could preempt no more than one claim on any one lode. Gulch or placer claims usually were measured 100 feet up and down the gulch, from bank to bank. Since water was an integral part of all mining operations, water claims were instituted, measured in feet up and down the streams. More extensive water rights were necessary for operating stamp or lumber mills, and these were usually designated as mill site claims, with the size determined by the amount of water required for a suitable dam or to keep a mill wheel operating. Not as common, but still of use, were timber claims for cutting trees in areas other than the mineral claims of the miner. And there were other variations: patch claims for diggings in placers outside stream beds or gulches; tunnel claims for digging into lode shafts; cabin claims and ranch claims.

Miners met to organize districts, regulate claims, and settle disputes.

A discoverer perfected a claim by staking off the site and marking on the stakes the name of the claim and the discoverer's name. The discoverer then had ten days, not counting Sundays, to record the claim and was given the right to one additional claim on the lode or gulch as an incentive reward for the discovery. Once the claim was recorded, others could locate on the lode, in numbered sequence in either direction from the original claim. No one under sixteen years of age could hold a claim, and all claims (except that of the discoverer) had to be improved or worked on. Satisfactory improving usually was accomplished by working one day in every ten until ten days of work had been completed. If the claim was not improved, it was declared vacant and could then be reclaimed by someone else.

These requirements were devised to be more than mere formalities. The codes were arranged to answer the need for protection of the miners' property and when disputes arose they were settled according to methods prescribed in the written codes. Although procedures varied, the method of deciding disputes in Gregory Diggings was probably typical. A miner claiming a grievance called on the district recorder who selected nine disinterested miners, and the parties to the controversy alternately struck names from the list until three remained. This panel of three arbitrators decided the case at once. If the miner did not agree with their decision, the recorder called a general meeting of all miners in the district who, by majority vote, could sustain or overrule the panel's decision. If the original verdict was upheld, then a party refusing to obey the verdict could no longer hold a mining claim in the district. Like most legal codes, that of Gregory Diggings underwent frequent changes, and the procedures of trial were refined in a pragmatic fashion. In time, the appeal stage was modified so that a jury of twelve men reviewed cases on appeal from the decision of the arbitration panel.

The process of creating legal codes was repeated in the several hundred mining districts organized in the Pike's Peak country in the first years of the gold rush. The governments were indigenously established, with no authority other than the "sovereignty" of the individual miners who agreed to place themselves under the districts' control. But such procedures were by no means unique to the Colorado mountains; they had been native to America since the Mayflower Compact of 1620. More directly related to the Pike's Peak experiences were the mining districts formed in California a decade earlier. The California districts had borrowed freely from Spanish customs and laws, and the hybrid results from the mixture of parentage worked well in the Rocky Mountains.

What worked for the miners in the mountains also worked for the agricultural settlers in the valleys. There squatters organized claim clubs to secure their tracts of land against latecomers and speculators. Here again, the techniques were borrowed from earlier frontiers, where claim clubbing had developed in Wisconsin and Iowa. An example was the El Paso Claim Club, organized in August 1859. The club operated under a written constitution with elected officers, including a panel of arbitrators to settle disputes concerning the validity of claims on some eighty square miles of land in the valleys of Fountain, Monument, and Camp Creeks. This land had not been surveyed by the federal authorities, so it was necessary to describe the claims of the members in terms of natural features like streams and trees. The Indian title to the land had not been extinguished and the major purpose of the club was to provide collective security to the settlers until such time as the federal government cleared the Indian titles, surveyed the land, and was ready to sell it at public auction. Although not nearly so numerous as the mining districts, one or more claim clubs were organized in each of the river valleys of the Eastern Slope and one club protected properties across the front ranges in Middle Park in 1860.

The town companies, designed principally to secure sites for specu-lation and profit, and the mining districts and claim clubs, whose main purpose was to secure and hold land claims, all provided rudimentary government for the settlers within their boundaries. They were all extra-legal, but, particularly in their early months, they served their purpose well. They protected personal and property rights until more legitimate governments were established, and they punished offenders in quick and simple procedures. Persons accused of wrongdoing were tried be-fore assembled citizens; once the verdict was pronounced, the guilty per-son usually was punished immediately, for the miners and tradesmen had neither time nor money to maintain prison facilities. Whipping, banishment, hanging—depending on the seriousness of the crime—were usual punishments. Horse thieves probably were the most common criminals of western America. But competing with them for notoriety were highwaymen, petty thieves, cheating gamblers—the usual host of depraved characters associated with a highly mobile society. In the min-eral districts and agricultural valleys, claim jumpers created problems. The elementary laws worked quite well, providing processes for re-straining disrupters of the peace.

Volumes have been written about the lawlessness of the rip-roaring frontier, and the Pike's Peak mining camps usually are not excepted from the general statements. Horace Greeley got into the act early by assert-ing that there were "more brawls, more fights, more pistol-shots with criminal intent in this log city [Denver] of one hundred and fifty dwellings, not three-fourths completed nor two-thirds inhabited, nor one-third fit to be, than in any community of equal numbers on earth." While it is difficult to describe accurately the extent of crime and unruly life in the mining camps, a good guess is that the Pike's Peak frontier was never as roaring as either Editor Greeley or later fiction writers have sug-gested.

Yet no matter how effectively the mining districts and the people's courts took care of local criminals, the Pike's Peakers sought more legit-imate, recognized government. Not only was state-making and senator-electing something of an American passion; the Pike's Peakers fully understood the advantages to be gained from political controls recog-nized by the federal government.

This explains why, in November 1858, during the first autumn at the diggings, the relatively tiny population voted at Auraria to send a dele-gate to Washington, D.C., to gain territorial status for the region. At the same time, with seemingly equal enthusiasm and, if later memories were correct, with equal fraud on both sides of a "wet" vs. "dry" split in the population, the voters elected a representative for the Kansas Territorial Legislature. From this shotgun method, one or the other might result in legitimate recognition. A. J. Smith traveled east to Kansas and was seated in the legislature there. Hiram J. Graham, who had defeated the "wet" candidate, William Clancy, to become the congressional delegate, carried with him to Washington a petition requesting the creation of a new territory. When he arrived at the national capital he found others already at work on the scheme. A bill was introduced for the formation of the Pike's Peak region into Colona Territory, but it died at birth in the House of Representatives in January 1859. Two other attempts that winter at congressional territory-making also proved unsuccessful.

In the spring of 1859, the Pike's Peakers decided that if Congress was not going to act, then they would establish their own territorial—or state—government. In April, at a meeting in "Uncle Dick" Wootton's store building in Auraria, delegates representing Fountain City, Eldorado, El Paso, Arapahoe, Auraria, and Denver City determined that a state was needed. The preferred name was Jefferson. A call went out for the election of delegates to a constitutional convention to be held in June. That convention, with fifty men representing thirteen different districts, convened as scheduled. But by June many immigrants were on their way home, disillusioned by their lack of success at gold mining. The number of "go backs" was great enough to raise the question again of whether a state or territory would best fit the needs of the communities.

Small wonder that the delegates were undecided; even today it is easy to be surprised at their actions, for "note the dashing boldness of these resolute pioneers. Here was a convention representing less than two thousand people, less than half of them fixed residents, before any great mines had been opened, or even discovered; before capabilities of the soil were known; before an acre of land had been planted, and whilst every soul was in doubt whether or not there ever would be a basis for support of even a small population, taking measures without precedent, without authority of law, and without the slightest prospect of ratification, for the creation of an independent commonwealth."

Unable to decide the question, the convention adjourned until August and then it nicely straddled the problem by drafting both a state constitution and a memorial to Congress requesting territorial status. The two propositions were presented to the people, who voted 2,007 for territorial status, 1,649 for statehood. It has been estimated that no more than one-fourth of the residents of the Pike's Peak area actually cast their ballots.

Nonetheless, acting on this indication of popular preference, a territory was manufactured in October, without any authority to do so by Congress. The voters elected Robert W. Steele governor of their creation—Jefferson Territory. He was to be aided in his administration by a secretary, a treasurer, an auditor, an attorney-general, a chief justice, two associate justices, a supreme court clerk, a marshal, and a superintendent of public instruction.

The constitution of the new territory provided for a two-house legislature. Elections for the legislators were held and a thirty-one-day session convened in November 1859. This Jefferson legislature enacted provisions for officers' salaries, a judicial system, the creation of counties, and the chartering of corporations. But it was one thing to pass laws and another to enforce them, particularly if they involved taxes. When the legislature levied a poll tax of $1 on each resident, hundreds of miners in the hills pledged to resist the collection of any tax imposed on them by the territory. In so doing, they repudiated the government itself.

Actually, as its founders well knew, Jefferson Territory could only be a temporary make-shift. Congressional approval was imperative for success. Thus, all through the days of the Jefferson experiment, agents and influence were used to prompt congressional action. The times, however, were not conducive to success; the slavery debate between North and South, and the approaching presidential election of 1860, absorbed the time and energy of Congress and the politicians to the exclusion of most other matters. One thing, however, did emerge from these attempts—the name Colorado.

Jefferson was not a popular name for the future territory; some people argued that Washington should be the only president honored by such distinction since all presidents could not be equally treated, and others, of the new Republican Party, were opposed because Thomas Jefferson was identified in memories with the rival Democrats. Many alternative names were suggested—Yampa, Idahoe, Nemara, San Juan, Lula, Weapollao, Arapahoe, Colorado, Tahosa, Lafayette, Columbus, Franklin—so many in fact, that as late as February 1861, a miner informed his correspondent to direct his letters "to Denver City with the name of this Territory, whatever Congress is pleased to call it." But gradually the name Colorado gained in favor, and it was ultimately assigned to the region.

Meanwhile, the government of Jefferson Territory became increasingly impotent. Control devolved into the local, popular agencies—the miners' districts, the claim clubs, the people's courts. Dissatisfaction with the state of affairs appears to have become rather widespread. One man complained: "We are neither in the Union or out of it. We are not sufficiently a territory to have laws, neither so far from it as to have the privilege of making our own laws with the power to enforce them. With what shameful neglect were we treated by that august body at Washington and also by the great father J[ames] B[uchanan]."

Another resident expressed the grievance this way: "This Rocky Mountain Country with its two hundred thousand souls has received just about as much legislative aid at Washington as the Fe Gee Islanders. No mail service for the next twelve months that can be relied on; no extinguishment of the Indian title; no territorial organization, and, in fact, no sort of governmental recognition for the advancement of our interests here . . . so we are compelled to adopt the squatter sovereignty doctrine, making our own laws."

This was the situation in the Pike's Peak area at the time of the 1860 presidential election. The victor in that contest was the candidate of the young Republican party, Abraham Lincoln. Southern representatives, consistent with their earlier warnings, now packed their bags and left Washington. As they withdrew, Kansas Territory, which in its six years of existence had contributed more than its share to the events now taking place, could be admitted as a free state to the Union. On January 29, 1861, Congress voted statehood for Kansas, with its present western boundary.

This meant that the new state's limits ended a long distance from the Pike's Peak gold camps, and the settlers in the mountains were in an even more disorganized status than before. But action to remedy the situation was soon forthcoming. A bill to create Colorado Territory was introduced into the Senate almost immediately after the vote for Kansas statehood. With fewer southern members to fear more free-soil votes, the bill passed the two houses. On February 28, 1861, the lame-duck president, James Buchanan, signed the "birth certificate" for the Territory of Colorado.

TEN

BATTLEGROUNDS

The infant territory called Colorado was brought into the world at the time its parent nation experienced the opening traumas of the greatest crisis in its history—the Civil War. From Fort Sumter in April 1861, until Appomattox Court House in April 1865, the convulsions of that war echoed within the territory, despite its relatively isolated geographic location. And before the end of the conflict had come, the territory would experience its own military problems, as the Indians of the Eastern Slope attempted to drive the white intruders from their hunting lands.

The argonauts had come to the Colorado mines from many home states, both from the North and from the South. Probably it was inevitable that some of the residents would reflect their native sections' cause. Considering the emotional appeals of both sides, however, it is remarkable that so few incidents occurred in Colorado. Southern sentiment appeared one morning in Denver, when the Confederate flag hung from a storefront, but loyal Unionists disposed of it in a hurry. The Unionists, who composed a majority of the settlers, limited their demonstrations to patriotic rallies, where they enthusiastically approved resolutions pledging support to the national government.

There was a curious tone of restraint in these resolutions, however. The declarations of loyalty to the Union were followed by protestations of peaceful intentions and hopes for harmony among all of the territory's people, not only, as they put it, because the framers loved peace but also in case they had "need of all for common defense against the Indian tribes around" them. The exposed and isolated situation of the mining frontier demanded that sectional differences be submerged in the interest of defense against more local dangers.

In one respect, at least, the Coloradans were fortunate, for the war did not begin until after the creation of the territory and its relatively stable government. President Lincoln selected an avowed Unionist, William Gilpin, as the first governor of the territory. Gilpin's views on the sectional crisis coincided with those of the majority of the residents; his leadership helped ensure the continued commitment of Colorado to the nation. Lincoln's choice was well received for another reason. Gilpin was familiar with the territory he would govern, for he had explored with Frémont, campaigned in the area during the Mexican War, and was known nationally as a western enthusiast.

After he arrived in the territory, in late May 1861, Gilpin set in motion the necessary procedures for operating the territorial government. In his work he was aided by his fellow officers who also had received presidential appointments: Secretary Lewis Ledyard Weld, Marshal Copeland Townsend, and Supreme Court Justices Benjamin F. Hall, S. Newton Pettis, and Charles L. Armour. Gilpin appointed additional officers, including an attorney-general and a surveyor-general.

The legislature was elected by the residents, as was the territorial delegate who represented Colorado's interests in the national congress. By September the first territorial legislature convened in Denver, and Republican Hiram P. Bennet—nicknamed "Garden Seed" after the campaign because of his promises to send voters free vegetable seeds—was on his way to Washington as delegate.

There was much work for the legislature's nine-member Council (upper house) and thirteen-member House of Representatives (lower chamber) to do in their first session. Basic codes were needed for both civil and criminal law. These were put together, with considerable borrowing from the law books of Illinois and other established states. The legislature carved the territory into seventeen counties and created machinery for their government. And of particular importance considering the times, the legislature enacted statutes creating the territorial militia.

The military defense of the gold regions, to this time, had been largely a federal concern. The settlers expected that the U.S. Army, from garrison forts in the region, would control any threats to their peace. The army had garrisoned both Fort Garland in the San Luis Valley and Fort Wise (Bent's New Fort, later renamed Fort Lyon) on the Arkansas River. But what in easier times had appeared to be adequate defense now seemed woefully insufficient.

For one thing, the garrisons were physically separated from the mining population, too far south to protect the new towns. Then, too, with the outbreak of the Civil War, the army might ignore frontier areas when it was so fully engaged in serious warfare in the East. And there were more threats to the peace than usual—in fact, three different, possible hazards. Southern sympathizers within the territory might attempt to wrest the area from Union control and attach it to the Confederacy, although this was the most minor of the threats. However, an area known as Mace's Hole, southwest of present Pueblo, did become a hotbed of rebel activity, and an attempt was made to organize an effective Confederate regiment from such areas as California Gulch and Georgia Gulch. A second possible danger might come from the Confederacy itself, for the gold of Colorado would be a great prize for the South, perhaps worth an invasion of the mineral regions of the West. This, as events proved, was no idle fear. Finally, the Indians, sensing the awkward state of the white defenses, might begin hostilities, with the aid, some thought, of Confederate agents. This, too, became a very real problem for the territory in the months ahead.

All these fears troubled Governor Gilpin, who realized that he could expect little immediate aid from the federal authorities. Since the dangers were great, he decided to act and, if necessary, explain later. Gilpin appointed a military staff, started to raise a volunteer infantry regiment, and began to gather implements of warfare. No public money was available for such purposes, but the governor issued $375,000 in drafts on the federal treasury, fully expecting them to be honored by the national government since they were to be used for the defense of the territory and the cause of the Union. And, in fact, Gilpin would later claim that before leaving Washington for Colorado, he had received verbal authorization from Lincoln to issue such drafts.

At first most of the Colorado merchants, tradesmen, and citizens were willing to go along with the governor's preparedness campaign. A few voiced objections, but they soon gave way when the governor and his aides suggested that the alternative to the drafts was outright confiscation of needed supplies. Gradually, however, an undercurrent of uneasiness began to grow concerning the validity of the drafts. When news from Washington corroborated rumors that the federal treasury was unwilling to validate the drafts, the consternation in the territory was enormous. Gilpin found himself a most unpopular man among the Colorado people; where only a few months earlier he had been warmly welcomed as exactly the sort of man the territory needed, now some citizens circulated petitions requesting his removal. The fact that the Gilpin administration had awarded the territorial printing contract to the *Daily Colorado Republican* (thereby angering the powerful and vocal *Rocky Mountain News* Editor William N. Byers) did nothing to help Gilpin's position. Beset on all sides, Gilpin decided to go to Washington to plead his case in person.

Meanwhile, whatever their legal status, the drafts had provided the funds necessary to organize and equip the First Regiment of Colorado Infantry, ten companies strong. In the summer of 1861 the regiment trained at newly constructed Camp Weld, near Denver. By the end of the year, the volunteers were a relatively well trained and equipped force, ready for action. And that action was soon forthcoming, for in the early winter of 1862, while Governor Gilpin was still in the East, the regiment was ordered south to join Colonel Edward R. S. Canby's Union forces in New Mexico. There one of Gilpin's worries had developed into an actual threat. General Henry S. Sibley was moving a Confederate army across the southwestern deserts, attempting to wrest the area from the Union.

By the time the Colorado volunteers reached New Mexico they were greeted with the news that the Texan army under Sibley had already taken the city of Santa Fe and was preparing an attack on Fort Union. In March, at a place called Glorieta Pass, between Santa Fe and Fort Union, the Colorado regiment performed with considerable credit to itself and to the territory. The Union men, with the Coloradans playing conspicuous roles, routed Sibley's Texans in the engagements sometimes called the Gettysburg of the West. That victory seemed to vindicate, for historians if not for contemporaries, the treasury drafts issued by the unpopular Colorado governor.

Unfortunately, the Union victory offered little immediate amelioration for the territory's financial problems. Gilpin's drafts had tied up most of the circulating currency and there was still no indication that the drafts ever would be validated. Eventually the federal treasury agreed to adjust the matter, upon presentation of itemized statements of claims by the holders of the drafts. But by that time Gilpin had been almost completely repudiated. If there had been no war, he probably would have been remembered as a very able first governor of Colorado. As it was, serious mistakes in judgment and attitude, including his assumption that all of his opponents were perforce rebels, contributed to his downfall. Effective in April 1862, President Lincoln removed him from the governorship.

As his replacement, Lincoln selected John Evans, a different sort of man. Both governors were staunch Union supporters, but where Gilpin's credentials for the office had centered in his previous experience and knowledge of the West and its problems, Evans's attractiveness was his proven ability as a successful organizer and entrepreneur in the Midwest. The new governor's first career had been in medicine, but he was also engaged in energetic and profitable enterprises in railroading and real estate. Combined with these experiences was an aggressive interest in education. He had assurances already that his midwestern activities would not be forgotten, for his name was perpetuated in the city of Evanston, Illinois, hometown of Northwestern University, which he had helped to found. He was, in addition, a friend of the president and had early supported his political career.

When Governor Evans arrived in May to take personal control of the territory, he found that some of the earlier fears that had so concerned Governor Gilpin no longer were major problems. The Confederate thrust in New Mexico had been halted, and there had been no eruption of Southern sympathizers within the territory itself. Two minor diversions would occur—a small group of Confederate officers attempting to enter the territory, and a brief raiding excursion by the guerrilla leader, James Reynolds, in the San Luis Valley—but these were disposed of very quickly. However, Gilpin's third fear—that of an Indian attack—had not ended. Before the Civil War ended, Indian-white bloodshed would bring an end to John Evans's governorship.

Evans's problems with the Indians, of course, had their roots in an earlier era. More than a decade earlier, at the Fort Laramie Treaty Council, in 1851, the Cheyennes and Arapahoes had agreed to accept the Eastern Slope stretches between the South Platte and the Arkansas Rivers as their designated hunting lands. Then gold was discovered, and the argonauts rushing to the Pike's Peak mines moved onto the reserved Indian lands, fully expecting that the federal government would extinguish the

Indian claims and ratify the gold seekers' precipitate actions. The expectations, in time, became demands. In the autumn of 1860, before territorial government was assured Coloradans, federal agents opened negotiations with the two tribes, or parts of them, at a council on the Arkansas River.

At that council the whites seemed to have their way. The Arapahoes and Cheyennes agreed to surrender all their former hunting lands, except a triangular-shaped reservation between the Arkansas River and Sand Creek. This new reservation was to be surveyed and divided so that each tribal member received forty acres of land. The federal agents promised the tribes a $30,000 subsidy for fifteen years, a grist mill, a saw mill, and schools for the arid reservation. With this help, the Cheyennes and Arapahoes were to begin the difficult transition from nomads to peaceful farmers.

On paper, the Indian "problem" was settled—only it proved to be less simple than that. For one thing, difficulties arose from the administration of Indian affairs at both the national and local levels. Political considerations, rather than competence for the job, often were involved in the appointment of agents, with the Indian service in some cases becoming a convenient dumping ground for relatives or friends of high officials in need of employment. Once appointed, Indian agents sometimes used their positions for personal gain; for example, it was charged that during the early 1860s Upper Arkansas Agent Samuel Colley, whose son Dexter was a trader, contributed to the misappropriation of treaty goods intended for the Indians under his jurisdiction.

As for the Arapahoes and Cheyennes themselves, there were neither fences around the Sand Creek Reservation nor soldiers at its boundaries to keep them on their lands. In addition, not all in the tribe were in agreement with the promises made by their chiefs at the council. Some claimed, in fact, that they had not been represented at the sessions. Younger braves, in particular, seemed increasingly angered. Some warriors undoubtedly argued that the white man's actions had now changed: Earlier fur trappers and traders had been as mobile as the tribesmen themselves, but since the gold discoveries white men had acted in a different fashion. They settled in permanent villages, brought their women and children with them, and showed no signs of ever moving away. The Indians also were aware of the embarrassing divisions within the white men's ranks. The Civil War had brought a sudden reversal in the flow of immigrants; the mining camps and supply towns were becoming less populated and less protected. Perhaps the time had come to drive out the intruders and redeem the tribal hunting grounds.

Although the Indians were contemplating such ideas, the relatively isolated and unprotected white settlers were also aware of changed conditions. Increasingly they faced the possibilities of a full-fledged Indian uprising. Their fears were based on a variety of factors. For one thing, they could hardly ignore former Governor Gilpin's earlier intense concerns. Now, in addition, disturbing news from the north reported that in the summer of 1862 the Sioux in Minnesota had made several attacks, leaving a trail of bloody destruction and death. In this atmosphere of uneasy apprehension, rumors could be, and were, believed that the Confederacy intended to aid the Indians of the plains. When the tribes increased their attempts to purchase horses and firearms, the frontier communities interpreted these actions, as all frontier settlers always had, as a certain sign of hostile intentions. Coloradans of Union sympathies had responded gallantly to Gilpin's call for soldiers to fight the Confederates earlier, and their New Mexican exploits had been warmly applauded in the territory. But that was considered "white man's warfare" against a "civilized" enemy. What all settlers—even those of self-proclaimed "neutral" disposition toward the Civil War—now faced was the possibility of a greater danger from those they judged to be "barbarians," psychologically a much more disturbing thought.

Following a not uncommon practice, John Evans had been appointed ex officio superintendent of Indian affairs as well as governor of the territory. The two positions were not really compatible, however, for as governor, Evans had to protect the citizens of the territory, while as superintendent of Indian affairs, he was responsible for the welfare of the Indians, who were not citizens. Moreover, although he was experienced in many areas, there was little in his background to equip him in dealing with the Indians. Nonetheless, John Evans was deeply immersed in the problem. One thing that could be done was to request the return of the volunteers from New Mexico. The First Regiment was brought back to the territory and scattered in small units to provide some protection to most parts of the region. But this was hardly sufficient to satisfy the settlers, and when the troops recruited in 1862 and 1863 were mustered into federal service, with the majority of them sent off to Kansas and Missouri, the gold towns found themselves literally drained of volunteers and still without adequate military protection against the Indians.

The alternative choices of action available to Evans were not promising. He could and did continue to plead with the federal authorities for army units to protect the frontier and for authorization to recruit additional volunteer units within the territory for home defense. In the light of experience, however, he could hardly hope for quick and favorable action on his requests. So he was left with the alternative of stop-gap diplomacy with the tribes, attempting to hold council with the Indians and demonstrate with words rather than action. The tribesmen, however, seemed uninterested in peace talks; their attitude was indicated by their complete indifference, in the fall of 1863, to the governor's invitation to meet for a treaty session on the eastern plains.

Until the spring of 1864, despite the tension that had been building in the white settlements for months, actual conflict had been confined to isolated incidents of harassment of traffic on the overland trails and occasional, limited stock-running and horse-stealing from the ranchers. But when warm weather returned to the area in 1864, the tempo of affairs increased. The tribesmen became less guarded in their actions, raiding ranches closer to settled towns, striking more often and with more daring at the freighters' wagons and stages on the South Platte Trail. Then, on June 11, a turning-point of sorts was reached when the Indians, in a brutal attack on a ranch about twenty-five miles southeast of Denver, killed Nathan Hungate, his wife, and their two daughters. When the scalped and mutilated bodies of the Hungate family were publicly displayed in Denver, the settlers braced themselves for a direct assault on the city, and at the same time they demanded immediate and complete revenge.

The governor, his advisers, and most of the military leaders, by this time, all seem to have concluded that a general campaign against the Indians was inevitable. But Evans, who was less impatient than many, recognized that some Indians were still disposed to peace. So he formulated a policy designed to separate the hostile tribesmen from those who were friendly. On June 27 Evans issued a proclamation "To the Friendly Indians of the Plains," directing all Indians who wanted to demonstrate their friendship with the whites to gather at federal forts, where supplies and protection would be offered to all who came in. "The war on hostile Indians," he warned, "will be continued until they are all effectually subdued." Perhaps the choice offered to the Indians was not fully understood by them; at least they did not respond to the governor's invitation. And while the raids continued, the undeclared and still largely undefined hostilities brought ever more serious problems to the territory. Mail service was disrupted; shopkeepers' inventories dwindled; prices increased dramatically as traffic on the overland trails ceased. More and more frequently whites now talked of an exemplary strike at the Indians—a total blow that would rid eastern Colorado of Indians, once and for all time.

In August, Evans proclaimed to the white citizens that any resident who desired to fight Indians could engage in such "private" warfare and keep the loot from his efforts. And the governor had at last secured authorization from the War Department to raise a regiment of soldiers, with enlistments valid for 100 days of service.

As for the Indians, whatever plans they might have had for a massive attack on the settlements did not mature. There is evidence that they had contemplated simultaneous strikes at the white villages in August; at least Elbridge Gerry, who lived in the South Platte Valley with the Indians, hurried to Denver to warn Evans of the possibility. But no such attack occurred. As autumn approached, Indians began to appear at Fort Lyon, especially some Arapahoes who indicated that they were finished with their raiding. The Cheyenne chief, Black Kettle, also indicated a desire to talk peace.

Major Edward W. Wynkoop, commanding officer at the fort, decided to escort seven chiefs to Denver for a parley with Governor Evans and his aides. It is at this point in affairs that events become highly confused and subject to a variety of interpretations. Some historians believe that Evans was dismayed at Wynkoop's actions, for by this time peace was no longer his goal. According to this view, Evans feared embarrassment might result from peaceful termination of affairs, because of his constant pleas for troops and general exaggeration of the Indian problem in his reports to federal authorities. Then, too, both Evans and Colonel John Chivington, at this time, were deeply involved in the political arena, especially in the abortive attempt to gain statehood for Colorado. Whatever the reasons, the council ended in a vague and inconclusive manner. Evans informed the chiefs that the "matter had been turned over to the military authorities with which alone they must deal." The army officers then suggested that the Indians' next move might be to their reserved lands. So there, on the Sand Creek Reservation, the Arapahoes and Cheyennes established their winter camp. Since they were now on their reservation—where they had not been for some time—and since they had been told to go there, they considered themselves at peace with and secure from their white neighbors.

Edward W. Wynkoop (left) and Silas Soule kneel in front of Chief Black Kettle (seated, center) at the Denver conference, September 1864.

The Indians might have considered the affairs settled, but the whites had other plans. At least some of the white leaders were now rigidly committed to a policy of tribal extermination, and they now had a military unit to begin the work. Evans's regiment of 100-day men was ready for service. What it lacked in discipline and equipment it more than made up in its eagerness for a campaign against the Indians. When the governor left the territory for a visit to the national capital, Colonel John Chivington, in command of the "Bloodless Third" Regiment, decided to strike the decisive blow. If his regiment was not used soon, the enlistments of his men would expire.

John Chivington, a Methodist clergyman, had attracted attention three years earlier when the First Colorado Regiment had been recruited, informing Governor Gilpin then that he preferred a "fighting to a praying" commission. He had been granted his request and at the battles of Glorieta Pass, during the New Mexican campaign in 1862, had distinguished himself and his command. Now, with characteristic energy, he prepared to "teach the Indians a lesson they would not forget" and, according to his critics later, prepare the path for a political career for himself. He moved his men to Fort Lyon and, joined by other troops from there, he continued, by a forced all-night march, to Sand Creek. He took special care that no news of his approach reached the reservation. At sunrise, on November 29, 1864, he sent his regiment in attack against the Indian camp.

The accounts of the engagement at Sand Creek that November day make unpleasant reading. Colonel Chivington seemed to lose control of his men early in the day. Subject to slaughter, mutilation, and reckless savagery, Indian men, women, and children alike felt the full force of white settlers. George Bent, the half-Cheyenne son of William Bent, who was in the camp at the time, described later what it was like. "The Indians all began running, but they did not seem to know what to do or where to turn. The women and children were screaming and wailing, the men running to the lodges for their arms and shouting advice and directions to one another." No two observers or later-day experts have ever agreed on the total number of Indians in the camp when fighting began or the number of Indians killed. Chivington's own estimate, in boastful tone shortly after the engagement, placed the number of Indians surprised by the attack at almost 1,000, with half that number killed. Lower estimates suggest that something closer to a total of 500 Indians might have been sleeping in their lodges when the attack began and that one-fifth of that number were killed.

The Sand Creek attack brought immediate and bitter repercussions, not only in the territory but all the way to the national capital. An investigation by the Congressional Joint Committee on the Conduct of the (Civil) War ended its deliberations by condemning Chivington for having "deliberately planned and executed a foul and dastardly massacre which would have disgraced the veriest savage among those who were the victims of his cruelty." A military commission spent months in another investigation. An indication of the violent opinions concerning Sand Creek can be seen in the never-punished assassination of Captain Silas S. Soule, an outspoken critic and witness against his fellow-officer, Colonel Chivington.

The commander was not without supporters. Some of his friends insisted that the only reason for the flare-up of hostile reaction was that Governor Evans and much of the Colorado bar were then trying to force the removal of the territorial judicial officers and that the judges had

This drawing on a page from a ledger book found on the Summit Springs battlefield depicts one Cheyenne warrior rescuing another whose horse has given out.

instigated the congressional investigation. Others claimed that the loudest opponents of Chivington were those who had lost trade goods in the attack and were bitter about their financial losses. Some whites insisted that the fresh scalps of settlers found in the camp were justification enough for the engagement. Many settlers, wearied by the months of incessant Indian troubles, and remembering the Hungates and others who had lost their lives in Indian attacks, unhesitatingly applauded the premise of quick, complete extermination of the tribes. So the arguments ran. The Chivington supporters proclaimed the engagement "a true battle" and exactly what the Indians deserved. The critics termed it an unjustified massacre.

The Indians now were stirred to revenge. Those who had escaped from the battlefield joined their brethren to counterattack white settlements. In January 1865, they sacked the station and stores of Old Julesburg in the northeastern corner of the territory. They returned to plunder Julesburg again in February, burning the place to the ground.

For the whites, the only satisfactory solution was to be found in federal policies of reservations and military patrols to ensure confinement of the Indians on those reservations. In October 1867, in the Medicine

Lodge Creek Treaty, the Cheyennes and Arapahoes agreed to move to the Indian Territory. They retained some hunting privileges off that reservation and, at times, they would encounter discipline from U.S. Army troops. In September 1868, an attack by some 1,000 tribesmen led by Chief Roman Nose pinned down a party of fifty army scouts from Fort Hays, in Kansas, on what later was named Beecher Island in the Arikaree Fork of the Republican River. The name honors Lieutenant Fred Beecher who was killed during the engagement. The siege lasted nine days, until units of the federal cavalry relieved the scouts. The following summer (1869) a band of Indian raiders was pursued by federal troops into northeastern Colorado and attacked at Summit Springs, about six miles from present-day Atwood. The white soldiers killed fifty Indians, including Chief Tall Bull, and freed two white women the Indians had captured in Kansas.

The Battle of Summit Springs was the final military engagement between whites and plains Indians in the eastern part of the territory. Westward, in the mountains, where the Utes still hunted, white settlers later would demand removal of the Indians. But for the immediate future, Eastern Slope Colorado now was available for whites to exploit with their railroads and irrigation ditches, cow herds and windmills.

ELEVEN

SMELTERS AND RAILROADS

Any American frontier opened for settlement during the years of the Civil War had cause for disappointment in its economic progress. With the nation locked in bloody warfare to decide the question of its continued existence, most peaceful pursuits had to await an end to hostilities. So it was with Colorado. And even after the war ended, the remaining years of the decade were filled with exasperating problems. Warfare between whites and Indians disrupted normal activities and other problems intruded, including the rumor that the gold mines were running out. Colorado—the epitome of the mining frontier—was threatened with the most formidable of possible economic dangers. The gold mines had summoned the population into the wilderness; around their continuing production many had linked their fortunes and their lives. Uneasy apprehension could so easily be converted into hysterical bankruptcy of the territory. It all depended on the good earth's treasures and what could be made of them.

For a time the idea that the gold-bearing ores were dwindling was unthinkable. This was especially true in the Little Kingdom of Gilpin—the county in which the most profitable mining properties were located and in which Central City, with its satellite towns, proudly proclaimed its importance, often taking precedence over the Queen City of the Plains, Denver. In Gilpin County the original Gregory Lode had been uncovered; here the Russells, returning from Georgia in the spring of 1859, had found their rich placers. And it was here, in the winter of 1863-1864, that the attention of eastern capitalists centered as Colorado mining stocks became a fad of investors.

Several elements contributed to the investment madness. A rise in the price of gold, nationally, played its part. So did the fluid capital available for investment in greater quantity than the country had ever known, the result of profits and profiteering during the Civil War. Colorado mining stocks happened to appear at a time when the demand for investment opportunities increased, and the consequences might have been predicted. As demands for shares of the golden harvest of the mines increased, the price for stocks climbed upward. The listing of nearly 200 Colorado mining companies' stocks on the New York and other eastern exchanges indicated the market for such securities. With such ready acceptance, it was probably inevitable that bad or worthless properties would be peddled along with the valuable and honest enterprises. It could not last, for in time some of the investors would find themselves without returns on their investments. When the bubble broke, as it did in April 1864, it left behind a bad reputation for Colorado mines.

Aggravating the situation was the rumor about the exhaustion of the territory's mineral wealth. It was a fact—not merely a rumor—that the easy ores were vanishing. The precious metal from the simply worked lodes and placers of the early years had been extracted, and although many kept faith in their conviction that the hills were still full of gold, there was little doubt that some new methods of mining and reduction of ore were needed. The easy, early ores had been no great problem. The gold was largely free gold, chemically unassociated with other elements. Washing, or crushing and washing, with amalgamation with mercury, sufficed to redeem the gold. Now, however, the ores brought to the surface of the mine shafts contained gold mixed with other elements, no longer separable by mere mechanical procedures. The day of the chemist and the metallurgist was at hand. Unfortunately, before sanity returned to the mining camps, an "era of process manias" came to pass.

In the circumstances, understandably, straws were clutched at, and any artist of deceit might make a fortune promising the new, the simplest, the least expensive, the only process that would bring about the alchemy necessary to divorce the gold from the natural allies with which it was found. When crushing in stamp mills no longer resulted in satisfactory separation of the ores (no more than one-fourth of the total gold in the ores reportedly was being recovered by the mills), many came to the conclusion that the ores must be roasted before the gold could be amalgamated. One invention for this purpose followed another; desulphurization, since many of the ores were identified as sulfides, became the abracadabra of the new alchemists. Speculators wasted thousands of dollars on sweeping claims of perfect successes put forward by deluded or deluding proprietors of patents.

This process mania, commencing in 1864 and continuing for almost four years, extensively damaged the reputation of the Colorado mines. Added to the losses investors in mining stock had suffered, it might easily have ruined the industry for a long time. About the only good aspect of it all was the fact that the situation lasted no longer than it did. What ended the process mania was the real success that Nathaniel P. Hill achieved when he opened his smelting operations at Black Hawk in 1868.

Nathaniel Hill, a professor of chemistry at Brown University in Providence, Rhode Island, had been sent to Colorado in 1864 by Boston capitalists to investigate their recently purchased mining properties. Intrigued by the local problems of ore reduction, Hill set to work to solve the riddle of the gold ores. Traveling to Europe twice to investigate smelting processes there, he finally arranged shipments of sample Colorado ores to Swansea, in Wales, for experimentation. Those tests proved that the ore could be smelted into mattes with copper bases and, in 1867, Hill organized the Boston and Colorado Smelting Company. The next year the company began smelting operations at its plant at Black Hawk. The process involved crushing the ore, then reducing it by concentrating the gold ores on copper mattes (in technical terms: by using a calcining furnace and a small reverberatory). These plates then were shipped to Swansea refineries for final treatment. By 1873 the Boston and Colorado would complete its own separating works, making the expensive European shipments unnecessary. That left only the gold to be worked out. For a few years the concentrates were sent to Boston, but by 1875-1876, the final process also would be introduced at the Hill plant.

Despite a multiplicity of problems—questions of proper purchase agreements with miners for their ores, costs of operation, and a general

Casting silver bricks at the Boston and Colorado Smelting Company in Black Hawk.

uncertainty of proper technical procedures at times—the Hill smelter was a success from the beginning. It made its originator a local hero as well as a wealthy man. The problem of the refractory ores had now been overcome, and the Colorado gold mines had been rescued from disaster.

The solution to the ore problem brought a promising ending to a difficult decade. Though mining in the 1860s had been based on gold, another metal—silver—was gradually gaining significance. As early as August 1859, stories of silver discoveries appeared, followed in the next few years by further reports, reflecting as much as anything else the general excitement over Nevada's Comstock. Silver had also been mined as a by-product in Gilpin County, but the first real mines were opened in 1864 near Georgetown. This camp, the first of Colorado's "silver queens," was the focus of interest that spilled over into the Snake River district across the Continental Divide into Summit County.

Despite excited hopes and high assay reports, silver mining languished because of the lack of an economical method of smelting. Lorenzo Bowman, a black Missourian with experience in the lead mines, helped develop a method that was successful on the surface ores. But the deeper ores were more complex and required more complicated procedures. Following the collapse of the gold speculation, it proved difficult to interest outside investors in an industry that promised only expensive trial-and-error experimentation before dividends could be declared. At the end of the decade, Georgetown had smelters, although experiments were still being conducted to find a more practical method; major production was imminent. The more isolated Snake River mines stagnated, awaiting the success of their neighbor and a cheap, rapid means of transportation before they too would bask in the glory of a mining boom.

The 1870s ushered in Colorado's silver era. Before the decade ended, discoveries would be made from Boulder County to Dolores County, on a southwest axis bisecting the state. Georgetown would be eclipsed as Leadville came into its own. The silver boom started in Boulder County with the discovery of the Caribou Mine in 1869, followed by a rush to the area the next year, which produced the camp of the same name. Here was the excitement, speculation, and promise of wealth that would be repeated so many more times before the era ended. Caribou was isolated, nestled as it was near the Continental Divide, and the most northerly of Colorado's silver camps, but it nevertheless attracted national and international interest. Eventually, a Dutch company purchased the Caribou Mine for $3 million, only to lose it three years later in 1876 at a sheriff's sale. Mismanagement, low ore reserves, poor mining methods and misrepresentation, if not complete dishonesty, on the part of the seller, plagued the company from the beginning. The new owners were Jerome Chaffee and David Moffat, constituting a partnership that lasted into the 1880s and affected Colorado mining significantly.

Such diversification of mining activities was promising. An economy that rested exclusively on gold might crumble and die overnight, as the process problem had illustrated. But whether the ore was gold or silver—or even the products of the expanding agricultural settlements—one problem confronted everyone in Colorado. Transportation was still *the* major economic concern. Despite near-heroic efforts all through the territory's first decade, a solution would not be reached until 1870. Yet each year brought more need for change. It is estimated that more than 100 million pounds of freight reached Colorado by wagon in 1865 and even larger quantities were brought in each succeeding year.

There was little argument about the type of transportation needed: railroads, and only railroads, would bring a satisfactory transportation system to the territory. But the method by which railroads were to be lured to Colorado was not as readily agreed to. At first most of the dreaming was intimately associated with a larger American dream—a transcontinental railroad, spanning the prairies and mountains, tying the nation together with bands of iron rail.

Colorado, astride the nation, contemplated a railroad that would place it on the mainline to the Pacific. The negative reports resulting from John Gunnison's survey before the Civil War should have been remembered, but they were not. In 1862, when Congress chartered the Union Pacific Railroad to build the eastern portion of the transcontinental line, Coloradans were elated at the prospect. Governor Evans, one of the 158 "commissioners" charged with the duty of organizing the railroad, on his first evening in Denver spoke of how it would benefit the community. Expectations soared that through his influence, and that of others, rails would come through the territory on the way to California.

Such optimism proved to be grossly ill-founded. Surveyors earlier had reported that better crossings of the Continental Divide lay to the north. No Colorado pass, not even recently discovered Berthoud, could match them. Despite Evans's continued promotional efforts while governor and afterward, Colorado would be disappointed.

The Civil War hastened the chartering of the railroad but delayed its construction. Not until the summer of 1867 did the Union Pacific build its roadbed and lay its rails across the Wyoming prairie. Then came predictions and prophecies that Denver and other Colorado communities would soon fade away. Cheyenne, to the north, blessed with the transcontinental railroad, loomed as the likely prospect to become the regional metropolis; "Denver was too dead to bury." Prophets who voiced such sentiments, however, reckoned without full appreciation of Colorado's leaders. Determined to save their investments and their hopes for the future, Coloradans soon worked out plans for building connecting branches—feeder lines—from the Union Pacific tracks south into the territory.

The Colorado Central Railroad Company seemed the most logical to make the initial connection with the Union Pacific. Golden's William A. H. Loveland, promoter, politician, mine owner, and rival of Evans and his Denver followers, had organized the road with the help of Edward L. Berthoud and encouragement from the Union Pacific itself. The town of Golden expected to profit from becoming the southern terminus. Though smaller in population than Denver, Golden never hesitated to compete with its large neighbor. If it could claim no other advantage, it was closer to the Gilpin County mines. Initially, Denver supported Loveland's idea, until it became clear that Golden would be on the main line and only a branch would serve its rival. Denver and Arapahoe County, which had previously voted to float bond issues to aid in construction, now refused to approve the bonds, not wishing to boost Golden to economic superiority. Here the matter temporarily rested, while both groups sought other support.

While Loveland planned his Colorado Central, another possible railroad connection appeared in the east. The Union Pacific Eastern Division, soon to be renamed the Kansas Pacific, building westward from Kansas City, promised to move trains into Denver at an early date. As long as its government aid for financing held out, the Kansas Pacific set a rapid rate of construction. But by late 1867, construction funds were exhausted and the railhead in western Kansas, still miles short of Denver, could not be pushed forward without additional help. To make matters worse, there were rumors that the Kansas road was seriously interested in diverting its line to the Arkansas Valley, bypassing Denver altogether.

These were dark months for Denverites. Railroad prospects for their city dimmed considerably. The Union Pacific was miles to the north; the Colorado Central had chosen to build from Cheyenne to rival Golden; the Kansas Pacific was bogged down in western Kansas. Property values in Denver began to spiral downward and tradesmen began to desert the MIle-High City. Only determined resistance to this flight from the "sinking ship" could salvage the city's future. Those who chose to remain optimistically organized the Board of Trade and, with organizational help from Union Pacific and Kansas Pacific officials, immediately announced their plans for a "home town" railroad.

They called it the Denver Pacific, to be built as a branch line from Cheyenne to the territorial capital. Financing, as usual, proved the major obstacle, despite imaginative efforts of the Denver leaders to seek aid in every direction. The citizens were summoned to contribute— cash, pledges, material, or labor, as their circumstances allowed. Arapahoe County, freed now from its former promise to aid the Colorado Central, underwrote a bond issue to further the enterprise, but all these efforts were not enough. It became quite evident that if the road was to be finished, more help from the outside was necessary. Both the Union Pacific and the Kansas Pacific looked favorably on the venture, hoping to use the branch line to tap the mining resources of the territory. They were willing to give some aid. Congress agreed to a 900,000-acre land grant, although it meant a merging of the 100-mile line with the Kansas Pacific. Now the track laying could proceed. In June 1870, the road from Denver to Cheyenne was completed in a traditional ceremony, including the driving of a silver spike presented by the city of Georgetown.

The Kansas Pacific also increased its federal land grants. With about 3 million acres of new lands as aid, the road successfully marketed additional securities and could resume construction. Its interests now tied directly to Denver's progress, the Kansas road forgot about the Arkansas Valley and determined to build as rapidly as possible to the capital city. When grading was started from Denver eastward toward the finished portion of the road, the crews working on the two ends of the line entered into a friendly competition. On the last day, the two crews recorded the remarkable feat of laying ten and one-fourth miles of track in ten hours' time. In August 1870, the first locomotive moved across the Kansas Pacific tracks into Denver. The Queen City now had two rail outlets to the rest of the nation.

That year, 1870, was also the year of birth for another railroad that was to become intimately identified with the territory and future state of Colorado. General William J. Palmer had supervised the construction of the Kansas Pacific line; he had also been a director of the Denver Pacific. He now began organizing a new road—the Denver and Rio Grande—designed to reach south to El Paso, Texas, and through connections there to form a link with Mexican railroads. Palmer's plan envisioned a north-south spine, with feeder roads west to the mining camps and east to the newly settled agricultural communities in the valleys. This scheme was a radical departure from generally accepted principles of railroading. Most roads in the American West were laid out on an east-west axis. Moreover, the Denver and Rio Grande was to be built with narrow-gauge trackage, three feet wide instead of the more standard width of four feet, eight and one-half inches. The narrow roadbeds would allow greater flexibility in surmounting the difficulties of construction over high mountain passes, up steep canyon floors, and around difficult curves.

The narrow-gauge road would become, in time, convincingly adapted to the mountainous terrain of Colorado. In later decades, it would become the "standard" for the area, completely fulfilling the prophecies of utility and, at the same time, inspiring respectable laughter for its picturesque qualities: "It doubles in, it doubles out, leaving the traveller still in doubt whether the engine on the track is going on or coming back."

Palmer planned and organized his road in 1870-1871; actual construction got under way in the spring of 1871. By autumn of that year the road had built its narrow-gauge bed and laid its thirty-pound rails from Denver to the vicinity of Colorado City. There, through its subsidiary, the Colorado Springs Company, it laid out a new town—Colorado Springs—with full expectation that the choice location would make it a fashionable summer resort. The next year the Denver and Rio Grande constructed its line south along Fountain Creek until it reached a site across the Arkansas River from Pueblo. There another of its subsidiaries, the Central Colorado Improvement Company, established another new town—South Pueblo. By the end of 1872, the road had also reached the coalfield area near Florence, again establishing its own townsite of Labran. Two years later the Rio Grande's locomotives steamed into Canon City.

By that time the capital city of Denver was in an enviable position. The Denver Pacific tracks north to Cheyenne gave it an outlet on the transcontinental; the Kansas Pacific rails tied it directly with Kansas City; the Denver and Rio Grande provided transportation to the southern part of the territory. Denver had clearly bested its rival, Golden, in the race for railroads. The Colorado Central had still not completed its connection with the Union Pacific. Unable to fulfill that promise, in 1870 Loveland's line did build tracks connecting Denver and Golden to take advantage of the railheads that city now enjoyed. And the Colorado Central had continued laying its track up Clear Creek Canyon. By 1877 its trains were climbing to Black Hawk and, the following year, to the riches of the Gilpin County mines.

Loveland had dreams of continuing westward, over Berthoud Pass, using narrow-gauge if necessary. But no realistic engineer could advise such an undertaking. The pass reaches an altitude of 11,315 feet and the grades are much more precipitous than even the wildest professional imagination could envision climbing with rails. Loveland considered using cable-buckets for the highest altitudes, but his road never moved beyond Georgetown and the Central City districts. In other directions, in time, the road was more successful. Starting north from Golden, after much delay, it tapped the new village of Longmont in 1872, and five years later it reached Fort Collins and a junction with the Denver Pacific, four miles from that town.

Tracks for the Colorado Central cut through Black Hawk in the late 1870s.

Although Loveland's Colorado Central never used its projected right-of-way across the Continental Divide, its plans blocked the original schemes of another Colorado railroad. Former Governor John Evans, inveterate railroad promoter, who had been a leading figure in the Denver Pacific road, helped organize the Denver, Georgetown and Utah

Railroad Company but found the way blocked by Loveland and a lack of financial assistance. Reorganized in 1872 as the Denver, South Park and Pacific, with Evans still the driving force, the company planned to build up South Platte Canyon and on into South Park, but the panic of 1873 made it extremely difficult to market the securities Evans had counted on for fund-raising.

The depression did not prevent the line's reaching Morrison, a settlement organized by a townsite company with which Evans was associated, where shipping revenue from the local stone and lime quarries paid company expenses. Local acclaim was gained by hauling summer excursions of Sunday School children, earning it the nickname "the Sunday School line." Though he continued his efforts, Evans was unable to find investors and experienced only frustration until 1876 when construction started. It stopped soon after, resulting in another reorganization. Finally, in 1877, construction was resumed and carried through to completion, spurred on by the Leadville silver bonanza. The Leadville rush brought prosperity to the road, and Evans found himself caught in the maelstrom of railroad-control struggles that hit the state late in the decade.

In the southeastern part of the territory, where the Denver and Rio Grande was extending its north-south road, other companies were planning extensions from the east. The Atchison, Topeka and Santa Fe Railroad, chartered in 1859, had begun to entertain transcontinental dreams. By 1873 it had built west as far as Granada in the Arkansas Valley, within the eastern boundary of the territory. There construction halted for two years in the wake of the financial panic. Both Pueblo and Bent Counties were induced to come to its rescue with financial aid raised by bond issues and, with that help, the tracks were extended to La Junta by December 1875. The following March the Banana Line—so-called because of its yellow coaches—had reached the city of Pueblo.

The Kansas Pacific road also revived its interest in the Arkansas Valley. At the town of Kit Carson, on its mainline through the Eastern Slope, the Kansas Pacific started building a branch southward to West Las Animas. By 1875 it also had reached La Junta. Within a few years, however, it became apparent that the area lacked sufficient resources to support the road, and the Kansas Pacific abandoned the division in 1878, removing the tracks from the right-of-way.

Meanwhile, south from Pueblo, the natural routes all led to Trinidad, near the historic Raton Pass crossing toward Santa Fe. Both the

Atchison, Topeka and Santa Fe, from La Junta, and the Rio Grande, from South Pueblo, were building toward that town. In 1876 the Rio Grande reached El Moro, its company town five miles from Trinidad. The Santa Fe moved its tracks directly into town the next year. There, in the months that followed, the two railroads would compete for possession of the pass into New Mexico. The Rio Grande was also building toward Santa Fe by the alternate route across La Veta Pass and on into the San Luis Valley, reaching Fort Garland in 1877.

Between 1870 and 1880, Eastern Slope railroad construction was in full swing, but other parts of the territory were less fortunate. There wagon roads, or perhaps pack trails, provided the only available transportation. Berthoud Pass was not climbed by rails. In fact, it was only after several abortive attempts that a wagon road was finally finished, and stages and freight wagons began to cross the Divide there in October 1875. Eventually the state would buy the road from its owner and Berthoud became the first free crossing from the Eastern Slope.

As the railroads reached out to tap the wealth of the mining districts, both prospered, because cheap transportation was a key to the success of mining. Before the rails, however, there were trails and wagon roads to pioneer the routes. It was in this business that Otto Mears, a Russian Jew, small physically but a giant in energy, gained statewide fame. Mears frequently sold his rights-of-way to the railroad and eventually organized his own lines. With the rise of rail transportation came the development of major smelter centers, such as Denver, with access to ore, fuel, and labor markets. Here at last were the factors that produced important improvements in smelting, so long dominated by small establishments scattered in the mining districts.

By 1880, with eastern Colorado served by a relatively extensive network of railroads, the transportation problems of the territory's first decade had ended. In their place, other problems had arisen. Much of the financing of the roads had come from outside the territory, and the control over those railroads remained in alien hands. Even a "home town" road like the Rio Grande would, in time, find itself engaged in a losing battle against outside financiers. And this was not the only difficulty. The Rio Grande itself had angered many Coloradans. General Palmer had played a dangerous game of seeking community support for his railroad but when his tracks approached an established town, he would place them in one of his self-made company towns next door. Residents of Colorado City, neighboring the new Colorado Springs, or those of Pueblo, viewing South Pueblo across the Arkansas River, had reason to be unhappy with the railroad builders. Even Denver merchants, who had seemingly emerged victorious in their struggles to gain rail connections, would in time come to realize that the potential power of the roads was something to be carefully watched. But whether viewed as curse or blessing, the railroads had come to stay.

TWELVE

UTOPIAS IN THE DESERT

Some Colorado communities owed their existence to goldfields; others to advantageous sites providing access to the mining gulches; some to the whims of the railroad engineers. But in the 1870s a new type of town building came to the territory—cooperative and semicooperative ventures in wilderness planting. Prompted by a series of hoped-for advantages, accompanied by some rather serious disadvantages, these colony towns of Colorado contributed a unique chapter to the history of settlement in the territory.

The colony plan of settlement, in many ways, was well adapted to conditions in Colorado. These settlements were designed as agricultural communities. As such, they would rely on irrigation for much of their farming and considerable advantage would accrue from constructing and operating irrigation ditches by cooperative rather than individual effort. The feared loneliness of farm life on the western prairies, with the accompanying dangers of possible Indian attacks, might be mitigated by group settlement. Perhaps better prices could be gained for the land settled upon if a group, rather than individuals, negotiated the contracts to purchase the holdings.

There were, of course, corresponding disadvantages. Any person who partook of the colony's benefits would have to pay the price in losing some individual freedom. The group's interests would take precedence over those of the single farmer. Management of the first class—intelligent, dedicated, diplomatic—was not particularly easy to enlist, as the failures of similar schemes in the East and Midwest had already demonstrated. There was also the possibility, if not the probability, that quarrels and friction would develop over the distribution of lots, farms, labor, and eventual profits.

But balancing the advantages and disadvantages, enough people were swayed into believing the plans would work to bring into Colorado Territory a rather unusual number of attempted colonies. Most of these followed a similar pattern. They were usually organized in some eastern or midwestern city. Arrangements were concluded for the purchase of land and cooperative settlement with a railroad company or a subsidiary land company organized to dispose of railroad lands. It was a nice meeting of interests, for the railroads not only had large stretches of federal land grants to sell but also recognized that until the land was taken up and agricultural products were available for freight, their lines would not fully prosper. Thus the railroads were interested in the colony schemes and widely advertised the settlements. With their help the agricultural colonies provided the instrument by which the farming frontier suddenly leaped from a diagonal line cutting across central Kansas and eastern Nebraska to irrigable lands in the shadows of the Rocky Mountains.

There were differences in the various schemes of colonization, although generally they all endeavored to be known as colonies. Some of the settlements were planned as completely cooperative ventures. Labor, capital, and profits were to be shared by the members. Others were semicooperatives, with certain details arranged by the leaders, yet allowing each free choice in many decisions. And, finally, there were colonies that were not cooperative at all, except that they used the word colony to induce people into believing that they were designed on a cooperative scheme.

The first colony actually to take up lands within the territory was a thorough-going, full-fledged cooperative endeavor. Carl Wulsten had come to the United States from Prussia before the Civil War. He had served in the Union Army and had then settled in Chicago where he edited a German-language newspaper. In that fast-growing, rapidly industrializing city he saw around himself, and his fellow-Germans, nothing but misery and dirt and long hours of back-breaking work in the city's factories. Prompted by a concept of communal living as a means to escape this plight, and envisioning an agricultural society somewhere in the Great American West where his fellow immigrants could again attain dignity and economic well-being, Wulsten organized the German Colonization Society in August 1869.

The society named a committee that came to the territory in November and selected a site in the Wet Mountain Valley. The society petitioned Congress for a special grant of 40,000 acres of land there. When the request was refused, the leaders decided to settle the colony anyway, depending on individual land claims for ownership. Back in Chicago, they helped their fellow colonists pack their belongings and hurried to purchase tools and equipment they would need in their new homes. In mid-winter 1870, the society, numbering about 300 men, women, and children, with their household furniture, tools, implements, and livestock boarded a train that carried them to the end of the Kansas Pacific tracks at Fort Wallace in Kansas. There they appealed to the U.S. Army for wagons to transport them the remainder of their journey and for troops to protect them against Indians. The federal authorities agreed to the requests, much to the amusement of many territorial residents who could not help but contrast these developments with their own, earlier experiences. They had come to the territory by their own devices; now the government was furnishing an escort "to cover the march of these teutons along the peaceful cornfields of Pueblo and Fremont counties."

In March 1870, the colonists arrived on their lands in the Wet Mountain Valley. Under the leadership of their president, Carl Wulsten, they built their homes, plowed their lands, and planted their first crops. They named their town Colfax, in honor of the then vice-president of the United States. Capital, labor, and profits, if any, were to be pooled for five full years in a communistic arrangement. But as had happened so often in other such ventures, dissension began to erupt immediately within the group.

The difficulties were numerous and, in the end, proved insurmountable. There was no common religious or social principle to bind the members together. Wulsten was often tactless—"hot-headed, arbitrary, and impracticable"—he proved less than a perfect leader. His successor, James Judd, was even less able. The crops planted the first season did not mature satisfactorily because of the short growing season in the valley and an unusually early frost. There was considerable hostility to the group in some parts of southern Colorado, based partly on the foreign character of the settlement and partly on the rumors that the Republican administration in Washington was championing the settlement as the first of several groups designed to provide a Republican majority in otherwise normally Democratic areas of the territory.

Society members who were unhappy with the experiment for one reason or another began to withdraw from Colfax. When federal officials seized shingles and lumber that the colonists had cut and sawed without paying the "stumpage" tax for taking timber from the public domain, the end of the affair was hastened. Most of the settlers then moved to other territorial towns—to Pueblo, Canon City, and Denver. Those who remained in the valley took up their individual claims on the government land. So ended the first chapter in Colorado colonization.

About the same time that Wulsten's group selected its site for settlement, Nathan C. Meeker, the agricultural editor of the New York *Tribune*, was touring the western territories. Meeker was an experienced hand at cooperative colonies. From 1844 to 1857 he had been a resident at the Trumbull Phalanx at Braceville, Ohio. By the time he returned from his western tour, Meeker was convinced that it would be possible to settle a cooperative community in Colorado. His publisher and editor, Horace Greeley, who had already seen something of the territory, endorsed the idea enthusiastically. Meeker called a public meeting for December 23, 1869, at Cooper Institute in New York City. There the Union Colony was born. Meeker, appropriately, was chosen president; a constitution was drafted; and memberships were offered for sale to temperance men of good character for a fee of $155.

The money raised by these fees was to be used to select and purchase the site for the colony. Each member would receive one town lot and a parcel of farming land in return for an investment. Meeker, Robert A. Cameron, the vice-president of the colony, and A. C. Fisk were appointed the selection committee. They viewed several sites in the territory and reportedly had almost decided on a stretch of land in South Park when William Byers persuaded them that the South Platte Valley contained the finest agricultural lands in Colorado. They chose an excellent location near the confluence of the Cache la Poudre and the South Platte Rivers. There they purchased a large block of land from the Denver Pacific Railroad (12,000 acres for $60,000), provisional title to an additional 60,000 acres, and a few private entries, to keep their colony cohesive—all of which would give them ample room to grow on. The colony also incorporated itself under territorial laws.

The Union colonists began to arrive on their lands in the spring of 1870. The town they established they named Greeley, although for the

Union Colony settlers established Greeley, shown here in 1870, and dug ditches to irrigate their crops.

first months it wasn't much of a town. To supplement the usual tents and temporary shelters, the colonists purchased a large building in Cheyenne and moved it down the Denver Pacific Railroad to Greeley. They fitted it up as a lodging house and christened it the Hotel de Comfort. That first season they surveyed the plot and laid out the streets of their town; they planted trees; they opened a school for their children. And, perhaps the most important of all, they dug their first irrigation ditch. Water was necessary if they were to harvest a crop the first season, and the ditch was a constant concern until they had turned water onto their fields.

All this was hard work, with small comfort for the present, but most of the colonists seemed willing to undergo the early hardships in expectation of better times to come. There were a few quitters who spread adverse reports, like the man who advised: "If you can't possibly stay where you are, *don't go to Greeley, Colorado Territory! That* is the last place on the face of this terrestrial ball that any human being should contemplate a removal to! Greeley, Colorado T., is a delusion, a snare—it is a fraud, a cheat, a swindle."

And since Horace Greeley himself and his newspaper were controversial, the political enemies of Greeley found much to scoff at in the new venture. When the great Horace arrived in town in October 1870, his lecture to the colonists was variously reported in the territorial press. One editor laughed at the idea of Greeley being able to advise western settlers: "What Mr. G. knows about farming is not likely to be more valuable in this Territory than the experience of the old settlers."

Either because of or in spite of Editor Greeley, the quitters and the scoffers were soon proved wrong. Sobriety, sense, or something led the colony to early prosperity. The economic base of the settlement was its agriculture. The irrigation system was added to each year, and the water and the fertile valley lands gave forth amazing crops. There was a problem of the wheat fields being trampled under by roaming cattle from surrounding ranches, but in time the Union colonists fenced their crops in and the neighbors' cattle out, with a wire fence around the perimeter of their holdings. This $20,000 fence became a point of ridicule among outsiders, who referred to the colonists as "saints" and jested that the fence had been erected to separate the "Bible-loving inhabitants" of Greeley from the "barbarians."

In the village of Greeley, diversification of the economy was attempted. A tanning plant for buffalo hides processed about a dozen robes a day, and for a time income ran as high as $2,000 a month. And the town also began to wear the mantle of a cultured society. A library, a lyceum, a farmers' club, and a dramatic association were organized. Theatricals—and dancing—were allowed by the "saints," but intoxicating liquors were strictly forbidden, in accordance with the original terms of organization. By 1880, when the colony ended its corporate status at the expiration of its charter, it had firmly developed the foundations for the town of Greeley and its surrounding farmlands to build on.

The rather spectacular success of the Union colonists made it inevitable that it would become the prototype of other such enterprises. Not all the imitators would enjoy the same success, but the Chicago-Colorado Colony, organized in the fall of 1870, came very close to matching it. In March 1871, this Chicago group, with cooperation from the National Land Company (the agency handling land grants for the Denver Pacific and Kansas Pacific railroads), located its site on Middle St. Vrain Creek and named the town Longmont. Lots and plots were distributed, irrigation ditches dug, and the place prospered. Part of its success was due to the intense desire of the settlers to "make good"; part resulted from the help of the colony's "fairy godmother," Mrs. Elizabeth Thompson of New York, who purchased memberships for poor settlers and in other ways encouraged the undertaking. Then too, the location was excellent; the irrigation water from Left Hand and Boulder Creeks, in addition to St. Vrain Creek, was more than adequate, and the management of the colony was intelligent and efficient.

South of Greeley, on the Denver Pacific Railroad, the remnant of a town called Evans furnished the site for another colony. Evans had originated when it served as a temporary terminal for the Denver Pacific Railroad, but once the road had finished construction to Denver, the place had all but died away. In 1871 a colony organized by the St. Louis–Western Company, launched in Illinois by a Reformed Presbyterian minister, the Reverend Andrew C. Todd, settled on the site. Evans was never to capture the sure success of Greeley, but it managed to stay alive and proved to be a thorn in the side of the Union Colony because it openly allowed grog houses and taverns within its limits—a temptation that sometimes lured colonists from Greeley.

There was almost magic in the word "colony" for a time in the territory. Promotional schemers who had little or nothing in common with the cooperative colonial endeavors used the word, hoping thereby to attract more settlers to their lands. The Platte River Land Company, for example, "boomed" its settlement called Platteville as a "colony" although it had none of the true features of cooperation and was strictly a speculation scheme to promote settlement on the land owned by the company. The Denver and Rio Grande Railway's subsidiary townsite and land companies also used the word "colony" in promoting Colorado Springs and South Pueblo. Although Robert A. Cameron, who helped General Palmer organize the townsite companies, had gained some of his experience in town planting in the Union Colony adventure, the railroad's towns, like Platteville, were ordinary speculative promotions.

None of the towns of the decade masquerading under the colony title carried the promotional campaign to greater extremes than David S. Green's Southwestern Colony town of Green City. On the South Platte River, twenty-seven miles downstream from Greeley, Green located two sections of government land and then set out to sell more than 5,000 town lots to people in the southern and border states. Green City tradition insists that some of the advertising circulars distributed by the promoters pictured steamboats at a wharf, suggesting that Green City would become a major commercial center as well as the hub of a prosperous farming area. Some settlers did move into the embryo town, but many lots were purchased merely for speculation. On such shaky foundations, no town could succeed and Green City was soon nothing but a bad memory of misleading promotion.

Farther down the Platte River, another settlement was begun at this time that in no way proclaimed itself a colony. Immigrants from Tennessee and Mississippi, dissatisfied with life in the southern states during the reconstruction days after the Civil War, began the town of Sterling in 1873-1874, about three miles northeast of the town's present location. When it was rumored that the Union Pacific Railroad was planning a branch line from Julesburg to La Salle, Sterling residents decided to try to gain the location of a division point between Denver and Omaha. They offered the railroad a donation of eighty acres of land as an inducement to locate the shops in their town, and when the offer was accepted, the future of Sterling was assured. The town then moved to its present location.

Westward, toward the mountains, Fort Collins came closer to satisfying the requirements of a true colony than many other new settlements. The site of Fort Collins had been a military reservation named Camp Collins. Abandoned by the War Department as a federal post, the site was bought up by a town company, which planned the new city of Fort Collins. Memberships in the Fort Collins Agricultural Colony were offered for sale to persons "of good moral character." Settlers could purchase memberships for $50, $150, or $250, entitling them to city lots, farming land, or both. Homes and commercial buildings were under construction by 1873, and the town ditch for irrigation was dug that same year.

Toward the end of the decade (1870–1880), other colonization schemes were effected that differed from the earlier ones. These later colonies were more closely tied to religious groupings. For example, Mormons created several agricultural communities in the San Luis Valley in the last years of the decade. Mormons from Alabama, Georgia, and Tennessee, led westward by a young missionary, John Morgan, eventually were settled on lands in the Conejos area by another young missionary, James Z. Stewart. Joined there by some families from Utah, and later by converts to Mormonism from Virginia, they created farming villages named Manassa, Ephraim, Richfield, and Sanford.

Some anxieties resulted from these developments. Several southern Colorado newspaper editors engaged in virulent editorializing against

Fort Collins in 1877, ten years after troops left the army post that gave the town its name.

this "invasion" of the valley. They disclosed a "Mormon plot" to establish a belt of colonies, twenty-five miles apart, all the way from Utah through Colorado to Nebraska. Some feared that the Mormons "would hold the balance of power in the politics of Conejos County which would result in political ruin for that part of the state." Actually, the Mormons proved more interested in farming than in politics, and friendships developed between them and their Spanish-speaking Catholic neighbors sufficient to quiet whatever fears the alarmist Anglo editors had raised among the residents of the valley.

Another colony of settlers arrived in Fremont County in 1882. Emanuel H. Saltiel, who owned silver mines at Cotopaxi, arranged through the Hebrew Immigrant Aid Society to settle sixteen families of Jewish emigrants from Russia and Poland on his lands. The experiment was not a particularly happy one. Although the farming lands were supposed to be located in the Wet Mountain Valley, the colonists instead were given rather barren lands for which no water was available for irrigation because of prior appropriations. In the view of some critics, the project's sponsors were more concerned with populating the town of Cotopaxi than in providing a new start in life for the refugees. When no satisfactory arrangements for aid could be negotiated with Saltiel, appeals were made to Jewish families in Denver for help. Finally the Hebrew Immigrant Aid Society advised the immigrants to leave Cotopaxi, giving families $100 each to help them settle in other places.

All these colonies—successful or not—were undoubtedly stimulated by the Board of Immigration that the territorial legislature created. Beginning its labors in 1872, the board induced many people to come to Colorado through its literature and promotional campaigns. As in other similar ventures, the claims of the board were sometimes exaggerated; the emphasis was perhaps too often placed on the attractive features of the territory and too seldom on those characteristics of Colorado life that required patience and concerted effort to overcome. More serious, to some critics, was the failure of the board to provide any help for immigrants after their arrival in the territory. "It is better to have no Board of Immigration at all," wrote one observer, "better not to waste time and money in advertising and entreating unless proper avenues are opened and the way cleared for such worthy people as may respond and are disposed to remain." Whatever the validity of such criticism, the Board of Immigration's efforts nicely illustrate the then contemporary public concern with peopling the territory and hastening the development of young Colorado.

THIRTEEN

CARPETBAGGER'S KINGDOM

For fifteen years—from 1861 to 1876—Colorado was a colony of the United States. Most of the territorial officers, from governor to justices of the Supreme Court, were appointed by the national government rather than elected by the people of the territory. Coloradans were allowed to select a delegate to the national Congress, but the delegate's powers were limited to participation in the debate without a vote. Some people in the territory, interested in full representation, worked to replace territorial status with a state government. And the desire for statehood was enhanced by the constantly shifting political scene in Washington. Each succeeding change in power there tended to be reflected in shifting officeholders appointed to territorial positions.

In many ways the story of territorial government and politics is a continuing chronicle of attempts to gain statehood for Colorado. The events were always played on two different and widely separated stages. In the territory itself, factions favored and factions opposed the anticipated conversion to "statedom" as they believed the change would benefit or harm their own interests. At the same time, political groupings in the national capital viewed statehood for Colorado favorably or unfavorably as a change in the status of the territory might be expected to bring good or ill fortune to them.

The presidential election year of 1864 marked the first major attempt to gain Colorado statehood. In that year, when the territory was a mere three-year-old, the Republican Party, hard-pressed by its lack of success on the battlefields of the Civil War, feared for its future in the political campaign. In addition to such precautions as converting the official name of the party to the Union Party and nominating as Lincoln's running mate a war Democrat from a border state, Andrew Johnson, the party pushed three enabling acts through Congress. (An enabling act was permissive legislation, allowing a territory to frame a constitution and submit it to the voters for approval; if such approval was gained, the president of the United States then could proclaim statehood for the territory.)

Colorado, Nebraska, and Nevada Territories were all given the chance to bring their expected Republican electoral votes to the polls that fall. Nine additional votes might ensure the margin of victory for the party. Nevada accepted the offer and became a state. Nebraska refused. Coloradans found much in the offer that was appealing. The obvious advantages of change included the benefits of home rule, the bolstering of local pride, a hoped-for influx of eastern capital to revive stagnated mining, and the advantages to be reaped from actual congressional representation. With two senators and a representative voting the territory's interests, "unfortunate" legislation like the Pacific railroad bill or a proposed federal tax on mining might be altered or enactment prevented. And, not least, unpopular territorial officials would no longer be able to hide behind the national patronage; "carpet bag" government would come to an end. All these motivations combined to build enthusiasm for statehood in the territory.

The enabling act required the summoning of a convention to draft a constitution for the proposed state. Haste was necessary, for the constitution would have to be written and approved by the voters in time for the president to proclaim statehood before election day if the votes from Colorado were to count in the presidential canvass. Independence Day that summer, 1864, found the delegates to the constitutional convention gathered at Golden to begin work. However, they soon adjourned to Denver, where facilities were less limited, and there they completed their deliberations.

From the beginning, those favoring statehood securely controlled the convention. The statehood advocates by and large were Republicans and Denver oriented, such as Governor John Evans, John Chivington,

Henry Moore Teller

William Byers, and Central City's Henry Teller, who was just beginning a long and distinguished career in Colorado politics. The necessity for haste appears to have led them into a serious procedural error. Blinded by their own enthusiasm for statehood, they underestimated a latent, largely unexpressed hostility to change and the role that personalities could play. In order to save time, they fashioned a slate of candidates for the new offices statehood would require; the voters then could ratify their choices at the same time they approved the constitution. They chose D. T. Towne for governor; Colonel John Chivington was to become the state's representative. Modestly reserving their own names from the slate, Evans and Teller presumably anticipated allowing the state legislature to reward them with the two U.S. senatorships.

From this maneuver an immediate hostility to the whole statehood movement resulted. Many citizens became convinced that the Evans-Teller group was more concerned with offices than with the welfare of Colorado. Some who had failed to secure places on the "ballot" moved over to lead the opposition to statehood. They soon discovered that there were other reasons for opposing the change. Many residents objected to the tax increases that would result when the federal government withdrew its subsidies for officers' salaries. Democrats saw no merit in hurrying three electoral votes for their opponents in the coming presidential race. Others were apprehensive about the extension of the federal conscription laws to Colorado, a change that would accompany the transition to statehood.

In addition, there was a bloc of antistatehood votes in the southern counties. No particular political friendship had ever developed between the Spanish-American settlers predominant in those counties and the Anglo-American settlers who formed the majority of the residents in the northern region. The barriers of culture and language undoubtedly contributed to the latent hostility of the southern counties to political domination by the northern sections. Since the Democratic Party was favored by the majority of the southern residents, Republican-achieved statehood and probable control of offices promised nothing of special attraction for them.

The combination of all these various forces was sufficient to defeat the statehood movement by a decisive majority: 1,520 for to 4,676 against. It was difficult for those who claimed Colorado residents were interested in statehood to explain the vote. Once the ballots were counted and the constitution and candidates rejected, the congressional enabling legislation was technically dead. But, surprisingly, a new movement for statehood rose like a phoenix, and interestingly its leadership included those recently opposed to the scheme.

Among them was Denver's urbane Jerome Chaffee, mining man and speculator but above all politician—perhaps Colorado's consummate politician of that era. He and Teller came to dominate the Republican Party, initially as rivals. The party was split into two factions, commonly referred to as the Denver and Golden crowds, each jealously guarding its own interests. The former had many of the territorial leaders—Evans, Chivington, Chaffee, and Byers—while the latter included Loveland and Teller, who switched sides after the 1864 debacle. For nearly a decade this split would have ramifications in various local issues.

With Chaffee's aid, a call was now issued for another constitutional convention to meet in the spring of 1865. The assumption was that if a constitution was drafted and accepted by the people, the national authorities would not refuse to admit Colorado to statehood on a mere technicality. But what the leaders failed to take into account was that Colorado's potential electoral votes were no longer needed. The election was over and the Republicans had weathered the crisis. Nonetheless, the statehood advocates continued in their plans. The voters ratified their constitution by a thin margin (less than 200 votes) although they rejected an accompanying proposal for black suffrage.

At this point it would have been wise to await word of presidential approval. But instead the statehood leaders sponsored an election for "state" officers. Three parties presented candidates: the Republicans, the Democrats, and a third group called the Sand Creek Vindication Party. The Republicans triumphed, capturing a majority of seats in the "state" legislature, electing the "governor" (William Gilpin, attempting another political career) and the "congressman," George Chilcott. When the unauthorized "state" legislature convened, it selected John Evans and Jerome Chaffee as U.S. senators.

The victory of the statehood faction and the Republicans in the "state" election proved short-lived, however, because the reaction in Washington was anything but favorable. Already lines were being drawn between the Radicals and President Andrew Johnson in the battle that would dominate the national political scene for the next few years. Johnson had no particular desire to increase the majority of Radical Republicans in Congress, and despite assurances from Colorado Republicans that they were loyal to his administration, he had reason to suspect they were wavering. Johnson refused to proclaim statehood on the grounds that the enabling legislation no longer was valid.

The statehood advocates then tried to convince the Radical Republicans to support a new enabling bill. They were not successful. The thin majority of voters favoring statehood alerted politicians to the divided local sentiments; Radical Republicans could not be pleased with the rejection of black suffrage. And the aftermath of the Sand Creek Massacre, with congressional investigation and the eventual removal of Governor Evans, eroded the support of some who might have advocated statehood.

Meanwhile, the territory continued to exist as a federal colony, governed by officials appointed in Washington. In the fall of 1865 Colorado received its third governor, Alexander Cummings of Philadelphia. Evans's removal from office had been considered for some time. His dismissal had been recommended by a committee formed to investigate the Sand Creek Massacre. Other motivating factors were a dispute about mining legislation and the fact that President Johnson probably wished to use his patronage for his own ends.

Cummings, one of the most controversial men to hold the governor's office during the territorial era, has been called by one historian "a hack politician, a spoilsman," and he earned from his contemporaries the title "His Turbulent Excellency." The petty quarrels that swarmed around him were generated partly by his adamant opposition to statehood. But his own personality—his stubbornness and unwillingness or inability to compromise on political matters—did little to win friends among influential Republicans in Colorado. He lasted only seventeen months in the office. In May 1867, Johnson removed him and named A. Cameron Hunt as governor.

The pattern of patronage and politics continued to rule the appointment of territorial officials. One of the most distressing facts of territorial status in the eyes of many Coloradans was the practice of the dominant political party to look upon the western territories as convenient "dumping grounds" for office-seekers with claims for partisan preference. Territorial offices were particularly useful for "taking care" of defeated, lame-duck officeholders. The coming and going of the governors was bad enough; lesser offices seemed to many to be filled with even less desirable appointees.

There were also a considerable number of patronage positions to be filled locally. These led to a constant scurry and scramble among the leaders of the dominant party in the territory, for continued control of the party often rested on the ability of a group to successfully juggle the spoils of office. Some of the positions were desirable because they legitimately carried with them large fees. The clerkship of the supreme court, for example, reportedly was worth close to $4,000 a year, "the best office in the Territory." Other posts presumably were desirable because they presented opportunities to engage in petty, and sometimes not so petty, graft. Besides appointive offices, the spoils of territorial politics also involved contracts for public printing and other services as well. Here, too, controversy seemed the rule rather than the exception. Rival newspapers and printing establishments jostled for supremacy in the affection of the officers who awarded the contracts.

It would be inaccurate to blame territorial status for all the shortcomings of Colorado's political life in those years. But many residents did believe that statehood would bring more responsible government. In 1866 those people were pleased by a brief resurgence of sentiment for statehood. Congressional leaders of the Republican Party, anticipating the need for additional supporters, passed a new enabling act for Colorado, with an eye on the off-year congressional elections that fall. President Andrew Johnson promptly vetoed the act on the grounds that the population in the territory was insufficient for statehood. Congress tried to override the veto but failed.

And in the territory, the fight had by no means ended either. With renewed efforts emanating from the statehood advocates, their antagonists girded for battle to defeat any move to elevate the territory's status. The Denver "ring," led by John Evans and Jerome Chaffee, worked diligently for admission to the Union. These men still controlled the unrecognized and nonfunctioning "state" administration of 1865, needing only national approval to become the government of Colorado.

Opposing them was the "Golden gang" led by Henry Teller, ready to take issue with the Denver Republicans on statehood or any other question. The split between the two groups was particularly focused on the commercial rivalry between the two towns, especially in their competition for railroads. The division of political spoils added another element to the rivalry. Then there was the controversy over the location of the territorial capital. The first legislature had been called to meet in Denver; during its session the members determined to convene in Colorado City for the second session. They had met there in 1862 but after a few days returned to Denver and its greater comforts. Golden then offered

Territorial legislators met briefly in Colorado City before moving to Denver in 1862.

the use of a building and free firewood, and the legislature accepted the offer and moved to that city.

From then, until 1867, both Denver and Golden claimed the honor of being the capital, and the legislature shifted sessions from one town to the other. Territorial Secretary Samuel H. Elbert, growing weary from moving the legislative furniture back and forth, reportedly muttered that the "first railroad needed in Colorado was the most direct line between its two capitals." Finally, in 1867, Denver was named the permanent seat of government.

Although Evans, Chaffee, and the Denver Republicans won the capital, the fight over statehood continued. Whatever might be said about the merits of the argument, Teller and his antistatehood group were winning many friends. Statehood was becoming less and less attractive to many Coloradans. In the spring of 1868, a last attempt was made to use the constitution and officers of the 1865 movement. The U.S. Senate Committee on Territories conducted hearings in Washington on the question—1868 was election year again! Evans and Chaffee submitted statements to the committee, emphasizing their estimates that population in Colorado was increasing rapidly and had reached a total between 75,000 and 100,000 people. In their view, the majority of residents were eager to enjoy statehood.

Teller, speaking for the other side, denied the population increases, insisting that no more than 30,000 people then lived in the territory. (Two years later the federal census would count fewer than 40,000 residents, an increase of only 5,000 since 1860.) Teller was also confident that a referendum among the voters would demonstrate a majority in the territory opposed to statehood. In Washington, Teller spent time with Senator Roscoe Conkling of New York and others. He did his work well; it was soon apparent that a statehood bill could not pass Congress. Evans and Chaffee, in a final, desperate move, "resigned" their never-sanctioned offices, hoping to eliminate some of the opposition. But the noble act did little good. From 1868 until the approach of the presidential election of 1876, Colorado statehood was a dead issue. "Carpet bag" government might be unpleasant, and even corrupt, but the statehood advocates had small success railing against it for the next seven years.

Even without electoral votes from Colorado, the Republicans experienced no great difficulty electing their candidate, U. S. Grant, to the presidency in 1868. He soon moved to employ the patronage of territorial offices, and Colorado prepared to welcome its fifth governor—General

Edward McCook. The new governor was no stranger to the territory. In 1859 he had joined the gold rush to Gregory Gulch and had practiced law for a brief time in Central City. Then, during the Civil War, he had attained the rank of major general in the Union Army. His career as Colorado governor was far from quiet. Determined to make the most of his powers, playing the customary game of spoils, McCook managed to alienate a large part of the Colorado political community during the next few years.

Not the least of his crimes against the commonwealth involved favoritism he showed his brother-in-law, James B. Thompson, whose insatiable appetite for public office led him to be the governor's private secretary, auditor of public accounts, and a special agent to the Utes (headquartered in Denver!). McCook, meanwhile, dabbled in land speculation, railroad projects, and cattle ranching. Together the two proceeded to use their offices to enhance their private welfare; for example, they made $22,000 net profit on a cattle transaction involving a sale to the Utes.

Anti-McCook sentiment brewed, especially in the Denver crowd. An investigation by David Moffat and Samuel Elbert uncovered some of the scandals, and Chaffee, now territorial delegate, presented the results in Washington. Petitions circulated demanding McCook's removal, and Grant eventually bowed to pressure, naming Evans's son-in-law, Samuel Elbert, governor. McCook did not surrender willingly and leveled some accusations and charges of corruption of his own. He convinced Grant of the justice of his case. The president, thus, in 1874 removed Elbert, who had been in office less than a year, and replaced him with McCook. The unpopular McCook had become a genuine liability to Colorado Republicans who split into factions over this latest example of carpetbaggism. This division allowed the Democratic Party, after a bitter campaign, to elect Thomas Patterson territorial delegate. This defeat was too much for the local Republicans, who feared what it portended for the future. They insisted that the governor must be removed, and the harassed Grant finally conceded to their demand. In three years, three men had been appointed governor. How much longer, Coloradans wondered, would they be victims of Washington's capriciousness?

With McCook's second removal, a general overturn of territorial offices followed. To have all except one judge removed and replaced created "a great sensation for a small western territory, which attributed the President's action to the results of a game of poker between himself and

Delegate Chaffee." To some, the shambles of expiring regimes followed so closely upon each other that all was confusion. The "revolving-door" character of the Colorado governorship impressed many observers as peculiarly unfortunate. The editor of the Laramie (Wyoming) *Sentinel* prophetically stated: "We don't reckon there was ever a territory or state that required so many governors for home consumption as Colorado, and her future historians will likely go crazy in tracing out and recording them."

The vacancy created by the second removal of McCook was filled by John L. Routt, the last of Colorado's territorial governors, destined to become Colorado's first state governor. Routt was a Kentuckian who had served as captain of an Illinois regiment during the Civil War. Grant is said to have noticed the officer's ability during the Vicksburg campaign. After the war Routt was named second assistant postmaster and from that office Grant assigned him to the Colorado governorship, in time to serve during the transition to statehood.

FOURTEEN

THE CENTENNIAL STATE

The year 1876 promised to bring to the American people one of the most exciting presidential elections in the history of the Republic. Despite the poor showing of the Liberal Republicans and Democrats four years earlier, when they had tried to match Horace Greeley against U. S. Grant for the presidency, the Republican leaders were worried. Grant was no longer eligible to be a candidate under the restrictive two-term tradition. Reconstruction governments in only three of the southern states were supported by federal troops, and most of the southern electoral votes were probably lost to the opposition. In addition, the disclosures of scandals and corruption during the Grant administrations would give the Democrats a surplus of ammunition to use in the campaign.

So once again the Republicans in Washington looked favorably on aspiring western territories, feeling again the need for the security of additional electoral votes. The Republicans confidently translated Colorado statehood to read "three Republican electoral votes." In the initial stages it was necessary to keep the Democrats content by linking the measure for Colorado statehood with an enabling act for New Mexico Territory, which in all likelihood would favor the Democratic Party. On the last day of the session, March 3, 1875, Congress approved the Colorado legislation. The New Mexico bill failed.

Thus Colorado again was given a chance to enter the Union. By this time the people of the territory should have been familiar with the procedures to be followed. A constitutional convention would be called. It would draft a basic charter for the new state, which, when finished, would be presented to the people for ratification or rejection. If the electorate approved the document, it would be forwarded to Washington. Then the president would complete the process by proclaiming Colorado a state.

The territorial leaders proceeded to set in motion the necessary steps in this procedure. First they summoned the voters to elect thirty-nine delegates to the drafting convention that would meet in Denver's Odd Fellows Hall in December 1875. The Republicans suggested a nonpartisan canvass because they had recently suffered the internal divisions brought on by Governor McCook. The Democrats, who had experienced their only political victories because of those divisions, refused. Nonetheless, the voters selected twenty-four Republicans and only fifteen Democrats as delegates. Actually, the partisan division was neither very important nor very apparent throughout proceedings of the convention. When divisions occurred, they resulted from other issues. Religious persuasions brought a cleavage between Roman Catholics and Protestants; the mining delegates sometimes differed with the delegates from the agricultural areas.

Much of what the convention did was routine work, rather easily agreed to by the delegates. The convention had no control over some of the provisions of the constitution. For example, Congress had stipulated that the boundaries of the state would be identical with the boundaries of the territory. Other features of the charter were taken wholesale from the constitutions of states already in the Union. A bill of rights listed traditional Anglo-American personal freedoms and privileges in considerable detail. These caused little debate, as did the plan to separate the state government into three branches.

The executive branch was to be headed by an elected governor. Six additional officials would also be elected to serve: a lieutenant governor, a secretary of state, an auditor, a treasurer, an attorney general, and a superintendent of public instruction.

The legislative branch was titled the General Assembly. It was divided into a senate of twenty-six members and a house of representatives of forty-nine members. The representatives would be elected for two-year terms; the senators for four-year terms.

The third branch, the judiciary, was to be headed by the state supreme court, originally composed of three members elected for nine-year terms. The justice with the least time remaining in the term would serve as the chief justice. An unusual provision of the judicial clause empowered the state supreme court to render "advisory" opinions when requested. In addition to the supreme court, the constitution established district courts and a county court for each county.

Most of these provisions were fixed without difficulty. Other sections of the constitution were more controversial, especially the attempt to determine the limits of the state's authority to regulate economic activity. The year was 1876; in the midwestern states "Granger" legislatures were at the peak of their power. Farmers and allied interests there, chafing under domination by railroad and storage companies, had used the previously social-minded Patrons of Husbandry, or Grange, organizations to elect their leaders to the state legislatures. In these chambers, the Grangers had successfully campaigned for regulatory legislation to limit fares and charges by railroads and terminal facilities. Granger sentiment had invaded some of the agrarian regions of Colorado and now was apparent in the convention debates.

At the same time, however, Colorado had other, opposite interests. The new state was still a frontier community without large domestic capital resources. The miners in the mountains and the farmers on the plains cried alike for capital investments to bring them into high productivity. That capital had to come from the East and from Europe. A harsh, inflexible code restricting corporations would create an unfavorable climate to risk investors. Thus the problem was "how to protect the interests of the people without scaring away the capital that was so essential for the economic development of the region."

In the end, the convention attempted to traverse a narrow line, avoiding both the extreme of rigid regulation on the one hand and the dangers of an unrestricted economy on the other. The delegates who feared the power of uncontrolled corporations were responsible for these provisions of the constitution: All incorporations were to be perfected under a general incorporation law, thus eliminating the hazards of private legislation; no irrevocable charters were to be granted; all out-of-state corporations were required to maintain an agent or a place of business within the new state; all railroads were to be considered "public carriers"; consolidation of parallel or competing railroad lines was forbidden, as were all unjust and unreasonable discriminations between individuals in their business with such corporations; the jurisdiction of the state courts was retained in case of consolidation of a state corporation with a foreign corporation, at least over that part of the corporate property within the limits of the state.

These restrictions and regulations placed the state a goodly distance from pure laissez-faire. But in comparison with the legislation that had issued from the Granger-dominated legislatures of the Midwest, it was a kind of "half-way" settlement. The constitution contained no provision for the establishment of a railroad or public utilities commission. There were no clauses specifying the right of the state, or its agencies, to determine maximum railroad or storage rates.

Although this problem of economic regulation undoubtedly presented the delegates with their greatest challenge, the convention generated much more noise and heat in its debates over the Deity. Many delegates believed that the absence of specific reference to God in the federal constitution was a serious omission. Other states had included an acknowledgment of Divine Power in their constitutions. The question of whether to include such a statement in the Colorado charter stirred considerable controversy. At length the convention decided to acknowledge a "profound reverence for the Supreme Ruler of the Universe."

Even more heated were the debates over the use of school funds. Congress, in the enabling legislation, had provided that two sections of land in each township were to be reserved for the use of the schools. Even if this land was sold eventually for only the minimum price, a windfall of $10 million would result. Immediately the delegates divided on the question of apportioning the grant. Was it to be used only for publicly supported schools or would it be more fair to include parochial institutions in the apportionment? The question pitted Protestants against Roman Catholics. In the final determination, the delegates adopted a clause specifying that "no state aid other than exemption from taxation for any sectarian institution" ever was to be provided.

A further problem that arose to delay the convention was the question of woman suffrage. In the centennial year of American independence, women's rights groups, local and national, deluged the delegates with petitions, suggesting the potential honor that Colorado might achieve by becoming the first state in the Union to provide full political participation for females. The drafters, however, decided to forgo heroism. They made a slight nod to the women by allowing them to vote in school district elections. But for a voice in honest-to-goodness partisan contests, women would have to await the decision of the general (male) electorate on a promised proposal for an amendment. Two years later, the question was placed before the voters and they rejected it.

The woman suffrage question, like that of economic regulation, actually was compromised as far as possible by the delegates. They were motivated primarily by their fear of controversy; their timidity followed naturally from their desire to shun any issue capable of seriously dividing the electorate and crippling the chances for ratification. Only in the matter of disposing of the school funds did the delegates take a strong position when they wrote the clauses upholding the traditional separation of church and state, and in this area they undoubtedly calculated the dominant strength of the Protestants. As for the constitution as a whole, it was probably much too long as it was written. Too much detail had been included, and matters that might well have been left to future legislatures were included in the basic charter.

After eighty-seven days of work, on March 14, 1876, the constitution-makers adjourned their convention. The members left Denver for their home counties to work for ratification of their product. The electorate balloted on the first day of July that summer. By a resounding majority— 15,443 to 4,062—the people of the territory accepted the constitution. All that remained was the arrival of good news from Washington.

President Grant did not keep the Coloradans waiting long. The national elections were fast approaching and Republican votes would be needed. On August 1, 1876, he issued the proclamation of statehood from the White House. Colorado responded with three Republican electoral votes that fall, which proved fortunate for the party since this was the disputed election when Rutherford Hayes's victory over Samuel Tilden rested precariously on a one-vote margin. Locally the entire Republican ticket for state offices, headed by John Routt for governor, was elected, and the party also won the majority of seats in both houses of the new legislature. Their only defeat came in the selection of a representative to Congress. A squabble over scheduling the election led to a contested decision, finally settled by the national House of Representatives, which gave the seat to Democrat Thomas Patterson. Republicans Henry Teller and Jerome Chaffee became the first senators from the new state.

Admittance to the Union proved an enthusiastic occasion for bolstering local pride. Not all Americans were as happy, however. A Pennsylvania editor growled: "Colorado consists of Denver, the Kansas Pacific Railway, and scenery. The mineral resources of Colorado exist in the imagination. The agricultural resources do not exist at all." And a New York newspaper was even more uncomplimentary: "There is something repulsive in the idea that a few handfuls of miners and reckless bushwhackers should have the same representation in the Senate as Pennsylvania, Ohio, and New York."

Easterners might sneer at the baby commonwealth, but to the citizens of the new state, such words were of small import. The East had traditionally been opposed to the "rising West" and Coloradans were not deflated in spirit by the critics beyond the Mississippi. The optimism of the decade from 1870 to 1880 was too entrenched to be driven away by mere words. Population alone refuted the pessimists. In 1870 the territory had counted only 40,000 inhabitants. Ten years later that number had increased almost fivefold, to a total of 194,327. Denver, which had registered the grand increase of exactly 10 people (4,749 to 4,759) between 1860 and 1870, now contained the amazing total of 25,000 people. In warm weather, there were even more people in the Queen City, for Denver was becoming a mecca for summer tourists. In 1878 the four main hotels in the city hosted 25,000 visitors during the summer season.

Not all the visitors were pleased with what they saw. Many would probably have echoed the sentiments of Isabella Bird, who, in 1873, had described Denver: "There the great braggart city lay spread out, brown and treeless, upon the brown and treeless plain, which seemed to nourish nothing but wormwood and the Spanish bayonet." But others found the place attractive, if not in itself, then at least as the gateway to the scenic wonders of the Rocky Mountains. The natural splendors of the peaks and valleys, widely advertised by railroads in their quest for passengers, became the objective of many visitors who came to look and to marvel. The natural scene was soon augmented with conveniences for these tourists. Although intended for more practical purposes, the Georgetown Loop, built to cover the mile and a half from Georgetown to Silver Plume, would soon become a favorite tourist attraction. The thrill of seeing massive mountains while riding across the Devil's Gate Viaduct was worth the price of the railroad fare.

The Royal Gorge enticed many others. Frank Fossett, in his guide for travelers, assured those contemplating a trip to the canyon of the

Denver as it appeared in 1874.

Arkansas River that as was the case with the Grand Canyon of the Colorado, thousands had visited it, but harm had "befallen none, for despite the seeming horror of the situation, the appalling depth and rugged paths, the fascination of the danger gives birth to the greatest caution."

The hot mineral springs in the hills also beckoned tourists, particularly the health-seekers. Colorado was now beginning to capitalize on its climate, proclaimed by many as ideal for the sufferer from tuberculosis. Fossett was almost rhapsodical in his prose: "The asthmatic forgets in the quiet of undisturbed slumber his nightly suffocation; the victim of chronic bronchitis discovers a new lease of life, and after the lapse of a very brief period he finds it hard to realize that he has been so recently afflicted with a cough so distressing, so violent, or so dangerous. The sufferer from malaria, in that most obnoxious form called fever and ague, is glad to have found a land where fever and ague never come."

The "pitch" was directed to all the infirm, but in particular eastern and midwestern physicians had begun to advise tubercular patients to seek relief in the Rocky Mountain region. They sometimes suggested that their patients plan the trip westward in several stages, making stops at Kansas towns along the way to acclimate the lungs to the changing altitude. Denver and Colorado Springs and other towns beckoned the sick and the near dead—the tourists who "ghostlike . . . glided through the corridors and shivered in the parlors and at the dining tables. Waiters were seen on the staircases carrying meals to the rooms of those who would never leave them again, and the direful echoes of hollow coughs resounded through the halls."

If the disease had progressed to its final stages, the invalid might not only find no cure but might also unfortunately meet an earlier death from the change in altitude. But many were more fortunate and added years to their lives by rest, diet changes, and the climate of new surroundings. By the decade of 1880–1890, perhaps one-third of all Colorado settlers could be classified as "health-seekers," an index to a facet of Colorado's development that has never been fully considered or described.

Infirm or not, visitors and tourists left their dollars in the Centennial State. But what were looked upon as even more desirable than tourists were genuine immigrants who came to stay. No effort was spared to spread the word that the former frontier was now a stable, permanent, culture-sprouting place. The advertisers had some facts to prove it. Consider, for example, the matter of higher education. Where less than thirty years before the Indians and the fur traders had bartered pelts there now stood no fewer than five institutions of higher learning. In Denver, Colorado Seminary had become the University of Denver. In 1867 the seminary had been forced to close its doors because of indebtedness. After twelve inactive years, the college reopened for classes in the fall of 1880 with a new name—the University of Denver and Colorado Seminary.

In Boulder, after existing on paper for some years, the University of Colorado was now a going concern. In 1877 its first class of forty-four students arrived for instruction. No need, of course, to dwell on the fact that President Joseph A. Sewall discovered that the students were poorly prepared for collegiate courses, necessitating emphasis on the preparatory school. Instead, concentrate on the fact that the first class was "on its way" and that by 1883 seven graduates would receive their diplomas.

The proud Coloradans could relate that Congregationalists had found General Palmer's new town of Colorado Springs ideally suited to their plans for a college in the Rocky Mountains and that, in 1874, they chartered Colorado College. Or that the territorial legislature, in the same year, had appropriated $45,000 to begin a School of Mines in the city of Golden on the campus of burned-out Jarvis Hall, a boys' school the Episcopalians had operated there. Or that Fort Collins promoted a college for itself and succeeded in gaining legislative approval for the establishment of the College of Agriculture. A land-grant institution, organized in accordance with the federal Morrill Act of 1862, the Agricultural College of Colorado opened in 1879 for its first enrollment of nineteen students.

Such good works made excellent topics for the local promoters. But as it turned out, none of them could compare to a different sort of magnet that soon enticed hordes to the new state. All the colleges and social institutions in the West faded in comparison with the attraction of quick and easy wealth. Gold had provided that impetus in the beginning. Now a new metal came to take its place. Suddenly, high and deep within the ranges of the Rockies, there was Leadville—and silver seemed to make all else dull and commonplace.

FIFTEEN

CARBONATE CAMPS

The discovery of gold and the subsequent Pike's Peak rush spawned the first large white population to settle in Colorado. In the decade that followed, gold mining continued to be the heart of the territory's economy. Gilpin County and its camps dominated the mining scene; it would take most Coloradans a long time to think in terms of other metals. Men like William Byers and William Gilpin could soar into flights of oratory describing additional mineral possibilities, but even after miners in Clear Creek County had discovered silver, prospectors and investors would not divert their attention from gold. Despite the Caribou silver mines and news of discoveries in the San Juans, gold continued to hold center stage. Silver triumphed, nonetheless. With Leadville and the proudly proclaimed title The Silver State, Colorado emerged as the greatest mining state in the country.

In the upper Arkansas River Valley, under the shadow of Mounts Massive and Elbert, prospectors of 1860 had stumbled onto a rich gold placer. Optimistically named California Gulch, it became the mecca for one of the larger intraterritorial mining rushes. For a season, Oro City, which grew up along the gulch without much planning or encouragement, had been considered one of the most promising new camps. Then, as the placer gold was panned out, people drifted away to more promising diggings. For a decade the district and the camp stagnated, seemingly forgotten relics of earlier days.

The discovery of the Printer Boy Mine, a gold quartz lode, at the head of the gulch, briefly renewed interest in the area in the late 1860s. Oro City was relocated near the mine, but the flurry proved short-lived. With a population of 251 in 1870 and declining mining, Oro City offered few incentives to newcomers.

Appearances can be deceiving and Oro City was an example. As early as 1873, the Oro City assay office reported silver in numerous ore samples, and in November the *Rocky Mountain News* published a story of a meeting of "prominent" citizens to discuss the erection of reduction works for "our silver ores." The problems were similar to those that hindered Summit County: the nearest mills were too far away to allow anything but extremely high grade ore to be shipped, and the real worth of the mines had not been proven.

The base was laid in 1876 for the rush that would follow in the next three years. Prospecting increased; the *Engineering and Mining Journal* reported that $21,000 worth of silver had been mined in Lake County that year. Oro City, however, was not destined to claim the glory of being the center of a bonanza silver district; this distinction went to the new camp of Leadville, a few miles to the northwest. There, in the summer and fall of 1877, discoveries were made eclipsing everything in California Gulch.

Throughout the winter, excitement mounted. A rush to Leadville began in the spring of 1878, with the curious, the hopeful, the tenderfoot, and the experienced prospector mingling freely in the giddy atmosphere of the 10,000-foot elevation. In April the Little Pittsburg Mine was discovered on Fryer Hill, the most important of the early mining areas. It launched Horace Austin Warner Tabor on a career that eventually put him in the U.S. Senate and made him one of Colorado's best-known legendary figures. Tabor, a veteran prospector and storekeeper in California Gulch, Buckskin Joe, and Oro City, had a change in luck when he grubstaked August Rische and George Hook, the men who discovered the fabulous Little Pittsburg. Tabor and his wife rose from comfortable middle-class respectability as Oro City's leading citizens to millionaire status. For the next three years, it seemed Tabor could do no wrong in mining or in investments. Eventually, his financial plunging led to his downfall, but not before he rejected his faithful first wife,

Augusta, to marry Elizabeth McCourt, better known as Baby Doe, creating one of the era's greatest social scandals.

Tabor, who moved to Leadville in the summer of 1877, had emerged as one of its leaders even before he had acquired his wealth. He worked hard to promote the camp, helped organize municipal government, and had been elected the first mayor. Larger horizons opened for him as his wealth grew. The Republican Party tapped him for lieutenant governor in 1878, and his improved status brought him into contact with many of the state's noted miners and speculators, including Chaffee and Moffat. He speculated with abandon; he purchased the Matchless Mine for "pocket money," and it produced for nearly a decade, supporting his other financial adventures.

Others found their fortunes almost as quickly. The hills of the district seemed to be stacked with silver. The first boom year of 1878 saw $2 million worth of the metal extracted; the count went up to over $9 million the next year. In the decade between 1879 and 1889, more than $82 million worth of silver was dug up, smelted down, and shipped from the Leadville region.

Founded in 1877 and incorporated in 1878, Leadville soon surpassed all Colorado communities but Denver in population, while Lake County, under this stimulus, grew from 500 to 24,000 people by the time of the census of 1880. Nearly astride the Continental Divide, Leadville lived high and grew fast, its mining history almost eclipsed by its town-making efforts. In many ways, Leadville was a repetition of other boom towns, but the spectacle of sudden growth was exaggerated. No other Colorado camp until Cripple Creek would compare with Leadville in numbers and wealth. All the ingredients of civilized life were wanting, and men and women were not hesitant about trying their hand at making dollars—one way or another—by catering to the needs of the new Cloud City.

Profiteering seemed the rule, not the exception. Staple groceries sold for four times the Denver prices. A barrel of whiskey reportedly could be made to work a $1,500 profit; hay sold for $200 a ton in winter. This sort of bizarre inflation came about largely because of the difficulties of freighting goods into the camp. Denver, Colorado Springs, Canon City, and Georgetown were the sites of the railheads, and all were at least seventy-five miles distant from Leadville. Some improvement came with the building of the "high line" wagon road over Loveland Pass in 1879. Then Georgetown, terminal of the Colorado Central, was only sixty miles away, and the trip, in good weather, could be made in one day with four-horse teams.

Leadville (above) was a mining town, Red Mountain (below) a mining camp. The differences in wealth, business district architecture, and size are obvious. Not so easily observable was the spirit that a town had naturally and a camp tried awkwardly to emulate. Horace Tabor spent more money (approximately $31,000) on his opera house than was invested in Red Mountain's entire business district.

Even after the goods arrived in Leadville, "chaos prevailed in the location and identification of freight. . . . Hundreds of loaded wagons arrived daily, and their cargoes dumped on confused heaps within twenty enormous warehouses, without attempt at sorting, classifying, or indexing. Merchants with waiting storerooms and clamoring customers were frenzied by their inability to secure consignments after arrival."

Under such conditions, travel and shipping rates were nothing but exorbitant. Passengers were charged 10¢ a mile from Denver to the terminus of the Denver and South Park Railroad; freight rates ran as high as $29 a ton—more than for goods shipped by water from New York City to California around Cape Horn. Only the construction of a railroad directly into Leadville would ease the situation, and more than one road was already heading in that direction. Colorado railroaders, boasting of their more than 1,000 miles of operating trackage in the state in 1878, discovered that until Leadville was included in the network their profits would never reach full potential.

The Denver and Rio Grande had quickly sensed the importance of the Leadville traffic and had begun its plans. But before it could act it had to wage a highly competitive battle with the Atchison, Topeka and Santa Fe road. The Santa Fe and the Rio Grande found themselves potential rivals for two points: Raton Pass into New Mexico and the canyon of the Arkansas River, leading to Leadville. Early in 1878 the Santa Fe began construction across Raton Pass, thus presumably blocking the Rio Grande's chances of entering the New Mexican capital by the old trail route. Almost simultaneously, work crews of the two roads appeared in the Royal Gorge of the Arkansas, determined to secure the narrow defile leading to the new silver camp. Before much actual violence was committed by either side, the roads' attorneys had transferred the contest to the courts. During the litigation the Rio Grande experienced humiliating moments, including a lease to the Santa Fe, and unleasing, and finally, the interjection of new ownership in the person of financier Jay Gould. Gould, also owner of the Union Pacific and Kansas Pacific lines, achieved a place on the Rio Grande's Board of Directors shortly after his purchase of company stock. Not until February 1880 was the complicated situation unraveled at a meeting in Boston between interested parties.

According to the Boston "treaty," the Rio Grande agreed to give up its plans to build south over Raton Pass to El Paso, Texas, acknowledging the historic crossing as Santa Fe country. It also promised not to build eastward toward St. Louis, a move that Gould had threatened. The

Santa Fe Railroad, in return, committed itself to withdrawal from the Leadville route and promised to forget its plans to build from Pueblo to Denver. The lucrative but long-delayed Leadville traffic would be carried over Rio Grande tracks through the contested gorge, with that railroad paying the Santa Fe the cost of its work in the canyon and a bonus for the settlement. The east-bound freight carried by the Rio Grande would be delivered on a fifty-fifty basis to the Union Pacific and the Santa Fe.

Two years had passed while the contest between the roads tied up construction toward the silver camp. Now, with a settlement reached, the Rio Grande hastened to complete the line. Building up the valley, the railroad company continued its town-building habits by buying up homesteaders' lots and laying out the city of Salida (South Arkansas) on the way. Before the end of 1880, it had reached Leadville.

While waiting to complete that line, the Rio Grande had pushed the construction of its other branches, especially the extension over La Veta Pass into the San Luis Valley. On July 4, 1878, the railroad brought its first train into the new town of Alamosa. This extension grew in significance after the Raton Pass route to New Mexico was closed by the Santa Fe construction. If the Rio Grande was to reach the New Mexican capital, it must do so by building south from the San Luis Valley. In 1880 what came to be known as the "chili line" connected Alamosa with Espanola, New Mexico. For some time, however, the Boston agreement prohibited construction of the remaining forty-four miles to Santa Fe.

While the Royal Gorge "war" between the Rio Grande and the Santa Fe captivated the public's imagination, the Denver, South Park Railroad also had designs on the Leadville traffic. By 1878 the South Park had completed its line from Denver through Platte Canyon to Bailey and was in an advantageous position to carry Leadville freight to the end of its tracks, from where the freight was hauled by wagon into the silver camp. But then, for reasons still obscure, instead of heading from Bailey directly to Leadville, the South Park swung in an arc through the mountain park and reached Nathrop in 1880, on its way to the Gunnison area. At Nathrop it intersected the Rio Grande tracks. Through an arrangement with that company, the South Park sent its trains up the Arkansas Valley into Leadville. The days of the South Park's independence proved to be as limited as the Rio Grande's. The Union Pacific, dominated by Jay Gould, bought the road and immediately extended a line from Como over Boreas and Fremont Passes to Leadville in 1884.

With control of the South Park, the Union Pacific was rapidly consolidating its hold over transportation in northeastern Colorado. The Colorado Central, Loveland's dream road, had fallen to Gould control in 1879, the year after the eastern financier had taken the Kansas Pacific into his hands. From the Colorado Central terminal at Georgetown, Gould envisioned an extension to Leadville, too. Under his auspices, the Georgetown, Breckenridge and Leadville Railroad was organized and, in grandiose style, the famed Georgetown Loop was constructed, lifting trains the 638-foot step above Georgetown to Silver Plume. A few miles west of there, at Graymont, construction abruptly halted.

For travelers on their way to Leadville, whether by Rio Grande coaches through the Royal Gorge, or by the South Park over Fremont Pass, or via Georgetown and the horse-drawn stage, the trip must have been tiresome. People going to Leadville wanted to get there in a hurry. When they arrived, they might very well have been disappointed at their first sight of the place. The hillsides had been denuded; the pine forests were cut down to make charcoal for the smelters because coal and coke were not available in quantity until the railroads reached Leadville.

In the first rush any type of construction was deemed appropriate; the startled visitor saw log cabins, false-fronted wooden stores, varied types of shacks, and even tents throughout the camp. These gradually gave way to brick and frame construction, though a lawn remained a rarity, while littering was common. Over all hung smoke from the smelters, the mine buildings, and the town. Mayor Tabor and the city leaders worked hard to provide a government with some controls, but the newness and tremendous growth worked against resolving sanitation, general nuisance, and criminal problems. The lack of a stable tax base hindered development of water works, street improvement, and the hiring of needed officials. The constant danger of fire spurred the formation of volunteer companies, which served until a regular fire department could be hired. Local mine owners, such as Tabor, furnished money for equipment and fancy uniforms.

A town did emerge, after passing through the camp stage very quickly. It had been born to serve the needs of the mines and miners, and serve them it did. A business census in the spring of 1879 listed among its findings 31 restaurants, 17 barber shops, 51 groceries, 4 banks, and 120 saloons. Lots that had been worth less than $100 two years earlier were now selling for thousands, and rents jumped correspondingly. At night Leadville put its best face forward, the soft lights masking the bleakness of a jerry-built community. At dusk the variety houses, dance halls, theatres, gambling halls, and saloons awakened from their day-long slumber. All types of entertainment were available, from the foulest dive to the handsome Tabor Opera House, which opened in November 1879. The red-light district claimed to be one of the country's best, a dubious distinction. Leadville had come of age as the silver queen of Colorado.

Though less noticeable because they were less spectacular, more significant developments contributed to the town's stability. The organization of numerous churches, the building of schools, and the growth of residential areas reflected the coming of families and the disappearance of the rough frontier trappings. Along with these came fraternal lodges and social clubs. Gas lights and telephones soon appeared in the business district and in some houses.

Above all else, Leadville was a sudden economic opportunity that created a frantic, feverish race to quick fortune. A variety of paths to the rainbow's end, other than mining, appeared. Two of the best lay in real estate speculation and the building of rental property. Many ignored mining and concentrated on services and supplies, where a steady if not spectacular income awaited the fortunate ones. Freighting, until the railroad came, was lucrative and even afterward the wagons went from the tracks to the more isolated camps. Some were content to labor in the mines, while others hired out only as a temporary expedient until they could find their own bonanzas.

The lucky prospectors and investors were really lucky. Tabor was not alone in his good fortune. Samuel Newhouse was one of those who prospered early; he would move from Leadville to become an important copper king and, in time, erect the famous Flatiron Building in New York City. John L. Routt, of contemporary political fame, the Colorado governor, bought part interest in the Morning Star Mine, which later sold for $1 million and netted the then ex-governor a goodly fortune. Alva Adams, of future political fame, banked his money from the Blind Tour Mine.

Those in smelting also prospered. By 1881 fourteen smelters and ore reduction plants were filling up the valleys with evil-smelling fumes. Among the earliest of these was the Harrison Reduction Works, opened in 1877, and the future Grant Smelting Company, dating from the following year. The Grant soon had seven furnaces in operation, treating 175 tons of ore each day, producing three carloads of base bullion every twenty-four hours. And it was at Leadville that the future "smelter king," Meyer Guggenheim, reached his first successes in the Centennial State.

Meyer Guggenheim had come to the United States in 1847 from Switzerland, a poverty-cursed nineteen-year-old. From peddler in Pennsylvania to commission merchant during the Civil War, he courted and won financial success. In 1879, with R. B. Graham, he bought the A. Y. and Minnie properties in Leadville. They were reported to bring him profits of $1,000 a day; a decade later they would still be valued at $14 million. Meyer sent his son Benjamin to Leadville to watch over the mining operations and it was through Benjamin that Edward R. Holden interested the senior Guggenheim in investing in his smelter at Denver.

As wood became scarcer as a smelting fuel, the operators began to use coking coal from Trinidad, which was more desirable than wood and charcoal although transportation costs kept the price extremely high. It was natural for smelter owners to try to locate their works in strategic centers. The Boston and Colorado had earlier discovered that by moving from Black Hawk to Argo, near Denver, they effected significant economies because of the added ease of securing coal. Although much of the Leadville ore was reduced locally, both Denver and Golden also grew as smelting centers. The giant Grant Smelter in Denver began operations in 1878.

Immense amounts of labor were needed to work the smelters and the mines. Italians, Austrians, Croats, Serbs, Slovenes—the newly arrived emigrants from southeastern Europe provided the majority of the unskilled laborers for smelter furnaces and mine tunnels. As though to emphasize the difference that had come to mining operations since the days of the earlier rush to the gold camps, the Leadville mines were a mere three years old when they were rocked by the first major labor disturbance in the state's mining history. The individualistic days when mines were owned by the same people who worked them, and when those who classified as day laborers shifted for themselves, were now past. Mining properties had become corporate enterprises and laborers had joined together into unions—in this case, the Miners' Co-operative Union, secretly chartered by the national Knights of Labor.

In late May 1880, the Leadville mines were hit by a strike that started with a walkout by the laborers at the Chrysolite Mine. For the next three weeks the town was gripped by the strike, which eventually so worried the "respectable" citizens, especially the owners, that pressure was brought to bear on Governor Pitkin to declare martial law and send in state troops. He did and his action broke the strike but not before threats of violence were heard from both sides. Reasons for the strike mystified contemporaries; explanations ranged from a demand for higher wages to an owner-motivated movement to mask the failure of the Chrysolite.

The strike hurt Leadville but less than other events of that same year—the failure of both the Little Pittsburg and the Chrysolite Mines. The Little Pittsburg, which had brought Leadville into its bonanza era, collapsed in February amid charges of stock speculation, overpromotion, and mismanagement. Many unhappy eastern speculators were left holding stocks that dropped in price from over $30 to $5 per share by April. This did little to increase confidence in Leadville stocks or in some of Colorado's well-known businessmen; Chaffee and Moffat, for example, were both involved. Just before the outbreak of the strike, rumors circulated that the Chrysolite was going the same route. Although it did not collapse immediately, it teetered on the brink of disaster and finally fell in late September. Chrysolite shares, which had soared to more than $40, now plummeted to the $3 and $4 range. Leadvillites took some solace in blaming eastern management and overexpectations, but Easterners were disenchanted and leery about further investment.

With these events the initial mining phase of Leadville's history came to an end. An era that had been born of excitement and nurtured by overoptimism was now closed. After the shocks of 1880 came a reevaluation of methods and development and a more conservative mining approach. There was still plenty of ore to dig from the hills around Leadville, and prosperity continued in the 1880s. But never again would the district be considered ripe for easy wealth.

The Leadville crash resembled the one that hit Gilpin County gold mines in 1864. In both cases all mining stocks suffered, and absurd inflation in values never returned. Another parallel between the Gilpin County gold mines and the Leadville silver camp developed. As the first mining gulches had filled up, sending crowded, excited prospectors scurrying over the surrounding areas to find other Eldorados, so a revived interest in mining at Leadville scattered prospectors far and wide over the state, into regions that had earlier been looked at and rejected as possible mining districts. In the immediate vicinity of Leadville, silver camps like Robinson and Kokomo and the Ten Mile district were opened very rapidly. Near the head of the Roaring Fork of the Colorado River, rich silver carbonates were uncovered. In 1880, Aspen came into being, soon to be elevated as seat of the newly created Pitkin County.

South and west of Leadville, only a few miles east of the boundary of the Ute Indian reservation, new life was injected into the area around Gunnison. In 1874 Sylvester Richardson and others had organized a town company with sixty $100 shares of stock and had laid out Gunnison. But it was the carbonate ores unearthed there after the Leadville strike that made it more than a straggling frontier townsite. Now, in a wide swath around the town, satellites sprang up at St. Elmo and Tin Cup, Irwin, and Gothic. Smelting operations in Gunnison were under way by 1882. South and east of there, in the Wet Mountain Valley, discovery of silver ores not far from the Rosita gold mines created Silver Cliff, founded in 1878.

As a sort of exclamation point to end the silver saga, in 1890 the mines at Creede were opened. This "last of the silver towns" created its own romantic history and even entered the realm of poetry in Cy Warman's words:

It's day all day in the day-time,
And there is no night in Creede.

Even though the new discoveries caught the public's attention and investors and the eternally hopeful flocked to Creede, it was not like it had been back in 1859 or at Leadville. It was easy to get to Creede—one could almost ride the railroad to the site. The pioneering phase passed quickly and so did Creede's moment of fame. The price of silver had fallen steadily and before long came the crisis of 1893, with the repeal of the Sherman Silver Purchase Act. Creede's production would never equal that of Leadville, but it was here that the curtain rang down for the last time on two decades of silver rushes.

Almost as feverish as the prospectors' race to new mining camps was the railroads' rivalry to follow them in. The Gunnison region is a good example. The South Park road had extended its line from Nathrop over Alpine Pass; the Denver and Rio Grande pushed a branch from Salida over Marshall Pass. Starting about the same time, the Rio Grande won the race when its trains arrived in Gunnison in late summer 1881. It was this "branch" to Gunnison, soon extended to Grand Junction, that became the road's "mainline" for many years. North from Leadville, the Rio Grande built to Robinson and by March 1882 to Red Cliff. The Colorado Midland and the Rio Grande both struck out for the ores of Aspen and again the Rio Grande won the contest, reaching that silver camp in 1887. The Midland arrived in Aspen the next year.

A busy street scene in silver-booming Creede.

   The railroads followed the passes and gorges that nature had carved through the mountain ranges, leading often to long and roundabout routes. The airline distance from Denver to Leadville, for example, is 75 miles; the shortest railroad route covered 151 miles. Aspen and Leadville are 30 miles apart by air; at one time it took 131 miles of railroad track to connect them. Yet twisting and tortuous though the transportation network might appear on the maps, without it the extension of Colorado's mining frontier would have been greatly delayed. Together, miners and railroaders were rapidly invading some of the last unoccupied wilderness in the nation.

SIXTEEN

OPEN RANGE DAYS

While men scrambled over the mountain slopes of central Colorado, seeking another Leadville, radical changes were also taking place on the plains east of the Continental Divide. The removal of the Cheyenne and Arapahoe Indians to reservations outside Colorado had created a huge expanse of unoccupied, unclaimed grassland. Within a short time a different kind of economic enterprise developed there, as this "open range" became dotted with cow herds, eating free and growing fat on the public domain.

Ever since the Spanish had penetrated the eastern Colorado prairies, a few cattle had lived on the plains, but those semiwild beasts were too limited in number to be of great importance. It was not until the gold mines had been opened, and Anglo-Americans swarmed into the Colorado hills, that cattle raising on the region's open plains became a major enterprise. Then, for about three decades, it flourished, leaving when it died a legend unsurpassed—a major episode in the national folklore—and, its direct descendant, the modern ranch cattle industry of contemporary Colorado.

Tradition has long related that the origins of the range cattle industry are to be found in the tales of prospectors who brought oxen to the goldfields in 1859 and freighters who carried supplies westward from the Missouri River towns. The argonauts and wagoners, so the story goes, sometimes turned their beasts loose on the plains after their arrival in Colorado. Instead of meeting early deaths, the oxen flourished on the native grasses, even during winter weather, thus educating people in the values of the prairie as cattle country. Why those who had seen buffalo survive on those same grasses should have been surprised to discover that domesticated cattle could live on them is something of a mystery. At any rate, some freighters and some prospectors came to realize that cattle might offer greater economic returns than transportation or mining, and they inaugurated the cattle industry in the territory.

A situation that encouraged such decisions resulted partly from the effects of the Civil War. After the Union Army won control of the Mississippi River, most of the Confederate markets for cattle could not be reached by Texas ranchers. It was unpatriotic to sell anything to Northerners, and the number of cattle in Texas multiplied in rapid fashion. As the supply increased, cattle sold so cheaply that ranchers could not afford to brand their stock. At the same time, beef cattle were selling in the North at war-inflated prices.

As the Civil War drew to a close, an unusual opportunity appeared. If the Texas cattle could be herded or trailed northward to the railroads that were being constructed across the prairies, they could be shipped eastward by rail to profitable northern markets.

The great grasslands that stretched from the line of agricultural settlements in Kansas and Nebraska, on the east, to the foothills of the Rocky Mountains, on the west, thus became the scene of trail herds driven north to railroad terminals. At the railheads, the cattle were separated, with parts of the herds sent eastward to slaughter houses, and the remainder driven westward to ranges for fattening. In addition, other cattle were driven directly into Colorado from Texas. The territory's grasslands offered ideal conditions for fattening the beasts. Much of the natural prairie grass was either buffalo or grama grass—low-growing plants that could survive trampling, close grazing, and drought, and still prove nutritious fodder in cold weather.

Trailing cattle into Colorado began in 1859, when John C. Dawson brought the first reported herd from Texas to the Territory of Jefferson. But it was not until 1864-1865 that stock were driven north in large herds. Then within a short time, several trails were developed and the bonanza days of the open range were born. By 1870, when the first railroads reached Denver, trailing into Colorado and then fattening the cattle became even more profitable, since transportation directly from the territory to eastern markets was more easily arranged.

A good cow trail provided certain necessary elements and avoided most undesirable features. Water was essential, and rivers and ponds spaced not more than five or six miles apart made an otherwise satisfactory trail quite superior. At most, water holes and camp sites were needed at least fifteen miles from each other, for herds could not be moved much farther than that in one day. Yet rivers had to be crossed with the least amount of hazard to the herd, so good fords were necessary. Farmers and their fences were avoided; rough, broken country and heavy timber were shunned. The trails were constantly shifted to avoid Indian reservations, quarantine legislation, and homesteaders. Today it is difficult to trace the exact location of many of the once prominent cow roads. Some trails that originally were pushed through Kansas, by the middle of the 1880s led into eastern Colorado. The trails were known by name—Chisholm, Western, Lone Star. The two best known roads entering Colorado were the Dawson Trail, which came into the Arkansas Valley, and the Goodnight Trail, farther west.

It would be difficult to decide whether gold prospecting or cattle trailing involved more economic risk. Many variables were involved in the cattle enterprise, each contributing to the eventual success or failure of a drive: branding expenses, herd size, number and training of men and horses, trail conditions, water courses, storms encountered, health or disease of cattle, the attitude of Indians, the frequency of stampedes— these and many other elements determined profit or loss.

The cost of trailing from Texas to the high plains was estimated at about $1 a head. The wages of the cowboys and the maintenance of equipment could both be covered by that sum. The feed along the trail was free—a gigantic government subsidy. Since cattle were worth more in Colorado than in Texas (in 1880, an average value of $14.50 compared with $9.30 a head), there was a workable margin of potential profit, even after trail costs had been calculated and paid.

The cattlemen prepared their herds for the drive by marking a "road brand"—a single letter or simple mark—on each beast. After sale, the new owners would brand the cattle again with their own symbols. At first, branding was a hit-or-miss affair, but in 1867, after the Colorado Stockgrowers Association was created, that organization's secretary recorded members' brands. Five years later, in 1872, a more formal

system was effected when the territorial legislature enacted a brand law, assigning each county a letter to be placed by the side of the owners' personal brands. The county clerks were thereafter charged with the responsibility of eliminating duplicate brands within their counties. After 1885 an even more centralized system was used, as all brands were then registered with the secretary of state. Lists and books of brands were printed and proved useful in identifying cattle and apprehending rustlers.

The trail herds generally numbered between 2,000 and 3,000 head of cattle. A larger herd was more likely to stampede; overhead expenses ran too high for smaller units. Perhaps the count on the herds crossing the Arkansas River at Trail City in southeastern Colorado from June 9 to July 20, 1886, was typical. Fifty-seven herds made the crossing between those dates; the largest numbered 3,300 head; the smallest contained 70 head.

The ratio of men to cattle on the long drive differed from outfit to outfit. Sometimes two cowboys were hired for every three hundred head of cattle; others worked at a ratio of twelve or thirteen men to 3,000 beasts. Similarly there were differences in the number of horses provided for the drive. At least two per cowboy were needed, but the number ranged upward of six or seven per man. Most of the cattlemen started their herds north from Texas early in March. With good luck, this would bring the drive to an end in Colorado in late June or early July—time enough to allow the cattle to become acclimated to the region before winter.

During its early years the range cattle enterprise offered a relatively free and open economic opportunity to anyone. The cattle themselves were the only major investment. Everything else—water, feed, cowboys' wages—was either free or very inexpensive. Those men with ability, energy, and initiative who "got in on the ground floor" were able to build large herds and create from them magnificent fortunes. In a relatively short time, these "cattle kings" became a dominant aspect of the open range. Greatest of them in Colorado was John Wesley Iliff. He had come to the Pike's Peak gold camps in 1859; two years later he began to invest in cattle. When the Union Pacific railroad reached the high plains north of Colorado, Iliff wrangled the contract to supply beef to the construction crews. By 1878 he owned 15,000 acres of range, much of it fronting the water courses of the South Platte River, stretching from Greeley to Julesburg in the northeastern corner of the state.

There were others. John Wesley Prowers, a man who had worked for the Bents as a freighter on the Santa Fe Trail, in 1862 purchased cattle in Kansas to start his herd. He concentrated on short-horned Herefords rather than Texas cattle. By 1881 he owned forty miles of river frontage on the Arkansas, giving him control of 400,000 acres of range land, enough to graze herds of 10,000 cattle. James C. Jones was another Arkansas Valley "beef baron." Coming to Colorado in 1879, later than either Iliff or Prowers, Jones preempted range lands south of the Arkansas and gained control of enough land to graze 15,000 head of cattle, all branded with the JJ brand.

Between 1870 and 1880 the individual cattle kings flourished, but their power was never absolute. There always were some restrictive aspects to the enterprise. For example, the roundup developed into a systematized, collective activity. It became a necessary adjunct of range life because each cattleman's herds roamed freely with others. Twice a year the stockmen in a wide area herded the cattle to one location. In the spring new calves were branded with the owners' marks. The fall roundup was used to count the stock and separate the beasts destined for the slaughterhouses.

In 1871 the Colorado stockmen reorganized their earlier association into a more efficient lobbying group. Partly as a result of its requests, the territorial legislature enacted a roundup law the next year, formalizing the procedures of the roundup. The commissioners of each county in the territory were authorized to set a time for both fall and spring roundups and to appoint agents to take care of the mavericks—the motherless calves. (The mavericks were either distributed proportionately among the stockmen or sold.) The roundups were big affairs. In the spring of 1877, 500 men, with 3,500 horses and 50 chuckwagons, started west from Holly in the Arkansas Valley Roundup. In time the county units proved too small for effective roundups and in 1879 the legislature divided the state into larger units called roundup districts. For each of the sixteen districts created, the governor designated inspectors to oversee the roundup events.

By the time the roundup district law was enacted, the cattle business was rapidly changing character, for investors at home and abroad had begun to see in western cattle an attractive investment field. English and Scottish investors were particularly active in the creation of corporate ranching, forming investment companies and anticipating rapid, large returns on their capital. The most spectacular of these ventures, in many ways, was the Prairie Cattle Company, organized in 1881. It put together an expansive cattle empire, with a northern unit in Colorado, a central unit extending through New Mexico and Oklahoma, and a southern unit in Texas. In Colorado it purchased the JJ brand stock of James Jones, added other holdings to that, and soon gained control of a fifty-mile-wide strip from the Arkansas River to the southern boundary of the state. The earliest years were exceptionally prosperous for the company. At the first annual meeting of stockholders, it was announced that the returns equaled 26 percent of the paid-up capital.

Ironically, almost simultaneously with the inception of corporate ranching, the years of trouble began. Many elements contributed to the collapse of the open-range cattle empire. The "nesters" were a major cause of irritation and trouble to the stockmen. Under the agricultural homestead legislation of 1862, farmers were allowed to cut the public domain into small parcels and set up fences around their acres. Immediately the formula for countless Western stories and movies was born. Most fencing was delayed until the perfection of the barbed-wire machine (1874), which allowed barbed wire to be sold at low cost. But after the machine-produced wire was available, a farmer could fence a mile for about $100.

The cattlemen turned to fencing too, but with a difference. They had no particular claim to much of the public domain they used for grazing. At first they were not hindered in closing off the government acres, but

Branding cattle on a San Luis Valley ranch, 1894.

in 1885 Congress enacted legislation forbidding fences on the public lands.

What the stockmen had hoped for these years was help, not hindrance from the federal government. At an earlier time the cattlemen had talked about the desirability of the government's withdrawing major parts of the arid plains from homesteading, restricting its use to livestock only. In the year of Colorado's statehood, the Interior Department had considered a suggestion that from the one hundredth meridian to the Sierra Mountains, the homesteading laws be forgotten and the area reserved for ranchers. A response to the idea was included in President Rutherford Hayes's message to Congress the next year: "These lands are practically unsalable under existing laws and the suggestion is worthy of consideration that a system of leasehold tenure would make them a source of profit to the United States, while at the same time legalizing the business of cattle raising which at present is carried on upon them."

The Colorado Stockgrowers Association also favored the idea. In 1878 that group petitioned Congress to set aside the plains region, which, it said, because of its lack of rainfall was unsuited for anything but "pastoral purposes." The stockmen thought that 3,000-acre homesteads for ranching would be more practicable than 160-acre farms. But the changes that eventually were made in the federal land laws came long after the open range was gone.

Farming settlements continued to disrupt range activities, and in 1884, in St. Louis, cattlemen in convention proposed the establishment of a permanent cow trail from the Red River of the South to the Canadian border. This roadway would be set aside from public lands, with private entries bought out in the places where they interfered. The trail, from five to fifty miles wide, would be completely fenced, with streams bridged and junctions with branch trails and railroads provided. Although Congress never enacted the necessary legislation, the concept alone demonstrates the changes that had come to the cattle industry.

Cattlemen would continue to consider farmers as particularly responsible for their problems, but the homesteaders' fences were not the only element hastening the end of the open range. In the river valleys, where irrigation was beginning to flourish, water ditches created obstacles. And quarantine laws, which the states began to erect at their boundaries, also checked the movement of cattle across the range. Colorado enacted such a law in the mid-1880s, forbidding the driving of cattle across the state lines unless the herd had been held for ninety days or inspected and certified as disease-free by a veterinarian.

Overstocking of the range also played a role in the collapse of the cow bonanza. With the investment corporations competing for profits, it was natural for each to try to make returns rapidly. As a result, many more cattle than could possibly be supported on the range were brought in and the predictable consequences were reaped, especially in the years of poor weather, such as the winters of the great blizzards of the mid-1880s.

During the years of the open range's decline, the Colorado cattlemen, particularly through their stockgrowers association, looked to the state legislature for help. This aid might take the form of creating a favored position in law for the cattle interests or regulating some phase of the range operations. Legislation of the first sort, for example, fixed upon the railroads, rather than the cattlemen, the responsibility for animals killed by trains. In 1886 a total of 2,242 head of cattle were reported killed by railroads in Colorado and compensation was sought. No matter how scrawny and scrubby the critter, owners always seemed to have lost prime beef. The railroads came to understand that it was less expensive to fence their rights-of-way than to compensate cattlemen for dead beasts.

However, the cattlemen were also beginning to realize that their own greed had contributed to their difficulties. Overstocking of the range, particularly with inferior cattle, had not been in their best interests. So they also requested and received legislative aid in regulating the number and quality of bulls on the open range and in quarantining to halt diseases among their herds.

In fighting one enemy, the cattlemen did not wait for legislative aid; they usually managed to win with their own devices. That enemy was the sheepman. In length of time, the sheep industry of Colorado clearly held priority over the cattle industry. The early settlers on the Mexican land grants in the southern part of the state had grazed sheep on lands around their villages before the gold rush. These had been relatively poor-grade sheep, but after the coming of the argonauts, both mutton and wool were in great demand in the new Colorado communities, and the sheep industry spread through the San Luis and Arkansas Valleys. In 1868 the Pueblo *Colorado Chieftain* reported 195,000 sheep in Conejos and Costilla counties, "Las Animas County has about 87,500 and Huerfano and Pueblo Counties about 35,000, totalling 317,500 sheep for southern Colorado." Although these statistics were probably exaggerated, they indicate sheep herding was well established in southern Colorado in the first decade of territorial government.

It was not until 1869 that fine-wooled Merinos were introduced into Colorado, and the beginnings of improved breeding were made. This event marked the origins of the sheep industry in Weld County, soon followed by a lesser industry in South Park. By 1886 the number of sheep in the state was estimated at 2 million head. In those early years, in northern Colorado, the sheep were driven into grazing areas by methods not unlike those of the long drives of cattle from Texas.

The story of the conflicts between sheepmen and cattlemen forms one of the less pleasant phases of the history of the open range. The cattlemen often resorted to brutality to force the sheepmen from the range, for the cattlemen believed that the grasses were destroyed by sheep because they cropped the grass closely; in addition, there was an ancient belief among cattlemen that cows would not drink at water holes used by sheep and that cows would not graze where sheep had crossed because of offensive odors left by the oil glands in the hooves of the sheep. As the poet put it:

A sheep just oozes out a stink
That drives a cowman plumb to drink!
Its hoofs leave flavors on the grass
That even make the old cows pass . . .
Sheep ranges, cattle sure won't graze,
But—cowboys hate sheep anyways!

That "hate" that existed "anyways" sometimes rested on an emotional antagonism between sheepmen and cattlemen, resting at least in part on ethnic differences between the two groups. Sheepmen sometimes were Spanish-speaking people; cattlemen were usually Anglo. Some cattlemen looked on sheep tending as a degrading, unprogressive occupation.

The sheepmen, in law, might have had as much "right" to use the public domain for grazing as the cattlemen, but the test of control often was based on the ability to wrest or maintain possession of the range. An organization known as the Cattlegrowers Protective Association, with members in many Western Slope communities in Colorado, dedicated itself to keeping the cattle ranges free from sheep. The association's common name was the Night Riders, which indicates its strategy in the contests. Often the cattlemen drew a dividing line, beyond which they warned sheepmen not to move their flocks. In the late 1880s and 1890s, Western Slope Colorado, especially the present northern counties of Routt, Moffat, Rio Blanco, and Garfield, was a scene of almost continuous warfare over the rangelands as cattlemen and sheepmen struggled to maintain or improve their control.

And the fight did not end with the collapse of the open range. It continued into the era of cattle ranching—as opposed to cattle ranging—and on into the twentieth century with its leased government lands and reserved grazing areas.

SEVENTEEN

BEYOND THE CONTINENTAL DIVIDE

The Continental Divide—separating the waters falling eastward and southward into the Gulf of Mexico from the waters falling westward to the Pacific Ocean—also separates Colorado into two major geographic areas. That portion of the state west of the Divide, irregular in shape and strangely varied in topography, is called the Western Slope. Much of this part of Colorado was not opened for settlement until after 1880; not until after the mineral discoveries in the San Juan Mountains in the southwestern corner of the state were made, the Ute Indians removed from previously arranged reservations, and railroads built for transportation did settlers come in large numbers to reduce the last Colorado frontier.

The mineral discoveries and the Indian removals are so interwoven that they are like two chapters of a single story. In 1863, while Governor John Evans was experiencing little but frustration in his attempts to arrange peace with Eastern Slope tribes, he managed a major success with the Ute Indians. At Conejos, in the San Luis Valley, the Utes agreed to cede that valley to the whites, promising to move to a reserved area on the Western Slope.

Within five years, however, the white settlers were ready for more land. Agents then escorted a delegation of Ute leaders to Washington to see the president and to be duly impressed by the extent and wealth of the white man's country. During their visit, the Utes were encouraged to negotiate a new treaty. That document, signed in 1868, provided that the Ute Indians would move onto a newly designated reservation, west of the 107th meridian (a little west of the present site of Gunnison), a piece of land about one-third of the total area of Colorado. The federal authorities agreed to establish two agencies on this reservation. One post would be located at the White River for the use of the Northern Ute bands. The other, in the south, would serve the Southern and Uncompahgre Utes. In return for the cession of lands, the agencies would disburse to the Utes annual gifts of clothing, food, and supplies.

The new plans to establish reservations had hardly been completed when a mining rush forced alterations. The San Juans were (and still are) one of Colorado's rich and varied mineral areas, and it was only a matter of time before the prospector came to stay. Earlier, in 1860 and 1861, interest in the area had been aroused primarily because Charles Baker claimed to have found valuable gold placers. A small rush developed, but the golden rewards proved small and the isolation and dangers great. But interest did not die and in the early 1870s prospectors returned to find gold and silver mines. This time settlers came to stay.

As the whites moved in, treaties were violated, tension increased, and demands mounted to modify previous agreements. A classic example of white-Indian confrontation unfolded and within a decade the Utes would be gone, not only from the mountains but from much of the Western Slope. Although they were trespassing on Ute land, the miners would not be stopped and the government pressured the Indians into ceding a large quadrangular area, which included the entire mining region. Known as the Brunot Treaty, the 1873 agreement temporarily calmed matters but provided no permanent solution.

The number of whites in the San Juans increased slowly in the 1870s, and by the end of the decade, mining camps were spread throughout the mountains. Some, like Silverton, Ouray, and Lake City, were supply points for a district; others, like Mineral Point, Capitol City, and Sherman, served only the nearby mines. Unlike smaller mining areas, the San Juans gave birth to numerous rushes in such districts as Red Mountain, Rico, Telluride, and La Plata Canyon. Here in microcosm was the mining history of Colorado: Discoveries were made, people flocked in, and camps rushed through a period of prosperity and then declined. Until well past the turn of the century, mining flourished, gold

The Highland Mary Mine in the San Juans, photographed by William Henry Jackson.

coming to replace silver as the foremost metal, as the miners dug deep into the mineral treasure house of the San Juans.

Isolated as they were, the camps and districts offered a bountiful opportunity for anyone adventurous enough to tie them together with a road system. Del Norte and Saguache were early supply points, and out of the latter came Otto Mears, who met the challenge by building both toll roads and railroads and emerged as the "king" of southwestern Colorado road builders. One of the early Mears roads crossed Poncha Pass; another connected Saguache and Lake City; a third was built between Ouray and Silverton. These toll roads, traversing 300 miles total at their zenith, brought the first freighting by wagon into many of the new mining camps as well as considerable income to their builder. Later Mears would build short railroad lines out of Silverton to tap nearby mining

Rico about 1900.

areas and the longer Rio Grande Southern from Durango to Rico, Ophir, and Telluride, before tying into the Denver and Rio Grande system at Ridgway.

Besides opening this new world of mining to whites, the Brunot Treaty had also designated Ouray as spokesman for the entire Ute nation. Federal agents disliked the uncertainties inherent in a situation where no one chief represented the entire Ute tribe and by government fiat ended this confusion. Ouray, who was part Apache, became the most famous Indian in Colorado history and until his death worked hard to maintain peace between his people and the onrushing intruders. Recipient of an annual salary of $1,000 plus a house, Ouray, in the eyes of the government, spoke for his people. Unfortunately, no chief could do that for all tribes and, especially among the northern bands, other leaders were more persuasive than Ouray.

Trouble was sure to come as the whites crowded into the San Juans. It culminated in the Meeker Massacre. However, even before this event the *Ouray Times*, December 22, 1877, was asking why "non-producing, semi-barbarous" people occupied land which "intelligent and industrious

Opening mines in the rugged San Juans, 1875.

citizens" could use. Feelings such as these were echoed by many on the Western Slope and soon the "Utes Must Go" slogan threatened to force the issue.

The events leading to the Ute removal began not in the mining areas but to the north at the White River Agency, where Nathan Meeker, of Union Colony fame, had been appointed agent in 1878. A sincere, dedicated man, who was also naive and somewhat impractical, Meeker took zealously to his task of turning the wandering Utes to a settled life. With great energy, but little patience, Meeker moved to the task before him. Step by step his plans for civilizing the Utes brought him closer to ultimate and tragic defeat. To end the nomadic habits of the Utes, Meeker planned an agricultural society; to educate the young in white ways, the agency provided a school. All around them, the Utes began to see hated symbols of oppression: fences, classrooms, farm implements—including a "monster" threshing machine. The Indians protested; the agent planned new methods of "reform." Something of the proverbial "last straw" was provided when Meeker ordered the plows to work on the Indians' racetrack, the scene of wild pony contests, accompanied by even wilder betting.

During the summer months of 1879 many Northern Utes left the reservation despite Agent Meeker's express orders against such wandering. Some of these Utes committed minor depredations and, more seriously, burned houses and fired forests. Others, free from "Father Meeker's" control, spent their time more constructively. Captain Jack and others journeyed to Denver to complain to Governor Pitkin about the agent and his policies.

Then Johnson, one of the Ute leaders, physically attacked the agent. Fortunately, other employees protected Meeker, but by then a general breakdown in all of the fine, utopian planning was obvious. Meeker decided that army troops were necessary for the "civilizing" process, and in response to his requests for aid the army sent a contingent of cavalry from Fort Garland to round up wandering Utes and bring them back to the reservation. And on September 21, 1879, from Fort Steele in Wyoming, Major Thomas T. Thornburgh led another force of soldiers toward White River to protect the agency itself.

After five days of marching, when Thornburgh's unit had reached the Yampa River, a parley took place with Captain Jack and other tribal leaders. The Indians alternated their remarks between denunciations of Agent Meeker and questions about why the soldiers were coming to the agency.

Meanwhile, Meeker had kept Thornburgh informed about affairs at White River; through this correspondence it became quite clear that it would be folly to try to move the entire contingent of soldiers onto the reservation. The Indians were extremely alarmed and the situation was too volatile to risk a full-scale threat against them. So Thornburgh agreed to halt his force some distance from the agency and to proceed with an escort of only five men.

These plans, unfortunately, were never realized. When the soldiers reached Milk Creek, near the reservation boundary, they were ambushed by the Utes. Major Thornburgh and thirteen of his men were killed in the skirmish. The rest of the force was pinned down and could not move. Finally the guide of the expedition, Joe Rankin, slipped away to the north. From Rawlins, in Wyoming, he summoned the aid of Colonel Wesley Merritt. The army also ordered the Fort Garland cavalry, already on the Western Slope, to hurry to the siege. They arrived first but were too exhausted to accomplish much. Merritt and his men appeared three days later.

As soon as the white soldiers began the battle to rescue the troops, the Utes raised the surrender flag. Ouray had managed to accomplish the difficult task of convincing the Utes that further fighting was futile.

Colonel Merritt and his men moved on to the agency where they found Meeker and eleven other men dead, and some of their bodies stripped of clothing and mutilated. Meeker's wife, his daughter Josephine, Mrs. Shadrack Price, and her two children had been carried away by the Utes. Under the circumstances, no pursuit or revenge was possible until the captives had been located and retaken. The former Indian agent to the Uncompahgre Utes, General Charles Adams, working with Chief Ouray, finally secured the release of the hostages. The women at first stated that they had not been mistreated during their captivity; later they would tell of Ute outrages on them. If such stories were manufactured for propaganda purposes, they were not necessary. Colorado citizens were already shouting loudly for punitive expeditions and raising the cry, "Utes Must Go."

During the uprising, uneasy tension had descended over much of western Colorado. Rumors that the Southern Utes intended to join their northern brethren brought the state militia into the field; federal troops were sent from Texas to Fort Garland and from New Mexico to Fort Lewis. But the fighting ended before it spread. Carl Schurz, the secretary of the interior, now readied an official investigation of the affair. The commissioners he appointed for the task were hard put to gather testimony from witnesses. Only women had seen the massacre and were alive to tell about it, yet Ouray stood his ground in insisting that the Utes would not accept as valid the word of females testifying against males. No Utes would testify at all. Ouray also demanded that any trials take place in Washington, D.C., claiming that a fair and impartial determination of charges would be impossible to reach in Colorado. The leader known as Douglas was the only Ute ever brought to trial. He served a short sentence at Leavenworth.

For the Coloradans, the Utes had provided the necessary stimulus for a final settlement of the Western Slope. Some of the residents, Senator Henry Teller among them, demanded punishment of the offenders. But Colorado's other senator, Nathaniel Hill, thought this a "narrow and selfish view." Probably representing the majority opinion in the Centennial State, Hill believed that punishment was less important than removing the Utes so that their lands could be opened for settlement. Echoing the sentiment, the Denver *Times* put it bluntly: "Either they [the Utes] or we must go, and *we* are not going. Humanitarianism is an idea. Western Empire is an inexorable fact. He who gets in the way of it will be crushed."

One of the arguments frequently used by Coloradans in their campaign to hurry the Ute removal was the high cost of maintaining the Indians on their reservations, although they never explained how the cost would be reduced by removing them to Utah: "The government might, with almost, if not equal propriety, plant a colony of Communists upon the public domain, maintaining them in idleness at public expense, as to leave the Colorado Utes in possession of their present heritage and present privileges; . . . even now . . . the Utes could be boarded at the first-class hotel in Chicago or New York, cheaper than at the present cost of their subsistence."

Early in 1880, a delegation of Utes, headed by Chief Ouray, was escorted eastward to the national capital. There, in March, one final treaty was put together. The Southern Utes were now to be restricted to a reservation on the La Plata River bridging southern Colorado and northern New Mexico. The Uncompahgre Utes were to be given lands near the junction of the Gunnison and Colorado Rivers—or, if land was not available there, they would be sent to the Territory of Utah. The White River Utes, too, were to be moved across the state line to the Uintah Reservation. In return for these removals, $60,000 in back annuities would be paid, along with $50,000 in new annuities after the actual removals. Before the treaty became binding, three-fourths of the adult males of the tribe had to sign, or mark, the document. There was some difficulty in obtaining the necessary number of signatures, largely because the Uncompahgre Utes feared that they would be sent to Utah. But the rolls were finally completed, and the legal formalities concluded.

In Washington, critics argued that the Coloradans showed indecent haste in the proceedings. Representative Belford answered them by asserting that in traveling to the capital from Colorado he had "crossed five states made up wholly of lands stolen from the Indians. 'And now gentlemen stand here in the name of God and humanity,' and say, while our fathers robbed and plundered the Indians, we want you to belong to the goody-goody class of people in the West."

The good Chief Ouray died on August 20, 1880, before the tribes had been moved to their new homes. He was mourned by the whites, for he had earned their respect and admiration. Even Ouray, however, probably would not have been able to help the Uncompahgre Utes in their desperate struggle to retain lands within Colorado. The whites were determined to make the removal complete, and the Uncompahgres were destined to move to the Uintah reservation. General R. S. Mackenzie, with six companies of cavalry and nine companies of infantry from Fort Garland, moved onto the Western Slope, establishing later-named Fort Crawford in the valley of the Uncompahgre River. The troops were there to help the Indian agents, if necessary, complete the removal.

On September 7, 1881, the last of the Utes passed the junction of the Colorado and Gunnison Rivers. "If one had stood on Pinon Mesa, what a march of a retreating civilization he could have seen! Here was the last defeat of the red man. Here the frontiers of the white man met, crushing the Utes in its mighty embrace."

Congress declared the Ute lands public and open for filing in June 1882, but actually many settlers had moved in and had platted towns before the official entry day. One of the more obvious sites for planting a white settlement was the junction of the Gunnison and Colorado Rivers. The protected valley, with water for irrigation, constituted one of the most desirable locations on the entire Western Slope. The advantages of the place had been sized-up by a group of men from the town of Gunnison. Headed by George A. Crawford, they laid out a town (which they first named Ute) on the site. They changed the name to West Denver and, finally, when they incorporated their venture, to Grand Junction.

Like all such new towns, it wasn't much at the beginning: a store, a saloon, a ditch company. But in 1882 the Denver and Rio Grande narrow-gauge line, from Gunnison through Sapinero and Montrose, reached the town (the railroad had secured half of the shares of stock of the town company) and the following year Mesa County was carved out of Gunnison County, with Grand Junction as the seat of the new jurisdiction. The town, with its fertile valley lands for irrigation, soon attracted enterprises sufficient to ensure it the status of the urban center of the Western Slope. When the Denver and Rio Grande put the place on its standard-gauge line in 1887, the future was assured. Among other early features of the town was the Teller Institute and Indian School, built in 1886 with federal funds on lands donated by Grand Junction citizens. This institution conducted regular scholastic classes and instruction in practical trades to Ute and, later, other Indian children.

After building to Grand Junction, the Rio Grande Railroad extended its line west to the Utah border where, in 1883, it connected with the Rio Grande Western Railroad. This enterprise also had been constructed by the Rio Grande and was soon leased to its parent; it ran westward into Salt Lake City and there, by connection with the Western Pacific Railroad, the Rio Grande reached an outlet to California. Colorado had finally achieved a circuitous but operable railroad to the west coast.

George Crawford, the "father of Grand Junction," was also the guiding spirit in the organization of the Uncompahgre Town Company. Begun in September 1881, this company promoted the founding of a settlement that, after several name changes, became the place called Delta, the seat of the county of the same name. Montrose, on the Rio Grande narrow-gauge, was laid out in January 1882, and like Grand Junction and Delta it housed a courthouse—for Montrose County. All three of these settlements were established originally on the basis of irrigated fields in the river bottoms, with cattle herds grazing away from the streams. Soon fruit trees had been planted, and the protected valleys and irrigation waters demonstrated the excellence of the area for orchards.

In the valley of the Colorado River, eastward from Grand Junction, was the site called Defiance. Here, in August 1882, the later-named Glenwood Springs was located. The hot mineral waters gave the site a quality lacking in most of the other Western Slope town sites. In 1887 the Rio Grande narrow-gauge from Leadville, on its way to Aspen, reached the town. Four years later, the standard-gauge tracks, built by the Rio Grande and Colorado Midland, connected Glenwood Springs with Grand Junction, making obsolete the toll road that had operated in the river valley between the two towns. That same year an English syndicate built an open-air swimming pool, bath houses, and a large hotel at Glenwood, anticipating its growth as a scenic spa in the Rockies.

Above the Colorado River, the huge northwestern wilderness of the state remained largely untouched, except for ranchers with their sheep and cattle. Here and there in the valleys, towns with small populations had been platted for a variety of reasons. The region around Hahn's Peak had been prospected in 1862; again in the mid-1870s miners had engaged in extensive, but only partly rewarding, work on the placers. Hot Sulphur Springs, a pet project of *Rocky Mountain News* Editor William

Frontier law: Durango's first public hanging, June 23, 1882.

Byers, who had homesteaded claims there, was named the county seat of Grand County in 1874. Farther west, Steamboat Springs dated from 1875, when the James Crawford family settled. These and other northwestern centers like Craig and Yampa would await the coming of the Moffat railroad, after the turn of the century, for their real development.

In the far southwestern corner of the state, Durango came into existence in 1880, thanks to the Rio Grande Railroad, which was reaching out to tap the San Juan mines. Older Animas City, which had spurned the railroad's offer to build to it, found itself quickly surpassed. In 1882 the narrow-gauge tracks pushed up the Animas Canyon, reaching Silverton and its mines, while Durango became the area's leading supply and smelter city. Located near coal and agricultural lands, Durango quickly grew and even had its own small nearby mining rushes. A varied economy and facilities for a transportation center gave Durango a much brighter future than its mining neighbors. The Rio Grande Railroad, meanwhile, came to make the San Juan country its own and, as long as the mines held out, the venture proved to be a very profitable one.

EIGHTEEN

DITCHDIGGERS AND SODBUSTERS

In 1862, the year after Colorado Territory was created, Congress enacted the Homestead Act, culminating a struggle for ever more liberal land policies that had its origins as far in the past as the creation of the national domain itself. The new legislation provided that any U.S. citizen, or person with intention of becoming a citizen, who was the head of a family and over twenty-one years of age, could gain title to 160 acres of land after five years of continuous residence on this tract and the payment of a small ($26 to $34) registration fee. If the homesteader desired, the title could actually pass into his hands after six months' residence and the payment of the minimum price of $1.25 an acre.

The Homestead Act of 1862 assumed that the average family farm should be 160 acres. Such calculations were justified by the experience of Americans in the humid regions where earlier land policies had been developed. A farm of 160 acres was certainly of adequate size in the well-watered valleys of the midwestern rivers. But when the pioneers crossed the fatal demarcation line of the one hundredth meridian, farmers practicing traditional techniques of agriculture were doomed. Superficially the prairies might not appear different from the older regions; settlement spread over the edges of the old into the new without fanfare or publicity. But once the one hundredth meridian was crossed, rainfall became a major concern. The average ten to eighteen inches a year fell far short of the minimum requirements for traditional farming, and the "averages" did not reflect the seasonal variation or extremely dry years when the usual western "unusual" weather brought even less moisture. Year in and year out, agriculture such as the American farmers were accustomed to could not thrive on the high plains.

To meet the challenge of these radically different climatic conditions, the homesteaders, where possible, made radical adjustments. They could not control some circumstances—the grasshopper invasions of the 1860s, for example. But they did alter traditional farming techniques, including irrigation in the river valleys, adopting moisture-conserving techniques on the high plains, and, in both, experimenting with new crops. Where irrigation was possible, intensive agriculture became expedient and the standard 160 acres allowed by the federal land laws might prove to be too much land for an individual farmer, faced with the additional expenditures for irrigation equipment. Where irrigation was not possible, grazing or, later, dry farming became standard alternatives to traditional methods of agriculture. In such circumstances, the old unit was much too small.

Congress did attempt some adjustments in the land laws. The Timber Culture Act of 1873, repealed in 1891, justified an increase in the size of entries by requiring tree planting on the land. Any person who kept 40 acres of timber in good condition could acquire title to 160 additional acres. The Desert Land Act, four years later, allowed a homesteader a full section (640 acres) of land if he put the land under irrigation within three years. But neither of these statutes gave much real relief. Most homesteaders tried to work within the basic land law.

The first Colorado farmers (except the Pueblo Indians) never experienced the need to alter their techniques of cultivation. The earliest irrigators were the Spanish-Americans from New Mexico who, by moving northward into the San Luis Valley, merely exchanged farms in one arid location for farms in another equally arid place. Shortly after their arrival in the northern valley of the Rio Grande, they began to dig their ditches and to transplant the irrigation institutions they had known in New Mexico.

On April 10, 1852, the settlers on the Culebra River commenced the San Luis People's Ditch, now the oldest irrigation canal in Colorado in continuous use. Four ditches on the Conejos River date back to 1855; eleven had their beginning in 1856. In comparison with later developments in irrigation, these early systems were miniature in size. The ditches were

A San Luis Valley canal, from the 1884 Immigrant's Guide to the Great San Luis Park.

short and narrow, providing water for only small fields of crops. The system was democratically administered, with one user each year selected to supervise the distribution of water and the maintenance of the ditch.

If language differences and geographic separation had not barred the way, the Anglo-American who began the irrigation of lands in the South Platte Valley could have learned much from the San Luis Valley farmers. But contacts between the groups were limited, and the newcomers tended to work out their systems on their own. Many of the argonauts had left farms in the Midwest to come to the mountains. When their enthusiasm for mining paled, with a practiced eye these typical offspring of an expansive and highly mobile farming frontier surveyed the area for signs of possible agricultural pursuits. Some of them took the plunge. Within a few years they would be joined by admitted agriculturalists, like the colony farmers of Greeley and Longmont, who brought themselves and their families to Colorado specifically to engage in farming. All these people, and many who came after them, embarked on a unique experience. They had "so much to unlearn" from their earlier farming experienced in humid areas that, as one person put it, "it is better to abandon all notions and begin anew."

In the valleys of the South Platte and Arkansas Rivers, and their tributaries, these first farmers, in pragmatic fashion, educated themselves to the ways of irrigation. David K. Wall is credited with the first successes among the Fifty-niners. He had been in California and had learned about artificial rainfall there. In 1859 he diverted water from Clear Creek at Golden over two acres of gardenland and cleared a promising profit from his vegetables. Soon others had copied and expanded his pattern. Within a few years, the lands accessible to the South Platte and Arkansas Rivers were dotted with small farms.

A progression of sponsorship in ditch digging ensued. The first canals—small, short, and generally confined to the "bottom lands" along the streams—resulted from individual efforts. The Greeley residents, beginning in 1870, expanded these single-farmer attempts into community or cooperative ventures, resulting in longer, larger canals that brought water to the table, or "bench," land above the riverbeds. Similar cooperative efforts from Fountain Creek, Huerfano Creek, and the Arkansas River proper began to appear in that watershed.

By the end of the decade (1870–1880), a further expansion of sponsorship brought company or corporate activity. Coinciding with the increasing interest in Colorado mines and cattle herds on the part of Europeans, particularly English investors, the water systems appeared lucrative enterprises for investment. The Colorado Mortgage and Investment Company, locally known as the English Company, completed construction of the Larimer and Weld Canal, as well as other large irrigation systems. The Travelers Insurance Company aided the financing of the North Poudre Canal. With such financial help, large canals that otherwise would have been too costly for individual or cooperative efforts were built. This was especially true in the Arkansas Valley. Almost all the larger ditches there were corporation projects: the Bessemer, Fort Lyon, Bob Creek, and Otero.

As the size and number of canals increased, the demands on the rivers and streams for irrigation water multiplied. Soon the need to supplement natural flow in the waterways was apparent. The complexities of irrigation increased as subsurface wells were sunk to provide additional water. Even more significant in portent for the future were the first searches on the western side of the ranges for water that might be brought to the Eastern Slope farms through transmontane tunnels. And as farmers shifted crops and encountered the need for extended irrigating seasons, reservoir construction was initiated to hold the all-precious liquid for release into the canals at the time in the growing season when it was most valuable. Large reservoirs were constructed in the South Platte Valley in the decade from 1880 to 1890; the Arkansas and Rio Grande Valleys were developed in the same manner somewhat later.

All the techniques of farming under ditches needed to be learned by the new settlers; they also had to revise traditional Anglo-American concepts of water law to fit the new conditions. In the more humid parts of the United States, the English common law protected both public and private rights in the use of water. The common law doctrine—known as riparian rights—allowed only a limited use of river waters to the owners of the land bordering streams. Since navigation and power for mill wheels constituted the major water uses, this doctrine prohibited any use that would diminish or alter the flow of the stream and denied to the users any proprietary rights in the water.

This system worked satisfactorily in the humid East, but the arid West required new rules, for there all settlers came to understand that "every drop of water that runs into the sea without rendering a commercial return, is a public waste." Water for irrigation had to be diverted from the streams, and to provide security of private property—a basic doctrine of the nation's legal institutions—those who invested capital and labor to perform the diversion needed protection in law that would ensure them continued right to draw the water necessary to irrigate their fields. As Chief Justice Moses Hallett of the Colorado Supreme Court phrased it, in 1872, "In a dry and thirsty land it is necessary to divert the waters of the streams from the natural channels, in order to obtain the fruits of the soil, and this necessity is so universal and imperious that it claims recognition of the law."

From this necessity there arose the Doctrine of Prior Appropriation, permitting the diversion of water from rivers and streams without regard to prior ownership of the land along the stream banks. It endowed the first users with a permanent right to water so long as they needed it and continued to use it beneficially. Priority of diversion established priority of usage rights, regardless of the geographical location on the stream where the diversion was made. Used sparingly in California earlier, the doctrine was taken up immediately by the Colorado irrigators and made official law. Congress endorsed the concept in 1866; the Colorado constitution-makers of 1876 wrote it into the basic charter of the state. Both federal and state courts have upheld it ever since in most of the arid states, for the "Colorado system" was soon adopted in Utah, Wyoming, Montana, Idaho, Nevada, Arizona, and New Mexico.

The adjudication of priorities and enforcement of the rights determined by the courts became a mammoth undertaking. It would keep lawyers and judges occupied as long as the system was continued. Priorities were determined by litigation in the regular judicial establishments, with determination of suits becoming matters of record for the future. But, in time, state officials were added to the system to oversee the general operation of the water code. Colorado was the first state in the Union to provide such official supervision of water distribution. In 1879 and 1881 the legislature divided the state into three water divisions and ten water districts, both of which would be increased in number later. The divisions followed the natural drainage basins of the major rivers. After 1887 a division superintendent was appointed for each. The water districts were entrusted to commissioners who were charged with the responsibility of insuring that the water was divided according to appropriation.

As demonstrated by their acceptance of the Colorado water institutions, western states and territories became aware of their unique problems regarding water. They began to encourage interstate sharing of knowledge and ideas. In October 1873, a convention of delegates from Nebraska, New Mexico, Wyoming, Utah, Kansas, and Colorado met at the invitation of Governor Elbert in Denver to consider the possibilities of a joint appeal for federal aid in reclaiming western lands. The delegates dispatched a memorial to Congress, requesting that one-half of the nonmineral public lands of the western states and territories be given to those local governments that, in turn, would use the money from their sale to reclaim arid lands for cultivation by building canals and reservoirs. Although no favorable response was given, this request marked the beginnings of interstate cooperation in western water affairs.

Even earlier, Coloradans had looked to Congress for help. Representative Belford had introduced a bill seeking $50,000 for aid in reclaiming lands in the Arkansas, Platte, and Cache la Poudre Valleys. The attitude of easterners had been apparent from the beginning. Belford was accused of urging Congress to "built a great series of expensive artificial lakes and ponds, and that at the next session he would go still further and demand the construction of a navy to float upon these still waters." Thus began the long and still-continuing dichotomy between East and West over the proper role of government in the reclamation of western lands.

Irrigation also brought the need for experimentation with new crops. Potatoes, in particular, received attention, beginning near Greeley in the mid-1880s. The crop demanded extensive storage facilities as well as reservoirs for irrigation during the later part of the growing season. A Potato Exchange was organized, which helped both in advertising the product and in initiating a marketing program. By 1890 more than 2,000 carloads of potatoes were shipped each year. Alfalfa, first grown in the territory in 1863 from seeds brought from Mexico, was studied intently at the Colorado Experiment Station and was soon planted in many irrigated areas. One flooding before each cutting sometimes produced three full cuttings of alfalfa a year.

Irrigation in the river valleys had become a well-proved technique before the agricultural settlers turned to consider the high plains that stretched between the rivers. Over the acres where the long-drive cattle had grazed and where the beginnings of the modern ranch cattle industry then were taking place, farmers now searched for a sign that would indicate possible success in plowing up the prairies.

In time the signs seemed to emerge. For one thing, the windmill had made its appearance, and perhaps enough subsurface water could be pumped by putting the prairie breezes to work to squeak through the driest months. It was largely a vain hope but considered by many. For fencing, the barbed-wire factories of the Midwest were now turning out a successful product at a cost low enough to afford protection for crops against the cattlemen's herds. James Oliver, by 1868, had perfected his chilled-iron plow, and from his factory at South Bend, Indiana, and others, instruments to turn the short grass sod were now available. And there were additional signs. From the Crimea, Mennonite farmers had brought hard red winter wheat. Although difficult to mill at first, after 1881 and the introduction of chilled-iron rollers, the wheat became accepted on the grain markets.

Finally, to provide the actual catalyst in the reaction, the "rainbelt" seemed to be moving westward during the decade of the 1880s. A cycle of years of above-average rainfall led land speculators and railroad agents to claim that the "rainbelt" had marched right up to the foothills of the Rockies. "So much rain now falls in the eastern portion of the arid lands of Colorado that it is no longer fit for a winter range for cattle," pronounced the Burlington Railroad, which had completed its Chicago to Denver tracks in 1882 and was energetically planting towns along its right-of-way. "What has brought about this great change[?] . . . In our opinion, the change is due to the extensive irrigation of land lying along the eastern base of the Rocky Mountains. Great rivers, which head in perpetual snow banks, have been turned into irrigation ditches; and the water which formerly

Everyone, including the horse, posed in front of this family's substantial sod house.

ran wastefully into the Gulf of Mexico has been turned on to the arid plains. There it soaks into the soil. The wind sweeping over the land sucks up a large portion of it. There is then moisture in the air and it is precipitated on the high lands of Eastern Colorado."

With such assurances, the sodbusters came in, spilling over at first from western Nebraska and Kansas. Lured on by railroad agents who had towns to build or grants to dispose of, they settled along the Burlington Road in proximity to such towns as Akron and Yuma and Wray, all three dating from 1886. Or they followed the right-of-way of the Missouri Pacific to Eads or Arlington or the Rock Island tracks to Burlington or Flagler, both dating from 1887. Eckley, Chivington, Springfield, Haxtun, Holyoke, Logan, and Otis—all date from the period of the late 1880s.

There were centers that had their origins earlier and now were infused with new energy, like Kit Carson, which the Kansas Pacific had moved from Sheridan in western Kansas after building across the eastern Colorado border. And there were new creations, like the Santa Fe railroad's town of Lamar. Although blessed with some irrigable lands in the Arkansas Valley, Lamar would share some of the dry land experiences. In May 1886, it was described: "Only five short weeks ago there was not a sign of human habitation in sight save a single log building down by the cottonwood belt that fringes the stream. From the river southward a desert-looking plain, partly covered by the short buffalo grass, extended up a gentle incline two or three miles. . . . Today there are five and twenty buildings completed or nearly so; many others are begun and active preparations are making to erect a large number more."

Around these towns the sodbusters settled on their lands, using the federal laws to advantage by preempting one quarter-section of 160 acres, taking another as a "tree claim" under the terms of the Timber Culture Act, and homesteading on a third quarter-section. On the prairies they found no wood, so they set up bricks of sod to build their houses and sheds. They planted their crops and watched with a wary eye the clouds on the horizon. For a few years they anticipated success. A "boom" in land values reflected their optimism. Unimproved land soon was selling for $3 to $10 an acre, while slightly cultivated lands were bringing between $8 and $20.

And then the years of trouble began. Dry years returned to the area in 1889 and 1890. The "rainbelt" hadn't moved at all; the rainmakers' promises never came true; "the only crop was bankrupts." A general crop failure engulfed the land and the easily discouraged started to move away. The state legislature appropriated $21,250 to provide seed grain to start anew, and relief in other forms was sent eastward from Denver to help those who decided to remain. Rainfall in 1891 and 1892 was more promising—in fact, 1892 was a good year for the dryland farmers.

But then the discouraging years came again, 1894 bringing the worst drought the region would know until the 1930s. The exodus from the plains turned into full-scale flight. Although relief again was sent to those who stayed—foodstuffs and clothing and coal collected by agencies like the *Denver Republican*—the enchantment had vanished. Those who clung to their homesteads began to turn to grazing, not daring to plant more failures on their plowed fields. Most of the settlers hurried to other regions. The first assault on the high plains had failed to sustain itself. After the turn of the century, others with new concepts of the way to wage war on the "desert" would write another chapter in the state's agricultural history.

NINETEEN

NEW FRONTIERS

The year 1890 marks a convenient dividing point in Colorado's history. With the exiling of the Utes and the opening of the Western Slope to white settlement, the days of the traditional frontier had come to an end. A frontier often is defined as an area of land with less than two residents per square mile. In 1880 the federal census had listed 1.8 people per square mile in the Centennial State, few enough to qualify as a frontier. But by 1890 the population average had increased to 3.9 people per square mile. The demographer's magic line had been crossed. And if other indications were needed to demonstrate the fading of the old frontier and the emergence of new challenges, they were not difficult to discover. In the nonmining regions, nomadic, grazing, pastoral pursuits gave way to settled farms and intensive agriculture, and in the growing cities the beginnings of industry were apparent by 1890.

The decade from 1880 to 1890 had been a time of growth and urbanization. Census statistics of every kind proved the assertion: the assessed property value of the state trebled; the number of farms quadrupled; railroad mileage almost trebled; the amount of capital invested in manufacturing increased sixfold. Denver grew from a town of 35,000 to a city of 106,000 people; Pueblo, becoming the state's "second city," increased from 3,000 to 24,000 people. In manufacturing, the number of establishments increased from 599 to 762; the number of employees from 5,000 to 9,000; the value of products from $14 million to $29 million.

Industrial growth depends on a few basic ingredients: a supply of fuel, a supply of labor, and markets in which to sell the manufactured products. Colorado could provide two of these three essentials without difficulty. Fuel was present and plentiful; the laboring force was, or would be, ready to move to the state when opportunities for employment existed. The only real problem for Colorado's industrial advance was then, as it is now, a lack of markets. The state is a great distance from the population centers of the nation; transportation was still a problem, for the mountain barrier had never been pierced satisfactorily.

Denver, the state's major population center, was at a great disadvantage in the freight-rate structure that then existed. The Union Pacific Railroad, with heavy investments in Cheyenne, Wyoming, preferred to feed goods through that town to Georgetown and Gilpin County, because Denver was a "pool point" and Cheyenne was not. The "pooling" arrangement meant a sharing of freight profits with other railroads. Wyoming, Utah, and New Mexico cities all enjoyed more advantageous railroad rates than Denver.

Nonetheless, Colorado still boasted potentials for manufacturing greater than many other western commonwealths. Adequate iron ore and coal deposits in Colorado could support a nascent steel industry. The coal mines of the state were centered in three general areas. There was a northern field in Jefferson, Boulder, and Weld Counties, the coal from which supplied Denver and other towns with fuel. A middle field in Fremont, Park, and El Paso Counties had been opened. And in the southern regions, coal deposits in Las Animas, Huerfano, La Plata, and Dolores Counties had demonstrated their superiority over the other regions. Almost all this coal was bituminous or subbituminous. The decade from 1880 to 1890 had witnessed a phenomenal increase in production from these fields: from 437,000 to more than 3 million short tons.

Coal from the Colorado mines was valuable for a variety of purposes: domestic heating, smelting ores, railroading, and fueling the emerging industrial factories. Most of the largest mines had been opened and were operated by railroad companies or their subsidiaries, like the Union Pacific's Union Coal Company with mines in the northern field and the Santa Fe's Canon City and Trinidad Coal and Coking Company with southern field properties.

One of the biggest coal operators was the Denver and Rio Grande ally, the Colorado Coal and Iron Company, with headquarters in South Pueblo. General William Palmer, visualizing this as one of the several "supplementary" enterprises for his railroad, formed the Colorado Coal and Iron Company in 1880 by merging three smaller companies and capitalizing the new organization at $10 million. The intent of the organizers was to convert Pueblo into the Pittsburgh of the West. Blast furnaces were going by 1881 and a Bessemer converter turned out its first steel (the first west of the Missouri River), and the first rails were rolled in 1882. This was the corporation that became, in 1892, following another merger, the Colorado Fuel and Iron Company.

Another Colorado industry attractive to investors was smelting. Leadville, in its boom days, was the great smelting center of the state, but Denver and Pueblo also attracted large ore reduction plants. Several large works existed in Pueblo even before 1888 when Meyer Guggenheim built his Philadelphia Smelter there at a cost of $1,250,000. The Philadelphia operated at a loss for some time, and it was only after August Raht introduced new metallurgical processes that Guggenheim's large investment began to earn handsome profits.

Smelters and iron works were soon joined by a third "native" industry—the manufacturing of mining machinery. This industry was a natural outgrowth of the simple blacksmith forges and small foundries that had fabricated machines for miners since the original gold rush. Denver, in particular, emerged as a center for mining machines. Factories like those of the Mine and Smelter Supply Company and the Hendrie and Bolthoff Company turned out ball and stamp mills, flotation and cyanidation systems, concentrating and "bumping" tables, "roughing jigs," and a host of other highly specialized machines to treat the ores of Colorado and much of the rest of the world.

The railroads of the decade helped to bring the material to the smelters and factories and to distribute their products. In 1870 only 157 miles of railroad operated in Colorado; in 1890 there were 4,176 miles. In 1880 only two eastern trunk lines had been built into the state—the Kansas Pacific and the Santa Fe. By 1890 these had been joined by four additional roads—the Union Pacific had constructed its lines from Julesburg to La Salle; the Burlington had built through Fort Morgan to Denver; the Rock Island had entered Colorado Springs; the Missouri Pacific now reached to Pueblo. Towns and cities along the Eastern Slope were in a much more competitive situation for their freight and patronage

Rounding a curve on the Colorado Midland's 1,084-foot-long timber trestle east of Hagerman Pass.

than ever before. Three lines now connected Pueblo and Denver, for the Santa Fe had constructed its road between the two cities.

The Denver, Texas, and Gulf Railroad had acquired the trackage of the Denver and New Orleans between Pueblo and Denver. Using the facilities of the Denver and Rio Grande from Pueblo to Trinidad, by 1888 it met the Denver, Texas, and Fort Worth there, and Colorado had a rail connection running south to the Texas gulf.

Railroaders were still extending their lines on Colorado's Western Slope too. Much of this construction continued to be narrow-gauge trackage, which reached its maximum mileage in 1890. However, the disadvantages of interchanging cars between standard and narrow-gauge had already become obvious enough to lead some lines to use a third rail so that cars of both sizes could be accommodated.

One of the most exciting features of mountain construction these years was the Colorado Midland Railroad, a standard-gauge road that had built from Colorado Springs via Manitou, Ute Pass, South Park, Buena Vista, and the valley of the upper Arkansas River to Leadville. Begun in 1885, it tunneled a 2,064-foot passage under Hagerman Pass, at an elevation of 11,528 feet, to accommodate the traffic across the Sawatch Range to the headwaters of the Frying Pan. At the junction of that stream and the Roaring Fork of the Colorado, the road branched in two directions. One line led up the Roaring Fork to the silver mines of Aspen. The other traveled downstream to Glenwood Springs and along the Colorado River to Newcastle, which it reached in 1889. From there the Midland's trains ran west to Grand Junction over a line operated jointly with the Denver and Rio Grande.

The critical point in the system was the crossing of the Continental Divide at Hagerman Pass. The Midland built the 9,394-foot Busk-Ivanhoe Tunnel, eliminating only seven miles in total distance, but lowering the elevation of the crossing 530 feet. By the time it was finished, in 1893, the Midland had been sold to the Santa Fe road.

Although Coloradans now boasted more miles of operating trackage than ever before, the state's railroad network also had come to be dominated more completely by one man than was healthful. Jay Gould controlled the Missouri Pacific, the Denver and Rio Grande, and the Union Pacific. This was a sizeable part of the Colorado rail system by itself, but delineated further, it meant that by controlling the Union Pacific, Gould also counted as personal property the Union Pacific's old subsidiaries— the Denver South Park, the Colorado Central, and the Denver Pacific. Traffic agreements with the Santa Fe, the Rock Island, and the Denver, Texas, and Gulf spread Gould's influence even further. Only the Burlington seems to have remained a free agent.

The capital city of Denver was the center of Colorado's rail network in 1890, as it had been in 1870. Despite Denver's increase in railroad facilities and the beginnings of an industrial complex, critics continued to complain that the city had no reason for existing. It was true that services, and its role as a distribution center, rather than industry, accounted for most of Denver's growth. But the place made short work of its critics as it had always done, refusing to believe that its destiny was not as magnificent as the mountain ranges that formed the backdrop of its location.

The Queen City now prided itself on such refinements as electric lights, electric street cars, and telephones. Denverites pointed with pleasure at the new buildings fronting the streets. British capital, organized

Horace Tabor's opera house was a Denver landmark until it was razed in 1964 to make way for the Denver branch of the Federal Reserve Bank.

by James Duff into the Colorado Mortgage and Investment Company, had constructed the far-famed Windsor Hotel. A second fabulous hostelry, the Brown Palace, opened in September 1892. Horace Tabor, with his Leadville profits, put up a handsome opera house, which had opened in regal style on September 5, 1881, with Emma Abbott and the Grand English Opera Company in *Maritana*. And in 1894, after fire destroyed an earlier structure, Denver's new Union Station was opened.

As befitted a commonwealth beginning a major chapter in its historical development, Colorado provided funds to build a new statehouse. On fifteen acres of land donated by Henry C. Brown, the cornerstone of the new capitol building was laid in July 1890. E. E. Myers of Detroit, who had planned statehouses for Michigan and Texas, was commissioned to design the $2,800,000 edifice. Architects styled his building, completed in 1894, a "free adaptation" of the national Capitol. It is unique only in the $4,000 worth of gold leaf placed on the exterior of the dome. The rest of the building, with granite exterior and dome features, is the usual statehouse of the period.

Many newcomers—both immigrants and tourists—by-passed Denver, traveling directly to General Palmer's town of Colorado Springs. Particularly as a tourist center, the Springs rivaled the state capital. In 1890 the Manitou and Pike's Peak Railroad opened for service. The peak that Pike had been unable to climb could now be scaled in the comfort of a railroad coach. Nine miles long, with grades as high as 25 percent (necessitating a rack system), the railroad proved a long-lasting magnet for the tourist industry of Colorado Springs.

But something much more exciting than cog railroads soon engulfed the Colorado Springs region. The decade of the 1890s had hardly begun when, not far from Palmer's town, the mines of a place called Cripple Creek were opened, bringing to Colorado its last big gold camp.

Gold seekers traveling the Arkansas River route in 1858–1859 had used the landmark of Pike's Peak to guide them to the mountains. The Peak had given its name to the gold rush and to the mining area before more official designations were made. It was natural, therefore, that the region around Pike's Peak was well prospected for placers and lodes in the early days. But from the time of the Lawrence Party in 1858 onward, many anxious argonauts had experienced the disappointment that awaited all who followed the natural instinct to search for Pike's Peak gold near Pike's Peak. Rather than the famous mountain, it was Cherry Creek, Clear Creek, and a host of other place names that came to identify the paying gold camps.

Not until 1874, sixteen years after the first gold seekers had guided themselves to the mountains, did the region around the Peak begin to demonstrate any mineral wealth. Even then, the first "boom" was short-lived. A few lodes were discovered, and a mining district named Mount Pisgah was formed about thirty-five miles from Pike's Peak. It ended almost as soon as it began, for the quantity of ore uncovered was very meager. Then a decade elapsed before, in 1884, another rush to the region occurred. This episode was even more ill-fated, for to the chagrin of the miners who hurried down from Leadville and other camps to cash in on the new field, it was soon discovered that Mount Pisgah had been liberally and unscrupulously "salted"—the claims were worthless. After this unfortunate incident, it seemed that the region had surely exhausted all possibility as a mining district. All that remained were herds of cattle grazing on the slopes and an evil reputation that lingered from the fraud.

Some of the grazing land in time came into the possession of two Denver real estate merchants, Horace Bennett and Julius Myers. Included in their holdings was the former ranch of Robert Womack. Womack himself remained in the area. For some years he divided his working hours between herding cattle for the ranch owners and digging in the hillsides, particularly at the site he called Poverty Gulch. Womack had gained some experience as a miner in Gilpin County but not enough to label himself as an expert. His persistence in searching for ore thus attracted little attention, although from time to time other prospectors would appear in the vicinity to try their luck.

Most experienced miners, however, were not interested. Everything about the region looked wrong. There were no outcroppings of ore to indicate lodes underneath. The slopes of the mountains were free of the deep ravines that usually indicated likely sites. In the volcanic rock structure of the region, the usual quartz indicators were missing. Add all this to the already bad reputation of the place, and it is easy to explain why Womack and others who kept digging holes there were considered "dreamers."

Yet it is Womack who is remembered as the discoverer of the riches of Cripple Creek. Late in the year 1890 he took ore samples from his Poverty Gulch hole into Colorado Springs for assaying. Although many still doubted, those assays indicated genuine gold. Other fortune hunters joined the prospecting cowboy until by May 1891, considerable activity was under way. Of necessity, chance would play a large role in the ensuing drama. Lacking the usual signs for locating lodes, the first-comers to Cripple Creek were forced into imaginative guess work.

Winfield S. Stratton's experience was not unusual, except that he was luckier than many others. Stratton was a carpenter who worked in Colorado Springs, but he had spent his vacations and free time prospecting over much of the Colorado landscape. The growing gossip about the Womack discovery soon captivated his attention. He tried several locations without any great success. Then he constructed a theory that the granite outcroppings on the slopes of Battle Mountain might mark the end-of-the-rainbow lode of his dreams. On the Fourth of July 1891, he pegged two claims there, naming them appropriately the Independence and the Washington. History not only records that they made carpenter Stratton a millionaire but also impressively relates that eight years later he sold the Independence to the Venture Corporation of London for $10 million, believed to have been the largest mining transaction to that time.

Stratton quietly built his properties into valuable mines; Robert Womack disposed of his findings for a few hundred dollars. Both patterns would be repeated many times during the first months of the new excitement. The Cripple Creek goldfields were concentrated in an area of about ten square miles. Into this relatively tiny region poured the usual population of a mining rush—seasoned, experienced prospectors from other camps, tenderfoot amateurs up from the valley towns to try their luck, fortune hunters from far-off cities and states who began long journeys toward the 11,000-foot elevations of the new camp. With their arrival began the usual process of claims, consolidations, suits, and countersuits as everyone scrambled in pursuit of luck and the valuable patches of gold-bearing ground.

Some startling differences distinguished this last major Colorado goldfield from its predecessors. Where the Fifty-niners had searched for free gold in gulch placers and mountain lodes, the Cripple Creek prospectors required re-education, for the gold of the district was largely found in combination with tellurium, in the compound tellurides called sylvanite, calaverite, and petzite. Washing, crushing, and amalgamation with mercury had separated the earlier free gold, but Cripple Creek ores required smelting, or even more complex chemical operations such as cyanidation or chlorination.

Yet much was also the same. The feverish haste to record locations still characterized the early days of the camp. The sudden influx of miners created the same necessities of goods and services and the same opportunities to supply them that the early camps had created. The same transportation difficulties of freighting over rugged mountain terrain would exist until railroads were constructed into the camp. And the same rivalries occurred between settlements aspiring for preeminence in the region.

Horace Bennett and Julius Myers, the Denver real estate men, surely had never planned a subdivision in their cow pasture; yet they were not slow to realize the opportunities presented, and they moved quickly to capitalize on their good fortune. Where their cattle had peacefully grazed along Cripple Creek, they soon boasted the town of Fremont, complete with hotel and bank. Residents of an earlier successful episode in town-promotion called Colorado Springs soon joined in an act of their own, laying out a rival settlement named Hayden Placer. The contest between Fremont and Hayden Placer settled into a fierce battle for the location of the U.S. post office. When Fremont emerged victorious,

Celebrating the Fourth of July, 1893, along Bennett Avenue in Cripple Creek.

a not unusual merger took place, with the new name—Cripple Creek—
adopted for the town. Incorporated in 1892, its population in the next
census was 10,147. In time the mining district would include many
other towns, most of them near mines and mills—Victor, Altman, Independence, Elkton, Anaconda, Arequar, Lawrence, Goldfield, Gillett. But
the city with the name of the district retained its lead.

Statistics of gold production tend to be impressive; the Cripple
Creek record still staggers the imagination. In 1892, when the district
opened, more than $500,000 worth of gold was dug. The following year
the total soared to $2 million and kept going up. Then came the really
astronomical figures: 1896, $7.4 million; 1899, $16 million in gold;
1900, a peak of $18 million; and, as late as 1917, over $10 million. Nothing in Colorado had ever generated such profits. It was a bonanza district indeed.

The pattern of organization for both mining properties and the society of the camp developed rather quickly. Individuals had discovered the
first mines; they tended to join together to gain the capital necessary to
work their holdings. As outsiders, with money to invest, became interested in the mines, the opportunity for exchanging shares in the organized

companies increased. One guide to the region, published in 1900, lists 496 separate mining companies with actual claims. Shares of stock in these companies were bought and sold, largely on the Colorado Springs Mining Exchange. In the last year of the century, that institution recorded 236 million shares of stock exchanged, with a total value of $34 million.

This type of mine ownership and operation led to a distinction within the district's population similar to that Leadville had earlier introduced into the state's mining history. The mineral properties were owned by shareholders in the companies; the actual development of the properties was entrusted to managers and superintendents hired by the companies. The owners, managers, and perhaps most of the professionals in the settlements tended to form one stratum of Cripple Creek society. The other stratum was composed of miners—the laborers who offered their services in exchange for daily wages. Both groups depended for their well-being on continued successful working of the mining properties, and both were eagerly interested in the specific welfare of their own group.

This division in the Cripple Creek society was of more than casual significance. The camp had been opened only a short time when conditions outside the region conspired to make Cripple Creek a focal point of collision between the two groups. In 1893 the United States suffered a devastating financial panic that ushered in a four-year depression. The silver mines of Colorado were particularly hard-hit by the economic crisis. Laborers from closed silver mines, joined by thousands of unemployed men from over the nation, converged on the still brightly active Cripple Creek field. This influx of surplus labor plus the uneasy apprehension of investors at the time combined to make Cripple Creek a theatre of war between capital and labor. Thus, the last of the major goldfields became one of the significant elements of a turbulent decade. To understand its role, however, it is necessary to examine the political and economic conditions in the rest of Colorado.

TWENTY

POLITICS AND POPULISTS

The Republican Party dominated the political scene in Colorado in the years following statehood. That party was formed of various, often competing interests and factions: Denver and Leadville carried the greatest political weight and aroused envy of their position; the mountain and plains counties were jealous of each other's influence; the Western Slope felt itself too often shunted aside; and the southern part of the state demanded some rewards, even if it did not carry much power. The tightly knit Republican leadership acted as political "broker," compromising the various demands by parceling out the "loaves and fishes." Denver usually received the largest share, followed by the mining regions. The first two U.S. senators, for example, were Jerome Chaffee from Denver and Henry Teller from Central City.

Into this situation, starting at Leadville, came the sudden influx of mining millionaires with money and political aspirations. Around them swirled intrigue and quite often success. The most sought-after prizes were the U.S. Senate seats, not the governorship. In the years 1877 to 1893, six men served as governor of Colorado: John Routt, Frederick Pitkin, James B. Grant, Alva Adams, Benjamin Eaton, and Job Cooper. Several of these men were closely connected with mining. The only two Democrats (Grant and Adams) both won primarily because the Republicans fell to fighting among themselves and were unable to heal their wounds in time to garner election victories.

The real power in the party and in the state resided in the senators, those whose names for the most part loom large, even today, in the annals of Colorado: Henry Teller, Jerome Chaffee, Nathaniel Hill, George Chilcott, Horace Tabor, Thomas Bowen, and Edward Wolcott. All were Republicans and all either powerful political figures or people of prominence and wealth. Bowen's, Tabor's, and Hill's fortunes were based on mining; Chaffee and Teller were closely allied with mining interests. These men had money to lavish on the Republican Party and they merited political consideration when they demanded it.

Although the governorship might be allowed to go to a lesser individual and be used as a pawn to gain a greater end, the party leadership played the Senate contests with deadly seriousness. Frank Hall, who observed the situation firsthand and from the inside, commented: "The bane of our political system is the eternal and almost frantic craze that possesses nearly every politician who assumes to be a leader, and which has governed the majority of our governors, to fill a seat in the Senate." The contests were fought in the state legislature, since U.S. senators then were not directly elected. This procedure permitted individual bargaining and made the money flowing from the coffers of a Tabor or Bowen that much more powerful. During a closely contested race, Denver became a hotbed of rumor and dealings.

The Republicans controlled every legislature during these years, making the Democrats, until the 1890s, a permanent minority party in Colorado. Even when the Republicans lost the governorship, as they did in 1882 and 1886, they retained legislative control. Not only did the party dominate the election of senators and governors, but after the initial single term of Democrat Thomas Patterson, it held the one congressional seat throughout the period.

Actually, the parties seldom seriously differed in outlook, and no permanent issues sharply divided them. Both Republicans and Democrats tended toward conservatism; both seemed more interested in offices and the resulting spoils than in any major reform issues (in this way they were not much different from their counterparts on the national scene). Nominations and elections often pivoted on personalities and money, and often degenerated into name-calling and personal slander.

The classic struggle of that period unfolded in 1882-1883 for the vacated senate seat of Henry Teller, who had been appointed secretary of the interior by President Chester Arthur. Tabor, Bowen, Pitkin, John Routt, and an old political pro, William Hamill, entered the race; but Tabor and Bowen had the inside track. Each had money and was willing to spend it to achieve his goal. After ninety-six ballots, consuming eleven days in January 1883, the two killed off all opposition, Bowen finally upsetting Tabor to win the six-year term; Tabor received only a token thirty-day appointment. Del Norte's Bowen, who had made a fortune in the San Juans and would become known as "Washington's finest poker player," had come to Colorado from Arkansas and had been one of the state's district judges. Charges were flung about who betrayed whom and for months afterward it appeared to be the political crisis of the age.

This sort of contest produced the highest excitement for politicians and electorate. Indeed, legislative elections were conducted with the idea of lining up support for a Senate race. When men like Tabor and Bowen faced off, real drama was produced; however, the people's will and formalities of politics might be ignored in the process. It would be a decade before political machines came to replace the individualism and the emotional following of these men who played for high stakes and backed their moves with thousands of dollars.

Occasionally a legislature would gain similar attention. Such was the case with the "Robber Seventh," which scandalously squandered appropriations in 1889 and 1890. An emotional clash of public and private interests, like the attempt to create a board of railroad commissioners in 1881, could generate heated debate and statewide interest. To resolve the financial malfeasance problem, the voters seemed to like the idea of electing Democratic treasurers, attorneys general, and superintendents of public instruction, hoping that they would serve in a watchdog capacity over the Republican governor and legislature.

This state of affairs lasted until the 1890s, when the political winds changed. The decade that brought the revival of gold mining in Colorado, led by Cripple Creek, was also a decade of economic crisis and political ferment. This was true throughout the United States, but Colorado seemed particularly vulnerable to the economic dislocations and peculiarly sensitive to the shifting political rearrangements.

One of the problems of the times, as usual, was money. In 1861 the mines of the United States had produced $43 million worth of gold and only $2 million worth of silver. But, by law, the coinage ratio was established at 15.988 ounces of silver pegged at the same price as 1 ounce of gold. This arbitrary balance of approximately sixteen to one, at earlier periods, had corresponded roughly with the "supply and demand"—or commercial market-ratio of the two metals. Now, however, silver was undervalued in comparison with its commercial price, and because a producer or owner of silver could receive a higher price on the commercial market, no silver had been presented for sale to the government for many years.

As the mining industry of the West developed, the relative production of the two metals tended to even out. In 1873 the quantities of gold and silver mined both were listed as worth about $36 million. This rapid increase in silver production brought a corresponding slump in the price of silver in the commercial market, and for the first time since 1837, silver prices fell below the old mint price established at the sixteen-to-one ratio.

That is, the price would have fallen below the mint price if there had been a mint price at the time. But, in fact, federal purchase and coinage of silver had ended. In that same year of 1873, Congress had legislated a new unit of currency, which, for the first time in national history, permitted the coinage of gold dollars. More than that, the gold dollars were to be used as the basic unit of value, replacing the silver dollar. The legislation paralleled the actions of Germany, France, and other European countries that had recently adopted a single gold standard.

If the supply of silver had remained short and the market price for commercial silver had remained high, there would have been little cause for complaint. But as the supply of silver increased, and the market price dropped, there were demands for a reestablishment of silver purchases by the federal government. Those directly interested in silver mines (the owners, managers, miners) and those dependent on silver mines in a less direct fashion (the smelting interests, the railroads, the suppliers—in fact, much of the population of Colorado) were concerned. So too were the people who opposed the deflationary policy of the government and who looked upon silver coinage as a method of inflating an otherwise restricted currency.

The inflationists had not always been enamored of silver. Their origins, in fact, were much more closely associated with a different sort of currency—paper dollars. During the Civil War the federal government had issued fiat notes, which had been dubbed "greenbacks." These notes had fluctuated in value all during the war period, reflecting both the uncertainty of the outcome of the war and the disposition the federal government might make of the notes after the conflict had ended.

There were, at war's end, some $400 million worth of the greenbacks still in circulation. They posed interesting questions. Should they remain in circulation—perhaps even be increased in quantity—to inflate the currency and provide "cheap" money? Or should the government deflate the currency by calling in the greenbacks, retiring them from circulation?

In 1875 the federal authorities decided to resume specie payments for greenbacks, retiring the paper currency and embarking on a deflationary path. To inflationists this seemed a gross error. What was needed, they argued, was not less but more money in circulation. In 1865 there were about $31 per person in circulation in the nation. Ten years later this amount had dwindled to about $19 per person. In ordinary times this would have been a rather rapid deflation. But, the inflationists insisted, these were not ordinary times. Agriculture, commerce, and industry had expanded since the war; the money supply should keep pace with that growth.

The inflationists gradually came to understand that their best hope of success rested on their ability to organize their own political party, since neither the Republicans nor Democrats were willing to contest the "tight" money policy. In 1876 they formed the Greenback Party. They never organized in more than eight Colorado counties, and even there the Greenbackers had little connection with the national movement. In 1878 they polled 8 percent of the state votes; two years later they garnered only 3 percent. In a few counties, particularly Boulder, they enjoyed local victories, but these often were the result of alliances with temperance or prohibition groups.

Nationally, after some successes in the congressional elections of 1878, the Greenback Party lost vitality. But that did not end the inflationists' programs. An expanded currency might be brought about in other ways. The inflationists gradually became interested in silver coinage. A reexamination of the history of silver brought into focus the legislation of 1873. The inflationists now argued that if the government would revoke that coinage law and begin to purchase silver at the former ratio of sixteen to one, the silver money minted would expand the circulating medium. Thus silver became the inflationists' new tool to gain cheaper (that is, more) money.

The silver interests—as differentiated from the inflationists—had also studied the history of silver. They had come to believe that the Coinage Act of 1873 was a ruthless action designed to ruin their properties. Soon they had applied the epithet "the crime of 'seventy-three" to the legislation, as they embarked on a campaign to bring congressional revision of the act.

In response to the demands of western silver interests and the growing voice of the inflationists, Congress offered a compromise. The Bland-Allison Act of 1878, passed over President Hayes's veto, met the silver champions half-way. A total return to the pre-1873 coinage was unacceptable to the "tight" money group; an alternative allowed the coinage of $2 million to $4 million worth of silver each month. The quantity would be set by the secretary of the treasury; and the mint price would equal the current market price rather than the old standard of sixteen to one. Perhaps one-half of the silver mined each year could be moved from the commercial to the government market by this legislation. The reduced supply, presumably, would be reflected in a rising silver price.

Coloradans were very much interested in such legislation. Mining, their chief economic activity, depended on silver. In 1874, for the first time, the value of silver mined in the state had exceeded that of gold. By 1881 Colorado was the leading silver producer in the United States, and throughout the 1880s production remained on that high level. This alone was enough to create deep interest, but the citizens came to believe that their very existence rested on silver mining: Residents of Leadville and the other silver camps were not the only ones vitally concerned. Almost all economic pursuits in the state were tied in one way or another to the mining industry; consequently, almost every Colorado resident had a vested interest in its success.

But the Bland-Allison legislation failed to live up to expectations. It did not allow a return to the old ratio price for silver, and the treasury secretaries were committed to deflation. The minimum amount was coined, when success required unlimited coinage at the sixteen-to-one ratio.

To this end Colorado leaders were active. In a Senate speech in January 1886, Henry Teller outlined what free coinage would do. It would, he reasoned, stimulate commerce and industry, provide more employment and better wages, and bring silver back to its old price. The appeal was broader than just Colorado, yet each point struck a responsive chord within the state. Horace Tabor made yet another appeal for free coinage, one that became increasingly frequent: "You wipe out silver off from the face of the earth and you just double the value of gold and the gold securities and the debt securities, which have to be paid in gold."

Under such conditions Coloradans soon organized to promote the free and unlimited coinage of silver. The first national Silver Convention met in Denver in January 1885 and formed the Silver Alliance, which quickly set up branches in all parts of the state. This was followed by state conventions and a Colorado Silver Association. Four years later Colorado sent forty-three delegates to a national silver meeting in St. Louis. By 1892, when a third national convention was called in Washington, D.C., the state was represented by delegates from 220 silver clubs, numbering more than 40,000 members. The foundation had been laid; the silver banner raised.

Given this interest, silver and politics were destined to join together. Colorado representatives and candidates, of both parties, consistently championed bimetallism—that is, a return to silver coinage. But despite their energy, and the work of their western colleagues and the enthusiasm of inflationists generally, they were denied a complete victory. In 1890, during Benjamin Harrison's administration, a "half-loaf" was achieved in the passage of the Sherman Silver Purchase Act. The measure was more or less bracketed with the McKinley Tariff Act of the same year. Westerners, without personal interest in the high rates of that tariff, supported the measure in return for enactment of their desired silver act.

Like the earlier Bland-Allison legislation, the Sherman act did not meet the full expectations of the silverites. It did, however, approximately double the amount of silver stipulated to be purchased by the earlier legislation: 4,500,000 ounces of silver a month, presumably enough to absorb most of the then current production in the United States. The price, again, was to be the market level rather than the fixed ratio.

At first it appeared that the Sherman legislation might work the magic. With increased government buying, silver prices began to climb. From the low level of 93¢ per ounce in 1889, silver reached more than $1.00 per ounce in 1890. Colorado, whose silver mines were now producing 58 percent of the total silver mined in the nation each year, had reason to applaud this initial effect. But the pace did not continue. The higher prices lasted only momentarily. Soon a continuing decline set in, and by early 1892 silver had not only fallen to its old level but had also kept declining. By 1894 it would sell for only 63¢ an ounce.

Disenchantment with the Sherman legislation reflected a similar disenchantment with the national policies of the Republican and Democratic Parties. Neither of the traditional groups seemingly dared to alienate its eastern supporters by championing western silver ideas. Into this vacuum came a new political grouping whose elements originated in a variety of reform and dissident factions—the People's Party, more commonly known as the Populists.

Historians often trace the rise of the Populists through the agrarian reform organizations like the Grange and its successors, the Alliances. But some Greenbackers also entered the Populist grouping, as did labor reformers and many others. The results can be seen in the variety of programs the Populists sponsored: a graduated income tax; government ownership and operation of the transportation and communication networks; the Australian secret ballot; an eight-hour day for labor; political devices like the referendum, initiative, and the direct election of U.S. senators; and—the most important in explaining the success of the party in western mining regions—free and unlimited coinage of silver at the legal ratio of sixteen to one. In time the silver issue became the lode-star of the party nationally as well as regionally.

The Populists organized a full ticket for the election of 1892 in Colorado, at the same time preparing to support the national ticket headed by James B. Weaver of Iowa, candidate for president. The party's candidate for governor, Davis H. Waite, who had moved to Colorado in 1879, was a man of considerable political experience. A Democrat before the Civil War, and then an ardent Republican, he had served in the legislatures of both Wisconsin and Kansas. In Aspen, he practiced law, became a justice of the peace and the first superintendent of schools for Pitkin County. He had also affiliated with the labor party there, serving as local secretary for the Knights of Labor.

Waite's conversion to Populism led him to newspapering. In 1891 he founded a radical weekly titled the *Aspen Union Era*. Unlike many of his followers, whose conversion to Populism extended only as far as the free silver plank, Waite was a thoroughgoing reformer, particularly convinced that the railroads needed curbing to provide protection for the state's consumers. He also consistently opposed all schemes of "fusion"—that is, alliances with Democrats espousing free silver or any other such group. "The two [old] parties," he is quoted as saying, "have only seven principles, and they are 'two loaves and five small fishes.'"

In the election of 1892, the Silver Democrats gained control of their party and brought it to the side of both the national and state Populist tickets, despite Waite's fear of "alien" support. The Republicans attempted to sit on the fence on the money issue. In so doing they gave a decided advantage to the Populists, for their out-and-out silver championing stood in stark contrast to the Republican attitude. The

Davis H. Waite, Colorado's Populist governor.

Denver *Times* might believe that "the average Colorado Populist is simply a Republican or Democrat with a grievance," but that grievance concerned silver, the state's major industry, and the election returns were indicative of its potency as a campaign issue.

Colorado, which had given its three electoral votes to Republicans Hayes, Garfield, Blaine, and Harrison, in 1892 voted for Populist James B. Weaver. The margin was impressive: 53,584 votes for Weaver; 38,620 for Republican Harrison. On the basis of the 1890 census, Colorado was now entitled to two representatives in Congress, and these seats were filled by Populists John C. Bell and Lafe Pence. At home, Populist Davis H. Waite was elected governor. With the aid of Silver Democrats, his party would control the newly elected state Senate, although the Republicans retained a one-vote majority in the state House of Representatives. Radicalism had triumphed at the polls. Time would tell how successful this new force in politics would be in promoting and legislating its reform programs.

TWENTY-ONE

THE SILVER CRUSADE

Eighteen-ninety-three proved to be an inauspicious year to test the tenets of Populism as advocated by Governor Waite. The price of silver continued to fall, threatening to carry with it the entire Colorado economy. Anxiety was evident in the Centennial State, but so was the determination to press ahead. The *Weekly Republican* (Denver) cheered its readers on January 4: "Colorado has such great resources that it cannot be crushed. The people have faith in the future and in their ability to develop its possibilities and bring about again an era of prosperity." But facts belied such rhetoric. Uneasiness appeared throughout the country, especially among eastern investors, who feared the demand for silver might force the government's hand and bring about inflation, based on the depreciated silver coin. And they were not encouraged as the government gold reserves steadily diminished, nearing the $100 million mark, then considered the magic point above which the gold dollars and the government were secure. By strenuous measures, the lame duck Harrison administration kept the amount barely above that figure until Grover Cleveland was inaugurated.

Other indications, meanwhile, pointed toward imminent financial distress. Commercial failures led banks into contracting loans; speculators began to dump their holdings on an already failing market. Many Colorado silver mines—some a decade or more old—were producing only lower-grade ores. Ominous news for the western silver interests arrived from abroad in June, when India ceased coining silver. The collapse of that market sent the price tumbling precipitately; in four days it dropped from 83¢ to 62¢ an ounce. For many Colorado mining and smelting businesses, this seemed the final judgment, dooming them to economic collapse. The owners declared that they would have to shut down their properties until a recovery in the price of silver allowed profitable operations.

And the mining camps and smelters were not the only scene of trouble. These years brought a severe drought to the agricultural areas, making life perilous on every farm and ranch and impossible on the Eastern Slope dry lands where homesteaders had followed the mythical "moving rainbelt," only to discover that they had settled where "normal" rainfall was practically nonexistent. The ensuing exodus from the high plains added another problem to those generated in the mines and mills.

The full force of the economic crash hit the state in July. Within a few days twelve Denver banks closed, smelters stopped operating, real estate values tumbled, and every newspaper from the mining regions brought further disheartening reports of mine closures and business failures. Failures, dismissals, foreclosures—it all added up to a sad picture; even the Denver tramway suffered, as people walked to save fares. The *Rocky Mountain News,* July 20, tried to rally Coloradans, "Shoulder to Shoulder, men, while the war upon Colorado continues." And it did seem like a war to those involved, a war upon Colorado's major economic pillar—silver. The chance for more silver legislation was nil; in fact, President Cleveland was about to call a special session of Congress to repeal the Sherman Silver Purchase Act.

Governor Waite gave the state some unneeded notoriety in July, when he addressed a mass meeting of delegates from throughout Colorado who had convened to discuss the deteriorating situation. In analyzing the current conditions, he insisted that civil liberties would need defense, asserting that "it is infinitely better that blood should flow to our horses' bridles rather than our national liberties should be destroyed." This phrase, taken out of context, earned the governor the nickname Bloody Bridles from the conservative press.

In Colorado, however, Waite's comments did not miss the mark by far. Devastating conditions covered the state and unemployment soared;

many of those out of work drifted to Denver in the vain hope of finding work. Tensions mounted as the burden grew almost intolerable for the city, which provided tents and food but could not continue to support the growing numbers. To encourage the unemployed to move out of Denver, railroads reduced or canceled fares. This relieved immediate problems, but Denver now was fully aware of the gravity of the times.

The Colorado Bureau of Labor Statistics, attempting to ascertain the depth of the crisis through a statewide mailing of questionnaires, issued a discouraging report on September 1. It listed 377 business failures, 435 mines closed (895 producing mines had been operating in late 1892), and over 45,000 persons out of work. Terms such as "gloomy, very bad, desperate, dull, depressing, blue and disheartening" were used to describe attitudes. An unidentified person in Bent County wrote, "Low prices of farm products and scarcity of money have made the condition of our people a deplorable one." Another correspondent from Aspen bemoaned, "The situation is bad and couldn't be very much worse. If we get no favorable legislation, Aspen and vicinity is a goner."

The panic of 1893, of course, was not confined to Colorado; it just appeared to contemporaries that the state was the hardest hit in a nationwide depression. Many interrelated factors had brought about the situation: the long-standing western and southern agricultural distress; overexpansion of industry, particularly the railroads; withdrawal of foreign investors; and a generally shaky international financial situation. Each of these contributed to the gold reserve drain and/or the panic, but a generation of eastern conservatives pointed its finger at a single scapegoat as being responsible—the Sherman Silver Purchase Act. President Cleveland, who had just been inaugurated when the $100 million gold reserve barrier was broken, concurred. Repeal of the act now became the panacea, for which Cleveland called a special session of Congress in August.

No joy was generated in Colorado over such action. Although the act had never been comprehensive enough to answer the silverites' demands, it was still the only positive legislation they had. Many were unhappy that no effort would be made to alter the tariff, which, in 1890, had been paired (to gain votes) with the Sherman act. The silverites now labored to prevent repeal; they were joined by others who favored inflation. All the old arguments and slogans were resurrected to acquire new significance in the urgency of this crisis. Colorado's two Republican senators, Henry Teller and Edward Wolcott, both exerted themselves valiantly in the debate. Teller was particularly effective. Ordinarily less of an orator than many politicians of the age, he now phrased the Colorado position neatly:

> We are neither cast down nor dejected. We know what nature had done for us, and we know that a State with more than 100,000 square miles of territory, with more natural wealth than any State east of the Missouri River, will be able to take care of herself. . . . We do not disguise the fact that we are to go through the valley of the shadow of death. We know what it means to turn out our 200,000 silver-miners in the fall of the year. We know what it means when every man in the State who has a little money saved must put his hand in his pocket and draw it forth to keep from starving the families of the laborers of our State. While we are ready and willing to meet the occasion, yet if anybody on this floor thinks for a moment that we are to be destroyed, I want him to understand that the State of Colorado will be infinitely stronger and greater than many of the States whose representatives are attacking us now by this infamous financial policy. But . . . the iron will enter our souls. We shall not forget that in this contest . . . the men with whom we have stood shoulder to shoulder in the economic battles heretofore have almost to a man forsaken us. We in the States of Nevada and Colorado have held those States in the Republican column for many a year. We have maintained a Republican majority in this Chamber by our votes. We have stood by our Eastern brethren who believed in the protective system . . . even when it would have been to our local interest to vote against certain measures.
>
> But how much aid . . . have we had from them? . . . We shall not abandon the faith that is in us. But when we shall be asked to yield our judgment to their judgment upon economic questions in the future, if we do not respond as promptly as we have in the past, I trust they will not be surprised.

Words, however, could not stem the tide. Repeal was voted by Congress. Since the federal government had demonstrated, by the action of Congress, an inability or unwillingness to rescue the state from its plight, Governor Waite now determined to resort to "home remedies." He summoned the legislature into special session and requested from the lawmakers a series of relief measures.

The Populist governor's program was doomed even before he presented it. Many of his own party were interested only in national silver legislation. The Colorado legislators did agree to minor modifications of the state laws regarding debts and interest rates. But these measures were designed to remedy the effects and not the cause of the troubles.

Governor Waite's basic proposal was presented as an alternative to the federal silver purchases, which Congress had recently ended. He suggested that the state of Colorado use its sovereign powers to buy the silver mined in the state, sending the metal to Mexico where it would be coined into dollars. These would be returned to Colorado to be used as a local circulating medium. Waite's opponents refused to be convinced. They labeled the proposed coins "fandango dollars" and almost laughed the scheme out of the legislative chambers. In the process they managed to further brand the governor a radical—perhaps even an un-American—schemer. And the governor's problems had only begun.

While the legislative session had been busily disposing of Waite's relief proposals, serious news began to emanate from one prosperous area of the state. For years the repeated mining rushes had acted as a safety valve to drain off surplus population from less prosperous districts. Now this release was gone; only Cripple Creek appeared booming. Men rushed there in hopes they could capture a share of the golden treasure; they found instead a surplus labor market, which favored only the mine owner. When the owners posted notices of an extension of the daily working shift from the usual eight or nine hours to ten hours, with no increase in wages, the miners demanded their former scale. And they sought recognition of the new union, the Western Federation of Miners, the first units of which had been organized in the district the previous year.

By the end of February, most of the Cripple Creek mines and many of the smelters were shut down. When the mine owners obtained a court injunction against strikers' interference, the union prepared for battle to keep nonunion laborers from working the properties. Soon there were three armed forces in the area: the union, with headquarters on Bull Hill, near the town of Altman; the sheriff and his deputies, representing El Paso County (of which Cripple Creek was a part until its separation in 1899 as Teller County), who seem to have acted largely on the part of the mine owners; and the state militia, sent to the district on orders of Governor Waite.

Violence threatened from all sides; there were some beatings and some dynamiting of mine properties. A battle between the militia and the sheriff's posse threatened. But finally, with the governor, union officials, and mine owners closeted for a conference on the Colorado College campus in Colorado Springs, cooler heads prevailed. The union and

National Guard troops march to Denver's City Hall at Fourteenth and Larimer streets during the 1894 "war."

the operators signed a settlement, returning the workers' scale to what it had been, with promises of no discrimination against workers. The Western Federation of Miners had won its first Colorado strike.

Although the Cripple Creek strike was settled in June 1894, it would become a major ingredient in the election campaign that fall. Waite and his Populist friends would receive the blame for the troubles in the gold camp and all the rest of the miseries of that unhappy time—continuing economic depression, unrelieved unemployment, and the affair known as "City Hall war."

Shortly after the legislative session had ended, early in March 1894, Waite had become embroiled in a conflict with the Denver Fire and Police Board. In those years, before Colorado cities gained home rule, the administration of Denver was an integral element of state government. Governor Waite dismissed two members of the Denver board, but they refused to be fired and locked themselves in City Hall, daring the governor to physically remove them.

Sides quickly formed. Supporting the board members were the police and fire departments and the notorious Denver "bunco king"— Soapy Smith—and his friends. They armed themselves and prepared to defend the bastion of City Hall. Waite summoned militia units, which drew up on Fourteenth Street with cannon loaded and small arms ready to storm the citadel. Federal troops arrived on the scene, along with thousands of Denverites who moved downtown to watch the battle. They waited all day, while Waite hesitated to order the attack. In the evening, he sent the militia to its barracks, having decided to take the issue to the courts. In time the courts would answer: A governor had the right to remove and replace officers but not to use force to do so.

Besides the burdens of "City Hall war," labor troubles, and economic depression, the Populists had a further liability in the campaign of 1894. The Democrats parted company with them in order to run their separate slate. The Republicans campaigned on promises to redeem the state from Populist "misrule." In the canvass that fall they won most of the state offices, electing Albert McIntire governor and sending John Shafroth to Congress. The election was notable as the first in which women voted. The year before, women suffrage had been approved, making Colorado the second state (after Wyoming) to provide political equality between the sexes.

The Republicans soon had an opportunity to demonstrate their ability to cope with a strike situation. In June 1896, the Western Federation of Miners, enjoying an enviable reputation among workers after its Cripple Creek success, struck the silver mines of Leadville for a $3 wage scale. Leadville was in trouble enough because of the falling silver price, and the strike soon turned the camp into a potentially explosive arena. As the miners left their jobs, they abandoned the pumps, and mines immediately flooded.

The patterns of Cripple Creek were soon repeated. The owners concentrated their attention on importing strikebreakers; the union struggled to seal off roads and mines to keep the "scabs" from coming in. When the union assaulted and fired ground-buildings of several mines that had managed to open with nonunion workers, the owners hastened appeals to Governor McIntire for help. Soon the militia was on its way to the Cloud City. But this time there was a difference, for the troops' presence allowed the owners to reopen most of their mines with imported laborers. The strike dragged to a close. What the Federation of Miners had gained in Cripple Creek in 1894 during Waite's administration, it partly lost in Leadville in 1896, under McIntire's regime.

During the summer of 1896, while the strike in the silver camp continued, national politics commanded unusual attention among

DON'T FORGET THE WOMEN WHEN YOU VOTE ON TUESDAY.

Equal Rights! Equal Responsibilities! Equal Suffrage!

Colorado women won the right to vote in 1893.

Coloradans. The nation was rousing itself for a presidential election. The Republicans met in convention in June in St. Louis. There the western silver interests in the party were completely submerged. When William McKinley won the nomination on a platform espousing the single gold standard, Henry Teller led a group of western Republicans from the convention hall, pledging to continue the fight for free silver in other ways.

When the Democrats met in Chicago, it was quite another story. The inflationists and silverites controlled a majority of the delegates' seats. They wrote a platform calling for free and unlimited coinage of silver at the sixteen-to-one ratio and awaited the appearance of someone to lead their fight. Enthusiasm developed among Democrats to name Senator Teller to a place on the ticket, believing he would draw silver Republicans to the cause. But William Jennings Bryan masterfully swayed the convention, and it stampeded for him as its champion. To the *Rocky*

Mountain News, July 11, 1896, Bryan was the very embodiment of the "new order of things, new issues, new men, new geographical groupings"; he was the man of the hour. Conservative Cleveland—Sherman act repeal and all—was repudiated by his own party.

Normal political relationships in Colorado were immensely disrupted by such proceedings. Some Republicans, like Senator Edward Wolcott, tried to ride out the split, insisting on loyalty to the national ticket and platform *and* free silver. Their attempts were generally unsuccessful. Other Republicans could not support the national policies of the party. Led by Teller, they organized the Silver Republican Party, thereby opening the gates to a wild process of "fusions" with other groups. The scramble for alliances finally resulted in the Democrats and Silver Republicans joining in one state ticket, while the Populists and National Silver factions presented another.

Both combinations endorsed free silver and William Jennings Bryan. The McKinley Republicans tried to enlist support for the regular party's position and candidates but with little success. The basic battle centered on the contest between the Democratic-Silver Republicans, championing Alva Adams for governor, and the Populist-National Silver group, led by M. S. Bailey.

The election of 1896—"the battle of the standards"—in both state and nation divided the country as it had not been divided since the fateful election of 1860. Silver was the token, but it represented much more than mere metal and mining. To the gold-minded Republicans who rallied around William McKinley, it was clear that "the underlying, fructifying element of this 16 to 1 movement is Socialism. It is the same old effort to get something for nothing." To the ranks of the Bryan supporters, it was equally clear that nothing but victory in the election would save the country from crucifixion upon "the cross of gold." Passions mounted right up to the day of polling. Not the strangest of many strange episodes during the campaign was the action of Colorado's "Mr. Gold" himself—Cripple Creek's Winfield Stratton—who endorsed free silver and Bryan. In fact, Stratton went even further. He announced a public wager of up to $100,000 that Bryan would win, a possibility that the regular Republicans believed would immediately and substantially reduce his own personal fortune.

No one offered to take Stratton's bet. Coloradans, at least, seemed to have decided early that silver would triumph at the polls. When election day arrived, they marked their ballots in full expectation of success. The count showed that the state's voters, for the first time, had given Colorado's electoral votes to a Democrat. William Jennings Bryan had overwhelmed Republican McKinley in the state, 161,269 to 26,279. Alva Adams was chosen governor and his Democratic-Silver Republicans slate captured the state offices. But in the rest of the nation, events followed a different pattern. McKinley carried the majority of the states; Bryan and Free Silver had gone down to defeat.

In Colorado, some people continued to hope for a return of free silver. But their hopes were destined to dwindle and, eventually, to die. Having fought a passionate contest over the issue once, the American people seemed content with their decision. Interest in the "money question" faded in the general prosperity of the United States in the years that followed. The death of silver left Colorado, however, with an inheritance of muddled political groupings and the challenge of building the state's economy on a foundation other than a government-supported market for the product of its silver mines.

TWENTY-TWO

THE GOOD OLD DAYS

Looking back on it now, it seems rather strange that the decade of turmoil and trouble described in the preceding chapters would later be remembered as the Gay Nineties and that future generations would hearken back to the time when the nineteenth century ended and the twentieth century began as the "good old days." The very fact, however, is useful in keeping human history in perspective. The grimness of the decade and the sporadic eruption of economic and political problems into violence are likely to dim the equally important fact that men, women, and children found time to live their lives, enjoy entertainments and recreations, and even glory in the advances of their society.

The years from 1890 to 1914 and the outbreak of World War I in Europe were, in many ways, years of transition. While the economic structures of state and nation were constantly undergoing violent stresses and changes, and political battles enlisted high passions, quieter, less spectacular social shifts were also occurring. These changes eventually created patterns of social life more similar to contemporary concepts than had ever existed before.

Many elements of society, of course, remained unchanged. Many aspects of life in Colorado continued from earlier times. The process of filling up the land with people, for example, despite the closing of silver mines and other economic setbacks, continued apace. When the census counters finished their survey in 1900, a 30 percent gain had been registered in Colorado's population, compared with a national increase of only 20 percent. The state now counted almost 540,000 people. The vast majority of the inhabitants (81 percent) were native born whites. Only 17 percent of the population was foreign born.

Although part of this increase in population is explained by the natural birthrate, immigration also added numbers. Labor difficulties, mine closings, and ill-fated attempts to settle the dry lands of the Eastern Slope did not bring an end to the movement of people into Colorado. Some of these newcomers followed the old pattern of health-seekers, searching for relief from tuberculosis and other ailments. Others followed the even older trail of the treasure-hunters, finding employment in Cripple Creek or Thomas Walsh's Camp Bird Mine. And during these years another old concept continued to attract immigrants—colony settlements.

Like the older colony endeavors, these group settlements varied greatly both in motivation and in success. A few examples will illustrate how different they were. In 1898 the Salvation Army established Fort Amity in southeastern Colorado between Granada and Holly on the Arkansas River. The ghost of Carl Wulsten survived in the scheme, for the plans envisioned moving underprivileged laborers and their families from slum areas of eastern and midwestern cities onto a thousand-acre tract. Families would be allotted ten acres of land, livestock, and implements. Thirty families from Chicago and Iowa, under the direction of Colonel Thomas Holland, settled the colony. Lands were plowed and planted to cantaloupes and, later, sugar beets. For a time Fort Amity prospered; the original 120 settlers were joined by others until 350 people resided in the colony. But exasperating problems also appeared. Particularly discouraging was the water seepage, which deposited alkaline residue on the lands, making them unfit for farming. Before the end of its first decade, Fort Amity was closed.

A second experiment involved emigrants from the Netherlands. In 1892, the Holland American Land and Immigration Company of Utrecht dispatched a colony of 200 adults and children from Amsterdam to a site in the San Luis Valley. On arrival in Colorado, these immigrants were housed temporarily at Alamosa, and almost from the beginning ill luck visited them. Diphtheria and scarlet fever broke out among the children, resulting in thirteen deaths. When it appeared that the company managers were totally neglecting them, the colonists organized their own government, but they could not reverse the misfortune that beset the colony. Eventually most of the group moved from Colorado to farmlands in Iowa.

A third colony followed a different pattern. In 1893, during the midst of the economic panic, ten people in Denver organized the Colorado Co-operative Company. From its inception, this was to be a utopian enterprise, where "equality and service rather than greed and competition should be the basis of conduct" and where Henry George's "single tax" concepts were to be practiced. The organizers issued 1,000 shares of stock at a par value of $100, with a maximum of one share and one vote allowed to each member. The company selected a site for its settlement on a mesa above the San Miguel River in western Colorado. By 1895 twenty members had established a town there, originally called Pinon. Ten years later the buildings were moved to a nearby site and the settlement was renamed Nucla.

They erected a sawmill and built fruit boxes for the orchardists in the Uncompahgre Valley. A large irrigation ditch was later completed, making farming on a more extensive scale possible. Despite internal crises, the expulsion of dissident members, and litigation between the colony and the Denver group, the settlement survived. Nucla thus marks one of the successful colonial efforts in the state's history.

A fourth colony, Dearfield, was set up in 1910-1911 between Greeley and Fort Morgan by O. T. Jackson, a black man. Inspired by Booker T. Washington's *Up From Slavery* and encouraged by the then governor, John F. Shafroth, Dearfield enjoyed initial success. Sixty families moved to the place during its first six years. But later discouragements set in. Since Colorado's black population was not large—in 1900 it composed only 2 percent of the total population—no sizeable continuing migration to Dearfield occurred. Many of the settlers lacked experience as farmers; some lacked the capital necessary to sustain themselves when crops failed. Gradually most of the families withdrew from the place.

Through colony-type plantings and individual immigrants, Colorado's population grew. The state also hosted thousands of temporary visitors each year as more and more vacationers embarked on western tours to see what remained of the American frontier and to enjoy the climate and scenery of the Rocky Mountain West. Many of these tourists were introduced to Colorado through conventions of national organizations that scheduled assemblies at Denver. One of the largest of these was the 1892

Dearfield founder O. T. Jackson poses with a child about the time the colony was organized.

conclave of the Grand Encampment of the Knights Templar. The American Federation of Labor met in Colorado's capital city in 1894; the American Library Association the following year; the first International Mining Congress convened there in the summer of 1897; the American Medical Association gathered the next year.

Tourists still arrived in Denver, Colorado Springs, and Pueblo by railroad and, for the most part, what they saw of the mountains was limited to the views from railroad coaches. In fact, excursion tours would continue for many years to form a major part of the tourist industry. But omens of a future change had already appeared. In the last year of the nineteenth century, the first motor car (electric) was seen on the streets of Denver. Two years later W. B. Felker entered his name in the history books by driving a steam-powered Locomobile to the summit of Pike's Peak, long before the famous automobile toll road had been constructed. By 1902 there were 200 vehicles in Denver alone.

Introduction of automobiles brought a new phase to an old problem of the area—transportation. The elementary components of the problem were obvious. Colorado's area is not only large (eighth in size in the Union); it is also rugged in topography. Yet the same terrain that made road building expensive was what tourists in the days ahead would want to drive through to see the natural splendor of the Rocky Mountains. The relatively small population of the state would be called on to maintain long stretches of highways that were extremely costly to build and repair.

Much of the impetus for road building came from the automobile clubs, which, in time, joined with the local group of the Good Roads Association. One of their major objectives was to have a highway commission developed within the state government. By 1908 this campaign had succeeded, but the battle had only begun. Appropriations for construction and maintenance of highways remained a continuing concern. One solution to the problem that gained favor in the early years was using convict labor to construct roads. In 1899 the state provided that all sentences (including life imprisonment) might be commuted for good behavior and work on the highways. A state road was constructed from Pueblo to Leadville, the Skyline Drive at Canon City was completed, and a road to the top of Royal Gorge was opened. These were actually designed as wagon roads, but the car enthusiasts welcomed their construction. Progress, however, proved slow: In 1914 the state had only 1,192 miles of improved highways compared with 38,588 miles of unimproved roads. By that time, 13,135 passenger cars had been registered under a new state licensing act.

In the years ahead automobiles would completely change the character of the industry of tourism. New needs would revolutionize the entire enterprise of luring travelers to the state and entertaining them during their visits. But the growth of the industry did not wait for that revolution to end—in fact, during the "good old days," some innovations to encourage tourists were developed that form unique footnotes to the history of Colorado.

In the southwestern corner of the state, in 1906, a long campaign to preserve the relics of the cliff dwellers culminated in the creation of Mesa Verde National Park. The crumbling edifices of the prehistoric people had first been seen by white men (as far as records tell us) in 1849-1850 when Lieutenant James Simpson reported seeing ruined structures in the walls of Mancos Canyon. A U.S. geological team surveyed in the area in the early 1860s, but not until 1874 was a scientific investigation of the ruins undertaken. Then the "photographer of the

West," William H. Jackson, led an official exploration and completed the first photographs of the dwellings.

The difficult access to the many areas of the mesa and the wide expanse over which the ruins are to be found made discovery of new sites a never-ending process. The Jackson party, for example, missed many of the larger ruins, including Cliff Palace, which was not found until 1888. Then three cowboys, Richard and Al Wetherill and Charlie Mason, searching for stray cattle on the mesa top, viewed it from across a canyon.

By that time pot-hunters were carrying away the artifacts they found. Amateur diggers and trained scientists like Gustaf Nordenskiöld, a Swedish archeologist, engaged in the sport. Nordenskiöld visited the mesa in 1891, taking with him when he left a collection of more than 600 choice artifacts that today are housed in the National Museum at Helsinki, Finland. As pot-hunters threatened to leave nothing but "ruined ruins," various groups in Colorado agitated for preservation of the mesa and its treasures. Particularly vigorous in this effort was the Colorado Woman's Club and its branch organization, the Colorado Cliff Dwellers Association. After years of work, in 1906, they and their allies persuaded the federal government to create Mesa Verde National Park.

Nine years later, in the northern part of the state, a second national park was set aside—Rocky Mountain National Park—405 square miles of mountain scenery and unspoiled wilderness. Here again, vigorous Colorado sponsorship was essential to success, particularly the determined crusade of Enos A. Mills. Federal authority also created Wheeler National Monument, northeast of Creede, an area of picturesque lava and rock formations, in 1908, and Colorado National Monument, west of Grand Junction, a site filled with grotesque natural structures of red stone, in 1911. All these held promise as tourist attractions for visitors to the Centennial State.

Tourists also were lured to Colorado cities where "palaces" were built. The movement began in Pueblo in the 1880s when members of the business community made plans for what they called the Mineral Palace. The idea was to call attention to Colorado's mineral resources and, of course, to provide a manmade structure for tourists to enjoy. This edifice was to be plated, both exterior and interior, with colored marbles, slates, mica, spar, pyrites, and quartz. Statues of King Coal and Queen Silver would reside within. Unfortunately, the committee ran short of funds and changes in the blueprints were necessary. The masons and

Leadville's Ice Palace, with its Norman towers and eight-foot-thick walls.

carpenters finished their labors in time for a splendid opening on July 4, 1890, as throngs flocked to see the "monstrosity" with its 25 highly ornamented domes.

Then Leadville decided to build a palace—this one of ice. In the winter of 1895-1896 a mammoth frozen structure of Norman design, covering five acres, enclosed a ballroom, skating rink, restaurant, and carnival displays within ice walls eight feet thick. The Crystal Carnival of the Cloud City proved only partially successful.

Other towns called attention to themselves in other ways. The "festival" concept seemed well calculated to attract tourists. Each autumn the newspapers commented on one of these: "On Thursday . . . September 5, Watermelon day at Rocky Ford will be celebrated. It is the oldest of the state's autumn festivals, and continues to hold an undiminished sway over the popular heart. The melon crop this season has been unusually large and of a fine quality, and tons of watermelon and cantaloupes will be on the ground for free distribution to the thousands of guests who are expected. The great Arkansas Valley fair will be in progress at the time,

Enthusiastic participants enjoy Watermelon Day in Rocky Ford.

with a magnificent display of the products of that section of the state, and the big beet sugar factory will be open for the inspection of visitors. In addition to these attractions a special programme of sports has been prepared. There will be running and trotting races for large purses, a five-mile automobile race and a five-mile cowboy race."

The Rocky Ford festival honored the melon; at Denver an even more grandiose festival most Octobers from 1895 to 1912 honored silver and the state's productivity in general at the Festival of Mountain and Plain. This celebration lasted a week. Designed to some extent on the well-established New Orleans Mardi Gras (with many of the floats for the first parades shipped from New Orleans and many artists imported from there to help in preparing them), the Festival of Mountain and Plain offered something of interest to everyone. Masquerades with street dancing, parades, and the Silver Serpent Ball with a Queen of the Festival attended by the Slaves of the Silver Serpent provided romantic illusions for escape from the grim realities of everyday life. During the week sporting events added thrills of participation and plenty of chances for "speculation." The holiday week in Denver provided a natural climax for a variety of contests: bicycle racing, fire runs, rock-drilling, and—for a time—rodeo events.

The bicycle races were reminders of that short-lived era before the advent of the motor car, when the craze for bicycle riding had generated bicycle clubs throughout the state and the thrills of novelties like the "century rides"—that is, rides of a hundred miles a day—or the actual construction of the first part of a projected cycle path from Denver to Palmer Lake. The fire runs, sometimes conducted at night as illuminated events, brought back to Denver the thrills of contests among volunteer fire companies racing as hook and ladder crews or hose companies to test their skill in laying hose or setting and climbing ladders. Denver itself by this time had "gone modern" by organizing a paid fire department. But throughout the rest of the state, the volunteer brigades still flourished, complete with handsome uniforms and a desire to capture the coveted prizes at state tournaments.

The rock-drilling contests furnished the most exciting of the festival's offerings. Competitive rock-drilling was a natural outgrowth of the state's most important industry. Local matches were held in the mining camps; counties then selected champions, often at Fourth of July celebrations; the county champions were sent to Denver to compete in the state finals at the Festival of Mountain and Plain. The rules governing the contests were rigidly drawn. Because the purses were large (as much as $5,000) and even larger sums were wagered on the contests, the judges administered the regulations carefully.

The contests lasted fifteen minutes. In single-jack competition a driller used a four-pound hammer and a three-quarter-inch drill; in double-jack performances one contestant handled a hammer weighing six to eight pounds and the other worked drills of various sizes. The passing minutes were called out by a timer. Several elements contributed to victory: speed of blows (with incredible records sometimes attained; as many as seventy-five blows per minute recorded); care with turning the drill, for the hole had to be smoothly rounded; the sharpness of the drill; the type of stone used. (Silver Plume granite, because of its hardness and uniformity, was usually employed.) Given the right combination, a double-jack team could drill a hole thirty-two to thirty-five inches deep in a fifteen-minute contest.

The rodeo events of the Denver festivals were natural reflections of another state industry. These years, however, they were not as universally popular as the rock-drilling contests. The Colorado Humane

Society, in particular, viewed the rodeo events with disgust and often intervened to eliminate the more brutal aspects of the contests between competitors and beasts.

Generally, though, not only at festival time but all through the year, spectator sports were becoming more popular—and more highly organized. Horse racing, the favorite diversion of the area, took a more eastern tone after the organization of the Overland Racing Association in Denver in 1887. Baseball, too, began to generate some of the enthusiasm on the part of spectators that would make it the "great American pastime." On Memorial Day 1902, nearly 11,000 persons attended games of the Western League, to watch the Denver team play the Milwaukee nine. And the athletic contests between teams of the state colleges brought out partisan spectators. The sports pages of the newspapers give something of the flavor of the times—for example, this headline from 1901:

RAN FROM FIELD
BOULDER FOOTBALL PLAYERS ALMOST MOBBED
BY STUDENTS AT FORT COLLINS
CHARGED AGRICULTURAL TEAM WITH EMPLOYING A
PROFESSIONAL AND THE TROUBLE FOLLOWED
GAME ORDERED FORFEITED AFTER AN EXCITING
CONFERENCE

Forfeiting football games was by no means the only problem the colleges encountered during the good old days. Some of the institutions were growing up, but financial difficulties impeded their progress. In 1900 the University of Colorado reported a total of 433 students in the collegiate program and another 356 in attendance at the preparatory school. Eighty professors, instructors, and lecturers taught these students and tried to convince the legislature of the need for larger appropriations. "If the state would direct more revenue its way," sympathetic editors explained, "such as the universities of Kansas and Nebraska enjoy," the university would be an even better school than it was.

The oldest Colorado institution for higher education—the University of Denver—was reportedly $165,000 in debt in 1900, with about $15,000 due in back salaries for the faculty. In 1892 the first building at the college's new University Park campus was finished. But there were threatened foreclosures and rumors that the building would be turned into a glue factory. Only the valiant efforts of Chancellor Henry Buchtel and William G. Evans kept the school from such an inglorious fate. At Golden, where the School of Mines was building an international reputation among mining colleges, student discipline seemed to be a problem. In 1900 the students went on strike because a professor of descriptive geometry flunked all but twelve members of a class of seventy.

In 1890 the residents of Greeley finally realized success in their campaign to house a college. They had lost to Fort Collins in a bid for an agricultural college and to Colorado Springs when the Congregationalists located their college. Now the state decided to establish its first normal (teacher training) school in Greeley. By 1911 the school's curriculum and the name had been changed to Colorado State Teacher's College. In answer to demands from Western Slope residents for similar privileges, the legislature established a second normal school at Gunnison.

In Denver, Colorado Woman's College was initiated. Patterned after schools such as Vassar and Wellesley, its founders looked to interdenominational support; Baptists, Presbyterians, Episcopalians, and Methodists were represented on the board of directors. The scheme for a "union" women's college did not materialize, but a building was erected and after leasing it for some years to an Oddfellows Lodge, in September 1909, the college enrolled its first students. The year before, the Presbyterians opened Westminster University north of Denver, a coeducational college, which became a boys' school in 1915 and two years later, suspended operations.

The last in the list of new collegiate institutions had its origins considerably earlier. In 1883, at Morrison, near Denver, the Catholics had established the College of the Sacred Heart. Five years later it was joined with Las Vegas College, moved from New Mexico, on a new campus nearer the city. The first graduating class of three gained their diplomas and the institution that in 1921 would change its name to Regis College had sent its first graduates into the world.

Education was not confined to ivy-covered halls. What today would be termed adult education had begun its tentative origins in a variety of fashions. The Chautauqua, with its lectures and moralistic entertainment, thrived with particular vigor at Palmer Lake and Boulder. State funds, in 1903, established a Colorado Traveling Library, so that books on wheels could find their way to the more remote areas of the state. The State Historical and Natural History Society, organized in 1879, successfully petitioned the General Assembly for money to construct a museum building in 1909. Six years later residents and tourists could view the artifacts and souvenirs of Coloradans who, just a half-century earlier, had rushed to Pike's Peak to dig gold.

Finally there were the daily newspapers—the "poor man's college." Crusading editors still existed: Dave Day, for example who moved his *Solid Muldoon* from Ouray to Durango in 1892, and Colonel L. C. Paddock, who edited the *Boulder Camera* from 1892 to 1940. But personal journalism was fading from the scene. High-speed presses and linotype machines brought enormous expenses and necessary attention to both advertising and circulation statistics. This revolution of the fourth estate was dramatically apparent in the Denver newspaper scene.

Thomas M. Patterson owned the oldest paper in the state, the *Rocky Mountain News*. He had made the journal the best known daily paper in the region. But this preeminent position was threatened by the *Denver Post*, begun in 1892, purchased by Frederick G. Bonfils and Harry H. Tammen three years later. Bonfils and Tammen turned Denver newspapering into a three-ringed circus or something worse. The *Post* owners intended to make money, if not set journalistic standards, and a wild, long-lived era of yellow journalism descended upon the city as the rival newspapers jostled for supremacy. Sensationalism and gallons of red ink were believed capable of augmenting circulation. If journalistic standards—or even good taste—were the test, the "good old days" already belonged to the past.

TWENTY-THREE

THE ERA OF INDUSTRIAL WARFARE

Despite the gloom broadcast over the Centennial State by the defeat of Bryan and Free Silver in 1896, new challenges in the opening decade of the new century were met with vigorous responses. The silver campaign had been predicated on economic intervention by the federal government; Coloradans had hoped that such outside aid would restore prosperity to the silver mines directly and to all of the state's economy indirectly. When the American voters rejected the silverites' scheme, they ended the hopes of many who had looked to Washington for help. Attention shifted to the local, internal scene. In the years that opened the new century, most Coloradans attempted to find their own solutions to their problems.

Yet paradoxically, it was largely forces reaching Colorado from far outside its boundaries that generated the major problems of the times. The new era of corporate organization had begun to invade the Rocky Mountain West, somewhat belatedly in comparison with its growth in more mature sections of the country. These new industrial organizations were designed to accomplish nothing less than nationwide control within their specific spheres. Mergers and consolidations of companies into "trusts" continued unabated, despite state and national legislation designed to eliminate their more dangerous or obnoxious practices. The East and Midwest had been engaged in debate over these economic "states within states" for some years; in Colorado the problem only now began to take shape.

A natural accompaniment of the "trust" was the corresponding growth of labor organizations. As business enterprises grew in size, the old-type relationship between employer and employee vanished, leaving the individual worker shorn of his stature and even his importance to the employer. No longer owning the tools necessary for the creation of the product, finding their skills less important as the labor market expanded, the individual workers hesitantly began to join together to form unions that, like their business counterparts, swelled in size and in power.

The economic dislocations of the years from 1890 to 1900 undoubtedly accelerated the growth of both trusts and unions. In the depression years, solvent industries were able to absorb less fortunate competitors and to seek strength by fashioning ever larger conglomerate structures. Laborers, desperate for work during the depression, often joined unions as the last resort to protect their wages or even their jobs.

No more obvious omen of these changes was afforded Colorado residents than the newspaper reports about the formation of what came to be called the Smelter Trust. Ore reduction in Colorado now was big business; the smelters that handled the telluride gold ores of Cripple Creek alone composed a major segment of the state's industry. The early Colorado smelters had been relatively small affairs, centered near the mining camps. As coke replaced wood as the fuel for the reduction operations, many plants had been relocated, and others had been built, in cities where railroad transportation eased the problem of fuel supply. Denver and Pueblo both had become important smelting centers, although cities closer to the ore sources, such as Leadville and Durango, also were famous for their reduction works.

In the year 1899, on April 4, Coloradans learned that this scene had been radically altered. On that day the largest smelting concerns, not just in the state but across the country, had joined together to form the American Smelting and Refining Company. Capitalized at $65 million, incorporated in New Jersey, this gigantic combination encompassed the Colorado Smelting Company and the Pueblo Smelting Company plants at Pueblo, the Durango Smelter at Durango, the Omaha and Grant and the Globe Smelters at Denver, and the Arkansas Valley and Bi-metallic

Built in 1882, the Omaha and Grant Smelter joined the American Smelting and Refining Company in 1899, about the time Denver photographer Harry H. Buckwalter took this picture.

Smelters at Leadville in addition to eleven companies located in other states. Coloradans also soon learned that one of the leading spirits behind the combination was H. H. Rogers, representing the interests of the Standard Oil Company, notorious in antitrust circles as the first American trust.

Such a huge combination, with control of so many of the country's smelters and reduction mills, presumably would be able to monopolize the industry, arranging prices and wages at will. But at the beginning, there was one important unit not included in the merger. The Guggenheims had not joined; their Pueblo smelter, the Philadelphia Smelting and Refining Company, along with their Mexican and Perth Amboy works, remained outside. It was rumored that the Guggenheims refused $11 million for their properties; commentators guessed that the family decided that too many of the merged concerns were unprofitable. The thing to do was to wait until these had been reorganized or eliminated.

However, negotiations between the trust and the family continued; within two years the monopoly was complete. In 1901 the Guggenheim brothers agreed to exchange their properties for one-third of the American Smelting and Refining Company's stock. They had also managed to purchase more than one-sixth of the trust's stock on the open market. They now controlled the trust.

Miners, mine owners, laborers in smelters and refineries, and consumers generally found much to fear in the trust. And if the American Smelting and Refining Company was the largest and most dramatic illustration of the new industrial concept, it was only one of several such examples. A related concern was the dramatic interjection of "outside" control and manipulation of "domestic" enterprises. As a frontier region, Colorado traditionally had looked to the East for investment capital; it would continue to do so. But a growing recognition that loss of control naturally followed outside investment alarmed many people, particularly laborers.

Anyone who had watched the dramatic battles for control of the Colorado Fuel and Iron Company at Pueblo, with its many ore and coal mines, should have been aware of the trends. John C. Osgood, who had headed the company since its formation in 1892, first engaged in a titanic struggle to retain control against the assaults led by financier John W. Gates. That battle had hardly been won when a second engagement pitted Osgood against E. H. Harriman. This time Osgood needed help and found it in the financial strength of John D. Rockefeller and George J. Gould. But "like the Briton of old, these two men . . . proved to be his Hengest and Horsa, for although he succeeded with their assistance in defeating his antagonist, he no sooner threw himself free from his grip than he found himself overshadowed by his allies, to whose influence he was obliged to succumb." With Osgood's retirement a short time later, Colorado's largest single industrial enterprise fell to "alien" control.

The industrial empire of the Colorado Fuel and Iron Company extended into ore mines and coalfields, particularly the southern fields around Trinidad where the best coking coals in the state were found. Corporate control of those coalfields accompanied the changes in ownership of the parent corporation. Much the same sort of consolidation occurred in other Colorado coalfields, for railroads had opened and operated many fields, and railroads, too, were pawns in the merger games.

The Panic of 1893 carried many of the region's railroads into receivership. On their emergence they took new, consolidated forms. An example was the Colorado and Southern Railway Company, incorporated in 1893. Into this new system were merged several historic Colorado roads: the old Colorado Central, the Denver Pacific, the Kansas Pacific, the South Park, the Denver and Fort Worth. Ten years after its formation, a further consolidation took place when the Burlington Railroad purchased the Colorado and Southern.

Another illustration can be seen in the history of General Palmer's Rio Grande Railroad. George Gould, the eldest son of financier Jay Gould, in 1901, became president of the Denver and Rio Grande's board of directors. Gould owned the Missouri Pacific system and he now pushed consolidation of the Rio Grande and the Rio Grande Western (the Utah extension of the Colorado road) with his other properties.

Just how difficult it was for a newcomer to compete against large corporate enterprises was well demonstrated when David H. Moffat decided to build a new railroad in the state. Moffat's credit rating, seemingly, should have insured him success, for his interests in the First National Bank of Denver and other banks and his investments in the Denver Tramway Corporation provided a reservoir of proven financial strength. Added to that was the profit from his sale of the Florence and Cripple Creek Railroad, which he had owned. But there was immense hostility to his scheme of driving a road—the Denver, Northwestern and Pacific—across Rollins Pass toward Salt Lake City.

Capitalized in 1902, at $20 million, Moffat's road reached Gore Canyon across the Continental Divide by 1907. Four years later Moffat died, his entire fortune invested in the endeavor and the railroad still not constructed to the coalfields of Routt County. Financial distress sent the road into receivership in 1912, leading to reorganization as the Denver and Salt Lake Railroad Company. Moffat had built the road over passes with extremely high grades, escalating operating costs. He had always considered this a temporary necessity. Some day a tunnel through the Continental Divide would be built to accommodate trains. From 1913 onward, after it became apparent that the revenue from the railroad alone would never be adequate to finance a tunnel, state aid for the construction was sought.

Paralleling the concentration of economic power in corporations was the gathering strength of organized labor. In this, the Colorado experience resembled the national pattern, except perhaps for the fact that the Colorado unions displaying the most "muscle" did not include the American Federation of Labor. Under the leadership of Samuel Gompers, the AFL had become the foremost organization of skilled workers in other parts of the country. In Denver and other towns, craftsmen had federated with the AFL. But other unions had organized the mining camps and smelters, where skilled workers formed only a small minority of the total labor force.

In the hardrock mining camps, the Western Federation of Miners had followed its early victory at Cripple Creek with rapid growth. In 1902, of the 165 local units of the Western Federation, 42 were to be found in Colorado, and the headquarters of the union was located in Denver. The coalfields of the state, however, were considered the province of the United Mine Workers of America, a national, industrial union that encompassed eastern, as well as western, coal miners.

Certain conditions, more or less peculiar to the Colorado scene, contributed to the explosiveness of the contests between capital and labor. One element was the number of unskilled laborers employed in the coalfields, gold mines, and smelting works. Newly arrived immigrants and unemployed workers could always be recruited into the ranks of nonunion workers during times of crisis. Thus, in many instances, the struggle between mine owners and labor unions focused on the question of hiring nonunion labor—a struggle on the part of the mine owners to import such workers and an equally desperate struggle on the part of the unions to intimidate, or drive off by physical force, the nonunion workers.

Another contributing feature of the Colorado economy was the relatively large degree of "paternalism" inherent in the mining industries (especially coal), which the unions came to resist and which the mine owners hoped to continue. Mines had often been opened in remote, inaccessible areas, where companies provided housing and stores. What began as a convenience developed into methods of control. The limitations of freedom for the worker who lived in company housing, bought groceries at the company store, perhaps was paid in company "scrip" (that is, paper currency valid only at the company store) came to be resented, and one of the objectives of the unions was to help workers untie the strings binding them to the company facilities.

An additional cause of stress in the Colorado industrial scene was the aftermath of the economic depression of the 1890s. While most of the rest of the nation bounced back into vigorous prosperity, the Colorado mining picture remained troubled. Cripple Creek gold found ready markets, but silver prices never recovered. Between 1900 and 1910 silver sold for prices ranging from 52¢ to 68¢ an ounce, far below the nineteenth-century levels.

Both capital and labor viewed the battle as occurring simultaneously on two fronts: legislative and direct action. Both sides engaged in attempts to persuade the General Assembly to enact statutes providing substantive gains or defenses against their opponent's actions. Labor, for example, was able to succeed in its campaigns for the establishment of a Bureau of Labor Statistics (charged primarily with enforcing labor legislation) in 1887; an antiblacklist law, in the same year; two statutes (1897 and 1899) allowing combinations of laborers to exist outside the conspiracy statutes but *not* including the "right" of collective bargaining; a semimonthly pay act, in 1901; and an eight-hour-day constitutional amendment, in 1902. Capital, however, convinced the legislature in 1899 that combinations of laborers should not be allowed to deter employees from continuing work if they wished or to boycott or intimidate employers. In 1905 the legislature also met demands of employers in providing that picketing or any method of obstructing or interfering with any worker's job was illegal.

The legislative battles often did not end in the chambers of the General Assembly. Laws on statute books and laws litigated often were very different. Both capital and labor defended their legislation in the courts; one of labor's constant refrains was that the bench was filled by conservative, business-allied judges who interpreted statutes for the benefit of employers.

The two groups also battled each other in more direct ways. The union, once established in an industry or mine, sought to convince the owners that since its voice represented the will of the workers, it should be allowed to bargain collectively for the work contract. To gain such recognition from the owners became the primary objective of most of the unions during these years; once that was achieved, the substantive details of labor contracts—hours, wages, conditions of work—could be negotiated. The strength of the union, and in its eyes, the welfare of the worker, thus depended on the ability of the union leaders to force recognition and the process of collective bargaining.

Employers were equally intent in their refusal to recognize the legitimacy of the union's demands for recognition. Denying completely the concept of collective bargaining, employers insisted that their relationship with each worker was an individual contract and on that basis only would the worker's right exist. The strike was the ultimate weapon (except for violence, which all too often characterized the ultimate method on both sides) in the hands of the union; by calling the workers out on strike the unions tried to force owners into negotiation. Owners tended to look upon strikebreakers, or nonunion workers, as an equally valid weapon. Let the union people leave their jobs; other workers would be glad to replace them, and the union would disintegrate.

Such concepts were well illustrated in the Telluride strike of 1901. The owners of the Smuggler-Union Mines refused to negotiate with the Western Federation of Miners in a dispute concerning the "contract system" of pay, which the union wanted abolished. The operators hired strikebreakers on exactly the same terms denied to the union. Finally, Federation members literally drove the nonunion workers from the district. Although the violent methods employed captured newspaper headlines, the significance of the event centers on the fact that the question of working conditions or wages was less an issue than union recognition.

In between, or perhaps above, the interest of labor and capital stood the general public's concern. Theoretically, this concern could be represented best by the duly elected officials of the community and state. All too often, however, the local authorities proved impotent to deal with the violence engendered, and state officials tended to be prejudiced in their action. Sometimes the prejudice, suspected or real, was directed to the side of the union, as many citizens believed was true during the Cripple Creek difficulties of 1894 under Governor Waite's administration. The unions believed, however, that more often the pattern of the company's call for protection and the penetration of the strike zone by the state militia (with an accompanying declaration of martial law) worked to the unions' disadvantage.

Industrial warfare erupted in many incidents during the years from 1894 to 1914, and a common pattern seemed to develop in most of the episodes. The specific complaint that led to the strike might vary; wages, hours, working conditions, or any combination might be the spark setting off the clash. The resolution of the strikes varied, depending on the strength of the union, its ability to control its members, the determination of the mine or mill owners and their ability to keep their properties operating with nonunion labor, and—often to a large extent—the climate of public opinion and the attitude and actions of the governor and the militia leaders. Notwithstanding these variables, the general patterns can be seen by examining, as illustrations, the strikes of 1903–1904 at Cripple Creek and the coalfield disturbances of 1910–1914.

The years 1903 and 1904 were punctuated by outbreaks of labor difficulties. Denver smelters and mines in Idaho Springs and San Miguel

County were struck for eight-hour-day contracts; coal diggers in both northern and southern fields engaged in strikes. But it was at Cripple Creek that the bitterest and most violent of the crises occurred, and it was there that the Western Federation of Miners suffered a major defeat. The Cripple Creek fields were still prosperous; they also were highly organized, on both sides. Under the dynamic leadership of Charles H. Moyer and "Big Bill" Haywood, the Western Federation had enlisted the majority of the fields' miners. The owners of the properties had organized a Mine Owners' Association. And in the governor's chair was James H. Peabody, a Canon City businessman destined to become a central figure in the conflict.

It was in the reduction works at Colorado City, where Cripple Creek ore was processed, rather than in the goldfields themselves, that the battle originated. The Western Federation of Miners, eager to complete its membership rolls among the mill workers, called out 3,500 Cripple Creek miners in a sympathetic strike to force union recognition in the mills. Although these preliminary difficulties in the summer of 1903, on the surface, seemed settled, the trouble had only begun. Soon the mill workers were out again, this time to secure a reduction from twelve to eight hours of work a day. By the end of October the gold miners were also on strike again.

As the mine operators imported nonunion labor from outside the district, the union formed armed camps to barricade the roads and railroads leading into the fields. After an appeal to Governor Peabody, the mine owners welcomed an investigatory committee and, immediately afterward, on its recommendation, the governor dispatched the militia to Cripple Creek. In his inaugural address in 1903, Peabody had pledged to protect lives and property. Those sympathetic to labor, however, felt that he shared the business community's hostility toward, and directed the power of his office against, the union.

Both sides recognized the value of propaganda in enlisting favorable public support, and soon more direct techniques appeared, even some that now presumably were illegal. The Western Federation published "scab lists" with pictures and descriptions of nonunion workers in a clear attempt to intimidate the strikebreakers by inviting retaliatory measures against them. The mine owners instituted a card system, blacklisting members of the union from further employment in the district.

As the strike continued it became warfare for unconditional surrender. Terror reigned in Cripple Creek as both miners and mine operators moved from intimidation and threatened violence to violence itself—raw and brutal. The climax was reached on June 6, 1904, when Harry Orchard, a professional terrorist in the employ of the union, dynamited the railroad station at Independence. Orchard had timed his foul deed to occur when a maximum number of strikebreakers would be present; his handiwork resulted in thirteen deaths and many more wounded among the nonunion workers. Although Orchard's identity as the perpetrator of the crime was unknown, each side blamed the other for the murders. The mine operators' strongmen now moved in, wrecking the office and plant of the *Victor Record*, a newspaper that had remained friendly to the union, rounding up strikers in wholesale lots, confining them in the infamous "bull pens" of the district, and driving many of them out of the camp. Seventy-three men were dispatched, under guard, to the Kansas border and there abandoned on the prairie.

Revulsion over the violence (for which the public blamed the union more than the owners), the continued support of the militia, and the drastic employment of martial law, along with the help of the Citizens' Alliance, all led to an operators' victory. By midsummer 1904, the strike was over, although the Western Federation of Miners never did terminate it officially. The owners reopened their mines with nonunion labor, and although the federation would later attempt to reestablish its locals in the area, it never again assumed its former significance in Cripple Creek.

In the years that followed this terror-filled strike, Colorado would experience continuing industrial warfare. But not until 1914, a full decade later, did violence again reach such heights. Then the scene shifted, from the goldfields of Cripple Creek to the coal mines of the state. For some years the United Mine Workers of America had engaged in sporadic strikes in both northern and southern coalfields. These were now climaxed, in September 1913, by an all-out effort. When the southern miners voted their strike, they listed as demands the recognition of their union, a 10 percent increase in wages, stricter enforcement of the Colorado eight-hour law, health and safety regulations, and the right to select their own living quarters, eating houses, and doctors.

John Lawson assumed the leadership of the Colorado units of the United Mine Workers. He was aided during the strike by the best talents among the union's national organizers, including the spectacular Mary Harris, the miners' Mother Jones—an eighty-two-year-old Socialist.

The usual pattern of events began to unfold. The mine operators, with the Colorado Fuel and Iron Company acting as speaker for the

Miners and their families in a tent camp during the 1913–1914 strike.

group, attempted to open their properties with nonunion labor; the miners bent every effort to keep the strikebreakers out of the fields. The owners hurried appeals to the statehouse; the governor sent the militia to the region. As the striking miners withdrew from the underground works, they formed tent colonies near the mines where they and their families were sustained by union funds.

Tension in the fields mounted and violence seemed inevitable as the soldiers sent to guard the properties and the miners living nearby scuffled with each other. The climax came on April 20, 1914, at Ludlow Station, eighteen miles north of Trinidad. When miners and militiamen tangled, the soldiers began to drive the miners from their tent colony, which housed about 900 men, women, and children. Five miners and one militiaman were killed; but even worse, fire burned through the colony and it was later discovered that two women and eleven children had been burned to death or suffocated in what the United Mine Workers immediately labeled the Ludlow Massacre.

And this was not the end, for a ten-day war of "burnings, dynamitings, and murders" engulfed the coalfields. Governor Elias Ammons decided that the situation was beyond state control and appealed to President Woodrow Wilson for help. By April 30 a contingent of U.S. troops reached Trinidad, ready to replace the militia.

With uneasy quiet enforced by the army, negotiations proceeded. The strike officially ended in December 1914. The United Mine Workers settled for less than complete victory. It was refused bargaining rights and withdrew from the Colorado coalfields, leaving the miners still unorganized. But the miners did realize substantive gains in protected conditions of work, better hours, and higher pay.

To replace the union the miners were denied, the Colorado Fuel and Iron Company established a "company union," which purported to give a vehicle for voicing workers' grievances. Hailed by many at the time as a sensible compromise to the labor disturbances that had rocked the state for more than two decades, the Rockefeller Plan in time demonstrated the flaws that trade unionists had always objected to in company unions. Despite the generous welcome that greeted the plan at its inception, it proved in many ways a weak friend to laborers.

TWENTY-FOUR

WATER AND SUGAR

The gold mines and coalfields were not the only Colorado arenas of change during the first years of the new century; agricultural techniques were also being transformed. More quiet than their counterparts in industry and mining, the agricultural changes were no less important. Both in the irrigable river valleys and on the dry-farming regions of the high plains, innovations wrought an evolution in crops and methods of cultivation that made farming in the Centennial State quite different from what it had been before.

The most apparent change on the arid plains during the first years of the twentieth century was the renewed interest of homesteaders in conquering the challenges of the Great American Desert. The new assault on the drylands was a much more sober, rational process than that which had occurred in the 1880s. Then enthusiasms had been buoyed by false hopes about shifting rainbelts and other impossible ideas. Now, as deserted homesteads that had been forsaken during early discouragements were taken up again, there was more understanding of the problems faced. Not all of the original settlers had moved out, of course. Some sturdy souls had managed to sustain themselves through the years of drought. But many of the farms had been left to revert to open range;

many of the sodhouses and shanties had begun to tumble and decay. Now the exodus had halted and the land began to fill up again.

Pioneering on the high plains would always be hard work. There were no shortcuts to success. But to a people who had grown up with a seemingly inexhaustible supply of free land, what was left of the frontier remained a place of promise to those who aspired, despite all the hardships, to success. American society still applauded the initiative and energy of the self-made, small farmer. From time to time the newspapers of the day would demonstrate that although it was fading fast, the American dream of an agrarian yeomanry still existed. For example, readers of a Denver newspaper undoubtedly applauded one Henry Engle "who lives near Kiowa . . . an example of what a man can accomplish on a homestead in a short time. Mr. Engle took up a homestead about six years ago, with a capital of one dollar and a half, and a family of eight children to support. He now owns his home, is out of debt, and has the following stock: Eighteen head of cattle, five horses, eleven hogs, and a lot of chickens and ducks."

To help homesteaders like Henry Engle, the resources of several public agencies were available. Both the state Agricultural College and the federal government, through its Department of Agriculture, experimented with seeds, soils, and methods of cultivation. From these experiments certain drought-resisting crops were propagated; new strains of seeds were evolved; tillage methods were studied until those best suited to the arid plains were recognized and encouraged. Thus the techniques of scientific dry farming spread. The farmers plowed their land deeply after each harvest, and after each rainfall they pulverized the top soil by disking to keep it free from weeds and, at the same time, to prevent evaporation of precious moisture into the spongelike atmosphere. Some farmers left half their soil uncropped but tilled throughout the summer months each year. Through the publications of the Department of Agriculture, the work of the state dry-land experiment station at Cheyenne Wells (dating from 1893) and the federal station by Akron (begun in 1907), and agencies like the International Dry Farming Congress (organized in Denver in 1907 and meeting in yearly sessions), the new approaches were publicized.

Since some farmers planted only half of their acreage each year, the dry-farming techniques emphasized anew the inadequacies of the national land laws. Larger expanses of land were an absolute necessity in the arid plains region. In 1909 the Enlarged Homestead Act revised the basic homestead unit from 160 to 320 acres. In 1916 a further modification allowed a full section of land (640 acres) under the Stockraising Homestead Act. This act was intended to offer grazers an opportunity to obtain ranch lands in desirable quantity. However, the action was "too little, too late"; more than a section was necessary to run even small-sized herds.

Nonetheless, the importance of homestead legislation in the development of Colorado should not be minimized. In the years from 1868 to 1961, homestead entries in the state totaled 107,618, involving 22,146,400 acres of land. Only Montana and North Dakota totaled more entries; only Montana and Nebraska recorded more acres of land taken up.

An indication of the effect of the land laws and the development of dry farming and ranch cattle industries can be seen by comparing population statistics from the 1900 and 1910 censuses. Kiowa, Kit Carson, Washington, Yuma, Lincoln, and Cheyenne Counties all showed remarkable increases in population, ranging from 313 percent increase in Kiowa County to a startling 635 percent in Cheyenne County.

Significant changes also were taking place in the irrigable valleys of Colorado. The legal structure of the doctrine of prior appropriation had already been gained. Now irrigators called upon the state to allow the creation of "district" irrigation projects. Individual, or even community, efforts, in many cases, were no longer sufficient to construct and maintain the larger projects desired. At the same time, investors of risk capital and corporations, which had been interested in financing such projects at an earlier time, had discovered that the dividends, if any, were slow in accumulating from such investments. Many of the privately capitalized irrigation projects built in the 1880s had gone into bankruptcy during the depression of the 1890s. The owners of the lands served by the canals and ditches took over the physical assets of the defunct corporations. Those farmers now desired legislation that would allow them to maintain and expand the systems.

The General Assembly responded in 1901 with the District Irrigation Law. It allowed land owners to organize irrigation districts capable of purchasing or constructing canals and reservoirs. These districts could issue bonds to raise capital and could levy taxes on the land served in order to pay off the indebtedness. The legislature also created the position of state engineer, an official charged with ascertaining equitable and regular water distribution.

Increasingly, irrigators looked to the state as a partner, an arbitrator, and a patron of their institutions. And the state seemed ready to accept that relationship. This became very apparent in 1901 when Kansas, on behalf of some of its citizens, brought suit against Colorado and sixteen large users of water from the Arkansas River. In the legal proceedings that followed, the state of Colorado took the initiative in preparing the defense of both the state and the private defendants against the Kansas charges. The *Kansas* vs. *Colorado* litigation over the distribution of water flowing in the Arkansas River also demonstrated the fact that water was becoming scarcer in the West. Where once individual towns or residents would argue about the equitable division of stream waters, now states were engaging in similar controversy. The importance of the litigation was apparently understood from the beginning; the *Rocky Mountain News* called it "the most important case . . . that ever reached the supreme court from a state west of the Mississippi."

The justices of the Supreme Court of the United States undoubtedly learned a lot about western agriculture before they had finished considering the Kansas-Colorado case. Kansas had been settled from its eastern edges inward, and its earliest settlers had enjoyed natural rainfall sufficient for cultivating their crops. As a result, the state had followed the common law rules of riparian rights. Colorado had rejected the older law and had adopted the doctrine of prior appropriation. Thus, two different systems of state water law collided.

Kansas claimed that its western lands were deprived of their natural waters from the Arkansas River because Colorado farmers and industries were diverting the entire flow of the river. Colorado argued that under its prior appropriation code, the earliest users of water had preference and that "thousands of cubic feet of water were used from the Arkansas . . . by farmers in Colorado . . . before there were settlers enough in western . . . Kansas to build an irrigation ditch, and when their people within the line of sufficient rainfall were boasting that they did not need to irrigate to grow crops . . . the water they rejected was appropriated by the farmers along the base of the Rocky Mountains."

The national government also became interested in the case. In fact, because the value of federal lands in the two states might be affected by the Supreme Court's decision, the federal government intervened in the suit. The question of national power, expressed through either the executive or legislative branches, as a possible regulator or mediator in dividing interstate river waters, was considered in the arguments. But the

Supreme Court rejected the suggestion. In the opinion, handed down in 1907, the justices specifically asserted that each state had complete control of the waters within its boundaries. This not only denied federal control of interstate stream waters; it seemed to give an advantage to Colorado, for Kansas was denied relief on the basis of the evidence presented at that time. In the future, should new evidence arise, Kansas could reopen the suit.

The opinion pointed new directions; the court, in effect, announced that it was to be *the* federal agency to decide such contests. In order to provide justice in quarrels between states, the court would undertake to determine similar controversies in the future, thus originating what came to be called the "doctrine of equitable apportionment." The Supreme Court seemed to say that regardless of the water law practiced in different states, each state had a right to some of the water in the rivers within its boundaries. In essence, the tribunal struck a severe blow at the concept of a state disposing of all the water within its borders, no matter how old the appropriations from the stream might be. Warning flags were now up; the Supreme Court would umpire future quarrels between states over irrigation water.

Colorado irrigators discovered in time what the new doctrine could mean in actual practice. The Laramie River flows north from Colorado into Wyoming. When Colorado irrigators in the Poudre Valley, on the Eastern Slope, began to construct a new tunnel to divert water from the Laramie River, Wyoming residents claimed that the additional diversion would interfere with their appropriations. The argument terminated in a lawsuit (*State of Wyoming* v. *State of Colorado*) instituted before the Supreme Court in 1911, with a decision delayed until 1922. There was no quarrel here between two different systems of water law; both states recognized the doctrine of prior appropriation. Rather, the argument concerned the quantity of water used by residents of the two states.

In the Kansas litigation, the Supreme Court had announced its equitable apportionment doctrine, implying that the substantive decision as to which state got what water might fall within the jurisdiction of the court later. The justices now proceeded, in the Wyoming case, to act on their former suggestion. After considering the evidence, they awarded the quantity of water they determined had been appropriated by Wyoming users to farmers there, allowing the new Colorado irrigators the remainder of the unappropriated flow, or not more than 15,500 acre-feet a year.

The handwriting was now plainly visible. Colorado might enjoy the fact that major rivers—the Colorado, Rio Grande, Arkansas, North and South Platte, and many of their tributaries—originated within the state, but in apportionment of water between Colorado and its neighboring states through which the rivers flowed, the Supreme Court would determine equity. More than that: The costly process of defending the state's rights in litigation before the court would continue to drain its finances and energy. No wonder these decisions provided great impetus for the negotiation of interstate compacts, or "treaties," by which the states themselves, with approval from the federal government, divided the flow of the interstate streams.

But while Colorado and the other western states soon indicated that they preferred to bargain around the conference table for their share of interstate waters, casting off judicial arrangements, those same states eagerly invited the help of the federal government in other aspects of reclamation and irrigation development. The quarrels between states over water were only another indication of the growing scarcity of the precious resource. The shorter the supply of available water, the more complex and costly became its proper management and use. By the turn of the century many westerners had come to anticipate a partnership with the national Department of the Interior in water affairs.

By that time, it was obvious that large projects, especially those involving transmontane carriage of water, would require greater financial resources than either private capital or state funds could offer. The era of huge dams and reservoirs would never appear if left to private investors, who shunned such projects because of the long period of waiting for dividends. State efforts at reclamation also had been less than successful. There had long been hope that the federal government, in some fashion, would encourage reclamation of desert lands. When Congress enacted the Desert Land Act in 1877, something of a beginning had been made. Settlers could claim a full section of land if they agreed to irrigate their holdings. But that legislation never greatly furthered reclamation.

Later Congress again responded to pleas for a comprehensive program of reclamation. The Carey Act of 1894 attempted a policy of federal-state partnerships. Up to 1 million acres of arid land in each western state were to be separated from the public domain and given to the states as a reward for their causing irrigation and occupation of the land. No federal funds were involved; the initiative was left to each state. But the states proved reluctant to join the partnership. Out of a total possible 7 million acres, only about 300,000 acres were actually withdrawn, demonstrating that something more tempting in the way of federal aid would have to be arranged to generate a vigorous policy of reclamation.

Thus far the record was discouraging, but those who believed that western deserts were as legitimately a congressional concern as sand-filled eastern harbors or tariff-begging midwestern manufacturers continued to press for federal aid. When, in 1901, Theodore Roosevelt became president of the United States, they recognized in the new chief executive a friend of the West, of conservation, and of reclamation, too. They were not disappointed in their anticipations. Congress now enacted, and the president signed, the epoch-opening statute of 1902—the Newlands Act.

This legislation provided that from a Reclamation Fund, to be amassed from the proceeds of the sale of public lands in sixteen western states, surveys, construction, and maintenance of irrigation works for storage, diversion, or transmission of water were to be initiated. The projects approved by the Department of the Interior were to be repaid by assessments on the reclaimed land in the form of use fees for water delivered. The payments would create a revolving fund from which the initial costs of other projects could be financed. Later, other legislation would bring more dollars to the fund from oil and mineral royalties. And, in 1911, the Warren Act expanded the concept by allowing surplus waters from federal projects to be sold for use on land already irrigated but suffering from insufficient water. This legislation was extremely significant for many parts of Colorado where irrigation had been instituted early, but enough water for full agricultural development had never been available.

As soon as the Department of the Interior, under the terms of the Newlands Act, established the Reclamation Bureau, one Colorado group presented plans for a project. On the Western Slope, in the valley of the Uncompahgre River, there existed an ideal situation for a pilot project. The original settlers in the valley had anticipated that the waters of the river would be sufficient to bring 175,000 acres under irrigation, but they had been sorely disappointed. By 1902 only 30,000 acres were actually being watered and often there was insufficient river flow to adequately irrigate those acres.

The Gunnison River flows parallel to the Uncompahgre River, just across the Vernal Mesa; the two streams join at Delta. But the lands to be

An early irrigating canal in the Uncompahgre Valley of western Colorado.

irrigated were above rather than below Delta. Unlike the Uncompahgre Valley above Delta, the Gunnison Valley has little land suitable for irrigation. From these circumstances arose the scheme of tunneling through Vernal Mesa to bring Gunnison water to the Uncompahgre Valley.

The scheme was no novelty in 1902. The Colorado legislature had been convinced of the practicability of the idea and had appropriated $25,000 to build a tunnel, but that sum had proved hopelessly small. Thus, it was natural to turn to the new Reclamation Bureau, which agreed to undertake the construction and maintenance of the diversion project, if the present and future residents on the irrigated lands paid for its costs through water use fees.

Under bureau approval, construction began in 1904. A decade and a half were required to fully complete the 5.8-mile tunnel and the extensive network of canals. But diversion of water did not wait for completion of the entire system. By 1910 water from the Gunnison River reached the Uncompahgre Valley. Problems would plague the residents there for years to come—construction costs had far exceeded estimates;

use fees for water required several adjustments; lands included in the original plans proved too alkaline or otherwise unfit for irrigation. But despite all the problems, the project was, and is, memorable as the earliest of the federally sponsored reclamation endeavors in Colorado.

Northwest of the Uncompahgre Valley, in the vicinity of Grand Junction, the Reclamation Bureau pioneered a second Colorado project. Here settlers had begun reclaiming arid lands in the early 1880s. In fact, the irrigation facilities were quite highly developed, with almost all the bottom lands of the Colorado River already under ditches and initial endeavors at pumping water to the higher lands underway. In 1902 surveys were made for the possible expansion of the system, but local interests then were averse to seeking federal aid, preferring continuation of development through private investment. Within the decade, however, the slow progress reversed sentiments, and the residents requested that the bureau intervene. After completing additional surveys, the bureau constructed a dam and canal system. The major canal stretched sixty-two miles along the valley; by 1917 the project became operable for water deliveries.

One of the many reasons for excitement over the expansion of established irrigation systems and the building of new facilities was the promising prospects for sugar beet culture. Probably no other single agricultural advance in the state, during the first part of the twentieth century, generated more enthusiasm. Yet the story of Colorado sugar beet dreams was far from new. Antiquarians take pleasure in pointing out that decades earlier, at the time when petitioners requested land grants from Mexico, those who were first given the Maxwell Grant had suggested that one of the advantages arising from their patent would be the cultivation of sugar beets on the land. They received the grant but evidently made no effort to grow the beets.

Then, shortly after the gold rush of 1859, pioneer farmers in the valley of Clear Creek grew some beets that were analyzed as of high quality and high sugar content. What was needed to develop a full-scale sugar industry was a factory to process the beets. The *Greeley Tribune* predicted that "a fortune awaits the man, or men, who will erect a sugar factory." For a time it was hoped that the state would play patron; in 1872 a bill granting a subsidy of $10,000 to the first beet factory in the territory failed in the assembly by one vote.

The faculty of the Agricultural College at Fort Collins continued to encourage the industry. In 1892 a sugar convention in Denver aroused interest from that city's chamber of commerce. Together with the college and the federal Department of Agriculture, the Denver chamber distributed beet seed to farmers, with promised prizes for the best results. Successful beet plants at Grand Island, Nebraska, and Lehi, Utah, stimulated interest. But if a fully developed sugar enterprise were to succeed, factories nearer the fields were essential in order to keep transportation costs from devouring all the profits.

A number of individuals merit special attention as originators of the Colorado sugar beet industry. Charles E. Mitchell and Charles N. Cox were particularly influential as promoters of a factory in the Grand Junction area. They succeeded in gaining a grant of funds from Mesa County to encourage the enterprise. John Campion, who had been fortunate in his mining activities in Leadville, supported the Grand Junction and other factories. Charles Boettcher became interested in beet sugar on a trip to Germany. He brought seed back to Colorado for distribution to farmers, finding excellent results in the irrigated regions of the South Platte Valley. He and Campion would work together in factory-building there. In the Arkansas Valley, George W. Swink of Rocky Ford, better known in Colorado agriculture as "the father of the cantaloupe," was a major exponent of the new industry.

The first sugar beet factory was erected in Grand Junction in 1899 by the Colorado Sugar Manufacturing Company. The returns were not as exciting as expected, and the plant continued somewhat disappointing after 1913 when the Western Sugar and Land Company purchased it. Results more closely matched expectations in the Eastern Slope installations, beginning with the American Beet Sugar Company's factory at Sugar City the same year. In 1901 the originators of the Grand Junction plant opened the first South Platte Valley factory at Loveland. The Greeley and Eaton facilities opened in 1902 and those at Fort Collins, Longmont, and Windsor the following year. Not all the towns were open-armed in welcome; some Greeley residents, for example, protested against the factory there because they feared that it would turn their town into an "industrial center."

As these plants were being built in the first decade of the twentieth century, hundreds of German-Russian families came to the South Platte and Arkansas River Valleys to labor in the sugar beet fields and factories. Descended from Germans who had first migrated to Russia in the eighteenth century, these thrifty and hard-working farmers often later purchased the land they worked. Today those who trace their ancestry to

Sugar beet factories were a familiar sight in many eastern Colorado towns. This facility was in Longmont.

these settlers compose the second-largest ethnic group in Colorado, and evidences of the German-Russian culture can still be seen in the homes and churches of many eastern Colorado communities.

In 1905 most of the South Platte Valley factories were consolidated in ownership and management into the Great Western Sugar Company. The leaders of this New Jersey–chartered corporation, capitalized at $20 million, included pioneers in the state's sugar industry like Charles Boettcher and Chester Morey, and others like H. O Havemeyer of the American Sugar Refining Company. Other Coloradans organized the Holly Sugar Corporation that same year. Its Colorado properties were centered, at first, in the Arkansas Valley at Swink (1906) and Holly (later moved to Wyoming). Later incorporated under a New York charter, the Holly Company bought and built factories in California, Wyoming, and Montana, as well as a plant at Delta, which opened in 1920.

The "sugar vision" was so exciting during those years that many Colorado communities caught the infection. In 1911–1913 the "virus" spread to the San Luis Valley where several factories proved short-lived ventures. But many of the plants continued their early successes; the rapidity of the industry's growth can be seen in the production values, which rose from a mere $100,000 in 1899 to $3,600,000 in 1901. By 1909, with 79,000 acres devoted to beet cultivation, Colorado became the leading producer among the states. The high altitude, cool weather, and controlled irrigation of the state's fields gave the industry elements that would continue the Colorado sugar industry among the first ranks in the nation. Beets gave Colorado farmers a fine cash crop, even though the continued prosperity of the industry would always rest upon tariff makers in the national capital and their willingness to protect the industry from foreign competition.

TWENTY-FIVE

THE PROGRESSIVE ERA

The history of almost any state in the American Union during any decade or generation may reflect the history of the nation itself, despite distortions that local conditions or traditions may provide. Certainly this is true of Colorado during the years from 1900 to 1920. Although Ludlow massacres fortunately did not occur in repetitious fashion in other states, and although transmontane reclamation projects and sugar beet factories could be counted as tokens of regional, local concern, the general pattern of events—and particularly the general aspirations of the population—paralleled those of the rest of the country.

The two decades that ushered in the twentieth century marked the high tide of reform sentiment throughout the United States. Many generations of Americans have been concerned with reforming squalid, corrupt, and evil conditions around them, but few generations have conducted such a vigorous battle on so many fronts at the same time. Few aspects of American life escaped the attention of the reformers; social injustices, economic discriminations, political corruption were all within the compass of their attention. Often these areas were merged, for one of the most immediate concerns of the reformers was the alliance (unholy in their eyes) between entrenched economic interests and the political machinery of government. But to many, this was only the first plateau on which to wage the battle. Once the political institutions had been cleansed and returned to the people for their own use, then social and economic injustices could be legislated away.

As in many other states at the time, the reformers in Colorado campaigned against the corruption in local government. From this opening battle emerged leaders for the larger campaigns to reform the state and eventually, the nation. This was more than a mere contest between entrenched holders of city hall vs. disgruntled "outs" in local politics. The major fight in Colorado centered in the only large city in the state—Denver—where almost everyone admitted public affairs were far from pure.

The reformers in Denver did not give their allegiance to either or any political party. They had long since grown disillusioned with promises by professional partisans that clean, democratic government would result from their being placed in office. For too many years Denverites had witnessed alliances between the franchised utility companies that provided tramway, electric, gas, and other services to the city, and the politicians who inhabited the city hall offices. For too many years elections in Denver had been degrading scenes of corruption, vote-buying, and small armed conflicts between active political partisans. Above all, for too many years Denverites had experienced the unhealthful situation in which state governors and legislators directly controlled the bureaus and boards of the municipality, thereby compounding the evils existing in state and local political life. "City Hall war" was continuous, with dramatic episodes like the battle of Waite's regime in 1894 merely emphasizing the difficulties.

Denver reformers concocted a scheme for action, beginning with a constitutional amendment to allow Denver the right to establish home rule. This change would divorce local politics from the vortex of state affairs. Then in order to eliminate unnecessary expense and to simplify the government of the municipality, they proposed that the City of Denver and the County of Denver be merged into one body politic, with provision for annexation of other areas in the future. In 1904 they presented their plan to the voters, who approved the constitutional amendment in the first major victory for the reformers, or as they soon called themselves, the "progressives."

The first progressive victory led to varied results. For some of the reformers, it was only the first step of a high ladder that would eventually lead through state reforms to national and even international goals. To others, home rule for Denver was the ultimate goal itself. It is easy to smile at the utopian dreams of those who believed that once the *procedures* of government had been changed, all would be well. We now know that these same people would soon discover that the battle never ended; that corruption might retreat, only to reemerge another day. Nonetheless, some notable achievements seemed to result from the successes of the Denver progressives.

Robert W. Speer became the first mayor of the newly organized City and County of Denver. His administration would greatly change the city's physical appearance. Denver's park system was expanded, with new boulevards and parkways laid out, viaducts built, and storm and sanitary sewers constructed. The old city dump along the streambed of Cherry Creek was cleaned up; the gulch was walled and landscaped. Construction of the city auditorium was begun, to be near enough completion in time to host the only national political nominating convention that ever gathered in Denver—the Democratic convention of 1908. In addition, the basic plan of Denver's Civic Center was blueprinted, aided greatly in design by Henry Read, the president of the newly formed Denver Art Commission. And to the west the city began to acquire the areas of mountain lands that would form the nucleus for the future municipal mountain park system.

Despite the accomplishments of the Speer administration, his opponents asserted that the mayor and his followers manipulated elections and were too closely allied with the corporations—that Speer was, however civic-minded, still a "boss." Moreover, Assessor Henry J. Arnold, who had come into office in 1910 as a Speer Democrat, charged that Denver's assessing system was discriminatory and riddled with inequities. Opposition to Speer crystallized late in 1911 when he summarily removed Arnold from his position. In the election of 1912, Arnold, running on the Citizens' ticket for mayor, defeated the Democratic candidate (Speer had chosen not to run) in a seeming repudiation of the mayor's policies. Regardless of the fact that many of Speer's methods were protested by reformers, however, the physical improvements of his administration were impressive. Other changes, less apparent, were also inaugurated. Two of these, in particular, translated progressive ideals into practice: Judge Ben Lindsey's Juvenile Court and Emily Griffith's Opportunity School.

The fame of Judge Ben Lindsey's experiment in social justice for young offenders spread far beyond the boundaries of Denver and

"'Send me, send my dog,' Billy Dunlop sobbed as Judge Lindsey sentenced the boy to the State Industrial School, so Judge Lindsey obliged the youngster by sentencing Trixie along with its master." Thus read the caption when the Denver Post *published this Juvenile Court scene, April 22, 1921.*

Colorado. Convinced that juvenile offenders should be treated separately from adult criminals, Lindsey, in 1907, established a special court for young people. Within a short time he had made his Juvenile Court a model of corrective institutions. His own deep interest in the problems of young wrongdoers in the increasingly complex industrial society helped to sustain the experiment during numerous attacks on it by those who feared that "misty-eyed" reformers had gone too far. Only later, another generation would question the paternalism and the insensitivity to children's rights that Lindsey's court epitomized.

That era's "society savers" were equally impressed by Emily Griffith's Opportunity School. Emily Griffith, a public school teacher in Denver, enlisted the aid of school board members, newspapers, and reformers generally, to establish an educational institution designed to meet the needs of all—children and adults alike—who, for one reason or another, did not fit the scheduled routine of ordinary classrooms. Opened in 1914, the Opportunity School combined many different functions: There were classes for adults who desired to learn such rudimentary subjects as the English language and simple arithmetic; there were shops

Emily Griffith, founder of Opportunity School of Denver.

and training rooms for those who wished to learn trades; night classes and day classes in both academic and vocational studies provided an all-inclusive opportunity for self-improvement.

Denver, of course, was not the only scene of such reform. Other Colorado cities also caught the pervading spirit of "progressivism," responding with experiments in new forms of local government and new campaigns for civic improvement. In fact, it became increasingly apparent during the first decade of the twentieth century that reform ideas were looked upon with favor by many of the Colorado voters. This being the case, partisan politicians considered converting their organizations to vehicles for progressive action.

Not all of the reformers' ideas were that easily handled, however. One, in particular, instilled fear rather than hope among practicing politicians. That was the concept of legislating a prohibition of the manufacture and sale of intoxicating liquor—a concept that gained many adherents during these years. Prohibition was fitted, in many ways, to the pattern of progressive thought. After the prohibitionists changed their emphasis from voluntary action to legislation, they tended to follow the same pattern as did many reformers who planned to use the public power to enact social legislation.

The antiliquor forces took a long time to unite their various programs. Groups like the Anti-Saloon League and the Women's Christian Temperance Union had always believed in gaining voluntary adherents to their cause. The Prohibition Party, however, had pursued a policy of direct legislation. Although the Colorado General Assembly had enacted a "local option" law, the Prohibition Party's efforts—continuous since the 1880s—to achieve statewide proscription of liquor had never met success. Finally the party came to believe that only a constitutional amendment, initiated by petition under new procedures allowed in Colorado, would bring victory.

In 1912 an amendment to prohibit the manufacture and sale of liquor was submitted to the electorate. The voters defeated the proposal, but that defeat stirred the various groups to common action. Submerging their differences, they sponsored another amendment two years later. This time the voters answered the question of ratification affirmatively, approving the experiment in social engineering, despite a two-to-one rejection of the amendment in Denver. The "wet" forces in the capital city threatened to use the new home rule prerogatives of the city to escape the effect of the law, but on January 1, 1916, prohibition became the rule in Denver and all of Colorado.

The liquor question had frightened partisan politicians, partly because the emotionalism on both sides of the issue was difficult to gauge and partly because it tended to blur other issues and to confuse the voters' allegiances. But there were other reform concepts of less danger, and in time many progressive issues became major ingredients of the campaigners' trade. The general atmosphere surrounding partisan politics in Colorado at the turn of the century probably contributed to the willingness of politicians to embrace progressive ideas. Since the last decade of the nineteenth century, when the silver question had burned brightly and fusions of factions had created a variety of temporary alliances, Colorado politics remained unstable and confused. Silver continued to be a political interest in the Centennial State; it brought victories to the Democratic Party in elections, for the Democrats continued to speak with hope of resurrecting bimetallism from the deep grave the McKinley Republicans had placed it in. But "liberalism" on the silver issue did not make the Democratic Party a vehicle for liberal policies generally. In fact, those they placed in the statehouse often were the older, conservative, professional party leaders.

The twentieth century began with a series of Democratic governors: Alva Adams served his second term (1897 to 1899), after which the combined silver and Democratic forces successfully wooed the voters for a two-year term for Charles S. Thomas, who was followed by a third Democrat, James B. Orman. This sequence ended in 1902 when the Republicans won the governorship. James H. Peabody, the new executive, inhabited the governor's office during two years filled with labor difficulties. Governor Peabody's actions, particularly in dispatching the militia to strike areas, set the scene for a bitter political struggle in the fall of 1904. The Democrats, who returned for a third time to their proven popular leader, Alva Adams, caustically criticized Peabody's handling of the Cripple Creek and other strikes. Adams and the Democrats seemingly convinced the majority of Colorado's voters that they would do a better job of ending the industrial warfare than Peabody and the Republicans could do.

The election of 1904 was not that simply ended. Despite Adams's apparent victory, the Republicans, in control of the legislature, insisted that fraud and corruption had dominated the balloting in certain counties. In fact, it seems clear that both parties used methods that prevented a free and open election. Since the legislature was charged with deciding contested seats, the Republicans declared enough vacancies to vote an unseating of Governor Adams. Peabody was then pronounced the victor, but on condition that he resign immediately after taking the oath of office, turning the governor's chair over to his Republican lieutenant governor, Jesse F. McDonald. Thus, on one day, Colorado had the questionable pleasure of having three different governors.

The revulsion of many voters at the circuslike atmosphere of the election of 1904 seemed to make something of an impression on the parties two years later. The Democrats then were split into two factions, with one wing of the state party devoted to U.S. Senator Thomas Patterson and the other following Denver Mayor Robert Speer. The Republicans decided to nominate a political novice for governor—a man who, they hoped, would appeal to the voters as uncontaminated by former corruption or even the suggestion of it—the Reverend Henry A. Buchtel, chancellor of the

University of Denver. The split in the Democratic ranks, and the expected relief from professional partisans, gave the election to the Republicans, who also captured control of the three congressional seats and the state legislature.

Those who had looked upon Buchtel's election as the beginning of a cleaner, more progressive era in the state's politics had some cause for disappointment in the early days of the new assembly's session. One of the first duties of the new legislature was to select a U.S. senator. The Republican majority had little difficulty deciding to retire Democrat Thomas Patterson, replacing him with Simon Guggenheim. But many voters, of both parties, considered the election proof that the politicians had not reformed their older ways. The Guggenheim selection seemed to follow the pattern of nineteenth-century senator-making when Senate seats had often rewarded men of great wealth. Guggenheim's election brought vocal protests from Democrats, union leaders, and reformers generally. Undoubtedly the incident furthered the growing sentiment in favor of removing senator selection from the legislative chambers and placing it directly into the hands of the voters. (This was accomplished by the seventeenth amendment to the federal Constitution, proposed in 1909, declared ratified in 1913.)

Yet despite this beginning, reformers found Buchtel's term promising before it had ended. Two statutes, especially, pleased the progressives: civil service legislation and a law creating a railroad commission. Although the federal government, since the 1880s, had engaged in a gradual transformation of the old "spoils system" of political appointments to a classified, competitive civil service, many of the states continued the older ways. As a result, the appointment and tenure of public employment remained a weapon in the hands of the dominant political party, providing a ceaseless arena for intimidation, corruption, and "unclean" government. In 1907, the Colorado General Assembly enacted the state's first civil service statute. Although it would be much amended and modified, and completely revised in 1915, it marked an encouraging beginning at cleansing one of the more notorious facets of state government.

The other epoch-making statute of the same session created Colorado's first effective railroad commission: a three-member board empowered to represent the public's interest in the railroad service and rate matters. The action was really the mark of final success for the concepts of Grangers and Populists from an earlier generation. Like much of the legislation sponsored by progressives, the railroad commission act was subject to litigation, and its effectiveness, in large measure, turned on judicial determinations. In this case, the act emerged from the courts mostly intact, dignified by a pronouncement of constitutionality. Seven years after its creation, the railroad commission was merged with the state Public Utilities Commission, also composed of three members, with powers to supervise rates and service of all utilities.

Although the two-year tenure of Governor Buchtel can be seen now as of more than casual significance in the development of reformed governmental policies, the governor and his Republican Party were to be denied the historic role of innovators. When the election of 1908 approached, a new reform group appeared to seize the opportunities for translating progressive idealism into action. John F. Shafroth was a man who had demonstrated popular appeal with Colorado voters as an earlier time. Born in Missouri, a graduate of the University of Michigan, Shafroth practiced law in Denver from 1879 onward. He had entered the political scene as a Republican and was elected to Congress in 1894. He was returned to Washington in the election of 1896, this time as a candidate of fusion Silver Republicans, Democrats, and Populists. Like Teller, he would move to the Democratic Party where he constantly championed William Jennings Bryan, anti-imperialism, and what was left of the silver issue.

As the Democratic candidate for governor in 1908, Shafroth campaigned strenuously on a platform calling for a variety of reforms. He led his party to victory and two years later he would win a second term. The four years during which Shafroth was governor produced a fruitful harvest of progressive legislation.

Merely to list all of the statutes enacted would require many pages; many of the laws were complex and their administrative history confusing. Generally, Governor Shafroth enjoyed greater success in sponsoring reforms of political devices than in the facets of his program concerned with social and economic problems. Among the major accomplishments, the constitutional amendment providing for initiative and referendum invoked enthusiastic expectations. A favorite of progressive concepts, it was believed that allowing more direct popular participation in legislating would result in a more direct representation of the citizens' interests. The legislature submitted the amendments to popular vote in 1910, and the Coloradans approved the amendments allowing citizens, by petition, to initiate both amendments to the constitution or statutes, and to approve or reject by plebiscite (at their option or the General Assembly's) statutes endorsed by the legislature.

Other progressive victories included a primary election law, a campaign expenses law, an election registration law, and the creation of a tax commission. Shafroth's administration also sponsored such milestone legislation as statutes providing for regulation of child labor, woman labor, an eight-hour day for hazardous or dangerous occupations, and a labor disputes act, the creation of a state conservation commission, a factory inspection act, and a coal mine inspection law.

Shafroth's four years in office resulted in a general identification of his wing of the Colorado Democratic Party with progressive legislation. But there were many Republicans as committed to reform; in fact, one of the complicating factors of the progressive movement, throughout the United States, was the fact that no one political party held a monopoly of the movement. There were many liberal, or "insurgent," Republicans who were certain that reform could best be worked through their organization. They had generally supported the Shafroth program, but they continued to work to make the state Republican Party the major vehicle for progressivism.

These men had national heroes to emulate, including Wisconsin's Robert M. LaFollette and former President Theodore Roosevelt. Looking forward to the election of 1912, they expected to see the national party provide a progressive candidate and platform on which they could model their reformation of the Colorado organization. Representing, generally, the small city or "outstate" interests, those progressive Republicans who favored working for reform within the party were led by Philip B. Stewart, a wealthy Colorado Springs businessman. Their hopes were dampened, however, when the regular Republicans gained control of the national nominating convention and selected William Howard Taft as candidate for a second time. But after Roosevelt had bolted the national organization and formed his "Bull Moose" Progressive Party, the Colorado reformers followed his lead and organized a State Progressive Party.

The leader of this new faction, which was principally urban oriented, was Edward P. Costigan. A Virginian by birth, Costigan had grown up in Colorado. He had graduated from Harvard and practiced law in Utah before he began his legal career in Denver in 1899. A Republican, he entered the ranks of the Denver reformers, working with Ben Lindsey, Irving Hale, and others in organizations like the Denver Voters' League to contest the power of the Democratic "bosses" of the city and to further home rule, civil service, and other progressive programs.

If the reformers were divided in their allegiance to political groupings, the same was true of their opponents. The Democrats might claim
with pride the accomplishments of Governor Shafroth, but there were
many in the party who clung to older ways. In fact, in the eyes of most
reformers, the Democratic "City Hall machine" of Denver was a "hydra
of corruption," conducting in ruthless fashion the patronage and spoils
of the state's largest city. If anyone doubted the division within the
Democratic ranks, he had only to remember the bitter, prolonged controversy in the party in 1911. U.S Senator Charles J. Hughes had died,
and the General Assembly, controlled by the Democrats, spent 123 days
and 102 ballots in a futile effort to select his replacement. The factions
of the party were unable to compromise, and for two years the state
counted only one representative in the U.S. Senate.

Among conservative Democrats and regular Republicans there was
agreement that reformers were potentially dangerous people. The conservatives viewed with alarm or horror the suggestion that the state
power be extended into so many aspects of citizens' activities. Such regulation and regimentation, they believed, would ultimately sap the individual's initiative; it was perilously close to, if not identical with, the
plans and programs of socialists. These men agreed with Henry Wolcott,
who had warned that continued progressive action would leave nothing
in Colorado but the climate and the scenery by the time the progressive
lawmakers had finished their work. There was particular fear that progressivism would drive away "eastern investors."

There was virtue in viewing the struggle, as Ben Lindsey and other reformers did, not as political struggle but rather as a contest between "people" and "privilege." Yet political contests are waged through parties, and
the election of 1912 demonstrated the application of the rule. That year
Coloradans witnessed a spirited campaign for governor among four candidates, a Republican, a Democrat, a Progressive, and a Socialist. The Progressives, in their first campaign, nominated Costigan for governor. They
hoped that the six speeches Theodore Roosevelt delivered in the state that
year would unite the majority of the reformers with them. But following
the national pattern, where the division in Republican ranks between Roosevelt and Taft opened the way for a victory to Democrat Woodrow Wilson, when the votes were counted the Democratic Party had also
triumphed in Colorado, electing Elias Ammons governor. In this election,
too, voters approved a state constitutional amendment providing for judicial recall, one of the most unusual experiments in progressivism.

Two years later the Progressives returned to the arena, again with Costigan as their candidate. For a time they anticipated success, for the Democrats labored under the real handicap of explaining away the uproar resulting from the Ludlow incident and the violence in the coalfields. In addition, the prohibition issue confused other distinctions. This year, it appeared, the voters who elected to stay with the reformers divided their votes between the Progressives and Democrats. As a result, the regular Republicans returned to office with George A. Carlson the new governor.

An indication of the momentum the Progressives had attained can be seen in the major legislative accomplishment of Carlson's term at governor. It was inevitable that industrial relations would concern the lawmakers, yet it is significant that the Republicans turned to a governmental device in seeking a solution to the problems that had generated the coalfield turmoil. The *form* was one reformers had often championed—an industrial commission empowered to investigate labor conditions, arbitrate labor disputes, prevent (when possible) strikes and lockouts. The new commission assumed many of the functions of the older Bureau of Labor Statistics, as well as the task of administering the new workmen's compensation program.

In such ways did progressivism permeate Colorado politics and law. But by this time the reformers had also broadened their objectives and had entered the realm of national affairs.

TWENTY-SIX

STATE AND NATION

Throughout the period of reform, Colorado progressives, regardless of party, viewed the local and state activities as only a part of an era of national reform. For that reason, they kept constant watch on other states where progressive experimentation developed, and also on pattern-producing events in Washington, D.C. Both Congress and the presidents—Roosevelt, Taft, Wilson—provided focus for the national reform movement. Generally, the federally sponsored reforms struck responsive chords among the Colorado progressives.

Vigorous national action by either the president or Congress, however, always carried with it the threat of penetration by the national government into the state's affairs. Out of this circumstance, Colorado, like all other states, grew to develop a policy of discrimination in viewing the effects of national progressivism. Some legislation was very welcome. Perhaps no state in the Union was more in accord than Colorado with Theodore Roosevelt's progressive reclamation policies. A "beneficial" tariff regarding sugar was considered essential to the welfare of the irrigation farmers. The direct election of senators and a federal income tax, both subjects of amendments to the federal Constitution, were warmly supported by Colorado reformers.

But there were other innovations that were not so welcome, and none probably excited more anxiety in Colorado than the progressive ideas concerning conservation of the country's natural resources, particularly federal forest policies. Actually, the problems of forest control and western anxieties about the problems antedated the surging progressive movement by several decades.

Coloradans consumed the timber of mountain and plateau areas for a variety of purposes. Lumber for cabins and houses, fuel for smelting, timber for railroad ties, wood for domestic fuel and general commercial use—all combined to deplete the timber resources. These raids were joined by the forces of nature that frequently destroyed the timbered slopes by fire, flood, and insects. For years most people had been unconcerned; if asked, they undoubtedly would have echoed General William Larimer's declaration in his Christmas celebration speech at Cherry Creek, back in 1858: "Our pineries are convenient, and will last for generations to come."

But there were a few individuals, as early as the 1870s, who were alarmed about the eventual depletion of the forest resources, and none was more significant than Frederick J. Ebert. He had come to Colorado, professionally trained in forestry at a German university; it was he who was largely responsible for the formation of a committee on forest culture at the constitutional convention, and he served as its chairman. Ebert proposed a state bureau of forestry to regulate timber cutting and establish nurseries for reforestation. The bureau was not created, but Ebert's committee was responsible for these clauses in the constitution:

> The general assembly shall enact laws in order to prevent the destruction of, and to keep in good preservation, the forests upon the lands of the state, or upon lands of the public domain, the control of which shall be conferred by congress upon the state.

> The general assembly may provide that the increase in the value of private lands caused by the planting of hedges, orchards, and forests thereon, shall not, for a limited time to be fixed by law, be taken into account in assessing such lands for taxation.

These sections of the Colorado Constitution of 1876 marked the first recognition of forest conservation ever included in a state's basic charter.

The legislature proved to be in no hurry to act on these instructions. An early effort to extend tax rebates for tree planting achieved no great success. But by the mid-1880s sentiment arose for more vigorous policies. The immediate concern was the possibility of inducing Congress to give the states control of forests on federal lands. This led to the organization of the Colorado Forestry Association, the major sponsor of the legislation creating a state forest commissioner in 1885. Edgar T. Ensign was appointed to the post, although no salary, staff, or budget was provided.

Of particular concern to Commissioner Ensign and to the forestry association were the headlands out of which the major rivers flowed. If those areas were used for agriculture, a denuding of the hillsides would destroy the river flow, with untold harm to the irrigation systems and flood safeguards. Thus, memorials and petitions to Congress were prepared and dispatched, first requesting state control of the watershed areas and, when that seemed impossible to obtain, demanding federal controls.

The national government's answer was the establishment of federal forest reserves. Beginning in 1891, forested lands were withdrawn from the public domain, halting private entries and exploitation of them. Some criticisms greeted the new policy. Public lands, to that time, had been traditionally viewed as eventually coming under private ownership via increasingly liberal laws. The withdrawal policy seemed to reverse long-tenured traditions, bringing cries of "socialism" against the federal program. But others, including Coloradans, hailed the law as a wise measure and when President Benjamin Harrison set aside the White River Plateau Reserve of more than 1 million acres in northwestern Colorado (the first in the state and the second in the nation), his action was applauded. Harrison, during 1891 and 1892, created four other forest reserves in Colorado—Plateau, Pike's Peak, South Platte, and Battlement Mesa. Since neither Presidents Cleveland nor McKinley established any additional reserves in the state, many Coloradans came to believe that the federal government was moving too slowly in the matter. By 1903, only 3 million acres, out of more than 13 million potential acres, had been withdrawn.

One reason for the lack of organized opposition to the federal policy during the first decade of withdrawals was the almost complete lack of enforcement. Not until 1897 did officers begin to patrol the reserves and bring to punishment individuals who violated the forest laws. When that began, immediate protests arose. Much of local citizens' indignation resulted from the seemingly arbitrary action of untrained, underpaid federal officials. But the grievances soon were elevated to terms of an unconstitutional demolition of states' rights by the federal government.

Undoubtedly mistakes were made. Not only were the administrative personnel poorly equipped for their assigned duties, but some of the federal procedures also needed correction. For a time persons who owned timbered lands within the reserves were allowed to exchange those areas for agricultural lands outside. All too often the lands were stripped of timber before the exchange was completed, presenting a spectacle of extremely poor administration.

But if sloppy administration was a cause of complaint, efficient administration created even more hostility. Theodore Roosevelt's personal interest in conservation and his decision to extend the forest policy brought the first real application of the program. During his administration the reserves were transferred from the Interior to the Agriculture Department and the enthusiastic conservationist Gifford Pinchot became chief forester. A fee system for grazers in the forest boundaries was inaugurated. Illegal enclosures within the reserves were eliminated; fencing was even physically destroyed, when necessary. The Forest Service personnel were upgraded, placed on civil service, and the laws were rigorously administered. Finally, President Roosevelt established fourteen new reserves in Colorado between 1902 and 1907. Older reserves were enlarged and by 1908 a total of 15,756,000 acres of Colorado lands had been withdrawn.

Hostility to this sort of "progressivism" in Colorado was widespread. Many felt personally injured by the new regime: newspaper publishers whose revenue from land office advertising declined; those who were engaged in land-location and lumbering enterprises; politicians who missed the patronage of the forest service; those who feared the fortified policy because it was new and untried; ranchers who had enjoyed free use of the reserve grazing lands; and those who were philosophically opposed to the extension of national power into such local activities. One Coloradan informed President Roosevelt: "My home is in the Reserve [the proposed Medicine Bow Forest Reserve, now the Roosevelt National Forest] and I earn my bread with a little 10-horse power sawmill, running the saw myself. If you wonder why I object to the Reserve, it is because I love liberty, hate red tape, and believe in progress. I like self government, but to be placed under a bureau and in a Reserve is too much like going back to the kind of government you impose upon your Indians."

President Theodore Roosevelt, a frequent Colorado visitor, sets out on a hunting expedition near Meeker in 1903.

A climax in the controversy was reached in June 1907, when a Public Lands Convention assembled in Denver. Most of the western states were represented by delegations, with the majority of the leaders, including Colorado's Teller and Shafroth, antagonistic to the federal policy. From Washington, D.C., came Interior Secretary James Garfield, Chief Forester Pinchot, and the head of the Reclamation Service, Frederick Newell, to defend the president's conservation program. The bitter debates afforded western opponents a chance to be heard, but there the matter ended. The policies were not to be reversed. But it would be wrong to suggest that the federal policies were arbitrarily imposed and lacked popular support. Outside the West, most progressives applauded the efforts to conserve what remained of the nation's natural resources.

The federal authorities did adjust minor matters. Congress forbade further withdrawals by the president without its specific approval. The reserves were soon combined and consolidated, and were renamed "national forests"—an indication of more sophisticated concepts of conservation. Instead of merely setting aside "reserves" of forest lands, the "national forests" were to be *used:* the timber would be scientifically grown and harvested, fires and destructive diseases would be controlled, the proper use for irrigation and grazing could be arranged in the watershed areas. In time these new ideas, through education and practical experience, would gain the support and loyalty of most westerners.

After the arguments over forest policy, if any doubt remained that the great crusades of the progressives had resulted in increased exercise of authority by the national government, that doubt surely was dispelled by the last of the great crusades—World War I. Of course, the impact of that struggle was felt by all people of all nations, and its effects were so far reaching that they penetrated almost all aspects of everybody's life. But the war years brought specific, and sometimes unique, changes to Colorado.

The general pattern of the times was unstinting cooperation and sacrifice on the part of the vast majority of Colorado citizens, even though many residents demonstrated reluctance to enter the war in 1917. In the fall elections the year before, Julius Gunter, a Democrat, had been chosen governor; the success of his party at the polls might have indicated general cooperation with Woodrow Wilson's administration. But when the vote in the House of Representatives on the war resolution was recorded in April, only one Colorado representative favored passage.

This attitude can probably be explained as a reflection of an older anti-imperialistic, isolationist one, hardly surprising when it is remembered that at the turn of the century, when Congress debated the resolution for declaring war on Spain, it was Colorado's Senator Henry Teller who sponsored the amendment guaranteeing a nonannexation promise to the Cubans whose independence from Spain was a major objective of the war. This pledge had not then resulted, however, in any lack of enthusiasm for the "little war with Spain." Coloradans had been as stirred as the citizens of other states by the events, and the general American rush to volunteer for service had not found Coloradans hesitant. The famed Rough Riders included many Colorado volunteers; Colorado troops under Colonel Irving Hale had distinguished themselves in the assault on Manila and in later guerrilla campaigns in the Philippine Islands.

In much the same way, once war was declared against Germany and its allies in 1917, the all-out effort to fight it rapidly and successfully engaged the energies of almost all Colorado citizens. Governor Gunter established a council of defense; the legislature, in special session, provided emergency appropriations for the war effort; citizens generally busied themselves with some form of patriotic sacrifice. One area of special concern, particularly during the anxious early months, was the exposed condition of the state's reservoirs and tunnels. Sabotage committed against them would result in extensive destruction of the state's industrial and agricultural facilities. When the Colorado National Guard was federalized in August 1917, one of its first assignments was to guard those essential works.

Like all the other states of the Union, Colorado was called upon to contribute to the drafted "citizen" army. In all, counting both volunteers and draftees, the state contributed 43,000 to the armed forces. Of these, 1,009 died in the service; 1,759 were wounded. Battle casualties, however, totaled only 326. The mustering into service of these recruits always provided an occasion for civilians to demonstrate their loyalty to the war effort. Gifts of tobacco, wristwatches, and mementos accompanied the soldiers and sailors on their way to the training camps. Volunteers and draftees would continue to be objects of concern for organizations like the Red Cross, YMCA, Salvation Army and, of course, their own families and friends.

Meanwhile, those left at home bought war bonds, paid increased taxes, planted war gardens in vacant lots, and cheerfully complied with the homefront campaigns of meatless, wheatless, lightless, gasless days or nights. By May 1918, it was reported that women's councils of defense had been formed in all but four counties of the state, and Colorado women sent clothing and supplies to war-torn Europe, helped organize Red Cross work, and provided information on food conservation. The La Plata County women's council, for example, established a community kitchen in Durango to instruct housewives in the preparation of war menus and the canning of fruits and vegetables. The younger generation also helped in the war effort; in June 1918, eleven thousand boys and girls from areas outside of Denver were enrolled in agricultural and garden clubs under trained supervision.

Coloradans young and old also watched the development in the state of some innovations in both agriculture and mining. Even before the nation's entrance into the war, the increasing demands for food in wartime Europe had led Colorado's farmers to increase their production. Consequently, by 1917, the state's wheat, sugar, and other farmers already were rapidly extending their efforts. With demands seemingly insatiable, it was inevitable that high prices would spiral even higher; wheat rose dramatically during the war years, reaching an average of $2.02 a bushel in 1919. With this sort of market, it is not surprising to find that enormous increases in planting resulted. In Washington County alone, for example, wheat acreage increased from 31,000 acres in 1917 to 175,000 acres in 1920. In Colorado as a whole, the 465,000 acres planted to wheat in 1913 had been increased by 1919 to 1,329,000 acres. Looking back at the feverish activity after the war had ended, critics found the source of much of the agricultural distress of the postwar decades in the careless fashion in which eager farmers converted the dry lands to plowed fields. But at the time it was both patriotic and profitable to engage in such bonanza farming.

Some problems accompanied the speeded-up tempo. Because of the wartime strains on the nation's transportation system and a shortage of freight cars, farmers sometimes found it difficult to get their produce to market, and at one time potato growers around Monte Vista were advised to build storage pits for crops that could not be shipped. Sugar beet farmers also faced a very real difficulty because they had always relied on German production of beet seed. With that source cut off, the Colorado sugar producers, especially encouraged by the success of the Great Western Sugar Company's endeavors, participated in a "crash" program of propagating beet seed. Generally, the war years were filled with optimistic agricultural expansion, and although the "mobilization" of the farms for the Great Crusade might have left a bitter heritage for the future, Americans were proud of the production they achieved.

In the mountains and plateaus of central and western Colorado, the war brought several significant changes to the state's mining industry. Although metals generally experienced a price rise similar to that of agricultural products, with silver, for example, reaching as much as $1 an ounce, the production of most metals declined during the war years. Labor costs increased, as factories, farms, and the government all placed drains on the labor pool. But, conversely, some metals were especially demanded for war production, and in three areas genuine "booms" occurred. One of these metals was molybdenum, used in hardening high-grade steel. On Fremont Pass, near Leadville, practically astride the Continental Divide, the Climax Company opened what proved to be the largest molybdenum mine in the world. Only the demand for this metal, resulting from the greatly increased need for steel, could have led to such a rapid development of the molybdenum properties in the very shadow of what was once Colorado's greatest silver camp.

Another metal in great demand during the war years was vanadium, also used in the manufacture of steel. Vanadium was mined as a byproduct of uranium, in the western part of the state, particularly in the Paradox Valley region. The metallurgy of uranium was still in its infancy; it had been identified as present in Colorado as recently as 1898. At that time the ores, called carnotite, were of greatest interest for their radium content, but with the advent of the war and the need for vanadium for steel alloy, the interest shifted. In the isolated valley where the Colorado Co-operative Society had planted its utopia only a few years earlier, reduction plants were constructed and a new dimension to the Western Slope economy emerged.

Finally, a third rare metal, tungsten, enjoyed a brief flurry of attention. Like molybdenum and vanadium, the tungsten industry resulted from the use of the metal in hardening steel. Like so many other mining stories, the Colorado tungsten saga had its beginning in earlier days, when the tungsten ore hampered miners in Boulder County who were searching for gold and silver. In this case, years elapsed before the element was identified, although it had been used in small quantities in steel making since 1859. The war increased demands rapidly, and a bonanza of short duration resulted, with the price leaping from $9.00 a unit ("one per cent of a ton of tungsten trioxide . . . which was about twenty pounds") in 1914 to $93.90 per unit in 1916. Again, the area of an old silver camp—Nederland—enjoyed renewed activity from the excitement of supplying the war needs with one of the earth's rarer metals.

But tungsten, vanadium, and even molybdenum did not ever attain the significance in Colorado's economy that gold and silver had reached at an earlier time. And after the end of the war, as in the wheat areas of the Eastern Slope, less exciting if not actually discouraging conditions set in. But for the brief time of the war months, Colorado's farms and mines, mobilized for the Great Crusade, contributed sensational harvests to the national effort.

TWENTY-SEVEN

THE TWENTIES

Crusading in Colorado, as in the rest of the nation, abruptly ended with the close of World War I. The "fall from enthusiasm" for high ideals and expectations set the stage for the decade of the 1920s—a decade in which both state and nation reverted to wishful thinking about "normalcy" and actions attempting to restore all the older virtues and none of the older evils of society. The emphasis of the age was derived from attention to material gain, personal well-being, and a return to Republican rule.

Indications of what was to come were apparent even before the war ended. Disillusionment in Colorado with Wilsonian concepts of international morality and domestic reform resulted in a Republican victory in the midwar elections in the autumn of 1918. John Shafroth was not returned to the Senate; rather, Republican Lawrence C. Phipps replaced him. Democratic Congressmen Edward Keating and B. C. Hilliard were retired to make room for Republicans William N. Vaile and Guy U. Hardy. In the state house in Denver, Oliver H. Shoup, a Republican, succeeded Democrat Julius C. Gunter.

The Republican restoration in Colorado proved somewhat less complete and of shorter duration than the victories of the party in national elections. Shoup won a second term as governor in 1920, but the rest of the decade resembled a tennis match of politics in the contests for the governor's office, with Republicans and Democrats succeeding each other. Democrat William E. Sweet inherited the office from Shoup. Sweet's victory over Republican Benjamin Griffith returned the Democrats to a single term of power, ending with a Republican resurgence and the inauguration of Governor Clarence J. Morley in 1925. Then the Democrats returned to hold the chair with an Alamosa rancher, William H. Adams, who would be elected governor three times.

The party affiliation of the governor, however, is not the best indication of party strength. During most of the decade, the Republicans controlled the state legislature. They also dominated the representative and senatorial offices from Colorado.

In many ways, politics from 1920 to 1930 were less confused than they had been for many decades in Colorado. All through the eras of Populism and Progressivism, fusions and party divisions had conspired to complicate alignments and allegiances. Now most of that maneuvering had ended. The older leaders of the progressive movement had either returned to the Republican fold or had sought refuge in the Democratic ranks. There was, however, a series of brief flurries that threatened again to entangle party divisions.

When the decade opened, there was a possibility that the Dakota-based Nonpartisan League's invasion of the state might be successful. But the league's program of "socialistic" aid to agriculture frightened many conservatives. In 1920, when the league endorsed James Collins, the Democratic candidate for governor, many Democrats crossed over to support Republican Shoup. It should be noted, however, that despite its failure as a political force, the league's concepts of agricultural aid remained of interest to many Coloradans.

A disturbing sign of the times was the anticommunist "red scare," which swept the state after World War I. Fueled by fears of labor strikes supposedly incited by "Bolsheviks," the Colorado legislature passed a law in 1919 prohibiting the display of the "red flag" in public. Suspected radicals were rounded up, the headquarters of the Industrial Workers of the World, in Pueblo, was raided, and a Denver ordinance was enacted forbidding any person from speaking out in a manner tending to incite "rebellion." The most dramatic manifestation of the red scare came during the summer of 1920, when unionized employees of the Denver Tramway Company struck to protest a wage cut. The company imported strikebreakers, and violence soon erupted, resulting in rioting mobs in downtown Denver who ransacked and overturned tramway cars.

By the end of 1920 the red scare had run its course. Yet many of the same forces that were at work during this brief spell of hysteria were apparent with the ascendancy of the Ku Klux Klan, another disruptive force on the political scene. This anti-foreign, anti-Catholic, anti-Jewish, anti-Negro organization recruited members in Colorado so rapidly that it threatened to become a dominant force in state politics. Under the leadership of its Grand Dragon, Dr. John Galen Locke of Denver, the Klan began its rapid rise at the precinct level in the capital city in 1924. By controlling the state Republican Assembly that year, it exerted influence in the nomination of Clarence J. Morley for governor. When the fall elections were finished, the Klan controlled not only the new governor but the new House of Representatives as well. Its legislative programs were less successful. For a time it appeared two measures might bring Klan victories: an anti-Catholic bill that would have prohibited the use of wine in the church sacraments, and a proposal to compel all students to attend public schools. Six Republican non-Klan senators joined Democrats to keep the bills from becoming law.

Although the Klan was a statewide organization, with local units spread from Julesburg to Durango, its greatest strength was in the Denver area. With a diversified membership that cut across occupational lines, excluding only the elite and the unskilled, the Denver Klan was led by business and professional people who helped to give it a measure of respectability. It counted as its ally the mayor, Ben Stapleton, and exerted its maximum oppressions against Catholic and Jewish business people by proclaiming boycotts. There, in the capital city, in its Monday night crossburning sessions atop Lookout Mountain near Golden, it provided its greatest excitement for the hooded members.

The decline of the Colorado Klan came almost as quickly as its sudden emergence as a political force. The Denver and other state newspapers contributed to its demise with a constant barrage of ridicule and opposition. Grand Dragon Locke also contributed to his organization's fall from power. Locke had always been an unorthodox Grand Dragon, using only those parts of the Klan program that pleased him and rejecting the rest. Pressed finally both by federal treasury officials and national leaders of the Klan for information about his income, Locke resigned his post in the summer of 1925. Without his leadership, the Colorado Klan quickly dwindled in size and power.

The entire Klan episode remains an ugly stain on the history of the

The KKK on parade along Seventeenth Street in Denver.

state, but a more specific indictment against the organization and those who utilized it for personal advantage can be made. Genuine problems of considerable magnitude that should have received the attention of citizens and politicians alike confronted the people of Colorado during those years. The two major economic interests of the state—mining and agriculture—were left in a disarranged condition as a result of the war years. If the efforts and enthusiasms that Locke and his cohorts had enlisted to combat minority groups had been directed to these areas, the state's welfare might have been greatly improved.

The Colorado mining camps emerged from the war years as greatly altered enterprises. The "ordinary" Colorado mines—silver, gold, and lead—had all declined in production. At Cripple Creek, for example, gold production, which as late as 1915 and 1916 had totaled $10 million to $12 million annually, had fallen to little more than $4 million a year in the early 1920s. During the war there had been hopes that the new metals—tungsten, molybdenum, uranium—would continue in demand and would take the place of the old. But the booms in the rare metals had ended. Cheap Chinese ores replaced domestic tungsten ores; Belgian Congo uranium replaced Colorado ores; no mining at all was done at the Climax molybdenum mines from 1920 to 1924. In addition, as the war-inflated prices of copper and zinc tumbled downward, mining operations for those products were suspended. Laborers from the mines, and from closed smelters at Denver, Salida, and Pueblo, joined discharged soldiers and sailors to glut the labor market in the postwar years.

An economic problem of equal magnitude descended on the dry lands of eastern Colorado during the same years. Less than a decade earlier, from 1914 to 1919, the spiraling wheat prices had brought great optimism for the future. Feverish haste to put land to the plow seemed only common sense when wheat prices reached as high as $2.02 a bushel. But now the situation had changed. By 1921 wheat had fallen to 76¢ a bushel, and genuine distress became visible in the dry lands. One indication of this downturn is apparent in the growing percentage of farm tenants in the state compared with farm operators who owned their own land. In 1920, only 23 percent had been tenants; in 1925 the percentage had risen to 30.9 and by 1930 it would reach 34.5.

One concept of relief for the farming communities found expression in the program of the Nonpartisan League, imported through the work of organizers sent into the state from the grainbelts of the Dakotas. Reflecting some of the ideas of the older Grangers, the league proposed to use state agencies to process, store, and transport agricultural products. In this way the middle man—the traditional foe of the farmers—would be bypassed. Although the Colorado League failed to gain control of the state government as the North Dakota farmers had done, they did anticipate success in 1923 when Democrat William Sweet, a vigorous advocate of some of their concepts, became governor. Sweet failed to persuade the legislature to sanction state-operated warehouses, but legislation was enacted to provide privileges for cooperative marketing associations.

During the following years, the expansion of cooperative associations stabilized some agricultural pursuits. The potato industry of the San Luis Valley is an example. Wartime demands for food had elevated potato prices and a great increase in production had resulted. Then, in 1919, prices began to plunge and producers looked for ways to protect their interest. They blamed part of their difficulties on the failure of railroads to supply freight cars at the right places at the right times. They came to believe that through organization they might provide better transportation services as well as more economical warehousing and more profitable sales.

In 1923 both the Del Norte Potato Growers' Cooperative Association and the Monte Vista Potato Growers' Cooperative Association were formed. Within five years these marketing groups had joined a statewide organization, the Colorado Potato Growers' Exchange. Although the original emphasis was on warehousing, grading and marketing of the potatoes soon became equally important aspects of the program. Something of the same development was seen in the Western Slope fruit industry, where organizations like the United Fruit Growers' Association of Palisade were strengthened by the Cooperative Marketing Act of 1923.

The postwar depression in agricultural prices emphasized anew that even in the irrigated farming regions, efficient management of land and water is essential for profitable farming. As farmers' income fell, the repayment on projects financed through the Bureau of Reclamation began to fall behind schedule, and the bureau was faced with possible bankruptcy on some projects. Dr. Hubert Work of Greeley was responsible for some attempts to rectify the situation. Appointed secretary of the interior by President Coolidge in 1923, Dr. Work directed endeavors to train farmers settled on irrigated lands in techniques of cultivation and marketing. Specialization of crops—whether potatoes or peaches, melons or lettuce—seemed to offer the best chances for success.

Probably the most significant change of the decade, however, was the inauguration of "treaties" with other states to ensure an equitable division of river water for irrigation and other purposes. By negotiating compacts for dividing river waters with competing states, the people of Colorado could secure their property interests and provide stability for future planning and growth in a less expensive and hazardous fashion than through litigation in the federal courts.

Delph Carpenter of Greeley is an excellent example of those who championed the concept of river compacts. He served as Colorado's negotiator on the first three "treaties" to which the state was party. Spurring interest in the compact idea was the long-delayed decision by the U.S. Supreme Court in the Wyoming-Colorado litigation over diversion of the Laramie River. That decision, in 1922, provided specific warning for Colorado that judicial determination of contested rights could prove dangerous.

That year—1922—became a milestone year in water development, for it marked success in negotiating the Colorado River Compact. The

Colorado River and its tributaries flow through seven western states. The upper basin commonwealths (Colorado, Wyoming, Utah, and New Mexico) are divided from the lower basin states (Nevada, California, and Arizona) by the great canyon of the river. Representatives of the seven states had met in January 1919 at the invitation of the governor of Utah and had formed the League of the Southwest to explore common problems concerning the river's waters. Subsequent meetings at Los Angeles and Denver both pointed to the desirability of a negotiated compact, for the federal government was interested in initiating ambitious reclamation projects on the river, and state and local interests needed definition and protection.

The Constitution of the United States forbids treaties between states without special congressional sanction, but by this time Congress had enacted permissive legislation, formally extending to states the right to enter into agreements with each other concerning water or forests. Upon the authority of those statutes, representatives of the seven states met in Santa Fe, along with Secretary of Commerce Herbert Hoover, who represented the national interests.

The negotiators assumed that the average annual flow of the Colorado River totaled more than 20 million acre-feet. This water was to be divided between the upper basin and the lower basin states in two ways. First, each group of states was guaranteed 7.5 million acre-feet of water a year, to be divided among themselves. Practically, this meant that the upper states guaranteed they would allow 7.5 million acre-feet of water to flow each year past Lees Ferry, the division point between basins. From the surplus water, the amount necessary to supply Mexico (presumably to be determined later by treaty between the United States and that country) would be drawn. If no surplus existed, both upper and lower basins would provide the necessary quantity to satisfy international agreements in equal portions. The remaining surplus waters, for the next forty years, would remain undivided. After that time, if the upper basin states had used their 7.5 million acre-feet, or the lower basin states had developed use for 8.5 million acre-feet, a further apportionment might take place.

The Colorado River Compact was scheduled to take effect after ratification by the legislatures of all of the signatory states and by the federal Congress. Six states and Congress approved; Arizona refused to ratify. Since the federal government was then proceeding with plans for the project known as Hoover Dam and thus was more than casually interested in the compact, in 1928 the Arizona objections were bypassed by a congressional decision that ratification by six of the seven states would suffice. In 1929 the compact was declared in force.

Three years after the Santa Fe meeting to negotiate the Colorado River "treaty," Nebraska and Colorado agreed to divide the waters of the South Platte River. The year 1897 was selected as a dividing date, with all Colorado appropriators of South Platte water prior to that year guaranteed their priorities. Even earlier, in 1923, New Mexico and Colorado representatives had sat at conference and agreed upon an equitable division of the waters of the La Plata River.

By then Colorado, Utah, and other relatively underdeveloped western states realized that unless they fully utilized their water resources, they might lose their rights to other states in negotiating sessions. To ensure adequate water resources for future growth, methods were needed to put surplus waters to beneficial use. It was this knowledge that caused Coloradans to begin planning large-scale diversions from the thinly populated Western Slope, where the greatest amount of surplus water was to be found, to the more heavily populated, water-poor Eastern Slope.

All the talk about division of river waters was based on the assumption that humans are endowed with capabilities to make beneficial use of available water. And in those days, when waters were moved under mountains and across long stretches of desert, who could question that ability? On June 3, 1921, however, a few moments of doubt may have occurred. On that fateful day, river and weather conspired to demonstrate their ability to devastate rather than benefit humanity. After three days of rain in the mountains, the Arkansas River became a wrecking flood, driving into and through the city of Pueblo and down the valley, carrying with it 600 houses and an estimated $19 million worth of property. More than 100 lives were lost in the calamity.

The Pueblo flood was so destructive that Governor Shoup summoned the legislature to special session. Out of the lawmakers' deliberations, rather unusual statutes emerged. All Coloradans were sympathetic to the Arkansas Valley and recognized the legitimacy of its claims for help. But in matters concerning public aid, the northern part of Colorado had indulged in ill-feeling toward the southern section of the state for some time. The issue that had generated the hostility was the question of state aid in completing a railroad tunnel under the Continental Divide. As recently as 1920 the northern tunnel interests had sponsored a plan that included a "middle area" tunnel at Marshall

Arkansas River floodwaters devastated Pueblo in 1921.

Pass to serve the Gunnison region and a southern tunnel at Cumbres Pass to pierce the San Juan Mountains, along with the long-talked-of northern tunnel. When a bond issue to finance the three tunnels was presented to the voters of the state, they rejected the suggestion, with the majority of the adverse votes registered in the southern counties of Pueblo, El Paso, and Las Animas. Voters there recognized that the plan would mean higher taxes and the eventual replacement of the Arkansas Canyon by a northern tunnel as the main railroad route through the Rockies.

Now, however, the situation had changed. The northern interests intended to take advantage of the exposed condition of the southern counties. By joining two issues—construction of flood control installations at Pueblo and a northern railroad tunnel—the special legislative session made history. In the south, a Pueblo Flood Conservancy District was created, with authority to levy taxes to pay for safeguards against future flooding. The companion feature for the north was the Moffat Tunnel Improvement District. It was allowed to issue bonds and levy taxes to finance a piercing of the Continental Divide for a railroad tunnel. The district encompassed the towns and counties on both sides of the Divide that would benefit most directly from the tunnel: Adams, Boulder, Jefferson, Grand, Routt, Gilpin, Eagle, and Denver Counties. Revenue was also anticipated from rentals to railroads for their use of the tunnel.

In many ways the building of the Moffat Tunnel was a heroic effort, even though the hoped-for completion date of 1926—the fiftieth anniversary of statehood—could not be met. The plans called for a pioneer bore, eight feet high and nine feet wide, driven ahead of the main tunnel to provide information about conditions and access to the main tunnel as it was advanced. The conditions discovered by the first bore were often discouraging. A greater amount of soft ground was found than had been anticipated, necessitating costly reinforcements. Water seepage far exceeded expectations; at one point all of Lower Crater Lake drained through a fissure. In February 1927, the pioneer bore was completed when the two crews—one working from the east and the other from the west—met deep in the mountain. A year later, after an expenditure of nearly $18 million (some $11 million more than the original estimate) and a cost of twenty-nine fatalities to work crews, the main tunnel was opened. Twenty-four feet high, sixteen feet wide, six and two-tenths miles long, the Moffat Tunnel was now an operating reality.

The tunnel eliminated the greatest operating problems of the Denver and Salt Lake Railroad (Moffat Road). Each year, more than 40 percent of the road's operating costs had been devoted to moving trains over the Continental Divide. Grades up to 4 percent had been costly to climb in good weather; in wintertime the snow had brought increased expenses and hazards. Although the tunnel eliminated only twenty-three miles of track, it had reduced the roadbed grades to 2 percent maximum, and the snow problems had been largely eliminated.

One feature of the tunnel's operation, however, caused constant complaint: The only railroad that could then use the costly hole was the Moffat Road, and its tracks ran only to Craig, for the original destination of the Utah capital had never been reached. Revenue from the railroad's use of the tunnel fell far below the optimistic expectations of the preconstruction days, bringing higher tax levies to the people of the improvement district. Even more discouraging, Denver still had not attained a direct western rail route, for the Denver and Rio Grande's mainline still used the Arkansas Canyon. But attention now began to center on the short forty-mile stretch between the Moffat line and the Rio Grande's tracks at Dotsero. In time, a "cut-off" would bridge the gap,

The Pioneer Zephyr *emerges from the West Portal of the Moffat Tunnel on June 16, 1934, the opening day of the Dotsero cutoff linking the Moffat line with Denver and Rio Grande tracks.*

and the Rio Grande's mainline between Denver and Grand Junction would be reduced by a total of 175 miles.

In many ways, the Moffat Tunnel's completion marked a dramatic end to the long struggle of Coloradans to build ever finer railroad facilities. A new day was fast approaching that would reduce the significance of the region's rail lines. In fact, the peak period of railroading had already been attained; in 1914, when the state had 5,739 operating miles of railroad, the zenith had been crossed. Automotive advances had begun to siphon interurban passenger traffic from the short-line electrics; many sightseers now toured the state in cars and buses rather than railroad coaches. Truck freighting was cutting deeply into railroad revenues. All these elements, added to the decline of mining in many parts of the state, brought death to historic Colorado railroads and contraction of services on others. The Colorado Midland died in 1918. Five years later the Colorado and Southern began to abandon the old Denver and South Park road.

Even more dramatic as an omen of future transportation was the introduction of regular airline mail service in Colorado in 1926. As in the quest for transcontinental railroad service three-quarters of a century earlier, Coloradans were disappointed in their first expectations of inclusion in the direct airmail service instituted between New York and San Francisco in 1920. Cheyenne, to the north, again became the closest stop. But in 1926 a branch service was initiated between the Wyoming city and Pueblo, with stops in Denver and Colorado Springs. "Celebrations marked the start of airmail from all three Colorado cities. Ten thousand people crowded onto the Colorado Airways field in east Denver on May 31, to watch the departure of the afternoon mail for Cheyenne. Two Curtiss-Standard J-1 biplanes, war surplus craft, transported 13,000 letters (325 pounds), the first forwarded from Denver by air to cities throughout the United States." Within a short time the flights from Colorado cities were carrying passengers and freight as well as mail. By 1921, only two years after it had been opened for service, Denver Municipal Airport (renamed Stapleton Field in 1944) counted 3,600 passenger arrivals and departures.

Airplanes and automobiles not only brought changes to the state's transportation pattern; they also revolutionized the fuel industry. Colorado railroads had depended on the local coalfields for their power; the new transportation consumed the products of oil fields. Colorado recorded its first producing petroleum well in 1862, when oil was discovered six miles north of Canon City. This was only three years after the Oil City, Pennsylvania, field had ushered in the "age of petroleum," making a Colorado well one of the earliest in point of time, if not significance. Later, in 1876, the Florence field had been opened, and Boulder County wells began production in the early 1890s. All these wells, however, were of limited significance, for most of their production was consumed locally. The year 1925 marked a turning point. Then the Wellington Dome near Fort Collins and the oil fields near Craig were brought into production. In the decade from 1910 to 1920, only 1,746,000 barrels of crude oil had been produced in the state; from 1920 to 1930 the total would stand at 12,398,000 barrels. For the first time, the last years of the decade would see production reach more than 1 million barrels of crude oil annually.

The railroads' dwindling use of coal coincided with an equally devastating reduction in the consumption of coal for industrial and domestic use brought about by the introduction of natural gas. In 1928 a pipeline from the Texas gas fields to Denver was completed, and soon the convenience of the new fuel wrecked another large market of the Colorado coalfields. Although natural gas fields had been discovered in many western states before 1928, it was not until seamless, electrically welded pipe was developed (in 1925) that it was possible to transmit natural gas over long distances.

Hard-hit from all sides during the decade, the coalfields were to undergo one additional crisis. In 1927-1928, the coal miners struck the operators for wage increases (to compensate for two wage cuts in 1925) and improved working conditions. The Industrial Workers of the World, which had recently organized the northern fields, claimed that its members could not obtain a redress of grievances through the legal machinery of the State Industrial Commission. The most violent of a series of clashes between miners and mine guards occurred on November 21, 1927, at the Rocky Mountain Fuel Company's Columbine Mine near Lafayette. The coal miners insisted on their right to enter the post office that was located on mine property; the guards refused entrance because of the proximity of the post office to shafthouses and surface installations. Six deaths and many injuries resulted from the incident. In addition, the "battle" brought a declaration of martial law to the area and, eventually, the breaking of the strike.

Out of the difficulties, however, a notable experiment in Colorado's industrial relations was born. John J. Roche, one of the owners of the Rocky Mountain Fuel Company, died in 1927 and his daughter, Josephine, inherited his holdings. Josephine Roche already had made some Colorado history as Denver's first policewoman (1912), an officer with Edward P. Costigan in the Colorado Progressive Society, and in various capacities with the Denver Juvenile Court. Her experiences in social work led her to conclusions that horrified other owners of the company; she decided that many of the miners' grievances were legitimate complaints. When other stockholders threatened to dispose of their holdings rather than invite the United Mine Workers to organize the miners and to enter into contract with the union, Josephine bought their shares and became the owner of a $10 million laboratory in which to experiment with her ideas.

In 1928 the Rocky Mountain Fuel Company signed a historic labor contract. Its stated purpose was "to establish industrial justice, substitute reason for violence, integrity and good faith for dishonest practices, and a union of effort for the chaos of present economic warfare." The road ahead proved rather rocky; in addition to the competition of gas and oil, the relatively high wage contract placed a financial burden on the company at the same time that rival companies were conducting a price-cutting campaign against Josephine's experiment. But in the spirit of the "new age," the miners lent the company funds to meet interest payments on its bonds. The miners also sold coal, with the slogan "Buy from Josephine" effectively used as a union label. Within a few years the production rate per miner, the days of labor per year, and the working wages of the Rocky Mountain Fuel Company had all outstripped other coal mines in the state. Many observers concluded that the experiment of the second largest coal operator in Colorado had been remarkably successful.

TWENTY-EIGHT

DEPRESSION DECADE

The decade from 1929 to 1939 conveniently marks itself for historians as the Age of the Great Depression. From the crash of the stock market in October 1929 until the outbreak of World War II in Europe in late summer 1939, the people of Colorado, the nation, and much of the world experienced the devastating dislocations of the most severe depression in their history. The economic collapse and the efforts to overcome its effects permeated almost every aspect of life.

Colorado's two major economic enterprises—mining and agriculture—had experienced their own depressions before the stock market crash. Gold and silver mining never had recovered its pre–World War I prosperity; the state's coal mines staggered under the impact of constantly decreasing markets. And despite recent harvests that were promising, the farmers of Colorado had endured equally troubled times.

The advent of the Great Depression brought even deeper agricultural distress. The drastic drop in the market price of agricultural products, plummeting even faster and farther than the most pessimistic observer of the troubled 1920s would have predicted, affected both irrigated and dry farmlands. A few examples illustrate the problems: Hogs that sold for $12.10 in 1929 brought not more than $3.10 in 1933; potatoes that found markets in 1929 at $1.40 a bushel were down to 24¢ a bushel in 1932; wheat prices during the same period slid from 96¢ to 37¢ a bushel. The harvests of ranch, farm, and orchard brought less at market than it cost to gather and transport them, and were often left in fields and on trees to rot.

Another ingredient, which added to the distress, was the unfortunate antics of nature, which chose the worst of all possible years to withhold precious rainfall, substituting dry, swirling winds instead. The combination brought the infamous dust storms of the early 1930s. The dry years seemed unending; huge billowing clouds of stifling dust lifted precious topsoil and carried it for miles. It did little good to think back to the bonanza years of $2.00-a-bushel wheat and realize that dust was the final harvest from lands that might better have remained grazing lands. In fact, there seemed nothing to do except watch the land being carried away. A few valiant individuals tried to pump subsurface water, but the results were as limited as the attempt was desperate. The answer, for many, was flight, as once again this farmers' last frontier witnessed an exodus of major proportions.

The flight from the farmlands became one of the familiar scenes of the decade. With falling income and no savings left to tide them over the long, lean years, farmers found their acres foreclosed on—many at tax sales. In some dry farming areas, more than 40 percent of the farms went through forced sales. As the inhabitants moved out, their deserted acres fell prey to absentee owners who had no intention of farming but leased the farms to tenants. All too often the tenants were "suitcase" farmers who stayed only long enough to try a crop or two, with no ambition or intention of improving the farm. Tenantry among farm operators continued to increase as it had since the end of World War I. The 34.5-percent level of the year 1930 had risen to 39 percent by 1935.

Many farmers, leaving the agricultural areas, moved to cities and towns, hoping to find relief from their economic troubles there. (Many others migrated to California and the Pacific Northwest; others headed west, but got no farther than the state's Western Slope.) A far from welcome sight greeted those who hoped to begin a new life in the city. Here an equally familiar scene of the decade was daily repeated. Sustained by soup kitchens and bread lines, contingents of people from the army of unemployed looked for work; desperation was visible on every face. In fact, in some ways, the fury of the depression was more apparent in the urban areas, for the contrast with what had come before was greater than in the farming regions. The agricultural areas had faced difficulties throughout most of the previous decade, but the "prosperous twenties" really existed in the cities and the towns. Then, with a swiftness almost too cruel to be recounted, the blows had begun to fall.

The state's lack of large-scale industrial plants had kept too great an army of unemployed from appearing at first, even though large producers of manufactured goods, like the Colorado Fuel and Iron Company at Pueblo, faced with growing inventories and few orders, discharged workers as production levels dropped. By 1933, Colorado Fuel and Iron was in receivership; in 1936 it emerged as the Colorado Fuel and Iron Corporation. Enterprises, both large and small, soon were being swept downward with the same dismaying results. Banks began to tumble— nearly one-third of the operating banks in the state closed their doors. The Denver and Rio Grande Railroad entered receivership again in 1935. It was ironic that the previous year had been a climactic moment in the railroad's history. The Dotsero Cutoff had been finished, linking Denver and Salt Lake via the Moffat Tunnel, giving Colorado its direct, mainline "transcontinental" route and fulfilling, at long last, the dreams of the pioneers of the 1850s and 1860s.

Just as Colorado's experiences during the onslaught of the depression were replicas of the national scene, so the groping attempts to redeem the economic system resembled those of the rest of the nation. Observers had pointed out that although the full impact of the stock market crash and the depression was delayed in Colorado in comparison with other states (largely because of the lack of industrialism), recovery from the depression would be equally delayed. The first thought was of local relief, where welfare agencies might extend the necessary help to take care of the destitute, while those with employment or savings conservatively managed their affairs until the storm had passed. But despite heroic efforts, private charity agencies could not keep pace with the worsening conditions.

Another response was the organization of self-help groups, such as the Unemployed Citizens' League of Denver formed in June 1932 by a group of unemployed professionals. During the year of its operation this cooperative venture provided food for members and engaged in a wide variety of activities; members worked a prescribed number of days to receive benefits.

It became increasingly apparent, however, that neither volunteer relief nor self-help projects were sufficient to meet the emergency, and demands for state action began to be heard. To entertain those demands, the voters placed a series of Democratic governors in the statehouse. William H. Adams, chosen governor in 1928, succeeded himself in 1930. Then for two consecutive elections, Edwin C. Johnson won the governor's chair. It was upon this long-time favorite of Colorado voters that most of the demands for state help fell. Johnson had come to Colorado in 1909 for his health. He had worked for the Midland Railroad, homesteaded in Moffat County, taught school, and managed a cooperative elevator at Craig. When, in 1937, he exchanged the governor's chair for a seat in the U.S. Senate, his party continued to hold the governorship, electing Teller Ammons, son of former governor Elias Ammons. Not until 1938 did the Republicans return to victory with the election of Ralph L. Carr as governor.

At the time the depression began, the state had neither an income tax nor a sales tax to provide revenue. This fact played a significant part in the reluctance of state officials to commit the commonwealth to a large spending program. Moreover, Colorado's outmoded administrative procedures were ill-suited to handle fiscal matters effectively, and the state also was facing a deficit from the 1931–1932 biennium. In its regular session in January 1933, the legislature sidestepped the question of direct appropriations for relief. Rather, the legislators took the position that it was the responsibility of county governments and municipal authorities to provide relief, supplemented with whatever they could obtain from federal emergency funds. But the federal authorities soon made it clear that they did not intend to continue funding programs without state contributions. So at a special session of the legislature in August 1933, a tax was levied on motor vehicles, the revenue earmarked for relief. The state Supreme Court soon declared the tax unconstitutional. Governor Johnson then summoned a second special session to meet in December. The legislature appropriated funds to buy cattle to feed the destitute and imposed an excise tax on gasoline, with a fraction of the proceeds designated for relief.

In this way, federal contributions could be continued. By the end of 1935 Colorado had received almost $48.5 million in relief funds from the federal government. Statistical analyses indicate that during the period 1933–1939 the western states benefited more than other sections of the country from New Deal programs on a per capita basis. Colorado ranked tenth of the forty-eight states in per capita expenditures of selected New Deal agencies. No wonder that it was to Washington, rather than Denver, that those searching for personal salvation turned their eyes.

There was, however, an ambivalence in that turning to Washington—an ambivalence that reflected regional attitudes. New Deal dollars hardly could be spurned in the needs of the moment; yet they brought with them penetration into local concerns by federal authorities that was anathema to many persons, including some Democrats and many Republicans. Colorado master politicians Alva B. Adams and Ed Johnson positioned themselves as anti-Roosevelt Democrats who, in 1940, would cross party lines to support Wendell Willkie for president. Such attitudes, of course, revealed continuation of the love-hate relationship that earlier federal policies in reclamation and conservation had exposed. And now, as then, there were many in the state who did not share the fear of centralization and who enthusiastically supported the national policies as they were applied in Colorado.

One of the earliest and most widely applauded programs of the federal New Deal was the Civilian Conservation Corps—CCC. Young men between the ages of seventeen and twenty-three were withdrawn from the lists of the unemployed and put to work building roads and bridges, fire lanes and parks, and generally improving the national forests and lands. Colorado, with a large part of its total land encompassed within boundaries of national forests, became the scene of much CCC activity. Working out of more than forty camps, more than 30,000 men during the years from 1933 to 1942 created needed improvements in the federally controlled areas.

Another New Deal action producing particular effects in Colorado was the 1934 abandonment of the gold standard, with the federal government calling for custody of all gold in the country and raising the price to $35.00 a fine ounce. Colorado mines that had been dormant since World War I now stirred to activity. At the time the mines had been closed, increasing labor and material costs, and the decreasing richness of ores, combined with a legally fixed and rigid gold price, had forced the closing. Now, with more efficient reduction methods, and a price rise from $20.67 to $35.00 an ounce, the Camp Bird, Cripple Creek properties, and other mines resumed operations on a modest scale. The effect of the price rise in Cripple Creek is apparent in the increase from the 1933 production value of $2,273,000 to the 1934 record of $4,479,000. However, production still was far below pre–World War I levels. Silver producers were helped temporarily by the passage of the Silver Purchase

Act of 1934, providing for government purchase of silver in such amounts as to balance the nation's monetary stocks at a ratio of one-fourth silver to three-fourths gold.

New Deal legislation brought changes for miners—and other Colorado workers—whether they were members of labor unions or not. The depression, with its armies of unemployed, had concentrated attention on the status of labor. Unions experienced increases in membership as laborers sought to protect their positions. The federal administration was convinced that unfair labor practices had played a part in bringing on the economic distress. Safeguards for labor, particularly the Wagner Act of 1935, legalized collective bargaining. Immediate adjustments were then necessary in Colorado; for example, the Rockefeller Plan that had been instituted in the southern coalfields before World War I was examined by the National Labor Relations Board on the charge that the plan actually established company unions. The board agreed with the charge and outlawed the plan. In addition, state laws prohibiting the use of boycotts and peaceful picketing by unions were declared void by the Colorado Supreme Court.

Agriculture was another area where the existing crisis offered a challenge to New Deal planners. The federal government acted on a variety of fronts in attempting to bring order to a confused, chaotic situation. The most massive, and most debated, of the programs were those designed to reduce the acreages planted to crops in order to produce a scarcity of marketable products. In one form or another, this concept has remained the basic foundation of federal farm legislation since that time.

A dramatic answer to the "dusted" Eastern Slope farmers' demands for help came with the offer to resettle those who were living on "submarginal" land. In 1938–1939, a group of families from eastern Colorado was resettled in the San Luis Valley near Alamosa. The Farm Security Administration built houses, farm structures, and a community center for use as a school and offices. The members of the new-style colony began the task of building new lives and raising potatoes on irrigated lands instead of wheat on arid acres. Other resettlement communities were "planted" near Grand Junction and near Delta.

Those who stayed on the dry lands began the slow reconstruction of both soils and personal fortunes. Federal and state programs to encourage soil conservation were initiated; dry farming techniques were adopted by almost all farmers on the high plains. Terracing, strip farming, contour listing, summer fallowing became universal practices. New

crops—Kanred and, later, Tenmarq wheat, sorghums, new oats, and bar-
leys—were tested at federal and state experiment stations; they gradually replaced older strains.

In 1934 Congress enacted the first comprehensive legislation to regulate grazing on public lands. The Taylor Grazing Act of that year provided that all unappropriated and unreserved public lands in western
states be withdrawn from entry until their usefulness as range lands
could be determined. A Division of Grazing was organized within the
Department of the Interior. This agency then established and controlled
(by licenses and fees) "grazing districts." Six Colorado districts regulated 6.5 million acres of land. It was hoped that the new provisions
would contribute satisfactory procedures for both sheep and cattle interests. The antagonisms between the two groups had been volatile since
early days; as recently as 1917 the hostilities had exploded into the
episode known as the "Gunnison National Forest war." Cowboys had
tied up a sheepherder and "rimrocked" his flock—that is, they drove the
sheep over a high cliff to their deaths below.

This brief, selected catalog illustrating New Deal agencies designed
to remedy the depressed and dislocated economy should include the
Works Progress Administration—WPA. Probably no other facet of the
Roosevelt program more radically changed the lives of Coloradans or the
landscape around them. The most visibly apparent results of the program (designed to provide jobs for the unemployed, at the same time
creating worthwhile public improvements or opportunities) were new
high school auditoriums, gymnasiums, and stadiums, bandshells and
bridges and playgrounds, town halls and courthouses. Unlike other relief agencies, the WPA imaginatively encompassed all kinds of unemployed—white collar as well as blue collar; skilled, unskilled, and
professional people. Artists and musicians, writers and teachers were
helped, along with manual laborers.

Among the many popular projects pursued under WPA auspices
were some especially welcomed by those interested in local and regional
history. Old Fort Vasquez was rebuilt; local records were collected and
inventoried; dioramas and other displays were constructed at the State
Historical Museum in Denver. There was also something quaintly and
picturesquely historical in the sight of the unemployed being taught the
rudiments of gold panning in Cherry Creek, where victims of an earlier
panic, almost a century before, had tried to find their fortunes in the bed
of the mountain stream.

Classes in gold mining were popular during the Depression.

Thousands of otherwise destitute people found work and hope through WPA employment. Early in 1936, almost 43,000 Coloradans (the peak enrollment) were WPA employees. When its activities ended in the state, in 1943, the WPA records demonstrated that the federal government had expended nearly $111 million in funds; local sponsors had added more than $33 million expenditures in material and labor.

Public works, used as depression-lifting devices, seemed to set a theme for the era, and none captivated the imagination more than the intricate schemes to bring West Slope water to East Slope users. Transmontane diversion of water under the Continental Divide had its origins much earlier, but the depression decade saw the first large-scale projects undertaken. Earliest of these was the completion of Denver's lining of the pioneer bore of the Moffat Tunnel, bringing water from the Fraser River on the West Slope through the tunnel and a pipeline to the capital city in 1936. Three years later, Denver finished a diversion project for additional waters (for sewage treatment) from the Williams Fork of the Colorado River, through Jones Pass Tunnel.

In the Arkansas Valley, a new diversion project was begun: to bring Roaring Fork water to the beet and melon fields of Rocky Ford and Ordway. The Twin Lakes Tunnel, under the Divide at Independence Pass, was built to carry water into the Twin Lakes near Leadville. From there it could be sent down the Arkansas River to the lower valley. A loan of $1.2 million from the federal Reconstruction Finance Corporation helped the project along. Some people hoped that the tunneling through the hills near Leadville might uncover mineral veins of richness sufficient to reduce the costs of the project. No such fortune appeared, but water diversion began in 1935, with 50,000 acre-feet of new water available for the fields.

Of all the projects initiated during the decade, none quite matched the ingenious, gigantic plans for the Colorado–Big Thompson project. The scheme for bringing Western Slope water to the Big Thompson and South Platte Valleys was complex both in engineering detail and in the maneuvering necessary to gain congressional approval and appropriations. About 600,000 acres of land in the Eastern Slope valleys, to be served by the project, were already under cultivation. The federal government, with one hand, was paying farmers to grow less; to use the other hand to build projects that would increase farm surpluses seemed idiotic to many people. Thus, from the beginning, the planners promised that the new irrigation water would be used only to supplement existing supplies for land already under irrigation; no new fields would be opened. It was a fact that the cultivation of sugar beets and vegetables was increasing in proportion to the quantities of wheat and corn, and that the newer crops demanded more water per acre. On this basis, the need for additional water for old lands was explained. This quieted some opponents, although it was never possible for the advocates of the project to deny completely the charges that more water, wherever or however used, would grow larger harvests.

The new water for irrigation—310,000 acre-feet a year—would be tumbled through generators on the eastern side of the mountains as it dropped down into the valleys. When completed, the project would produce more electric power than was then used in all of Colorado. The estimates of cost were set at $44 million. Of this, the water users would pay back $25 million; the electric power sales would repay the balance.

Initially introduced in Congress in 1936, the scheme encountered a barrage of opposition. Since the proposed diversion tunnel was to run under Rocky Mountain National Park from Grand Lake to the vicinity of Estes Park, opponents argued that ugly surface installations at both ends and a constant fluctuation of the level of Grand Lake would mar the beauty of the reserved park area. They also insisted that the project would set a precedent leading to exploitation of other park lands. Reclamation Bureau promises to clear all debris and to maintain a minimum fluctuation in Grand Lake water levels partly silenced the opponents.

Others predicted that the farmers of the Eastern Slope would never be able to pay their cost of the project. This was a particularly cogent argument among national taxpayers, who saw little personal benefit from the suggested project. In answering these critics, the defenders of the scheme argued that four decades would be allowed for repayment. Since the price of water in the South Platte Valley then exceeded $2 an acre-foot, the annual payment of more than $600,000 would satisfy the contract for debt reduction.

The most serious obstacle, however, was the fact that the Colorado congressional delegation was not united. Colorado River water from the West Slope was to be used in eastern Colorado, and Western Slope interests feared that such a mammoth diversion might dry up the river during drought years. Before they would support the project, they demanded an expansion of the plans to include reservoirs to hold the spring waters for late summer use on the Western Slope. The Platte Valley advocates hesitated to meet these demands for total costs would

Shadow Mountain Reservoir, part of the Colorado–Big Thompson Project, forms an extension to Grand Lake (left) in this 1947 view. Grand Lake Village is visible in the foreground.

obviously increase. However, without a unified state delegation, victory could not be achieved. Other states, such as Oklahoma, were complaining that Colorado had already received far more than its fair share of reclamation funds. Thus, with reluctance, the Eastern Slope leaders committed their constituents to pay the cost of Western Slope reservoirs in order to achieve victory.

Reintroduced in Congress in 1937, the Colorado–Big Thompson bill gained the approval of both houses. President Roosevelt signed the measure on December 28 of that year. The system as outlined (in its basic elements) would consist of two dams on the Colorado River west of the Divide. These dams would store the waters of Granby Reservoir and Shadow Mountain Lake. The water collected at Granby Reservoir would be pumped 186 feet into Shadow Mountain Lake above. From there it would flow by gravity into Grand Lake, then through a thirteen-mile, nine-foot tunnel under the Continental Divide, through a power plant at

Estes Park, into the Big Thompson River, and then through a system of siphons, canals, and reservoirs into the farm ditches of the valley. Ultimately four power plants would be built in addition to the generating installations at Estes Park. Only the last plant was essential for the operation of the system, however. Power produced there was to be sent back through the tunnel to operate the Granby pumping station on the Western Slope.

Construction got underway in 1938. Almost immediately, two elements conspired to wreck the schedule. Inflation pushed the project's price tag constantly upward, and wartime priorities slowed the work. It was not until 1947 that the system was brought into partial operation when the first water flowed through the Alva B. Adams tunnel to the East Slope farms.

TWENTY-NINE

LIFE IN COLORADO
BETWEEN TWO WARS

From the end of World War I until the outbreak of World War II, that is, during the two decades from 1919 to 1939, the population of Colorado changed very little. Not since the 1860s, with their Indian wars, Civil War, refractory ores, and transportation difficulties, had the state failed to record population increases each decade of at least 100,000 persons. But in the years from 1920 to 1930, only 96,000 additional people were counted, a reflection of both decreased birthrate and decreased opportunities for employment. The next decade, 1930 to 1940, registered an even smaller total gain of 87,500 people

Not only had the population growth slowed; the residents of the Centennial State seemed to maintain an unusual stability in their distribution. Unlike much of the rest of the nation, which experienced radical declines in rural population and corresponding increases in the number of urban dwellers, Coloradans remained fairly constant in their location. In 1910, 50.7 percent of the state's residents were classified as urban; comparative percentages were 48.2 percent in 1920 and 50.2 percent in 1930. In other words, population increases were rather equally divided between farm and city; Colorado towns were no more lively than ranches in population growth. Compared with earlier records or

Life in Colorado was quiet and stable between the two world wars. This peaceful main street is in Longmont.

with the startling increases that would occur after World War II, Denver's growth from 256,491 persons in 1920 to 322,412 residents in 1940 could only be described as "ordinary." Only three Colorado cities—Pueblo and Colorado Springs, in addition to Denver—counted more than 25,000 residents in 1930.

During the same decades the population of Colorado seemed to grow more homogeneous. Smaller numbers of foreign-born persons found their way to the state than ever before. This was partly the result of the new, restrictive "quota" system that had been written into federal immigration laws and partly caused by the decline of mining and smelting operations, ending opportunities for large numbers of unskilled workers to gain employment. The foreign-born residents of the state had accounted for 15.9 percent of the total population in 1910; by 1930 this percentage had shrunk to 8.2.

There was one exception to this trend. In the sugar beet fields, where the work of planting, thinning, and harvesting required enormous amounts of hand labor, families of migrant workers from Mexico were employed. During the 1920s this seemed to be desirable, for they performed the labor cheaply, and no other group except Japanese-Americans from West Coast areas competed with them for the jobs. From time to time a few voices of protest were directed against the state for its failure to regulate the working and living conditions of the migrants, but it was not until the depression decade that the migrant labor system became a major issue.

Then, when relief rolls were expanding and many were unable to find jobs, antimigrant sentiment flourished. To bring additional laborers into the state to compete with "native" laborers seemed to many an unjust policy. Reflecting this viewpoint, Governor Ed Johnson announced, in the spring of 1936, a prohibition against importing migrant workers. He proclaimed martial law in the areas along the southern state boundary, stationed the National Guard at the highways entering the state, and attempted to turn back all incoming laborers. Such actions raised serious constitutional—to say nothing of humanitarian—questions. After a few days, the governor lifted the restrictions and the migrants again appeared to labor in the beet fields.

The fact that it was the economic question rather than humanitarian or social considerations that finally attracted attention to the migrant labor policy is indicative of the change that had come to the social scene in the years since the reforming Progressives had administered public affairs. In the 1920s there was little need to be concerned with the cost of public welfare—or the tax rate for relief—for no programs existed in Colorado outside the county level. Until 1933, for example, the only provision made for elderly indigents in the state was the institution known as the poorhouse. These caretaker facilities existed, if at all, at the direction of individual counties, without supervision or aid from the state government. Not until late in the decade was any change in the structure contemplated.

In 1927, in a belated beginning at welfare for older persons, the legislature awkwardly attempted to institute a statewide policy of assistance. This first program was based upon continuing action by individual counties, with no state funds involved. Each county, if its commissioners desired, could provide a levy to raise revenue to financially assist (in their homes) needy people seventy years or older. The attempt was doomed from the beginning. Not only was a system of state financing withheld; opponents immediately raised the constitutional question of whether it was legal for county commissioners to act in a "judicial capacity." When the courts agreed with the opponents, the act became a dead statute.

Six years later, in 1933, a new approach was taken. By this time the effects of the depression had so dramatically illustrated the need for old-age assistance that the long-prevailing barrier against the use of state funds for relief vanished. The General Assembly now instituted a mandatory program under the control of county judges (to escape the unconstitutionality charges of the earlier enactment) with state funds to be augmented through county levies. Maximum payments were set at $1 a day for subsistence. The one grave defect in the legislation, aside from allowing the counties the option of adding to state allocations, was the decision to distribute available monies on the basis of population rather than need. Since only one county imposed a tax to increase its revenues for the program, the state funds were distributed in such a way that the amount available to qualified pensioners might vary from $5 a month in one county to $27 a month in another county.

Meanwhile, plans for a federal social security act were progressing, and in 1936, after the enactment of the national legislation, it was necessary to change the Colorado policies to allow participation in the federal program. Some of the more restrictive eligibility requirements of the state law were eliminated, maximum pensions were set at $30 a month, and a finished program for old-age assistance seemed established. But as events soon proved, this was only a beginning.

The Great Depression spawned a variety of schemes designed to bring social justice to almost every group in American society. In the case of older citizens, the needs were drastic and the suggestions offered were radical. When payrolls had to be trimmed, employers often eliminated older workers; investment failures and dwindling income from savings created especially bleak conditions for older persons. From California, Dr. Francis Townsend called for payments of $200 a month to every citizen over sixty years of age, with the stipulation that the pensioner retire from work and spend his allotment during the month it was paid to him. Townsend's ideas, and those of other "social engineers," spread across the nation during the dark depression days.

In Colorado, the National Annuity League was the agency responsible for initiating the scheme of old-age pensions. In November 1936, voters accepted its plan for payments of $45 a month for pensioners sixty years of age or older. The customary liens on property of pensioners were wiped away, allowing retention of personal property and inhabited real estate. A "jack pot" provision required the balance in the state pension fund to be evenly divided among all pensioners at the end of each year. This clearly ignored the concept of "need"; in the future, as revenues increased, part of the state's total revenue was distributed each January among the older citizens.

To fund the program, the amendment designated the state sales and use tax (which the legislature recently had adopted) a permanent tax, earmarking 85 percent of the levy for the pension fund. By freezing the pension program into the constitution, its advocates insured maximum protection against change. Not until the 1950s, and then only after a strenuous campaign of education to gain approval for another amendment, was the state to recapture some of the sales tax revenue for other purposes.

Old people were not the only group whose plight during the depression years called for consideration; children were equally a concern. Dependent minors, who could not be cared for by their mothers or guardians, earlier had come under the sympathetic eye of the Progressives. In 1913, a Mothers' Compensation Law provided optional county welfare payments for dependent children. As late as 1934 only 33 of Colorado's 63 counties administered such a program. The 1936 Dependent Children Act mandated county participation, a provision essential for ensuring continued federal benefits.

In this, as in other programs, the need to meet minimum federal requirements motivated the state. If federal funding was possible, the state intended to arrange its programs to meet stipulated requirements. In the early years of the New Deal it was not easy to ascertain where the state and federal roles separated. Colorado's attempt to match its administrative agencies charged with directing welfare programs to the expanded nature of the programs illustrates the situation.

In 1891 the state created a Board of Charities and Corrections with authority to investigate public charities and to examine the conditions of correctional institutions. However, the board was only an advisory agency, with no control functions. In 1923 the General Assembly abolished this board and created, in its place, a Department of Charities and Corrections, with a secretary directly responsible to the governor. An appropriation of funds for two years enabled the secretary to expand the department's work, but then, for eight years, no funds were allocated. A part-time secretary acted as clerk in matters concerning the penitentiary and other correctional institutions. By 1933 it had become obvious that the state's welfare agencies could not be adequately administered without reorganization and funding. A new agency—the Division of Public Welfare—absorbed the duties of the older board. Three years later its name was changed to the Department of Public Welfare; it supervised and administered all welfare activities (including child services, outdoor and indoor care of needy persons, assistance to the aged, and the blind) and, in the years ahead, would be assigned additional responsibilities. In the restructuring, care was taken to conform to federal regulations and requirements.

In 1936, when the Colorado voters approved the pension amendment, they also gave sanction to an amendment providing the first state tax on individual and corporation income. The proceeds of this tax, for the first years, were designated for use as a public school fund. Until that time the only source of state aid for schools had been the income from the state school lands; all other financing had come from local district levies. Consequently, little uniformity existed among the public schools, even though an earlier "minimum teachers' salary law" had been enacted. The cost per student in public schools might vary from the $41.14 per student enrolled in Costilla County in 1932 to the $165.34 per student in Summit County the same year.

Once the state embarked on revenue-gathering through income taxes, the concept of equalization of educational facilities was debated. Many of the mining areas were losing population; their assessments on real property fell drastically during the depression years. Many citizens believed it was wise to offer equal educational opportunities to all children, regardless of the county's or town's financial condition. Not until 1943, however, did the state begin equalization through school funding.

Competing with the public schools for state revenues were the publicly supported colleges and universities. In the early 1920s, the state's second teachers' college, at Gunnison, initiated a four-year course leading to the baccalaureate degree and changed its name to Western State College. In 1925 the first students were enrolled in a third teacher-training institution, Adams State College at Alamosa.

During these decades the first modern junior colleges in Colorado were established. Designed to provide both introductory college courses and vocational training, junior colleges opened in 1925 at Trinidad and Grand Junction. Pueblo Junior College began instruction in 1933. That year also marked the opening of Fort Lewis Agricultural and Mechanical

College at Hesperus, where the buildings that had housed Fort Lewis in the previous century, and had later been used as an Indian school, and following that an agricultural and vocational high school, now formed the campus of a publicly supported junior college. The General Assembly, in 1936, enacted legislation allowing a county, or group of counties, to create a taxing district for the support of such institutions. The first school formed under this law was the junior college at Lamar.

The instruments that brought the greatest changes in the lives of most Coloradans, however, were not junior colleges, the teachers' colleges, or old-age pensions. It was the mechanical triumphs—the radio, the airplane, and the automobile—that most dramatically changed society between the two world wars. The state seemed suddenly to dwindle in size with the new transportation and communication techniques; mountain ranges no longer isolated the state as they had in the past.

The beginnings of scheduled commercial air flights challenged the remoteness of the Rocky Mountain West from the rest of the United States. And in communication, much the same effect was achieved with the inauguration of regularly scheduled radio broadcasts. In 1920 W. D. Reynolds started a radio station in Colorado Springs. The next year he moved the station to Denver where it became KLZ. Three years later General Electric started broadcasts from its Denver station, KOA. By 1940, the fifteen stations in Colorado were so located that almost every area of the state was served by one or more.

The automobile changed the daily lives of Coloradans even more dramatically than the radio or airplane. Mass-produced cars allowed those people who lived on farms, ranches, and in isolated towns to travel to urban centers at pleasure and in comfort. Mass ownership and operation of automobiles brought a continuation of earlier demands for better highway construction and maintenance. The mileage of improved roads in Colorado increased in the 1920s, largely because dollar-matching funds for construction were now available from the federal government. But a major assault upon the problem did not come until 1935. Then Governor Ed Johnson proposed, and the legislature accepted, a state bond issue of $15 million to initiate a major paving program for the state highways.

Although none of these changes were distinctively peculiar to Colorado, for all of the nation was experiencing them, there were unique features in the Colorado situation. The combination of unusual climate and spectacular mountain scenery had long marked the state as a tourist

Early travelers negotiate a curve in Glenwood Canyon.

mecca. As the shift from railroad travel to automobile touring took place, Coloradans needed to maintain the best possible highways to attract tourists. Visitors wanted more than good highways to drive on; accommodations and entertainment became part of the growing tourist industry. The city of Denver, for example, purchased Overland Park and, in 1921, converted it to a motor camp for the use of the "gypsy motorists." The tourists provided their own cooking and living equipment and settled down for long stays at such campgrounds. Denver remodeled the Exposition Building at the park for a grocery store, soda fountain, and public laundry. City organizations scheduled concerts and lectures to entertain the tourists during their residence at the park. By 1925 this camp and two others operated by the city had housed an estimated 76,000 tourists.

Of course, many tourists wanted to see more of Colorado than its capital city. Among attractions, the two national parks in the state ranked high. An indication of the change that the automobile had brought to tourism can be seen in the ambitious program initiated in 1929 when the federal government began the construction of Trail Ridge Road through Rocky Mountain National Park. Because of the high altitude, construction was restricted to the summer months; it took four seasons to build the road from Estes Park to Grand Lake. When it was finished, tourists could drive on a highway running for more than ten miles above timberline, and almost half of those miles were above 12,000 feet. The highway enhanced the popularity of the park immensely. Records indicate that in 1933 a total of 291,000 visitors, in 83,000 automobiles, entered the mountain park gates.

Although it is more remotely situated, Colorado's other national park, Mesa Verde, also registered increases in visitors during these decades. In 1921, only 3,000 tourists (651 automobiles) were recorded at Mesa Verde. In 1933, there were 16,000 visitors (4,000 automobiles). Perhaps the most exciting innovation at this park was the completion of the first instrument to date scientifically the ruins of the cliff dwellers. In 1929, Dr. Andrew E. Douglass of the University of Arizona finished his tree-ring calendar. This archeological tool, based on the natural growth of trees—with thick rings in wet years and thin rings in dry years—provided a master time chart for timber. By comparing cross sections from the poles used in the cliff dwellings with the new calendar, one could date ruins back to the eighth century. The veil hiding these mysterious, prehistoric Indians from modern knowledge had been drawn back a little farther.

In addition to the national parks, tourists also were lured to the national monuments. In 1932, 46,000 acres of land on the west slopes of the Sangre de Cristo range were designated a national monument to preserve the great sand dunes. Three years earlier, the natural Mount of the Holy Cross in White River National Forest had been set aside as a monument, although in 1950, because of the difficulty of maintenance, the designation would be withdrawn. President Hoover, in 1933, proclaimed the creation of a monument in the Black Canyon of the Gunnison River.

The continuing expansion of federally controlled lands in the state—either by the creation of monuments or the expansion of earlier designated areas—met some local protest. Citizens complained that expansion removed lands from potential taxation rolls of local and state governments; unlike the national forests, where grazing was conducted under a license and fee system, the national parks and monuments were closed to sheep and cattle. Only in times of emergency—such as war or extreme drought—and then only under limited conditions, was the general prohibition lifted. Consequently, both cattle and sheep interests felt threatened by the encroachments of federal action. Probably, however, the majority of Coloradans favored the new designations, both because they preserved the scenic wonders of a fast-fading frontier, and also because they added to the growing tourist attractions.

Not all of these attractions were federally created. In fact, one of the noteworthy endeavors to provide first-class recreation and entertainment for summer visitors resulted from the work of a dedicated group of Colorado women and their male allies. Ida Kruse McFarlane and Anne Evans (daughter of Colorado's second territorial governor) originated the concept of the Central City Festival, destined to become an outstanding example of a new type of tourist attraction. By the 1920s, the days of Central City's glory had long since passed. The town was "falling to pieces"; the famed Opera House—often termed the finest west of the Mississippi—had suffered neglect and ruin. The concept of a festival was centered around a renovation of the Opera House and the importation of quality entertainment during the summer season.

The McFarlanes inaugurated the program of rehabilitation by donating the theatre to the University of Denver, thereby ensuring a tax-free status for the enterprise. The women then initiated a series of teas and functions to nourish interest in their project. They used the funds they raised to rebuild the roof of the Opera House, to restore the frescoes that had been ruined in the years when the building had housed a movie theatre, and generally to refurbish the structure. "Memorial chairs" were sold to increase the funds for the project. By July 1932, a transfigured Opera House was ready for the opening of the first Central City Festival. Lillian Gish opened the house in a production of *Camille*. One of the nation's most successful festivals had its birth that night. In the years since then, the charm of seeing and hearing operas and plays in a unique nineteenth-century mining-town theatre has proved irresistible to tourists and Coloradans alike.

THIRTY

DECADES OF BOOM, YEARS OF BUST

For twenty years—from 1919 to 1939—Colorado was a quiet place. The population grew very slowly; both mining and agriculture suffered from sicknesses that even the radical prescriptions of those years failed to cure. Casual observers might have predicted that the glorious days of the Centennial State had passed, that never again would excitement like that generated by a Leadville or a Cripple Creek lure the fortune-seekers and fortune-makers. They would have been wrong.

World War II changed everything. No other single event in the state's history and no other national crisis—not the Civil War, not World War I, not the Great Depression—transformed Colorado to the extent that World War II did. Much of what constitutes contemporary Colorado arose from the rapidly changing events of the years from 1940 to 1945.

The story of the impact of the war on Colorado is really two stories. One of these is reminiscent of Colorado's role in the earlier world war. Volunteers and draftees once again climbed aboard trains to be carried to training camps; heavy demands on fields and factories forced them to mobilize their resources for war. Bond quotas and daily sacrifices were required to win the ultimate victory over the enemy. Simultaneously, in a pattern quite different from that of the first war, World War II brought to Colorado military installations and scientific developments that would give direction to the complexion and character of the state after the war ended.

The first of these stories can be told rather simply, although it is impossible to recapture the dedication and personal sacrifice such an effort produced. It is, for example, an easy task to record that, during the war, 138,832 men and women enlisted or were drafted into the service of their country. This number represented approximately one-eighth of the state's population. Scarcely a family in Colorado—as in all of the nation—was not affected to some degree by the seemingly insatiable, continuing call for personnel for the armed services. Of those who left the state for training, approximately 2,700 gave their lives during the conflict.

These statistics are simple facts. What is not so easily described is the heartache of broken homes; the waiting and working for the momentous events termed VE and VJ days; the increasing demand for news from the fronts as the war progressed; the ration books and limited consumer goods—all the daily fears and frustrations of those who stay behind during a war.

Again, as in the period of the First World War, the demands on farm and factory brought radical expansion of planting and fabrication facilities to already existing installations and, at the same time, spawned a host of new enterprises. The abrupt reversal of farm policies from those of previous years created a paradox. Throughout the depression decade, farmers had reduced production to induce price increases. Now the government encouraged them to expand their operations to meet the demand for foodstuffs. The new bonanza produced familiar results. Growers became intoxicated by the high prices and abundant crops. Again they played agricultural poker with the same reckless abandon as they had during World War I. With the improved economy, driven by unprecedented demand, land values shot up. Land that Colorado farmers had abandoned during dust bowl days now sold for $40 an acre. The rising land values reflected the spiraling prices of wheat, corn, sugar, and beef during the war years.

Agriculture responded to wartime needs with the greatest production in Colorado's history; not until 1949 did farm income start to slip. Of course, the hazards of rapid expansion still weighed heavily. During the war, any soil that would germinate seed was put to use. And after the war, during the days of the Marshall Plan and of economic aid to less fortunate parts of the world, the demand for grain stayed high. So the Westerners kept at their task of ripping up sod and searching for more soil in which to plant. A conservation writer, visiting the area near Cheyenne Wells, Colorado, in the spring of 1946, watched farmers at work and remarked: "They were plowing again the land reclaimed from the dust by Government help and sowed back to grass in the 1930s. They were also turning over native sod on shallow soils never before plowed. This was but a sample of the mischief going on in a dozen other localities along a 600-mile front."

Factory workers, like the farmers, found ready and eager markets for their products. As did the farmers, manufacturers not only converted their existing facilities to war production, they also soon found cause to expand their capacities or construct new installations to meet the demands of the crisis. The federal government pumped $360 million in contracts into the state's economy. Virtually every industrial plant in the state was touched by the effort, whether a massive enterprise like the Colorado Fuel and Iron Corporation (CF&I) at Pueblo or a small establishment such as the Heckethorn Company at Littleton, which was only a few years old when the war began but was soon engaged in ordnance work. These enterprises turned out an impressive variety of war goods. Land-locked Denver even built ships. Workers constructed hull sections for escort vehicles in the Denver steel yards, beginning with the U.S.S. *Mountain Maid,* "launched" in the spring of 1942. Army barges were also fabricated in Denver factories before the war ended.

The Denver Arms Plant, which the federal government built in 1941, became one of the largest of the new facilities. The Remington Company and, later, Henry J. Kaiser, operated it as an arsenal and ammunitions works. At the height of its operation, almost 20,000 workers were employed in manufacturing cartridges, shells, and fuses. In 1942, north of Aurora, the federal government constructed the Rocky Mountain Arsenal—a chemical weapons plant that soon employed 15,000 people. Other federal facilities included a medical depot in northeast Denver and an ordnance depot at Pueblo. The plants and depots that were built in Colorado during World War II exemplify the dramatic difference between this war and the earlier conflict, when almost no expenditures were designated for the state.

During the 1940s, the state's population increased by more than

200,000, a greater jump than in any of the other mountain states except Arizona. Many of the newcomers had been "wartime visitors" who decided to return. The growth was almost exclusively urban, especially on the Eastern Slope. The population increase in Denver and the three adjacent counties—Adams, Arapahoe, and Jefferson—represented 78 percent of the state's increase for the decade. In the census of 1950 these four counties held 42.5 percent of the total population. All the mountain counties, which depended chiefly on mining, lost people during the 1940s. And these were not the only ones to decline; the census revealed that thirty-five out of the state's sixty-three counties had decreased population figures.

Other effects are more difficult to define precisely. The scientific aspects of some wartime installations left a "residue" at war's end. This residue and the determined effort of Colorado leaders attracted new industries, as did major cooperative efforts by existing institutions and industries. The result was a complex series of scientific-research-military installations centered along the mountain base from Pueblo on the south to Fort Collins on the north, which gives contemporary Colorado one of its unique features.

Colorado's location far from both coasts made it an ideal host for a number of military bases. Each provided civilian jobs and gave a boost to the local economy. Lowry Air Force Base and Buckley Field near Denver, Peterson Air Field near Colorado Springs, the Pueblo Army Air Base, and the La Junta Army Air Field all trained air force personnel. Camp Hale, beyond Leadville in Holy Cross National Forest, became home to the famous Tenth Mountain Division. The largest military installation, Camp Carson, provided training facilities for the 89th, 71st, and 104th divisions before they departed for overseas. Late in the conflict, the camp also housed German prisoners of war.

"Prisoners" of a different sort resided temporarily in another area of Colorado during the war years. In the Arkansas Valley near Granada, on a tract of 11,000 acres, the federal government established the Granada Relocation Center for interned Japanese-Americans moved from the West Coast. The first of the camp's detainees arrived in August 1942. Most of the men and some of the women worked in the area's agricultural fields, harvesting sugar beets and potatoes. At least two-thirds of the residents of the camp (peak population, 7,500) were U.S. citizens; many of the young men enlisted in the nation's armed services and displayed their loyalty to the United States on the battlefields. In

The scene is pastoral, but this is Amache, one of the World War II Japanese-American relocation camps. Briefly, the residents made the prairie bloom.

Amache, a small city that blossomed on the prairie, the Japanese-Americans soon established an internal government for the camp, along with school facilities and a newspaper for the residents. Although in an admittedly barren and restricted form, life continued for these relocated American citizens. The camp closed in July 1945, even before VJ Day.

Other installations were shut down after the war. But Lowry Field stayed open for business as a permanent training school for the air force, and Camp Carson served as a mountain troop summer home for Camp Hale ski troops. Later, during the Korean conflict, thousands of basic trainees were schooled at Carson. In 1954 the Defense Department des-

Vetsvilles *were common sights near colleges and universities after the war. This one was at* Colorado College.

ignated the camp a permanent installation, changing its name to Fort Carson.

The end of the war brought little change in the population of wounded and recuperating veterans in Colorado's military hospitals. Fitzsimons General Hospital, which the army had first located in Aurora during World War I, absorbed many service personnel for treatment. The navy had used Hotel Colorado at Glenwood Springs for a convalescent hospital, and since 1922, the Veterans Administration had operated a hospital at Fort Lyon on the Arkansas River. Now, as thousands of ex-GIs needed care, the Veterans Administration selected two additional sites for hospitals in Colorado. Major medical centers were created at Grand Junction, which opened in April 1949, and at Denver, completed in 1951.

Mining in the 1940s enjoyed prosperity and endured hard times, reminiscent of earlier years. During the war, numerous government agencies underwrote intensive exploration and development in Colorado's mineral areas to uncover needed supplies of essential metals. Simultaneously, federal government regulation of the industry mounted. Uncle Sam intervened to the point of stipulating who could mine and what could be mined. For example, Gold Limitation Order L-280 closed nonessential mineral mines by refusing their operators access to replacement machine parts or materials and prohibiting work other than maintenance. Gold and silver mining slumped, and molybdenum, under pressure of wartime demands, became the state's most valuable mineral. The Climax Molybdenum Company continued to be the world's largest producer, a ranking it maintained from 1924 to 1946.

A brief postwar upswing in precious metals suffered a setback when the Cripple Creek mines were almost completely shut down at the end of the 1940s, primarily because of the closing of the Golden Cycle Mill at Colorado Springs. Teller County had been Colorado's leading gold producer.

Coal production rebounded during World War II but dropped off steadily afterward, when the demand lessened and the competition from oil and gas increased. Oil, ever an also-ran in Colorado mineral development, showed an astonishing jump in production from 1.7 million barrels in 1940 to 58.5 million sixteen years later. The Rangely and Denver-Julesburg Fields spearheaded this turnaround.

Colorado mining took an exciting turn in the late 1940s when a uranium rush invaded the Colorado plateau. The excitement, a byproduct of the atomic age and the Cold War, got its spark in 1948 when the Atomic Energy Commission (AEC) concluded details of a major program for uranium exploration. For the next decade uranium lured the adventuresome, just as gold and silver had done. Attention quickly focused on Uravan and the Paradox Valley, where the ore had been mined earlier. Grand Junction became the natural base for much of the activity; more than one hundred uranium companies established their headquarters there, and the town took on the feverish expansion trappings familiar from earlier mining days.

Gone from the scene were some old standbys of previous days—the burro, mining pan, pick, and shovel. In their place came jeeps, low-flying airplanes, and Geiger counters. Thousands rushed into the region, spurred by stories of rich discoveries. Some writers of popular magazine articles sought to romanticize the rush and others presented the "true" picture, in attempts to attract nationwide attention. This endeavor was not to be undertaken by the ignorant or the unprepared—the land was rugged, dry, and vast—but they came anyway. The AEC financed road-

A wartime necessity, a postwar excitement—uranium mining focused on western Colorado. This mill was at Durango.

building programs to the isolated sites, paid bonuses for production, and tried to keep some control from its office in Grand Junction. As in the old days, however, promoters soon reared their heads. Stock speculation in penny-and-up shares seemed an easier way to wealth than trudging through canyons and over mesas. Small towns, such as Moab and Monticello in Utah, and Rifle, Uravan, Naturita, and Dove Creek in Colorado, prospered.

In other areas, like Caribou in Boulder County, miners unearthed uranium ores; companies were organized and work started, as the demands of the Cold War stimulated an all-out effort to find more sources of the metal. Mills and reduction plants to process the ores, for both war and peacetime uses, were authorized by the AEC in various Colorado locations. They were soon operating in such scattered towns as Durango, Gunnison, Canon City, Grand Junction, Rifle, and Uravan.

From 1948 through 1960, Colorado produced uranium ore valued at about $133,456,000. Production in the 1960s declined gradually to approximately $20 million in 1968 and $17 million the next year, with Montrose and San Miguel Counties producing over half the total. The boom had receded by then; the lonely land that had recently buzzed with activity reverted to a more placid condition. Isolation, increasing costs of operation and exploration, cutbacks in government support, lower prices, and depletion of older deposits all contributed to the decline. So did public concern over potential dangers from nuclear power plants.

The last Colorado mining rush left typical scars on the landscape: pollution, abandoned buildings, and roads that wandered nowhere. But it also left evidence of a different kind: radioactive waste. The wind had been sown; the whirlwind was yet to come.

The war years and their immediate aftermath marked a division in Colorado history. As in the gold rush years of a century earlier, an abrupt transition had occurred, which ushered into existence a new era for the people of the Centennial State. Colorado could never return to what might have seemed a more romantic era.

The new era was one of boom, with a few dips and slips, for nearly forty years, the longest in Colorado's history. Colorado's economic patterns of earlier years persisted. Manufacturing became more diversified than ever, particularly with increased activity in the aerospace industry and the movement of eastern-based companies to Colorado, especially in the Denver-Boulder-Longmont triangle. Martin Marietta, IBM, and Ball Brothers migrated from outside the state, while others, like Storage Technology Corporation, were homegrown. Compared to a fully industrialized state, however, Colorado remained underdeveloped.

Colorado also mirrored national industrial trends. Pueblo's steel mills shut down, forcing layoffs and creating other complications for the once regionally dominant CF&I Steel Corporation. Foreign competition and declining national demand again proved fatal. Several companies tried to keep going, but steel would never again dominate Pueblo's economic life. Colorado suffered another blow when Frontier Airlines, its pioneer major line, quit flying. The victim of overexpansion, poor management, and deregulation, it was swept, along with the older Denver & Rio Grande Western Railroad, into history's dustbin. The D&RGW had merged with other lines and eventually its name, if not its tracks, disappeared.

No longer masters of their own destiny, Coloradans were faced with economic reality. As Governor Richard Lamm and others warned, the Rocky Mountain West had become a "colony of the East." The fact that the same accusation had arisen a century earlier made it no easier to face in the 1980s and 1990s.

The increased role of government agencies—local, state, and national—became evident in 1990, when they employed 14 percent of the state's workforce. No other mountain state could match Colorado's 53,000 federal employees. That figure, however, constituted only a third of the total number of local government workers. White-collar employment increased, while the number of blue-collar jobs continued to decline.

A major economic shift during the 1970s and 1980s came with Colorado's conversion to a service-based economy in line with the national trend. Colorado again led the mountain west with 256,000 employed in 1987 in a variety of businesses, such as hotels, advertising, amusement parks, legal services, and funeral parlors. Employment in the health services, in particular, surged as the population of America turned gray and demonstrated intensified concerns about health care. In general, service sector companies paid lower wages and included fewer employee benefits. Part-time jobs predominated in this kind of job market. One observer said, "To generalize and say they're all bad jobs is not true, but there are maybe fewer jobs in the middle that are OK."

As changes came to the state's economy, two of its old reliable pillars began to crumble. Agriculture still dominated in the nonmountainous counties for decades after the war, with beef cattle, wheat, sugar beets, grains, and truck garden projects undergirding it. The state ranked high nationally for irrigated lands, in 1987 ranking fifth in the number of irrigated acres. But small farmers and ranchers soon found it more difficult to persist in the face of rising costs and a relatively static income. Their plight produced much soul-searching but little concrete improvement in their situation.

Great Western Sugar and Holly Sugar both closed their mills and plants in the late 1970s, and sugar beet plantings and tonnages dropped drastically during the decade. Outdated facilities, low prices, a world sugar surplus, and cheaper foreign imports brought them down. In the end, the sugar beet story became the story of farming throughout Colorado, tied as it was to national and world markets and conditions. The proud independence of the farmer lingered more in fantasy than in fact. The decline in farming was evident in the continuing flight of much of the rural population to cities that seemed to hold a brighter economic future.

Most Coloradans remained unaware of or uninterested in the farmer's predicament as they rushed to buy land outside urban areas. "The stability of the agricultural structure is at stake," warned Morgan Smith, Colorado's agriculture commissioner in 1979. "We will have to make the case to protect agriculture. Making all state citizens aware must be a goal of the eighties." Smith concluded by saying, "People don't go to Yuma County, which is one of the largest corn-producing counties in the country, and when they go to the Western Slope, they see Vail and Aspen, where agriculture already has been preempted."

Mining, the original bellwether of Colorado's economy, fell to even further depths. Several events generated moments of false hope. One came in the early 1960s, when the price of silver was freed from government regulation. Early optimism about another silver boom evaporated, however, when all the cost factors were weighed carefully. New life flowed into Colorado's precious metals mining industry in 1979–1980. A tense international situation produced unheard of prices—$40 an ounce for silver and $800 an ounce for gold—bringing an economic transfusion unknown since the 1930s. A new generation of Horace Tabors, Thomas Walshes, and Winfield Strattons planned extensive prospecting tours for the spring, but a drop in prices dampened their enthusiasm. Regardless, mining was again, briefly, very profitable—for big corporations and those already in the industry. There would be no repeat of the 1859 rush; government regulations, declining prices, and environmental laws now kept the industry in check. By the 1980s, environmental regulation had become part of the life of a miner, despite heated emotional protests. Die-hards expressed their views vehemently on bumper stickers: "Ban Mining. Let the Bastards Freeze to Death in the Dark."

Mining never sank that far, though hard times did befall it. By 1990 the value of the total state production dropped to $861 million (mostly coal, aggregate, and molybdenum). Colorado's general postwar boom emulated mining, ending in the early 1980s. Suddenly, economic matters became a statewide concern, more so than at any other time since World War II. Colorado's economy slumped as it had not done since the 1930s. Part of the decline reflected a national recession that hit the state in 1982 and hung on tenaciously in both urban and rural areas. A hoped-for energy boom died when the international price of oil plummeted; the high-tech industries suffered from cutthroat competition that damaged this once-promising segment of the economy. When conservative President Ronald Reagan implemented retrenchment of government programs and spending, federal money, a long-time Colorado bulwark, could no longer be relied upon to invigorate the state's economy. Construction leveled off, and tourism and skiing failed to expand as expected. Unemployment increased, bankruptcies mounted, growth almost stagnated, and vacancies on Main Street and in high-rise office buildings soared to new heights.

Those previous stalwarts of the economy, mining and agriculture, suffered from a collapse that coincided with national and international crises more than with any specific Colorado problem. The tragedy was more personal and local in nature than statewide; both industries had already faded to mere shadows of their formerly significant selves, making up only about 3 percent of the workforce. Few contemporary Coloradans fully appreciated what these two industries had once contributed to their state. For Colorado, the symbol of the former high-riding days and the new reality was Denver's Silverado Banking, Savings & Loan. Its meteoric decade rise ended in late 1988 with a federal takeover and taxpayers left holding the bag of nearly $300 million in bad debts. Shoddy business practices, overly ambitious ventures, unwise loans, "creative bookkeeping," and poor management duplicated events elsewhere in the country. For Denver, the failure symbolized the last years of the "good times." The crash was devastating to a generation that hardly remembered the 1930s depression. Bankruptcy petitions peaked in 1989, and a year later 2,077 businesses failed. The number of workers in the construction industry plummeted from more than 80,000 to 61,000 in three years.

By the early 1990s Colorado was on an economic rebound, the recession relegated to history, it was hoped. Only a decade away from the twenty-first century, Coloradans expectantly awaited a return to prosperity. Their forebears of a century earlier had experienced the same feelings.

THIRTY-ONE

COLORADO AND THE NATION

Washington and the federal government had always played a pivotal role in Colorado and, despite some disclaimers, Colorado had always been a part of the United States. World War II intensified and increased Washington's involvement and emphatically reinforced the presence of the government. The years that followed only accelerated the pace.

Western historian Richard White wrote, "On one level, the economic and social changes that followed World War II seemed to make the American West a less distinctive region within the United States." Colorado lay on that level. Television, interstate highways, expansion of the federal government, the changing economy, water projects, and air travel all helped eradicate the isolation, independence, and distances that had once characterized life in Colorado. The proliferation of agencies and influence of the federal government affected all corners of the state. Uncle Sam had always been a presence in Colorado, but now he could be seen almost everywhere, from agricultural regulations and highway construction to making America energy independent. He had come for supper and decided to move in!

Massive wartime federal contracts, construction, military needs, and agency relocations had changed the face of urban Colorado. Denver was nicknamed the "second national capital" because of the number of federal agencies housed there. Many of those agencies were headquartered in the old Denver Arms Plant, which, after World War II, was converted into the Denver Federal Center. Other Colorado cities also provided homes for federal agencies, including many national park and forest headquarters. Boulder acquired both the National Center for Atmospheric Research and a branch of the National Bureau of Standards (now the National Institute of Standards and Technology).

The military complexion of Colorado cities like Denver and Colorado Springs, which came with the war years, was diminished to some extent by the reconversion process during the first years after the war. But it had not been completely erased when the Korean conflict brought renewed defense activities to the state. And since then it has continued to grow. Colorado Springs, particularly, retained a military ambiance, partly from the Fort Carson activities, from the decision in 1957 to locate the North American Air Defense Command at Ent Air Base there, and, additionally, from the selection of that city's doorstep as the site for the Air Force Academy.

In 1949 the secretary of defense, James Forrestal, created a committee to recommend a general system of education for service officers. Within a year, this advisory group reported that only an air academy, separate from both West Point and Annapolis, would meet the needs of the air force. When Congress authorized creation of the institution in 1954, the secretary of the air force launched the site selection process. Three "semifinalists" emerged from the screening: Alton (Illinois), Lake Geneva (Wisconsin), and Colorado Springs. In a remarkable display of state, county, and city cooperation, Colorado won the prize. The land, situated at an altitude of 7,900 feet, bordered Pike National Forest and encompassed such scenic attractions as Monument Creek and the limestone formation called Cathedral Rock.

The bulldozers and earth-movers soon were at work, and the glass, aluminum, steel, and white marble buildings began to take shape, creating startlingly rectangular silhouettes against the mountain backdrop. The Cadet Wing moved to the academy from its temporary campus at Lowry Field in late August 1958; the following June, the first class was graduated from the permanent campus. By that time, $140 million had been expended on construction of the academy, not including such extras as the football stadium and the golf course, which private funds made possible.

Tourism expanded after World War II, placing increased pressure on scenic and historical activities. Tours to Balcony House at Mesa Verde had to be limited.

The Air Force Academy, which became a major tourist attraction, was only one facet of Colorado's new relationship with Washington. Military needs had underwritten the building of bases, and the uranium excitement and the military-industrial complex permeated the state's economy. Martin Marietta built missiles, including the rockets used to land astronauts on the moon, and Ball Brothers, Honeywell, and other smaller companies reaped military and aerospace contracts. The Rocky Flats Nuclear Weapons Plant opened in 1951, mushrooming into a massive operation, and the Rocky Mountain Arsenal's chemical weapons and pesticide plant sat on a 27-square-mile plot in Adams County. Thousands of jobs were created by the military, aerospace, and civilian defense industries. The economic influence of defense did not stop there. University of Colorado officials estimated in 1982 that 23 percent of the school's research funds came from defense, energy, and space contracts.

By 1988 nearly 8 percent of the Defense Department's research and development budget was spent in the Denver-Boulder area.

Federal money helped finance the Rulison Project (1969–1970) near Grand Valley and the Rio Blanco Project (1973), by which the government attempted to use nuclear energy to release natural gas. Though exciting in concept, the projects raised protests against radiation, pollution, and safety compromises; in the end, they failed to produce results. Evidence of public concern came in the form of a citizen-initiated law to require a statewide vote on future underground nuclear blasts; it appeared on the 1974 ballot and was approved. A new era had dawned.

More federal involvement and Colorado's expanded role on the national scene came with the attempt to develop the oil-shale industry. Oil shale (a rock containing hydrocarbon capable of yielding oil) had intrigued mineralogists since early in the century. It generated a "madness" in the late teens and early twenties, which included grandiose plans for extraction, stock speculation, and projected prosperity for northwestern Colorado. DeBeque briefly enjoyed its status as an "oil shale capital." The immense deposits there promised "in the near future to become one of the most important sources of petroleum production in this country" (*Colorado Year Book*, 1923). Those hopes dimmed because of the high costs of retorting the oil shale and other technical problems.

Interest in oil shale was thus subdued until the 1970s. Then came the energy crisis caused by the rising international price of oil, America's gluttony, and the instability of the oil regions in the Middle East (the Arab oil embargo of 1973 brought the matter to a head). Colorado residents, like everyone else, found the price of gas and heating oil rising steadily, sometimes spectacularly, and always contributing to an increase in the cost of living. The old days of cheap energy had vanished.

In desperation, the country launched a search for new sources of oil, gas, and other fuels to allow it to become energy independent. As a leading national source of coal, uranium, and oil shale, Colorado entered the limelight and was faced with a dilemma. Exploration and development promised an energy boom that would spur the economy, encourage growth, and invigorate some otherwise economically sluggish areas of the state; but these activities also threatened the environment and promised to invite the developmental problems of another exploitive rush that would also extract a high price in human and natural resources. The controversy between need and impact divided Coloradans;

Strip mining coal produced more tonnage and raised environmental questions. This operation was between Hayden and Oak Creek.

they appeared to be at the mercy of the future rather than masters of their own fate.

Indeed, the fate of Colorado seemed to lie more with Washington and international circumstances than with Denver and local communities. The state had the resources and the country needed them; for some individuals, the issue was as simple as that. The impact was immediately evident. Denver fared well in the late 1970s when many energy companies arose or relocated there, and it quickly proclaimed itself the energy capital of the United States. On a more sour note, Craig and the district surrounding it mushroomed into a complex of strip mines and power plants. Somewhere between the two circumstances lay a glimpse of the future. Colorado's environment and its quality of life had become pawns in the nation's strategy to satisfy pressing demands for more fuel and energy.

While oil shale grabbed the headlines, coal produced the goods. In 1979, the previous all-time tonnage production record (1918) of 12.5

million tons of coal was easily surpassed: nearly 20 million tons was mined in 1980. The coal came from forty-nine underground and twenty-five surface mines, primarily in Routt and Moffat Counties, followed by Gunnison, Delta, and that old-time producer, Las Animas. Coal reigned again as king of the energy industry, thanks largely to its use by utility companies to generate electricity. All this activity obviously affected Colorado with air pollution, transportation problems, and unregulated local growth. The fearsome specter of cheaper strip mining lurked in the background. It trailed a reputation for environmental devastation, despite a new emphasis on reclamation.

For all the significance implied in coal's resurgence, oil shale promised an even greater impact, if it could be developed. Long overshadowed by other fuels, Colorado's vast shale deposits might be a means of relieving energy pressures on the country. Exxon, the world's largest oil company, envisioned an industry that would produce a stunning 8 million barrels of oil daily by the year 2010. In 1980, it set to work on its Colony Project. This project, the company predicted, would recruit 1.5 million Coloradans to mine and retort and give rise to a metropolitan region of Denver's size in northwestern Colorado. Staggering to imagine, the plan had unprecedented sociological, ecological, and economic implications. A *Denver Post* editorial on June 29, 1980, warned that Colorado had failed to prepare adequately for the development of those reserves and had now to take a more active role: "A surging shale industry doesn't have to do simply with oil. A surging shale industry involves roads and schools, law enforcement and medical services, domestic water supply and pollution control—a myriad of human concerns, all of which are Colorado's concerns."

Concerns mounted, but Exxon was having its own problems, including cost overruns, retorting problems, and changing international oil prices. On "Black Sunday," May 2, 1982, Exxon announced that it was abandoning its Colony Project; 2,200 people immediately became unemployed, which was just the beginning of the ripple effect. Depressed, disillusioned, and bankrupt, former employees drifted away over the next couple of years. A philosophical resident of Parachute lamented, "Everybody was here for money. Heck, I was. But we just couldn't make it."

The long-anticipated oil-shale boom busted, the victim of international oil prices and the continued failure to find a profitable method of retorting. The economy of Grand Junction and Craig—and Mesa and

Garfield Counties—sagged along with that of the new community of Battlement Mesa. (The last did manage to rebound as a retirement community later.) Colorado's oil and natural gas companies slowed their exploration and drilling, laid off workers, and waited for better days.

As Governor Richard Lamm accurately observed, "This is part of the boom-and-bust cycle the West has been experiencing throughout its history." Even with the support of Washington and Exxon, the Western Slope had "busted" twice since World War II; the energy crisis had boosted expectations higher and busted them lower than ever before. The willingness to back any boom had led to trouble once again. Looking for scapegoats, Coloradans zeroed in on those old bugaboos: big business and the federal government. They took to the political stump as they had in the past. Politics acquired new vigor with the energy issue.

Coloradans, always mavericks when it came to voting and political preferences, had demonstrated further evidence of their capricious nature after the war ended. Both major political parties pointed with pride to election victories during the two decades from 1950 to 1970; neither could claim a monopoly on the voters' affections. The fall election of 1950 gave state control to the Republicans, who elected Dan Thornton as governor. Thornton won a second term before the Grand Old Man of the Democratic Party (and one of the leading Colorado politicians of the era), Edwin C. Johnson, led his party to victory and seated himself in the governor's chair in 1954. Johnson, involved in state politics since the 1920s, served one term and was succeeded by Democrat Stephen McNichols, elected twice. One of his terms was the first four-year governor's term in Colorado. The Democrats dominated the governorship in the 1950s, a trend reversed in the 1960s.

John A. Love led the Republican resurgence. He won a term as governor in his very first attempt at elective office in 1962. A Colorado Springs lawyer, educated at the University of Denver, Love retained his office through the next two elections. Despite victories by Democrats Johnson and McNichols, the Republicans also garnered the state's six electoral votes throughout the 1950s and lost them only once in the next decade—to Lyndon Johnson in the landslide of 1964. The Republicans also controlled the U.S. Senate seats, except for the single term of John Carroll (1957–1963). Gordon Allott (1954) and Peter Dominick (1962), both conservative Republicans, withstood Democratic challenges. Colorado was one of the ten most Republican states in the United States, based on statewide and congressional elections in the 1960–1990 era.

Popular President Dwight D. Eisenhower enjoyed visiting Colorado, the home of his wife Mamie. Here Ike has just finished a day's fishing after the Republican Convention in 1952.

The Republican trend did not prevent the Democrats from faring better in the House, where they shared a two-two division with the Republicans and controlled the delegation after 1964. This record reflected the political durability of Wayne Aspinall, who represented the Fourth (Western Slope) District from 1949 to 1973, and Byron Rogers from the First (Denver) District (1951 to 1971).

The state was split politically, much as it had been in the 1880s, although the bases of party strength had shifted somewhat. The Democrats held Denver, the Republicans the suburbs, duplicating national patterns. The eastern plains supported the GOP, while the southern counties and Western Slope generally responded to Democratic appeals. In his successful campaigns, Governor Love managed to hold his districts and make crippling inroads into Democratic areas, while the Democrats proved unable to find either candidates or issues attractive enough to reverse Love's fortunes. A change was coming. The 1964 U.S. Supreme Court decision, "one man, one vote," assured the eventual dominance of urban Colorado.

In the presidential election of 1968, 71 percent of Colorado's eligible voters turned out to give Republican Richard Nixon slightly more than 50 percent of their votes. Nixon repeated his victory in 1972. On the major political question of the 1960s—the Vietnam War—Colorado, like the rest of the country, seemed uncertain and divided. Demonstrations, parades, sit-ins, and disruptions of speeches marked the movement by youth and peace groups; "hawks" and "doves" each had their own spokespersons. Unrest on some university and college campuses angered conservatives (and some moderates), while street politics and confrontations continued to demonstrate the highly emotional nature of the complex issue.

The inevitable outgrowth of the turmoil was change. Aspinall, Allott, and Rogers lost their constituencies, and Governor Love resigned (1973) to become director of the Office of Energy Policy in Washington, D.C. Proof of the changing order came with the election of the first woman to Congress from Colorado. Pat Schroeder won her House race in 1972 and during the next two decades provided the state with a knowledgeable, energetic, and controversial congresswoman.

Water and public lands controversies stirred up a "sagebrush revolt" throughout the West in the late 1970s. It was an old song with a new title, and the villain this time was the federal government. No longer merely an intrastate squabble, the water feud had long before evolved

Colorado's first woman representative, Patricia Schroeder, caught baseball fever in the 1990s.

into a regional, national, and international dispute. When President Jimmy Carter issued his famous "hit list," which temporarily halted the planning of western and Colorado water projects, the state and region arose in anger. Coloradans in large numbers raised the banner of states' rights and reviled the excesses of big government, overbearing bureaucracy, and federal red tape. Anger raged and sectionalism cried out for attention. Water, energy development, federal land ownership (36 percent of Colorado), and taxes all generated controversy. When they took their case to Washington, however, Coloradans and other Westerners found themselves, as usual, long on resources but short on capital and votes. Colorado has always promoted growth and enjoyed federal subsidies, taking more from Washington than it has ever given back to benefit the country.

The revolt looked potent for a season. Coloradans had fought this battle earlier, and if history were to repeat itself, the issues would dissipate after a short time. The revolt died in the early 1980s but not the issues. Carter had little to lose politically in either the state or the region; neither one had given him a majority in 1976. Politically nonconforming in politics for most of the 1970s, Colorado elected two Democratic senators and a Republican-dominated state legislature. Democrats also held the edge in the state's delegation to the House of Representatives. Richard Lamm won the governor's chair in 1974 and then bickered with the Republican-dominated General Assembly over a multitude of issues. He appeared to be extremely vulnerable when he sought reelection but won easily in 1978. During Lamm's administration, Democratic choices for lieutenant governor claimed two firsts: the first African American, George Brown, in 1974, and the first woman, Nancy Dick, in 1978.

The Republicans were revitalized as the decade closed, winning one Senate seat with Bill Armstrong and solidly retaining the Colorado statehouse. The other senator, Democrat Gary Hart, won easily in 1974; he skillfully represented Colorado's interests in Washington during the following crucial years and was reelected. Colorado politics exemplified the turbulent changes of the 1970s. The state, as one analyst saw it, was propelled out of a low-key, easy-going era into a new period of turmoil.

Growth gave Colorado a sixth seat in the House of Representatives in 1982. Always politically unpredictable, the state remained so in the 1980s—the Republicans won the presidential election and did well in state legislative races, while the Democrats maintained their hold on the governorship and persevered in congressional elections. Majority

Republicans in the legislature, more often than not, found themselves at odds with Governor Lamm, who finished his third term in January 1987.

All the squabbling, the rural versus urban conflicts, and the lack of farsighted leadership led to an unimpressive record for the legislatures of the 1980s. The deterioration of Colorado's highways gave dreary evidence of legislative indecision. Cutbacks in Washington and the weak economy did not ease the task of the legislators, but the fault ultimately lay with them and the voters who sent them to Denver.

Part of the problem became evident in a June 1986 poll, which found that only 29 percent of Coloradans interviewed could correctly name both of their U.S. senators; 13 percent knew their state senator. A dearth of leadership from business, education, and politics can also be blamed for the lack of direction in the 1980s.

After twelve challenging and controversial years, Richard Lamm decided to step down. "Politics, like theater, is one of those things you've got to be wise enough to know when to leave," he admonished at the end of his third term. No other Colorado governor had ever held the position so long, and no one before him had so continually attracted national attention to the state because of his thought-provoking opinions on such topics as health care, immigration, and America's future. With a broad vision of what Colorado and the West could be, Lamm was a refreshing rarity in state and national politics, "a candid, yet far seeing philosopher," who gave new dimension to the office.

For the first time in Colorado history, both of its senators, Gary Hart and Bill Armstrong, were seriously discussed as presidential candidates. In 1984 Hart made a strong bid for the Democratic nomination; anticipating another try in 1988, he retired from the Senate in 1986, but his second try for the nomination was aborted early in 1988 amid the rumors of marital infidelity. Colorado's stature in national politics had never been so high, and its congressional delegation had never before been so active on the national scene. How a normally insignificant state, politically speaking, could acquire so great a voice mystified observers. Obviously many of Colorado's best leaders had gone to Washington, not to Denver.

The pressures of politics intensified over the years, as Representative Ray Kogovsek testified: "I had lost all control of my life." The problems of a 56,000-square-mile district (from Pueblo in a wide sweep to Grand Junction), mounting campaign expenses, and the constant travel led to his decision to retire from office in 1985 after three terms.

In the 1980s politicians of both parties resorted more and more frequently to mudslinging and negative advertising—tactics that were prevalent across the nation. Another disturbing trend was the rising cost of campaigning. Never before had Colorado politics been so expensive—in 1986, $3.1 million was spent on the governor's election and $7.5 million on the Senate race.

When the 1986 campaign was over, voters had given the Democrats much to cheer about. They had elected Roy Romer governor (and re-elected him in 1990 and 1994), Tim Wirth U.S. senator, and split the House delegation, with three going to each party. The Republicans increased their majority in the Colorado Senate, the Democrats in the House. Women also improved their lot; twenty-nine were elected to serve in the legislature, an all-time high. They had also played more key roles in the year's top campaigns than ever before, befitting their rising involvement in politics. Moderates in both parties also made inroads.

As the 1980s drew to a close, Colorado politics remained as unpredictable as ever. Although Republicans cornered most of the votes, an attractive and hard-working Democratic candidate had a good shot at winning. "It's a Republican leaning state, yet appealing, pro-business and pro-Colorado Democrats can win there," noted political scientist Thomas Cronin. Protests and debate aside, Washington, as always, played a major role in the state. Colorado's legislature still wrestled with generations-old problems. Nonetheless, change came and Tennyson was on the mark when he wrote, "The old order changeth, yielding place to new."

THIRTY-TWO

URBAN COLORADO

High mountain villages, eastern plains ranches, and southwestern Colorado farms coalesced to form an idyllic image of a picture-perfect rural state. But that picture was distorted. The 1990 census takers found that 82 percent of Coloradans lived in an urban setting. The population was concentrated along the front range, with over 80 percent settled in the corridor from Fort Collins to Pueblo, making Colorado one of the most urban states in the United States.

Colorado's dramatic postwar population growth was swollen by emigrants from both the East and West Coasts, who brought with them the very pollution and overcrowding they had sought to escape. The state's population rose from 1,325,089 in 1950 to 3,294,394 forty years later. The rate of growth in the 1950s was 28 percent, a record 30.8 percent in the 1970s, and 14 percent in the 1980s. Another perception of the change comes from the people-per-square-mile figures: In 1969, it was 20.2; in 1990, 31.8. Though not yet crowded by eastern standards, Colorado had less and less elbow room. The disparity in population across the state was evident in the fact that Denver had 3,050 residents per square mile and Hinsdale County .4. In 1990 Colorado was the second most populous of the mountain states, behind Arizona, and ranked twenty-sixth nationally.

Meanwhile, some areas of eastern, southern, and southwestern Colorado lost population; rural counties did not show the same growth as their more prosperous neighbors. From 1950 to 1990 the population decreased in San Juan County by 46 percent, in Kiowa County by 56 percent, and in Costilla County by 53 percent.

Not since the halcyon mining days of the previous century had the state been so urbanized. World War II invigorated the urbanization process, and postwar migration flowed largely to the metropolitan areas. The strength of urban Colorado steadily increased relative to rural Colorado, as the latter became an ever less powerful satellite of the former. This shift did not occur without some wrenching conflict and heartbreak. Yet, through it all, the venerable nineteenth-century "grow or die" philosophy flourished, pointing inevitably, it would seem, to a prosperous future. Along with the prosperity, the growth proponents argued, would come lower taxes, more jobs, and urban landscapes better suited to the pace and style of modern life. Their arguments sounded compelling, and many Coloradans were predisposed to believe them.

Much of the urban growth resulted from federal activity and the surge of corporations into the metropolitan area, which did increase personal income in those regions. The state's per capita income in 1990 averaged $14,821, but Adams, Arapahoe, Boulder, Douglas, and Denver Counties, for example, ranged up to $7,000 higher than that average. On the lower end of the scale were such rural counties as Costilla, Huerfano, Mineral, and Conejos. Urban dwellers also tended to be younger and better educated than their rural counterparts.

Statistics alone, however, cannot begin to tell the complete story of changes in Colorado after 1945. Even Denver, which reaped the biggest benefits, suffered through its share of trauma. Journalist John Gunther wrote in 1947, "Denver is Olympian, impassive and inert. It is probably the most self-sufficient, isolated and self-contained city in the world." The transformation of the city began with Quigg Newton's victory as mayor over Ben Stapleton, who had held the office, except for one term, since 1923. The old guard gradually changed, as the city council also got a housecleaning. With these people went some of the old attitudes. Faced with a city housing shortage, Stapleton had said in 1946, with a certain blundering accuracy, "If all these people would only go back where they came from, we wouldn't have a housing shortage."

Investors and corporations brought money in from outside the region over the following decades, and their impact was clearly seen in the city's rapidly changing skyline. New movers and shakers replaced rigid traditionalists, and some decisions about Denver's future were coming from outside the city. The "sleepy, self-satisfied" town was awakened as it had not been in the twentieth century. The capital's shiny new face could not, however, disguise the fact that the city was facing drawbacks common to all modern urban communities: pollution, inadequate public transportation, traffic congestion, a decaying core, negligence of minority rights, and unresponsive government. Denver was growing up but not nearly so fast as it was growing out.

The suburbs expanded far faster than the core city. Railroads and streetcars had shaped early Denver and Colorado, but automobiles reshaped both the cityscape and human lives. The clearest example was the Boulder-Denver Turnpike, which opened in 1952. By 1966, 13,774 travelers a day were paying the 25¢ toll; in September 1967, the accumulated profits allowed the tollbooths to be removed. Westminster, Broomfield, and Boulder benefited immediately, as did eventually Longmont and other nearby communities.

A few statistics illustrate the impact of growth on Denver's once sleepy, rural suburbs in the hectic postwar decades from 1950 to 1990. Littleton's population soared from 3,300 to 33,600, Aurora's leaped from 11,300 to 222,100, and Arvada's from 2,300 to 89,200. Some of these communities were nearly as old as the 1859 gold rush, others were quite new, but all of them had in common the postwar boom. Boulder, nearly alone among the booming communities, worked to control the explosive growth that overwhelmed its neighbors. Strict codes regulating building, open space, and land use terrified their critics but ultimately paid public and private dividends. Even so, the university city's population grew from 19,000 to 83,000.

Though tied to its suburbs by proximity and new development, Denver related to them in much the same way as it had to the federal government—with ambivalence. Many of the problems perceived as "metropolitan" actually arose from regional economic and social conditions that transcended the city's boundaries. Denver, called upon to solve them, had no "stick" to force the suburban communities to help pay for solutions.

By the 1960s Denver was home to a significant number of minorities and its tax base had declined; at the same time, the surrounding suburbs had remained predominantly white and Anglo and maintained a solid tax base. The white exodus from the inner city was not unique to

Water has emerged as the issue throughout Colorado. Shown here is the Englewood Dam under construction.

Denver. Elsewhere, as in Denver, the social services, and medical, public, and cultural facilities provided by the city benefited the outlying towns, which balked at supporting them. Denver tried to shift some of the financial burden, without much success.

Annexation of surrounding areas by the capital city also fueled anger and resentment. Finally, in 1974, Coloradans passed a constitutional amendment (popularly known as the Poundstone Amendment) that required Denver to gain voter approval not only from the area to be annexed but also from the county that stood to lose ground. Denver's geographical growth was effectively ended that year. The vote exhibited a fear not only of Denver's plans and power but also of its integrated schools and their court-mandated busing.

Water also caused controversy. Denver had enough, thanks to the powerful Denver Water Department. As historians Thomas Noel and Stephen Leonard observed, "With single-minded purposefulness, the

DWD redirected statewide water flow to the metropolis." Some suburbs were not blessed with so powerful an agency and the long-range planning it provided. The proposed Two Forks dam in South Platte Canyon was intended to be a joint project between Denver and the Metropolitan Water Providers to ensure plentiful, cheap water and promote economic growth. Opposition arose from environmentalists, recreationists, and the state of Nebraska concerning water flow, wildlife, and other issues. When the Environmental Protection Agency denied the permit in 1989, some suburbs wanted to pursue the fight, but Denver abandoned it. An effort at cooperation between Denver and its suburbs died amid a barrage of name-calling, leaving a legacy of hard feelings.

Jealousy and fear of Denver has existed since 1859 in both rural and urban areas. Though Denver has had its share of problems, no other city in the state has ever come close to challenging its number one position.

Other parts of Colorado either failed to grow or saw their populations decline. Rural areas, particularly the eastern plains and the San Luis Valley, experienced the worst problems. Limited job opportunities, poverty, the lack of development, fewer facilities (such as medical), and isolation hindered the best attempts to reverse the downturn. The efforts of one state administration after another and expenditures of millions of dollars failed to alleviate the chronic economic stagnation in these areas. Former Governor John Vanderhoof aptly summarized the 1970s when he grimly stated, "There just aren't a whole lot of things the state can do. I wish it wasn't true but it pretty well is." Unfortunately, a lack of understanding by Denver and the urban areas handicapped renewal efforts. A marked unwillingness to invest and settle in the rural regions persisted on the part of Denverites and outside companies.

An obvious change—and a crisis—came to farming when the so-called family farm became more a relic of the past than a reality of the present. As large mechanized operations began to dominate the agricultural scene, the need for workers and their families evaporated. As a consequence, business receded in farm communities and the population melted away, continuing a trend that would last for decades. Young people financially able to start farming on their own literally became an endangered species. Rising land values, taxes, debts, day-to-day costs, and wildly fluctuating prices (usually low) plagued the farmer. In despair, many of them sold out to developers or more successful neighbors. All these changes were occurring in Colorado at a time when world food shortages mandated even larger increases in food production.

Not all urban areas boomed in the postwar years. In 1957 Silverton reflected only a little of its mining past, but tourism was coming.

The crux of the farmers' plight lay in declining farm income. Totally aghast, Colorado Agriculture Commissioner J. Even Goulding remarked in 1978, "It is stunning to see so much decline in farm income," which was 48 percent lower than it had been only three years earlier. In the fine tradition of their ancestors, Colorado farmers protested heatedly. Agitation stirred in depressed southeastern Colorado in the small farming community of Springfield. Farmers, calling themselves the American Agriculture Movement, threatened to strike. In September 1977, the call went out for a nationwide farm strike in December. Before the tumult died, tractors rolled in protest to Washington and elsewhere, and farmers plowed under some crops, attracting a good share of television and press coverage in the process. Congress passed emergency legislation in response. Like their Populist counterparts of the 1890s, the farmers had spoken and acted, but had anyone listened? Urban Coloradans only

Three-term governor Richard Lamm shows Colorado's new international role as he signs a wheat contract between Chinese and Colorado farmers in 1978.

noted or, at best, vaguely understood. Crop prices, meanwhile, failed to improve and taxes and farming costs continued to rise.

The 1980s brought no improvement in their lot. The domino effect hit eastern Colorado particularly hard; towns and counties lost population and jobs as businesses and banks failed. In Hereford, near the Wyoming border in Weld County, the bank and grain elevator closed in the fateful summer of 1984, and with the closing went most of the town's reason for existing. Resident Judy Werner pinpointed another major problem: the migration of young Coloradans from rural counties. Heartbroken but empathic, she lamented the departure of her own children and those of others from Hereford: "Most of 'em leave, I think it's a shame." Without jobs, these youth had no future; without the young people, the Herefords of Colorado faced a bleak one.

Larger communities in decline suffered equally devastating blows. A Yuma farm equipment dealer spoke for many when he described his business in 1986, "I'd say, to be frank, we've dropped off at least half in the last three years. It's getting hairy." From Montezuma County to Sedgwick, agriculture diminished; neither individuals nor state and federal programs were able to reverse the trend.

Commenting on the loss of the farm and ranch culture, State Representative Richard Bond, whose district included the Greeley area, perceptively summarized the what and why: "I think it's going to be a loss for the whole country. And yet I recognize that the price of time and progress is change. And I guess we have to make change. I think you're dealing with the heart of the human dilemma and some would say, the human tragedy."

For rural Colorado, the Western Slope provided a microcosm of the entire state, both in its promises and in its problems. As the potential site of most of the future energy developments, it was threatened with great changes. Craig, during its brief energy boom, gave dramatic evidence of unplanned instant urbanization—trailer-court sprawl, increased crime, family dissension, and overwhelmed county and town governments. The exorbitantly expensive, tinsel, jet-set community of Aspen ("The Land of Peter Pan," *Sports Illustrated* called it in a 1977 feature story) exemplified the horror of overexploitation of skiing and tourism. Somewhere between these two extremes sat the remainder of the Western Slope. The search for a broader economic base went on; the hope was to find "clean" (nonpolluting) industries to complement agriculture, tourism, and mining.

Residents of the Western Slope had very little political influence; they cast about 10 percent of Colorado's total vote in the 1970s elections. Not much improvement came in the next decade, when only Grand Junction and Durango topped 10,000 in population. A poor country cousin politically—rural, isolated, and exploited—the Western Slope (a colonial appendage that included some of Colorado's most spectacular scenery) placed its future in the hands of outsiders.

Perennially at odds with the Eastern Slope over water, the Western Slope confronted Denver and other eastern cities that had their eyes on Western Slope water, the only major surface source left. Frustration and fear mounted. There was even some talk in the West about seceding from the rest of Colorado, which was "far away" and seemed to have no interest in solving the problems of the Western Slope. Denver was the lightning rod that attracted all the attention and received much of the blame. Yet without the help and tax support of the Eastern Slope, the Western Slope would have had a hard time maintaining itself. The complaints were as old as Colorado.

Urban Colorado had new things to worry about. On one crucial issue, civil rights, Colorado was right in step with the nation. Minority

Coloradans were demanding their rights and government response to their collective grievances. African Americans, Chicanos, Hispanics, and Native Americans, many in urban situations, began to assert themselves.

Denverites felt the impact of minority unrest when de facto segregation in their public schools generated complaints. Minority groups predominated in some schools; inferior facilities and tacit, if not overt, segregation by means of redrawn school boundary lines led to a court challenge to force school desegregation. The case eventually was heard by the U.S. Supreme Court, which ruled that Denver tolerated de jure segregation and a dual educational system. The Court ordered busing to achieve racial balance, a solution that riled residents of Denver as much as those of other cities. But when the schools opened in the fall of 1974, the first term under Court order, Denver's residents generally acquiesced peaceably, and there was minimal protest as buses transported students. For the next two decades Court-ordered busing continued.

The rapid movement of minority groups into previously all-white neighborhoods generated hostile reactions, which, along with the increasing inner-city problems, drove residents into the suburbs in search of the "all-American" way of life. The goal obviously proved elusive (because there is no such thing), and the problems migrated right along with them.

Denver exhibited a less-than-admirable side, too. As the largest urban center, it attracted minorities struggling for social, economic, and political equality. Housing discrimination, dead-end and low-paying jobs, police "brutality," and closet racism affected them all. Tension and trouble accompanied their striving for a better life. Opposition to busing, racial disturbances, city council bickering, and the activities of the Ku Klux Klan and other white supremacist groups played a role in Denver's reaction to integration, which was much the same as that of other U.S. cities. On the positive side, minority integration came to politics on the congressional and city levels; the election of Mayor Federico Peña, a Hispanic, in 1983 was a major breakthrough. By 1990 Denver had an African American district attorney, city auditor, and manager of safety; two African Americans sat on the city council.

Demands for minority rights were not limited to the capital city, and they were not only related to race. Women continued to lobby for rights long denied them. In the political arena they made strides throughout the state; the election of Pat Schroeder as congresswoman was an outstanding example. Several women served as mayors of such diverse communities as Silverton, Sterling, Walden, and Kremmling, and by 1990 they held the majority of city council seats in Denver and other communities. They also worked as fire and police chiefs, parks and recreation directors, and city attorneys, and were elected to various other town, county, and state positions. Nevertheless, it took the prodding of federal officials to persuade mine operators to offer underground coal-mining jobs to women in 1973. Women's athletics stirred a wave that buffeted institutions of higher learning and incited strong feelings. But the women persisted, and under federal prodding, athletic programs moved slowly toward equality of the sexes. Women were appointed presidents of several Colorado colleges and universities, were better represented in the professions, and invaded the higher echelons of business and management. A backlash inevitably arose and precipitated an attempt to repeal the Equal Rights Amendment, which voters had previously approved in 1972.

Mexican Americans are the only ethnic group found in large numbers throughout much of Colorado. They, too, struggled to improve their position. Local schools and health care were targeted for improvement, along with the lot of the migrant worker, the permanent rural Hispanic, and those crowded into the slums of towns large and small. Both violent and nonviolent protests were organized; small gains came slowly. In Center, in the San Luis Valley, Hispanics controlled the town council, secured representation on the school board, and pressed other issues in a new, forceful manner. In Denver, Rodolfo "Corky" Gonzales and his Crusade for Justice focused on the plight of the metropolitan Chicano.

The decades-old division between the Anglo and Spanish cultures, long unspoken, came into the open at Center and many other places. Some serious efforts were made to bridge the gap. The Cultural Resource Center at Alamosa, for example, made bilingual and bicultural materials available to schools and teachers in the San Luis Valley. Although comments such as "Their culture has to fit into ours," or "We do not have the problem here" demonstrated a continuous lack of awareness and sensitivity, the inherent problems were being recognized. Active reformers were challenged to seek equitable solutions.

In southwestern Colorado, the Southern Utes and the Ute Mountain Utes inhabited two reservations granted to them a hundred years earlier. The Southern Utes adjusted well to twentieth-century life, living in a triethnic culture around their tribal government at Ignacio. To the west, the Ute Mountain Utes in the Towaoc area dwelt in near poverty on a reservation that lacked water and held out little hope for the future. In truth, more Indians lived in Denver than on the two reservations combined; most migrated to the city from the plains reservations. They tended to place more importance on civil rights than on tribal rights and often made common cause with other minorities. Their White Buffalo Council sponsored the annual Indian Exposition and public performances of tribal dances. Like other minorities, some adjusted well to urban living, and others found the road more difficult.

Pondering all the problems of the 1960s and 1970s, Governor Lamm, in a sober inaugural speech that launched his second term, predicted that Colorado was "on a painful collision course with the future." Was Colorado ready? Were Coloradans prepared? That future depended on the answers. It would have to be decided by all Coloradans, both urban and rural, and by all ethnic groups.

THIRTY-THREE

THE OLD AND THE NEW

Another star is added to Columbia's galaxy, and that Colorado is the Centennial State in good earnest. It is as a sovereign state, mistress of herself and her destinies, Colorado will now conquering and to conquer, pursue the path of prosperity.

William Byers prophesied thus on July 2, 1876. Coloradans a hundred years later might have wished the same for their state, but their world was greatly different from that of Byers. Colorado's centennial came and went with appropriate pomp and ceremony, but it was somewhat overshadowed by the nation's bicentennial. A few citizens saw the commotion as a waste of time; others involved themselves enthusiastically. Most Coloradans seemed to take the occasion in stride, partaking of what struck their fancy and ignoring the rest. At least this celebration had proved more authentic than an earlier one: In 1959, the centennial of Rush to the Rockies had paled in its attempt to imitate the original gold rush.

Whether in 1859, 1876, or 1976, the vagaries of nature remained a constant factor. The disastrous South Platte flood of June 14–17, 1965, inundated more than $500 million worth of both rural and urban property and disrupted transportation. Modern manipulations—dams, improved stream channels, and other engineering efforts—could not stop it. Nature dealt a cruel centennial card on July 31, 1976, when the Big Thompson flood killed 151 people, destroyed 52 businesses in the canyon, swept away 323 homes, and did millions of dollars damage. It was a painful way to commemorate the state's centennial.

A 1977 drought hurt skiers and farmers alike; in July 1980, the worst forest fire in Colorado's recorded history burned over 10,000 acres of the White River National Forest. A tornado almost destroyed Limon in June 1990, and myriad hailstorms over the years ruined many crops and damaged vehicles and buildings. Avalanches took a steady toll of careless or unfortunate backcountry skiers and closed highways; and the winter of 1992-1993 produced some record snowfalls for southwestern Colorado. Old scourges rose to bedevil the modern day.

Water continued to be the subject of an enduring saga. East Slopers squared off against West Slopers in an ongoing debate, while Colorado and other states went to court over water rights. The environmental movement further complicated matters by the 1970s, creating a scenario in which only water lawyers stood to gain.

Water bubbled into headlines on a multitude of fronts. In 1956 Congress authorized the Upper Colorado River Project, which included plans for reservoirs, dams, and power plants in Arizona, Utah, New Mexico, and Colorado within a 110,000-square-mile basin. The major purpose of this sweeping plan was to provide an equitable division and apportionment of water in the Colorado River system. It also prescribed water storage, flood prevention, and electric power. Each state would receive an allotment of water to be used during the year, and a river commission would be established to oversee the operation. Launched with enthusiasm, the project would, it was hoped, "promote interstate comity." As it turned out, ingrained biases and state self-interests proved hard to overcome. Extended planning and high costs of operations ensured complaints and bickering.

However, an indication of the financial success of the venture came with the nearly $98 million in revenues for the twelve-month period ending September 30, 1970—$25 million more than the preceding year. Sales of electric power and water were greater than anticipated, allowing more rapid project repayment than the Bureau of Reclamation had predicted. Among the participating projects in the Upper Colorado system were the Blue Mesa Dam on the Gunnison River, Rifle Gap Dam near Silt, and Lemon Dam on the Florida River in La Plata County. Local irrigation and reclamation benefited, and all the projects proved to be magnets for tourists.

Congress also approved, in 1962, the Frying Pan–Arkansas Project for transmontane storage and water diversion to assist the southeastern part of the state. This system collected water west of the Continental Divide and tunneled the diverted water to the Eastern Slope, where it was stored in reservoirs for later use for irrigation and municipal water supplies. Protests arose again from residents of the Western Slope about the loss of their water, but the project went ahead nonetheless.

By this time, Colorado's water position, in relation to competing states, was fairly stable. It appeared that at last the way was clear to resolve the water problems that had so long baffled and irritated the populace. But the exceedingly rapid growth of two of the so-called lower-basin states, California and Arizona (particularly the Phoenix area), had created new demands on old interstate compacts by the end of the 1960s, resulting in another round of water and dam planning.

As the 1960s ended and the 1970s opened, federal projects were becoming harder to secure, and issues associated with them had grown more complex. The history of the Animas–La Plata project, a water storage and irrigation facility planned for southwestern Colorado, clearly evidenced the change. A generation of planning, debating, arguing, and lawsuits went by as costs mounted and construction seemed as far away as ever. The project appeared to have a life all its own. While the Animas–La Plata was mired in the mud, the neighboring Dolores Project survived a similar battle and intense federal scrutiny as it proceeded to completion. Words such as environmental impact statement, endangered species, Indian water rights, aquifer, acre-foot, and salinity assimilated themselves into Coloradans' vocabularies.

Local opposition to the Animas–La Plata project proved that potential environmental changes produced by federal projects would thereafter prompt serious and penetrating investigation; that unquestioned compliance with rearranging nature's work would no longer prevail. The newer, more sensitive concerns would challenge other so-called improvements, from highway construction to activities at the Rocky Mountain Arsenal.

Denver had its eye on water from the Western Slope—the only major surface source left—and so did others. Advocates lobbied for more dams and storage reservoirs; opponents argued just as emotionally that the impact on the environment and the cost would negate any benefits of the projects. The demise of the Two Forks project proved the impact of environmentalist efforts. Several suburbs looked to buy water rights on the Arkansas River, while some individuals and companies talked of selling unused water rights to California and Nevada.

In old battles and new, water attracted attention and remained on the front page. No longer confined to intrastate squabbles, water had emerged very early as a regional, national, and international issue. Water and water projects, it seemed, brought out the worst in people. East and West Sloper, rural and urban, industrialist and farmer—all were involved in the controversy at one time or another. For example, the U.S. Supreme Court held in 1983 that nontributary groundwater was not subject to appropriation; that ruling put an end to several years of litigation. More than 100 lawyers represented various concerned parties at the hearing. A completed project proved unable to produce harmony among warring factions—a group of farmers claimed that they could not afford the Dolores Project water and sued the Bureau of Reclamation, alleging misrepresentation of the cost of the water to them.

Permeating all of these plans and projects was a growing concern for the environment. Coloradans were beginning to realize that they could lose something irreplaceable. Evidence of the attitude conversion came dramatically in the early 1970s. The debate over the state's hosting of the 1976 Winter Olympics provided unequivocal evidence of the changing concerns of Colorado residents. Enthusiasm for securing the games had been elicited as part of the centennial and bicentennial celebrations. Rigorous international competition from other potential sites failed to thwart Colorado's bid for the honor, which was awarded in May 1970. The Denver interests that had led the fight and stood to gain the lion's share of publicity and profit hardly had time to congratulate themselves before heated opposition rained down on their parade. Objections quickly zeroed in on site selection, transportation logistics, costs, air quality, and environmental impact.

Citizens for Colorado's Future, the organized opposition, launched a petition campaign to allow Coloradans to vote on whether state funds should be expended for the Olympics. A 1972 referendum placed the issue squarely before the voters. A door-to-door campaign and other strategies were used to create awareness of the issue and promote discussion of its ramifications. The Denver Olympic Committee, meanwhile, sought to counteract criticism by rearranging the sites and initiating a well-financed campaign of its own. Its cause was not helped initially by estimating the cost to the state at only $14 million, a projection that escalated to $35 million within two years. "Sell Colorado" had been a perennial theme; now there was fear that it had been oversold.

When the votes were counted, the amendment to prohibit the expenditure of state funds for the Olympics had passed by nearly 180,000 votes, sweeping almost the entire state. Even Denver voters supported it. Governor Love, who had backed the games, said he was disappointed, embarrassed, and "somewhat ashamed." Obviously, most of the electorate felt otherwise. They did not so much oppose the Olympics as they favored protection of the environment and better use of the taxpayers' money.

And it was not just the Olympics that forced the issue. The "brown cloud" hanging over Denver gave the city and state some undesirable publicity; a "second Los Angeles," some called the city. Heavy automobile use (Colorado has one of the highest car-per-person ratios in the world) has generated insidious smog, which hovers mainly over the Eastern Slope's urban corridor from Pueblo to Fort Collins. Too many two- and three-car families, and too little use of public transportation, have exacerbated the problem, along with wood and coal smoke; efforts to clean up the air have ranged from enforcing no-wood-burning days to requiring the use of oxyfuels (specifically blended gasolines designed to cut carbon monoxide emissions). Improvement has been noted, but the once healthful, clear atmosphere that Colorado is famous for disappears some days. Other towns, such as Aspen and Telluride, have limited wood burning and regulated fireplaces and stoves.

Those relics of yesterday, uranium tailings, contaminated land from Denver to Grand Junction and Durango, and places in between. The Environmental Protection Agency and the state, after much feuding over whose responsibility it was, launched a cleanup campaign. To remove the tailings from the Durango site cost $15 million—and that was just a start. The EPA also looked into other messes, such as the ones at the Rocky Mountain Arsenal and at Rocky Flats, and concluded that the cleanups there would be neither cheap nor easy.

Acid rain was falling on the mountains, mountain cabin cisterns and privies were polluting streams, and litter could be found almost every place to which the public had access. Well-known resorts like Aspen and Grand Lake were facing crises brought on by overpromotion. The crunch of increased population and tourism promised that the situation would only worsen unless some drastic measures were taken or the public could be persuaded to change its habits.

Tourism increasingly emerged in postwar Colorado as virtually the

Protestors surround Rocky Flats Nuclear Weapons Plant in the early 1980s.

only industry in many parts of the state, albeit a growing, vital one. Thanks to the federal government, the state's parks, mountains, and resorts were more accessible than ever before with the construction of four-lane divided highways, beginning in the 1950s. Running north and south, Interstate 25 connected the cities strung along the Front Range, while Interstate 70 carried tourists into the central Rockies on an east-west route. After the Eisenhower Tunnel, on I-70, was completed in 1973 at a cost of more than $1,000 *per inch* for the 8,941-foot tunnel, skiers no longer had to brave the icy slopes of Loveland Pass to reach many popular ski areas. Reflecting, in large measure, the efforts of veterans of the Tenth Mountain Division, some of whom returned to Colorado after the war, skiing became increasingly popular and profitable. It provided year-round tourism potential from Telluride to Eldora and attracted more participants each year. In the well-known resorts, like Vail and Aspen, thousands crowded onto the slopes on brisk winter weekends. The winter stillness of the mountains was also broken by a relative newcomer—the snowmobile—which brought both economic assets and potential environmental liabilities with it.

Even more tourists landed in the summer, seeking out such long-time favorites as Rocky Mountain and Mesa Verde National Parks. The mountains, as always, were the magnets that attracted visitors from out of state. New and convenient camping vehicles and equipment added different dimensions and requirements to the tourist business. Mounting pressure on space forced the government to consider limiting the number of people who could visit Mesa Verde each day. Hot disputes erupted on how best to use the recreational space: Should it be preserved as a protected wilderness, available only under specified conditions? Or should it be opened expansively to accommodate as many people for as many purposes as they wanted?

The tourist industry affected almost all Colorado communities. A town such as Cortez prospered greatly from its proximity to Mesa Verde and its location on a main highway. It could provide gas, food, and rooms to all who traveled through; their purchases filled the coffers of the business people and the city as well, through taxation of goods and services. Hinsdale County depended on tourists for its very existence, as did Estes Park, which had been relying on them for years.

Aspen is a blatant example of a community that sold out to tourism. This former silver camp languished for decades until it underwent a renaissance, beginning in 1948. Walter Paepcke, a Chicago industrialist, initiated the conversion of Aspen into a health, sports, and cultural center. In the wintertime, it offered skiing and in the summer a music festival. Aspen boomed as it had not since the 1880s. What Aspen achieved, other towns dreamed of duplicating. In the end, however, the price of success was to force lower and middle-income people out of town. Homes were sold to newcomers at an average price of more than $1 million.

Not the least of the attractions that lured visitors and residents to the ski town of Aspen—and to the summer opera and theatre season at Central City, the melodrama in Cripple Creek, and the narrow-gauge train trip from Durango to Silverton—was the chance to relive the days when "the West was won." The Centennial State has much to offer in this respect and capitalized on it in the postwar years.

Overcommercialization threatened to render this heritage a tawdry tourist trap, and some ties with the past, like the Tabor Grand Opera House and the Windsor Hotel in downtown Denver, succumbed to the wrecker's ball. An awakened appreciation for the historic and economic benefits of preservation managed to save some of the state's best-known landmarks. Preservation ordinances were enacted and boards formed, from southwest to northeast Colorado, as Coloradans fought to preserve their heritage.

Coloradans also constantly faced the mounting costs and demands of education. Legislature after legislature wrestled with school finances, while school boards sought sources for more money at the local level.

By the 1980s, tourism had become one of the mainstays of Colorado's economy. Even rainy days did not keep tourists from sightseeing.

Large school districts gradually replaced the chaotic system of small districts, and children were bused to central facilities instead of going to neighborhood schools. The loss of local autonomy was a debit, but greater efficiency and wider educational opportunities were an asset. By the 1980s, over half the state budget went to public and higher education.

In 1940 fewer than 10,000 students were enrolled at state-supported senior colleges. Then came the impact of World War II and its aftermath, which brought scores of veterans to institutions of higher education, as they took advantage of the GI bill. By 1960 the count was 26,000 students, and by the 1970s the legislature had imposed enrollment ceilings on the larger institutions. The University of Colorado, Colorado State University, and the University of Northern Colorado (formerly Colorado State College at Greeley) neared or topped 20,000 students. CU, meanwhile, opened campuses at Colorado Springs and Denver.

Some citizens looked to the establishment of junior colleges for relief from the problems inherent in large campuses. But junior colleges have a way of growing up too. Fort Lewis, begun near Hesperus as an Indian school, evolved into a high school, then a junior college, and finally relocated its campus to Durango and upgraded to a four-year curriculum. The junior college at Pueblo traveled a similar route to become the University of Southern Colorado, and Mesa Junior College in Grand Junction took a like path in the 1970s to the status of a four-year college. Other innovations were implemented to attract students. Colorado Mountain College had campuses at Steamboat Springs, Aspen, Rifle, Breckenridge, Vail/Eagle, Leadville, and Glenwood Springs; and Colorado Northwestern Community College (Rangely) provided service-area centers at Meeker, Hayden, Yampa, and Craig.

Metropolitan State College of Denver, the multi-campus Community College of Denver, and the University of Colorado at Denver offered educational options to the urban student. Sharing the Auraria Higher Education Center, on the site of Denver's earliest settlement, the three institutions cooperated in administering a library and other centralized facilities, while retaining their separate identities and programs. The University of Colorado emerged as the state's "flagship" institution and a regional research center, as demonstrated by Professor Thomas Cech's winning of the Nobel Prize for chemistry in 1989. Cech was the state's first Nobel Prize winner.

Governance of these various schools remained a problem, as did financing. Both Fort Lewis and Southern Colorado came under the CSU system, governed by the State Board of Agriculture, while many smaller colleges were controlled by another board—the State Colleges in Colorado. Colorado had thirty-one public two- and four-year colleges and universities.

To avid sports fans, higher education meant a fall football game or a winter evening's basketball game. CU rose to national prominence in football in the 1980s, and the Air Force Academy and CSU provided opportunities to experience other "big time" sporting events. The college fan had many teams to cheer for, as did all Coloradans. Professional major-league sports teams found a home in Colorado: first, the Denver Broncos of the American Football League (which became the American Football Conference) in 1960; then the Denver Nuggets (Rockets, until 1974) basketball team later in the decade. These teams were followed in the 1970s by soccer, rodeo, and the Denver Racquets, who aced their debut by winning the league tennis championship in 1974. Despite their winning ways, the Racquets left for Phoenix in 1975, when no local investors could be found to purchase the franchise. Denver gained a World Hockey Association team in the spring of 1975, only to lose it in 1976 because of poor attendance; a later National Hockey League franchise did no better. Local perception aside, Denver was not the sports mecca it was envisioned to be.

Even with poor early management and a losing record (the best in the 1960s, 7–7), the Broncos emerged as a strong and popular franchise and finally achieved winning ways in the 1970s. Then the Broncos reached the Super Bowl in January 1978; though they lost the game to the Dallas Cowboys, long-suffering fans were only temporarily depressed. "Bronco-mania," as it became known, unified Coloradans as nothing else had done for years and created a multimillion-dollar economic bonanza, which featured everything from Orange Crush T-shirts to ballyhoo-style books. The 1980s brought the Broncos twice to the Super Bowl, and they played again in 1990, but they suffered three more defeats. The aftermath of their second consecutive crushing Super Bowl defeat (January 31, 1988), at the hands of the Washington Redskins, 42–10, was likened by historian Tom Noel to the boom-bust cycles of the nineteenth century and the dashing of Denver's high hopes during the silver era.

The Denver Bears baseball team could boast that it was Colorado's oldest continuous professional sports organization. With the glory days of the 1950s, when they were affiliated with the New York Yankees, behind them, the Bears had their ups and downs in the American Association; but interest in baseball never waned. Attempts to acquire a major league baseball team in these years failed, however, and Denver remained, for the moment, on the outside looking in on its field of dreams.

Coloradans had always had their dreams. Perhaps as they moved through the postwar decades, they should have taken a moment to reflect on where they had been and where they were going. In the words of Colorado's poet laureate, Thomas Hornsby Ferril, from his poem *Stories of Three Summers*,

> Out of the time-slosh of the tides
> We've learned to crawl
> And race the stars so soon,
> We can't remember who we were tomorrow,
> We can't remember who it was
> Back in those quaint old days
> Who walked the moon.

THIRTY-FOUR

"WE CAN'T REMEMBER
WHO WE WERE TOMORROW"

As the 1990s move into the realm of history, a new millennium lies only a few years away. A thousand years ago, the Anasazi were getting ready to build their homes in the caves deep in Mesa Verde. Today Coloradans admire—or berate—their new Denver International Airport, cheer the Colorado Rockies, fret about taxes, and crowd the mountains on weekends. Thomas Hornsby Ferril understood this change and its impact; he wrote in his *Stories of Three Summers*

> For centuries are only flicks
> Of dragonflies
> Over the granite mountains.

Change, the one constant in Colorado's history, has, so far, dominated in the twentieth-century's last decade.

The population exodus was stemmed in 1990–1991. In October 1993, for example, the Denver metro area reached a population of 2 million,

Delays in the opening of Denver International Airport caused controversy and cost money.

only thirty years after passing the 1 million mark. Colorado attained a certain degree of status as the eighth fastest growing state in the nation. Nine of the top ten states were in the West, but California was not one of them. Disenchanted Californians migrated in droves to the Rocky Mountain states, bringing with them mixed blessings. Towns like Durango saw real estate prices rise alarmingly, as the housing supply and available lots dwindled. High as it seemed to Coloradans, the market presented Californians with the opportunity to invest windfall profits reaped from the even higher one they had left behind.

Not all Coloradans found the boom touching their town or county and some that did discovered it to be a troublesome trend. Ouray and other resort towns—Telluride, Aspen, Vail, for instance—faced a major crisis in affordable housing. "It's a problem of success," observed Tom Baker, Aspen/Pitkin County director of housing. "Given the limited space and the amount of demand, it's not a problem we can solve." The price of a home within fifteen miles of Aspen averaged $1.5 million, and the number of people who lived and worked in the town dropped from 65 percent to 45 percent in a ten-year period. The economy of Steamboat Springs moved from agriculture and mining to tourism and recreation. Observers bemoaned the passing of all that had made the town attractive. Rancher Vernon Summer pinpointed a concern of many locals. "It seems people all around have sold their places for high prices. But I'm doing what I want to do. This is my home."

Karval, a "small community [Lincoln County], marked by a tree-filled cluster of houses and abandoned old buildings," had problems of a different kind, the *Denver Post* reported May 20, 1993. With fewer than 100 residents, it faced an uncertain future. So did the scores of other Karvals scattered throughout the state, which reflected a national pattern for rural America. Young people were leaving, older people were dying. As the population shrank, schools and businesses closed, precipitating further decline. Rural towns near a city could convert to bedroom suburbs and survive, but remote villages and counties were forced to rely on their own resources.

Brush succeeded in demonstrating that it was possible for a town in decline to turn itself around. By attracting new industries, revitalizing its main street stores, and lowering unemployment, the community earned a 1991 City of the Year award. As the Chamber of Commerce president explained, "We're looking for good, solid growth that's going to be here a long time and beneficial to the town and area."

That statement summed up the sentiments of many other communities. Through reinvigorated discussion, people tried to come to grips with what Colorado was and would be. Rural residents observed the urban sprawl of the front range and wondered if they actually had a future in Colorado. One disgruntled rural writer, Ed Quillen of Salida, even questioned the need for Denver in a long article in the *High Country News* (May 3, 1993). He concluded, among other things that Denver had quit investing its wealth in building up its hinterland, instead using it to grow suburbs. "But as things are going, it's becoming just another isolated, isolationist Front Range city."

He was not alone in his opinions. Sad to say, urbanites often held badly distorted perceptions of their rural neighbors. As Bill Hornby wrote in the *Denver Post* (October 3, 1993), "The attitude canyon between big-city Coloradans and their country-side neighbors is still as wide and deep as our Royal Gorge, with bridges few and far between." Each side bore some responsibility for the misunderstandings. What

should have been a partnership degenerated into name calling and accusations that harkened back to Colorado's early years. The future of
Colorado would depend to a great degree on the outcome of the dispute,
which encompassed issues ranging from politics to tourism, environment, and water.

Once again, water seemed to be a factor in everything from urban
growth to wilderness designation. It took the U.S. Congress twelve years
to approve a new Colorado Wilderness bill (1993), which set aside over
700,000 acres of spectacular high country. Said one participant, "It has
been a damned nightmare." The issue of water was one of the primary
deterrents to the bill's passage as environmentalists and water developers sought to preserve their perceived rights. Rural and urban Coloradans fought the same fight they had been for decades.

Water, the saying goes, flows toward money, and the urban areas had
most of that. Thornton, Aurora, and other front range communities pursued or purchased rural water rights. But their efforts in doing so were
not clandestine—in the "vast majority of cases, farmers, not cities, are
initiating these water deals by offering to sell." The reason was simple:
Rural Colorado was "in a dire financial situation," as people left the
farms in droves. One person explained the predicament this way, "Why
work your buns off for $10,000 a year ranching when you can sell your
water and retire on the money?" Why, indeed? The balance of power between rural and urban was irrevocably changing. An interesting statistic
confirmed that change: The fall of 1993 marked the first time in Colorado history that people outnumbered cattle and sheep.

The defeat of the Two Forks dam and the continuing debate over the
Animas–La Plata project made it obvious that the days of water projects
had run their course. Conservation of water resources, cooperative projects, and other new ideas would chart the future of water distributions.
The rivalry between the federal government and the state government
for control of water would dominate every proposal.

Colorado voters made a major change in their lifestyles in 1990,
when they approved limited stakes ($5 limit) gambling for three historic
mining towns in decline—Central City, Black Hawk, and Cripple Creek.
Casinos opened in all three in 1991. By virtue of a U.S. Supreme Court
decision (*California vs. Cabazon*, 1987), the inauguration of gambling in
the state allowed the Southern Ute and Ute Mountain Ute tribes to operate their own reservation gambling; both soon launched casinos. Black
Hawk emerged as the big winner among the three Colorado towns,

Gambling came to Central City, Black Hawk, Cripple Creek, and the two Ute reservations. The Sky Ute Casino is in Ignacio, Colorado.

primarily because it provided better parking than canyon-confined Central City. The state literally hit the jackpot when revenues proved greater than projected. By law these tax monies were to be distributed to the gambling towns and counties, to the state historical preservation fund, and to the Colorado general fund. Preservation projects throughout the state benefited from the profits from the 28 percent of the gaming revenue designated for that fund.

All that glittered was not gold; there was another, darker side to the story. A *Wall Street Journal* article (September 23, 1992) gave voice to what happened: "Certainly, the towns have gotten more than they bargained for." Fading rural communities dealing with the question of how to invigorate their economies without changing their essential character found that there were no simple solutions. The problem proved particularly acute when their survival relied on gambling.

Most retail stores were converted to casinos, and Gilpin County lost its grocery stores and gasoline stations, for example, by the time gambling reached full swing. Property values—and then taxes—soared, forcing old-timers out. Multi-storied casinos elbowed out "mom-and-pop" stores. The rush to cash in on casino profits created a market glut and resulted in fifteen casinos closing or going bankrupt in the first year; others followed suit in the winter of 1992-1993. Additional entrepreneurs who intended to ride gambling's coattails failed—both of the slot machines maintenance schools failed, and only two of seven dealer schools survived two years.

The quality of life deteriorated in unanticipated ways, and local governmental debts mounted as towns and counties scrambled to keep pace with the consequences of a major boom. The Central City Opera saw its attendance decrease by 15 percent in 1992; other tourist attractions were hit even harder. These towns were no longer oriented toward family entertainment. Increased levels of noise, pollution, traffic, and construction spiraled in all three towns. Gilpin County witnessed a 559-percent increase in traffic citations and more than double the number of criminal and misdemeanor cases; Teller County courts had a 242-percent increase in domestic cases and a 172-percent increase in criminal cases. To keep pace, police forces and city government rapidly expanded.

The needs of tourist hordes exceeded the capacity of sewer systems, a situation that required immediate attention. Central City's government grew from seven employees and a $300,000 annual budget to a staff of fifty and a budget of nearly $6 million within a year. Casino gambling had proved no gold bonanza, though the second year was less hectic.

Despite its obvious drawbacks, gambling still held an allure for communities desperate to revive their economies. A host of initiated gambling bills reached the 1992 ballot. Twenty-six towns hoped to reap the benefits of the gambling craze. Coloradans voted them all down. Rejecting the voters' decision, Trinidad and other towns continued to agitate for gambling, but voters in 1994 rejected more gambling. The Wall Street Journal reporter was right when he said that some Coloradans had become "addicted to a revenue fix." Colorado's experiment was the most ambitious effort yet "to use gambling as a rural economic tool." It will be years before a true assessment of gains and losses can be made.

Over 75 percent of Coloradans voted in 1992. As maverick as ever, they managed to pass an anti–civil rights amendment that caused a national controversy, including an unsuccessful boycott of the state, and one that gained it the unenviable title "hate state." The object of the amendment was deceivingly simple. It prohibited Colorado, any community, or public agency from enacting, adopting, or enforcing any statute or policy granting minority or protected status or "claim of discrimination" to any person of "homosexual, lesbian or bisexual orientation." The amendment ended in the state courts on constitutional grounds and was struck down. That decision was appealed to the United States Supreme Court.

Potentially more likely to have wide ramifications was a voter-approved, tax-limitation amendment, which curbed the taxing authority of school boards and state and local governments. A conservative bloc composed largely of El Paso, Jefferson, and Mesa Counties spearheaded the movement that had barely lost a close election in 1990. This group exemplified the antitax, antigovernment, and antiestablishment sentiment evident in many parts of the country. How Amendment 1 will actually affect Colorado only the future will tell, but Coloradans have already found ways to circumvent it. As Governor Roy Romer observed, "What's on my mind is we have not yet realized what we have done to representative government by the change we made [by passing] Amendment One."

A majority of Coloradans voted for Democratic presidential candidate Bill Clinton, returned Patricia Schroeder to Congress from the First District (there were also 35 women serving in the Colorado General Assembly), and promoted Ben Nighthorse Campbell to the Senate in 1992. The Republicans could take solace in the fact that they had captured four of the six House seats.

In the off-year election of 1993, Coloradans tried another innovation: the mail-in ballot. Utilized in thirty counties, mail-in balloting posted over a 50 percent turnout; counties employing polling places had a slightly less than 30 percent turnout. In the only statewide issue, voters defeated a measure to restore the tourism tax, a fund to promote tourism. Other results were mixed. Boulder County increased its sales tax to raise money for open space, but Eagle County rejected an increase in its sales tax to support a bus system. Commenting on the election, a *Denver Post* (November 4, 1993) reporter remarked, "If there was any consistent message . . . , it was that voters want to know exactly how government is spending their tax money."

It was a Republican year in Colorado in 1994 and throughout the nation, although Democrats continued to hold on to two House seats. Roy Romer proved an exception as he easily won reelection in, unfortunately, a "dirty" campaign (including innuendos, falsehoods, name-calling) waged by his opponent. Fortunately, Coloradans seem to reject the increasingly popular dirty campaigning trend.

Senator (D) Ben Nighthorse Campbell was a hit in the Tournament of Roses and Inaugura-tion parades in 1993. Always a political maverick, Campbell joined the Republican Party in 1995.

Colorado's problems in the 1990s are not limited to politics, water, and growth. The economic gap between the rich and poor is widening faster in Colorado than in all but three other states. The inequality is most evident in the Denver area and in the thriving mountain resorts. Economists attribute the gap to a low-wage economy that is transforming the West, combined with layoffs of skilled workers and a national tax structure that favored the rich until a 1993 change under President Clinton's administration. Whatever the reasons, over 11 percent of Coloradans live in poverty, according to the 1990 census; for them, life has become a struggle to pay bills and afford homes.

Environmental issues have never been far from the front page. The worst by far, the Summitville mining disaster (southwest of Del Norte), gave that industry a black eye and raised serious questions about the effectiveness of state and federal regulation. A poorly conceived and executed cyanide-leaching operation by a Canadian mining company failed, creating an environmental nightmare. The runoff contaminated streams and water supplies, and turned a mountain into "a toxic stew of cyanide and heavy metals" (*Denver Post*, February 21, 1993). As 1993 moved toward 1994, the Environmental Protection Agency had hired fifty-five full-time workers and was spending $33,000 a day to prevent the disaster from worsening.

Fortunately, other mining cleanup projects have progressed more smoothly, including the Red Mountain District between Ouray and Silverton. After nine years of lawsuits and negotiations, both sides reached an agreement for revegetation and cleanup programs. Mining, however, is not the only environmental polluter.

The cold war left behind Rocky Flats, and with it an unwanted heritage of radio-active waste and other pollution. Federal, state, and local governments continued to discuss and argue about responsibility and what to do as they had for years. The answers will prove to be expensive. Despite some improvement, Denver's noxious brown cloud still hovers over the city and surrounding areas; other communities have their own clouds, largely generated by car exhaust and smoke from stoves and fireplaces. Trash, litter, and other pollutants threaten the quality of life throughout the state. The struggle to preserve Colorado's environment is far from over.

On a more happy note, 1993 welcomed the Colorado Rockies to Denver, the state's first major league baseball team. Decades of anticipation became reality in 1991, when baseball executives selected Denver

The Colorado Rockies' first season was amazing, setting a major league attendance record. Catcher Joe Girardi's tag was too late here as the Rockies lost to the Marlins, 2–1.

as one of the two National League expansion cities. The next year focused on organization of a minor league system, selection of uniforms, a draft of players, the choosing of a spring training site (Tucson, Arizona), and ground breaking for a new ballpark, Coors Field. Baseball fever became epidemic, as the first season approached.

The Rockies' inaugural season exceeded expectations: The franchise drew a major league record attendance of 4,483,350. Along the way, the team set many other attendance records, including ones for opening day, night games, and season average per game. Fan enthusiasm and the Mile High Stadium playing site made these feats possible. The economic impact on the city and state also outran forecasts. In the words of Dante Bichette, one of the first Rockies' heroes, "It was a fairy tale." Not bad for a team that finished the season 67–95 but rewarded their fans with many thrills, including Andres Galarraga's winning the National League batting championship with a .370 average. A strike cancelled the last part of the 1994 season and delayed the start of the 1995 season, and fans saw another side of the owners and players. It was not a pretty picture.

The other two major professional franchises, the Nuggets and Broncos, did not have outstanding success. Although the Broncos continued to pack Mile High Stadium, they disappointed their fans by once again losing the Super Bowl (1990)—for the fourth time. Other professional sports had their adherents, and Colorado attracted moments of national attention (Durango, for example, hosted the World Mountain Bike Championships in 1990). The University of Colorado continued to be a national power in college football, and Colorado State gained that status after a highly successful 1994 football season. The Air Force Academy experienced less success, but some of the smaller colleges did well, such as Adams State and Western State in cross-country, wrestling, and track. Women's sports made strides on the high school and college levels, especially the University of Colorado's basketball team, but athletics at all tiers became more expensive while education budgets remained static.

Colorado gained some desired and some undesired headlines in 1993 and 1994. As 1993 drew to a close, three things drew national, and even international, attention to Colorado: the Rockies' amazing success; the World Youth Conference (August 1993), which brought Pope John Paul II to Colorado; and, finally, the September 6, 1993, issue of *Time* magazine with its special cover story, "Boom Time in the Rockies." The article summed up the situation in the state and the region: "Rocky Mountain home of cowboys and lumberjacks has become a magnet for lone-eagle telecommuters and Range Rover–driving yuppies. So far, it's been a booming good time." Boom had returned. Will it last? History says no.

The Denver International Airport drew attention, controversy, and embarrassment throughout 1994 with repeated opening delays, cost overruns, construction disputes, and airline company quarrels. While this proved embarrassing for the city, the airport did eventually open in 1995. What this attention has meant to Colorado can easily be seen in renewed publicity, in the costs of unmanaged growth, the clash between old and new values, environmental degradation, and soaring real estate prices.

Governor Romer believed six basic issues face Colorado—education, environment, health, law and order, infrastructure, and the business climate (regulation and taxes). As he stated in his January 12, 1995 State-of-the-State Address, there are two parallel tracks toward taking care of our people and our state:

One is to develop our human potential and the other is to keep the beauty and the quality of the place.

Some have said that if we reform welfare, build prisons, crack down on crime, cut government and cut taxes, we will have done our work. But if that is all we do, we will not secure the kind of future that Colorado deserves and can have. [T]he people of Colorado are frustrated and worried because government isn't solving problems. They see a world that is rapidly changing, and they worry that they won't have the skills to compete. They worry that their children won't be able to live the kind of life they themselves have been able to live.

How Coloradans respond to these issues and others frames the opening of the twenty-first century. The future rests on every Coloradan. As Thomas Hornsby Ferril wrote in *Time of Mountains,*

So long ago my father led me to
The dark impounded orders of this canyon,
I have confused these rocks and waters with
My life, but not unclearly, for I know
What will be here when I am here no more.

THIRTY-FIVE

COLORADO IN THE
NEW MILLENNIUM

The truth of the popular saying of the late twentieth century, "What goes around, comes around," was obvious, as Colorado turned the corner of a new century into a new millennium. The opportunities and the problems of the last generation had not gone away. They had intensified, in fact—growth, education, water, pollution, quality of life, rural issues, boom and bust, and transportation made up a list that went on almost endlessly. Colorado, in the 1990s, was a fascinating place, and the future promised to be equally so. Coloradans of the past would have completely understood most of the underlying issues, if not some of their consequences.

Growth remained an overwhelming issue, even as the legislature, citizens' groups, and many city and county governments tried to cope with it. No easy answers existed, because such issues as water, pollution, governmental programs, and transportation were tied intimately to growth. And the elusive "quality of life" always lurked in the background. Front Range growth far surpassed that of the eastern plains or the Western Slope. Some counties in those two areas, for example San

Juan, Jackson, Kiowa, and Baca, continued to lose population. Indeed, eleven of Colorado's counties jibed with the census bureau's nineteenth-century definition of "frontier"—fewer than two people per square mile. Most of the growth came in the ten metropolitan Front Range counties, which make one long swath from Fort Collins to Pueblo. Denver's population, meanwhile, reached an all-time high of 554,636. The distribution was startling: More people now resided in those counties than had lived in the entire state a decade earlier. Hispanics were the fastest growing of the state's minority groups, nearly doubling in number to 735,000.

A composite portrait of Coloradans at the century's turn found 84 percent of the highly educated population living in an urban environment. Only about 37 percent belonged to or attended church regularly, well below the national level of 52 percent. Also, Coloradans had a higher divorce rate than the national average and led the nation in marijuana use.

According to the 2000 census figures, slightly more than 1 million people had arrived in Colorado since 1990. The state, with a population of 4.3 million, thus gained an additional seat (the state's seventh) in the House of Representatives and the distinction of being the third fastest-growing state in the nation (nearly 31 percent since 1990), following its western neighbors Nevada and Arizona. Utah came in only a step behind. The West gained a total of five seats in Congress and more potent political clout.

The question was how state lawmakers would redraw district lines for that seventh seat. For the first time since 1961, Democrats controlled the Colorado senate, if only by a slim one-vote margin, which pitted them against a Republican state house and the Republican governor, Bill Owens. It looked like a special session would be required to decide the issue. An independent commission tackled the reapportionment of the state legislature's thirty-five senate and sixty-five house seats. This issue remained unresolved as of July 2001.

While those in state government pondered that question, the public became aware of an undercurrent of resentment toward newcomers. Frustrations and challenges faced old and new citizens of the state. For example, one out of every four Coloradans crowding the highways and byways of the state had not been a resident ten years earlier. One long-time resident complained about growth, "You just can't get away from it. I get so frustrated." Former governor Richard Lamm put it in perspective, "The question really isn't a physical carrying capacity, it's the social carrying capacity."

It could be Denver, Durango, Aspen, or any Colorado town. Crowded roads reflect the problems of growth throughout the state.

Drivers traveling on Interstate 70 on any Sunday (headed in the summer for a day in the cool mountain air or in the winter for a skiing outing) witnessed the effect of population growth on Colorado's roads. As they approached Denver, they were likely to find themselves in a traffic snarl. Eisenhower Tunnel carried record numbers of cars each year. Traffic jams could also be found in mountain-locked towns like Glenwood Springs, Telluride, and Black Hawk, although for different reasons. Traffic there tended to be funneled to one main street. The introduction of rapid transit systems in Denver and its suburbs gave rise to a growing network of buses and trains, but the congestion soon increased beyond the capacity of the public transportation system. Meanwhile, the condition of Colorado's roads grew worse, and the legislature worked to find funds to try to catch up and keep up with repair and construction.

One road continued to receive praise: Interstate 70 through Glenwood Canyon. Long hailed as one of the "most environmentally sensitive highway projects in the country," this 12.5-mile stretch has received many awards, including a 1993 Outstanding Civil Engineering Achievement Award, "which is considered the Oscar of highway awards." In 2000, it was given the Presidential Design Award. The beauty of the canyon was preserved by fitting the road into the "eye-popping" environment rather than the other way around.

There was a positive aspect to growth: Development fueled a decade-long boom. Growth, economist Tucker Adams pointed out, "is the price that is paid for economic success." Colorado's average household income ranked high nationally throughout the decade. Growth allowed Douglas County to lay claim to being the fastest-growing county in the country. It also was the nation's richest county, with a median household income of $77,513 and the nation's lowest poverty level, 1.9 percent. The other side of the picture was less glowing. The county gained the "honor" of being featured in National Geographic as "the symbol of suburban sprawl."

The gap between the rich and the poor was no more clearly shown than in a comparison of Douglas and Costilla Counties. In the latter, the estimated median household income stood at $18,700. Nearly half of Costilla County's children lived in poverty. The two biggest employers were the school district and the county. Bemoaned a county official, "Other than [those two], there's not very much employment here." The boom of the nineties had not reached the southern San Luis Valley and other areas of the state.

The median household income in Colorado was $45,252, seventh in the nation, a 1999 report showed. The state also came out well in "the poverty rankings," having the nation's third-lowest percentage of residents living in poverty. Economists attributed these rankings to a combination of extraordinarily strong job growth and a tight labor market, which forced employers to raise wages. At the same time, however, housing costs rose rapidly, making it difficult for many families, even those above the poverty line, to purchase homes. Affordable housing emerged as *the* issue in a host of counties and communities.

Growth, or a lack thereof, promoted much of the dichotomy. Tucker Adams saw both the positive and the negative in growth. She cautioned, "We don't want to turn Colorado into Southern California or northern New Jersey, which would happen if [we] kept growing at the rate we had." Echoing what had been thought and said before, she admonished, "You hate to think what another decade of this kind of growth would bring."

Metro Denver already showed what the future might bring. It received the dubious honor from the Federal National Mortgage Association of having the nation's fourth worst case of urban sprawl. Not only did that "honor" affect the quality of life and give the region a bad image, it obviously worried Denver officials. One official commented that if the assessment received "wide dissemination around the nation that Colorado has a problem with sprawl, that hurts our long-term economic sustainability."

Growth also gave Colorado a greater return on the federal dollars that its citizens sent to Washington in the form of taxes, which meant more funding for highways, housing, social services, Head Start, and other educational programs. In addition, Denver's population had surpassed 500,000, the "magic number" the city needed to compete for larger federal grants. Growth was a double-edged sword—it could help and it could hurt.

As the debate continued, many Coloradans realized the time had come to make difficult and perhaps unpopular decisions. The people would have to reach a consensus about being stewards of the land and maintaining the quality of life. The issue could no longer be ignored.

Growth management was not the only serious problem. Education was a close second. The differences in finances, student performance, school facilities, and teacher qualifications that divided rural and urban and rich and poor school districts widened during the 1990s. Local school boards and the legislature wrestled with these issues throughout the decade with mixed results. In an attempt to solve the problems, voters approved a constitutional amendment in the year 2000 for funding public schools. The purpose of this amendment was to increase per pupil funding and "total state funding for special purpose education programs." The governor, the legislature, members of both political parties, and educators held various opinions about how they would use the money to accomplish these goals.

Various additional approaches to problems in the educational system were tried or discussed. Some communities created charter schools as an alternative to public schools. These schools created some controversy, but less than the idea of issuing vouchers of public funds and having students and parents select a school they preferred. The emphasis might be new, but the debate was not. As with the growth issue, no easy or simple solutions existed and feelings ran deep.

The administration of Governor Roy Romer came to an end in January 1999. He would be the last governor of Colorado to serve twelve years. In 1990 voters had passed an eight-year term limit for state officials. Romer's administration had been marked by ups and downs, but his willingness to listen and his energy highlighted those years. One former lawmaker noted that it was not always a smooth ride, but "the state got its money's worth with Roy Romer."

Unlike his predecessor, Richard Lamm, Romer initially promoted growth as he commented, "Colorado is open for business." His approach had worked. Then came the 1992 Taxpayers Bill of Rights (TABOR amendment), with its strict limits on state spending. His focus turned to "smart growth," and he worked with local governments for orderly growth. He then returned the state to the growth management policies pioneered by Lamm.

Romer energetically presided during a period of general economic boom, and the expansion was more closely tied to the national economy than ever before. The tie extended to politics as well, as evidenced by the fact that Romer served as chairman of the Democratic National Committee during his third term as governor, and former Denver mayor Federico Peña served as President Bill Clinton's energy secretary in 1997 and 1998, after serving as secretary of transportation in Clinton's first term. Clinton's secretary of state, Madeleine Albright, also had Colorado ties. Connections between Colorado and Washington continued into the new administration, when, in 2001, former Colorado attorney general Gale Norton was selected as President George W. Bush's secretary of the interior.

Sixth Judicial District Attorney Sarah Law is sworn in for her second term in January 2001. She was one of the first women district attornies in Colorado and was the first to be reelected in a contested election.

Throughout his years as governor, Roy Romer had confronted a Republican legislature, as Colorado's role as a political maverick continued. The voters supported Republican presidential candidates but split on congressional and statewide races. They continued to use the old Populist tools of initiative and referendum to get a variety of amendments and referenda on the ballot every election year. Most of them promptly went down to defeat, putting the issues back in the legislature's lap. Coloradans talked of change but generally seemed slow to embrace it.

When Romer left office upon the inauguration of Republican Bill Owens, who had won the 1998 election, he took on the daunting challenge of being superintendent of the Los Angeles, California, school system. Education, which had always been high on Roy Romer's agenda (he twice intervened to settle labor disputes in the Denver Public Schools), continued to hold an important place in his life after he left office.

Republican Bill Owens placed education, roads, and tax reduction high on his agenda. As had his predecessors, Owens found it tough going in the Colorado legislature. The controversial issue of educational reform was the topic of heated debates. Whether students would take standardized tests and whether schools would be evaluated according to their students' test results raised concerns among parents, school boards, and educators from rural and urban Colorado. The results, good or bad, were still forthcoming as of the summer of 2001.

The same could be said for discussions about the problems of growth. After the legislature failed to enact any significant legislation controlling growth, despite widespread support among Coloradans, Owens called a special session of the General Assembly. The session opened the morning after the 2001 regular session ended but died in partisan wrangling. In response to this, citizens started a movement to put a constitution amendment on the 2002 ballot.

Like Romer, Owens worked to bring business to Colorado. In a spirited effort in 2001, Denver competed with two other cities to land Boeing headquarters. Colorado lost to Chicago. It appeared to many at times that Coloradans had "landed" in a fantasy world, as they continued to lure new businesses to the state and at the same time to struggle with controlling growth.

The Denver metro area experienced two changes in 2001. The first was the creation of a new county: number 64, Broomfield. The rapidly growing community had been spreading into several nearby counties, which generated a host of taxation, political, jurisdictional, and legislative problems. Broomfield was the first new county since 1915, when Moffat County was created.

The second change involved the two major Denver newspapers, the *Rocky Mountain News* and the *Denver Post,* which had battled each other for more than a century. In an era when the number of major metropolitan newspapers was declining, Denver proved an exception by having two. In the West's "most spirited newspaper war," the *News* changed its name to the *Denver Rocky Mountain News* and basically served only the region in and about the capital city. The costly contest produced operating losses, particularly for the *News,* as a result of a fierce promotional war. Finally, the two papers signed a joint operating agreement—and the Justice Department concurred—to form a new company combining the papers' business operations. The two would publish separate editions during the week and combined editions on the weekends under a joint nameplate. The *News* also dropped the word *Denver* from its name and returned to the time-tested, familiar name.

Sheep released in a reintroduction program scamper in the snow-covered San Juan Mountains.

A third change touched everyone in the state. The computer age affected Coloradans, as it did all Americans. Through their schools and workplaces and in their homes, the young and adults took to their computers. Computer businesses set up shop in various areas of the state, but particularly along the Front Range. They generally made profits, and another "boom" set in. Then came a downswing, and computer stock prices tumbled.

Colorado gained two new national parks, both of which were upgraded from monuments—the Great Sand Dunes and the Black Canyon of the Gunnison—and a new national monument to honor the original inhabitants of the Four Corners region—Canyons of the Ancients. Much as the truce between the two newspapers was indicative of the changing times, so were these shifts in federal lands. Objections, as expected, were heard about the loss of rights and the trampling of western heritage, but they could not stop the actions.

Agriculture's role in Colorado's economy continued to slip away. While much of Colorado experienced growth, rural areas continued to face decline in a variety of areas, from population to tax base to political clout. The jobs, Internet connections, educational opportunities, medical facilities, and transportation were simply not available to entice businesses and people. The only exceptions were cities like Grand Junction, Denver, Durango, and Greeley, all of which succeeded in turning their nearby rural ranching and farming land into suburbs.

For Colorado's professional teams and their fans, the second half of the decade of the nineties proved an exciting, cheering, and rewarding time. The Rockies made the National League playoffs in their third year of existence, and the Avalanche won the Stanley Cup in 1996 and again in 2001. Long-suffering Bronco fans finally received their due when their team won two consecutive Super Bowls (1998 and 1999), behind quarterback John Elway. The Colorado sports legend retired after the second championship.

The Avalanche and Nuggets played in the new Pepsi Center, and the Rockies moved to Coors Field, a beautiful ballpark modeled after some older, venerated parks. Mile High Stadium, which had been built in 1948 and which first bore the name Bears Stadium, was torn down in 2001. The Broncos played on a new field, which, after a long, emotional, and sometimes heated debate over its name, was christened Invesco Field at Mile High. Denver had decidedly come of age as a major league sports town—although all the women's professional sports teams collapsed. The American Basketball League, which opened in 1996 and included the Colorado Xplosion, died in 1998. The professional football team and league did not even make it through the inaugural 2000 season.

Tourism remained a significant economic pillar for most parts of the state. When the numbers slumped at the century's turn, concern mounted. In the 1990s tourism had seen both a boom, as national parks were over-loved and over-crowded and at times almost a bust. Ski areas, for example, faced the problems of low snowfall, more expensive lift tickets, "the graying of America," and out-of-state competition. Higher gasoline prices and the general rising costs of travel also hurt.

The shortage of winter snows also affected agriculture, and Coloradans again became worried about drought conditions and their water supplies. After the second longest wet cycle in the state's history, 1982 to 1999, it seemed inconceivable to newcomers that drought could be a problem. The dry conditions became obvious in 2000 when major fires struck various locations in the state. Mesa Verde National Park had to be closed after more than 25,000 acres were burned in August, severely hurting the area's summer tourist business. Earlier that season, the East-

Mesa Verde may look deserted in this photo, but we are loving our national parks to death.

ern Slope lost more than 20,000 acres in two major mountain fires. The cost of fighting these two fires neared $10 million. As subdivisions and homes were built in the mountains, the number of homes lost and damaged jumped, as did complaints and worries. Beleaguered rural fire departments faced mounting problems.

Two Colorado State University climatologists warned that a drought "will come" and that increasingly thirsty and crowded Colorado needed to be prepared. "When drought returns to Colorado, as it surely will, it will be challenging to see just how far we can stretch our water." Nature still prevailed in the state, and humans not aware and cautious of it paid the price. Old-timers could have told newcomers of nature's perseverance and sometimes seeming capriciousness, but, unfortunately, it seems to be a lesson that repeatedly needs to be learned.

Some ski towns and other Colorado communities faced a housing crunch. Workers could not afford, for example, to live at Vail, Aspen, or Breckenridge and had to settle in neighboring communities and drive long distances to work. Leadville became a bedroom community for nearby ski resort workers and even opened a twenty-four-hour child care center to accommodate their needs. In larger cities like Denver or in smaller ones like Durango, the need for low-cost housing emerged as a serious problem. In some areas, the average price of a home topped $200,000.

Shortly after Coloradans approved limited stakes gambling, they learned that gambling did not provide the cure-all for three depressed communities (Central City, Black Hawk, and Cripple Creek), as some had hoped. Of the three communities that opened casinos in 1991 and 1992, only Black Hawk prospered, but at the cost of remaking itself into a pseudo-mining town that fronted casinos and of turning surrounding areas into parking lots. Despite preservation efforts, old buildings were amazingly transformed, moved, or disappeared. Central City suffered severely from its neighbor's surge and finally decided, after much controversy, to build a road up Russell Gulch so gamblers could bypass rival Black Hawk. Cripple Creek came in second in gambling revenue, but the expected general prosperity of the town failed to materialize.

Certainly, gambling produced revenue. The year 1999 set a record of $551.3 million, and more visitors than ever came to the gambling towns. Yet, as the Denver Post (February 13, 2000) reported, "Owning a casino is still a crapshoot." Eight of them closed that year, primarily because their cash flow failed to cover operating costs and debt. That brought the total to eighty-six casinos that closed since gambling began in 1991.

Central City, Black Hawk, and Cripple Creek are no longer particularly enjoyable places to grow up in according to a Post article (March 21, 1999): "Gambling leaves little room for kids." Said one teacher at the Gilpin County School, "There's nothing for them—no theater, no bowling alley, no grocery, no arcade." This was one of many implications of legalized gambling in the first decade of its reintroduction in Colorado.

The ramifications of Denver International Airport were more what ardent supporters, including former governor Romer and Denver's former mayor Peña, expected. After a rocky 1995 opening, a slow start, and a few problems that needed to be ironed out, passengers and traffic increased. It soon became the nation's sixth busiest airport. The Wall Street Journal, in January 2001, ranked it as one of the five best airports in the country. A pleased Denver Mayor Wellington Webb said, "We have a world-class airport that is providing a powerful economic engine for this entire region."

However, two of Colorado's formerly strong economic pillars showed signs of weakening. Mining joined agriculture in playing a less significant role in the state's economy and the number of farms declined, as did the total farm acreage, while the average acreage per farm soared. That change reflected the national trend. Mining, hardly a shadow of its former self, hung on in several counties. One reason for mining's troubles was the price of an ounce of gold: in 1980 it reached $875; twenty years later it dipped into the $260 range. Coal mining slipped as well along with molybdenum. Uranium mining had long since disappeared.

The now-dominant service industry in its many forms had taken the place that these older two once held. Meanwhile, Colorado's work force, which was better educated than ever before, ranked fourth in the nation, with 36 percent of the working age population (ages 25 to 54) having college degrees. A 2000 study also revealed that the state had the highest percentage of working women in the nation.

As the debate died away about whether 2000 or 2001 was really the start of the new century and the new millennium, forecasters looked into the future. They predicted an informational revolution and continued stress over growth. Would Colorado continue to lead the nation economically? Some thought so. Rural Colorado would finally boom again, one envisioned. Colorado would prosper, according to a cheery forecaster's crystal ball. But all realized that water issues would not go away. Something new, something old—the next decade promised to be a fascinating ride. Coloradans seemed flexible and resilient, so the future should be as challenging and exciting as the past.

Suggested Reading

The following bibliographies offer suggestions for those who wish to delve more deeply into particular topics. We have attempted to list relevant books and articles published through 2000, with emphasis on more recent scholarship and on those works that, for the most part, are readily available in major libraries. In addition, since the seventh edition of *A Colorado History* appeared in 1995 the Internet, especially the World Wide Web, has emerged as a significant resource for historians. Most libraries are now online, and numerous organizations have their own web sites. For a good introduction to this new world, see Dennis A. Trinkle and Scott A. Merriman, *The History Highway 2000: A Guide to Internet Resources* (Armonk, N.Y., 1999). We have included a few references to web sites in the Readings; the addresses, we believe, were accurate and current when this book went to press, but researchers should be aware that changes can occur at any time.

General Works

The Colorado Centennial in 1976 saw the publication of several major works on the state's history, including three one-volume accounts: Robert G. Athearn, *The Coloradans* (Albuquerque, 1976); Carl Abbott, *Colorado: A History of the Centennial State* (Boulder, 1976; 3d ed. with Stephen J. Leonard and David McComb, Niwot, 1994); and Marshall Sprague, *Colorado: A Bicentennial History* (New York, 1976). David Lavender offered a personal, illustrated view of his native state in *David Lavender's Colorado* (New York, 1976).

Older works that still have value are LeRoy R. Hafen, *Colorado: The Story of a Western Commonwealth* (Denver, 1933); Percy Fritz, *Colorado: The Centennial State* (New York, 1941); and *Colorado: A Guide to the Highest State* (New York, 1941), a product of the Work Projects Administration Writers' Program, reissued as *The WPA Guide to 1930s Colorado*, with an introduction by Thomas J. Noel (Lawrence, 1987).

Multivolume histories of Colorado include Frank Hall, *History of the State of Colorado* (4 vols., Chicago, 1889–95), valuable for the author's firsthand knowledge of many of the events; Jerome C. Smiley, *Semi-Centennial History of the State of Colorado* (2 vols., Chicago, 1913); Wilbur F. Stone, ed., *History of Colorado* (4 vols., Chicago, 1918–19); James H. Baker and LeRoy R. Hafen, eds., *History of Colorado* (5 vols., Denver, 1927); and Hafen, ed., *Colorado and Its People: A Narrative and Topical History of the Centennial State* (4 vols., New York, 1948).

Accounts for young people include Thomas J. Noel and Duane A. Smith, *Colorado: The Highest State* (Niwot, 1995); Smith, with Kate Shuchter, *Colorado: Our Colorful State* (Niwot, 1999); and Matthew T. Downey and Fay T. Metcalf, *Colorado: Crossroads of the West* (1976; 3d ed., Boulder, 1999).

Biographies of noteworthy Coloradans can be found in John H. Monnett and Michael McCarthy, *Colorado Profiles: Men and Women Who Shaped the Centennial State* (Evergreen, 1987) and Abbott Fay, *Famous Coloradans: 124 People Who Have Gained Nationwide Fame* (Paonia, Colo., 1990).

Excerpts from first-person accounts, novels, and poems are featured in W. Storrs Lee, ed., *Colorado, A Literary Chronicle* (New York, 1970); Carl Ubbelohde, Maxine Benson, and Duane A. Smith, eds., *A Colorado Reader* (Boulder, 1982); Frederick R. Rinehart, ed., *Chronicles of Colorado* (Boulder, 1984); and Eleanor M. Gehres, Sandra Dallas, Benson, and Stanley Cuba, eds., *The Colorado Book* (Golden, 1993).

For pictorial views, see Clifford P. Westermeier, *Colorado's First Portrait: Scenes by Early Artists* (Albuquerque, 1970); Terry William Mangan, *Colorado on Glass: Colorado's First Half Century as Seen by the Camera* (Denver, 1975); Richard N. Ellis and Duane A. Smith, *Colorado: A History in Photographs* (Niwot, 1991); and Christian J. Buys, *Illustrations of Historic Colorado* (Ouray, 2000).

Guides and Bibliographies

With more than nine thousand entries, by far the most comprehensive Colorado bibliography is Bohdan S. Wynar, ed., *Colorado Bibliography* (Littleton, 1980). An older, selective guide is Virginia Lee Wilcox, ed., *Colorado: A Selected Bibliography of Its Literature, 1858–1952* (Denver, 1954).

For information on newspapers, see Donald E. Oehlerts, ed., *Guide to Colorado Newspapers, 1859–1963* (Denver, 1964). Updating Oehlerts's work, the staff of the Colorado Newspaper Project conducted a survey between 1987 and 1991 to locate, catalog, and microfilm all surviving Colorado newspaper titles. The information then was entered into the national Online Computer Library Center (OCLC) database, accessible via First-Search through many academic and public library on-line catalogs. In addition, the OCLC catalog entries are available in printed form in the Stephen H. Hart Library of the Colorado Historical Society (www.coloradohistory.org). More details on the program can be found at www.neh.fed.us/preservation/usnp.html. For newspaper indexes, see Walter R. Griffen and Jay L. Rasmussen, "A Comprehensive Guide to the Location of Published and Unpublished Newspaper Indexes in Colorado Repositories," *The Colorado Magazine* 49 (fall 1972): 326–39.

The Colorado Magazine was published by the Colorado Historical Society from 1923 through 1980. A subject guide (1923–80), two cumulative indexes (1923–60), and several indexes to individual volumes are available. As well, a combined index to all fifty-seven volumes was completed in 2000 and deposited in the Hart Library.

As a continuation of *The Colorado Magazine*, between 1983 and 1994 the Colorado Historical Society published scholarly, documented manuscripts in *Essays and Monographs* in *Colorado History*, composed of two separately numbered series, *Essays in Colorado History* and *Monographs in Colorado History*. Beginning in 1997, *Colorado History* has provided a similar forum for both traditional journal articles and longer, book-length works. *Colorado Heritage*, a quarterly magazine for general readers, has been published since 1981. Reviews and notices of new books on Colorado and the West are available through the Colorado Book Review Center, established in 2001 as part of the Society's web site, www.coloradohistory.org.

For the West generally, useful reference tools include Charles Phillips and Alan Axelrod, *Encyclopedia of the American West* (4 vols., New York, 1996) and Howard R. Lamar, ed., *The New Encyclopedia of the American West* (New Haven, 1998). On western literature and culture, see *A Literary History of the American West* (Fort Worth, 1987; sponsored by the Western Literature Association) and Richard W. Etulain, *Re-Imagining the Modern American West: A Century of Fiction, History, and Art* (Tucson, 1998).

Bibliographical guides include Oscar Osburn Winther, *A Classified Bibliography of the Periodical Literature of the Trans-Mississippi West, 1811–1957* (Bloomington, 1961) and, with Richard A. Van Orman, the *Supplement (1957–1967)* (Bloomington, 1970); Rodman W. Paul and Richard W. Etulain, eds., *The Frontier and the American West* (Goldentree Bibliographies in American History; Arlington Heights, Ill., 1977); and Charles F. Wilkinson, *The American West: A Narrative Bibliography and a Study in Regionalism* (Niwot, 1989). Current articles and dissertations are listed in the *Western Historical Quarterly*, published by the Western History Association since 1970. Opportunities for further research are suggested in Etulain and Gerald D. Nash, eds., *Researching Western History: Topics in the Twentieth Century* (Albuquerque, 1997).

For the Southwest and the Borderlands, see Ellwyn R. Stoddard et al., *Borderlands Sourcebook: A Guide to the Literature on Northern Mexico and the American Southwest* (Norman, 1983) and Daniel Tyler, ed., *Sources for New Mexican History, 1821–1848* (Santa Fe, 1984).

Several recent works examine the historiography of the American West. Gerald D. Nash provides a masterful overview in *Creating the West: Historical Interpretations, 1890–1990* (Albuquerque, 1991). See also Roger L. Nichols, ed., *American Frontier and Western Issues: A Historiographical Review* (Westport, Conn., 1986). On western historians, see Michael P. Malone, ed., *Historians and the American West* (Lincoln, 1983); John R. Wunder, ed., *Historians of the American Frontier: A Bio-Bibliographical Sourcebook* (New York, 1988); and Richard W. Etulain, ed., *Writing Western History: Essays on Major Western Historians* (Albuquerque, 1991). Eugene H. Berwanger assesses Colorado and its neighbors in "The Absurd and the Spectacular: The Historiography of the Plains-Mountain States: Colorado, Montana, Wyoming," *Pacific Historical Review* 50 (November 1981): 445–74.

Since the mid-1980s, western historians have been engaged in a debate over the "new western history," launched by such works as Patricia Nelson Limerick, *The Legacy of Conquest: The Unbroken Past of the American West* (New York, 1987). To sample the dialogue, see Limerick, Clyde A. Milner II, and Charles E. Rankin, eds., *Trails: Toward a New Western History* (Lawrence, 1991); Limerick, Gary Holthaus, and Charles F. Wilkinson, eds., *A Society to Match the Scenery: Personal Visions of the Future of the American West* (Niwot, 1991); William Cronon, George Miles, and Jay Gitlin, eds., *Under an Open Sky: Rethinking America's Western Past* (New York, 1992); Milner, ed., *A New Significance: Re-envisioning the History of the American West* (New York, 1996); Forrest G. Robinson, ed., *The New Western*

History: The Territory Ahead (Tucson, 1998, published also in the *Arizona Quarterly* 53 [summer 1997]); and Limerick, *Something in the Soil: Legacies and Reckonings in the New West* (New York, 2000). General works that reflect the influence of this movement include Richard White, *"It's Your Misfortune and None of My Own": A New History of the American West* (Norman, 1991) and Robert V. Hine and John Mack Faragher, *The American West: A New Interpretation* (New Haven, 2000).

Research Collections

Major collections of research material can be found in the Stephen H. Hart Library of the Colorado Historical Society; the Western History/Genealogy Department of the Denver Public Library; the Western Americana Collections in the Archives, University of Colorado Library, Boulder; the Center of Southwest Studies at Fort Lewis College, Durango; and, for public records, the Colorado State Archives in Denver. Many college and university libraries have strong collections, as do a number of public libraries; a noteworthy example is the Carnegie Branch Library for Local History of the Boulder Public Library.

In addition, the student of Colorado and western history should not overlook the resources of the National Archives and Records Administration (NARA), both in Washington, D.C., and at the Rocky Mountain Region branch at the Denver Federal Center. For more information, see the *Guide to Federal Records in the National Archives of the United States* (3 vols., Washington, D.C., 1995), available also on the Archives web site, www.nara.gov; the multivolume series compiled by Robert M. Kvasnicka, *The Trans-Mississippi West, 1804–1912: A Guide to Federal Records for the Territorial Period* (Washington, D.C., 1992–); and John Porter Bloom, "Records in the National Archives for Colorado Territory and the West," in Daniel Tyler, ed., *Western American History in the Seventies* (Fort Collins, 1973), 50–56. *Prologue,* the NARA quarterly journal, provides current details on programs, acquisitions, and publications.

Prologue: The Land

Frank H. Tucker, "A Song Inspired: Katharine Lee Bates and 'America the Beautiful,'" *Colorado Heritage* (Issue 3, 1989): 32–42, tells the story behind this American classic. Works that examine the Colorado environment include Kenneth I. Helphand and Ellen Manchester, *Colorado: Visions of an American Landscape* (Niwot, 1991); Cornelia Fleischer Mutel and John C. Emerick, *From Grassland to Glacier: The Natural History of Colorado and the Surrounding Region* (1984; 2d ed., Boulder, 1992); and Thomas P. Huber, *Colorado: The Place of Nature, the Nature of Place* (Niwot, 1993). See also Huber, *Colorado Byways: A Guide through Scenic and Historic Landscapes* (Niwot, 1997).

On the Front Range, see Gleaves Whitney, *Colorado Front Range: A Land Divided* (Boulder, 1983) and Thomas T. Veblen and Diane C. Lorenz, *The Colorado Front Range: A Century of Ecological Change* (Salt Lake City, 1991). Charles Wilkinson examines the Colorado plateau region in *Fire on the Plateau: Conflict and Endurance in the American Southwest* (Washington, D.C., 1999).

Works that deal with Colorado geography include Mel Griffiths and Lynnell Rubright, *Colorado: A Geography* (Boulder, 1983); Kenneth A. Erickson and Albert W. Smith, *Atlas of Colorado* (Boulder, 1985); and William Wyckoff, *Creating Colorado: The Making of a Western American Landscape, 1860–1940* (New Haven, 1999). Thomas J. Noel, Paul F. Mahoney, and Richard E. Stevens, *Historical Atlas of Colorado* (Norman, 1994) provides maps on geography, political boundaries, agriculture, transportation, settlement, and recreational and historical areas. Erl H. Ellis, *Colorado Mapology* (Frederick, Colo., 1983) details the development of state and county borders. On place names, see Maxine Benson, *1001 Colorado Place Names* (Lawrence, 1994).

Aspects of Colorado weather past and present are covered in Mike Nelson et al., *The Colorado Weather Book* (Englewood, 1999); Phyllis Smith, *Weather Pioneers: The Signal Corps Station at Pikes Peak* (Athens, Ohio, 1993); and William E. Wilson, "Georgetown Weather Observations: A Historical Perspective," *Colorado History*, no. 1 (1997): 107–46. James Grafton Rogers offers a sensitive view of the changing seasons around Georgetown in *My Rocky Mountain Valley* (Boulder, 1968).

Chapter One: A Prehistoric Prelude: The Dwellers in the Cliffs

Tammy Stone furnishes an overview of the prehistoric peoples of Colorado in *The Prehistory of Colorado and Adjacent Areas* (Salt Lake City, 1999). See also Dennis J. Stanford and Jane S. Day, eds., *Ice Age Hunters of the Rockies* (Niwot, 1992) and Bruce Estes Rippeteau, *A Colorado Book of the Dead: The Prehistoric Era*, published as vol. 55 (fall 1978) of *The Colorado Magazine* and as a separate monograph.

On the Indians of Mesa Verde and the Southwest, see Don Watson, *Indians of the Mesa Verde* (Mesa Verde National Park, 1955) and H. M. Wormington, *Prehistoric Indians of the Southwest* (Denver, 1959). See also Wormington, *Ancient Man in North America* (Denver, 1957) and Alfonso Ortiz, ed., *Southwest*, vol. 9 of the *Handbook of North American Indians* (Washington, D.C., 1979). General accounts of Mesa Verde sites and artifacts include David Muench and Donald G. Pike, *Anasazi: Ancient People of the Rock* (Palo Alto, 1974); William M. Ferguson, *The Anasazi of Mesa Verde and the Four Corners* (Niwot, 1996); and David Roberts, *In Search of the Old Ones: Exploring the Anasazi World of the Southwest* (New York, 1996).

On Colorado archaeology, see E. Steve Cassells, *The Archaeology of Colorado* (1983; rev. ed., Boulder, 1997) and Philip Duke and Gary Matlock, *The State of Colorado Archaeology* ([Denver], 1992). Works that focus on archaeology in the Mesa Verde and Four Corners region include Duke and Matlock, *Points, Pithouses, and Pioneers: Tracing Durango's Archaeological Past* (Niwot, 1999); David Breternitz, "Mesa Verde National Park: A History of Its Archaeology," *Essays in Colorado History*, no. 2 (1983): 221–34; and Florence C. Lister, *In the Shadow of the Rocks: Archaeology of the Chimney Rock District in Southern Colorado* (Niwot, 1993), *Prehistory in Peril: The Worst and Best of Durango Archaeology* (Niwot, 1997), and, with Robert H. Lister, *Those Who Came Before: Southwestern Archeology in the National Park System* (1983; 2d ed., Tucson, 1994).

Reports of Mesa Verde archaeological investigations by early archaeologist and park superintendent Jesse Walter Fewkes include *Antiquities of the Mesa Verde National Park: Spruce Tree House* (Bureau of American Ethnology Bulletin 41, Washington, D.C., 1909);

Antiquities of the Mesa Verde National Park: Cliff Palace (Bureau of American Ethnology Bulletin 51, Washington, D.C., 1911); and "Far View House—A Pure Type of Pueblo Ruin," *Art and Archaeology* 6 (September 1917): 113–41. Portions of Fewkes's Bureau of American Ethnology studies are reprinted in Jesse Walter Fewkes, *Mesa Verde Ancient Architecture: Selections from the Smithsonian Institution, Bureau of American Ethnology, Bulletins 41 and 51 from the Years 1909 and 1911*, with an introduction by Larry V. Nordby ([Albuquerque], 1999).

For other reports, see Deric O'Bryan, *Excavations in Mesa Verde National Park, 1947–48* (Medallion Papers 39, Globe, Ariz., 1950); Robert H. Lister, *Contributions to Mesa Verde Archaeology* (University of Colorado Studies, Series in Anthropology, 9, 11, 12, 13, 15, Boulder, 1964–68); and Douglas Osborne, *Contributions of the Wetherill Mesa Archaeological Project* (Salt Lake City, 1965). Artifacts used in studying the Mesa Verde people are described in Earl H. Morris, *Archaeological Studies in the La Plata District, Southwestern Colorado and Northwestern New Mexico* (Carnegie Institution of Washington Publication 519, Washington, D.C., 1939).

Chapter Two: A Spanish Borderland

David J. Weber, *The Spanish Frontier in North America* (New Haven, 1992) is the best modern introduction to Borderlands history. See also John Francis Bannon, *The Spanish Borderlands Frontier, 1513–1821* (New York, 1970) and David Lavender, *The Southwest* (New York, 1980). Early Spanish experiences in the Southwest are described in Cleve Hallenbeck, *Alvar Nuñez Cabeza de Vaca: The Journey and Route of the First European to Cross the Continent of North America, 1534–1536* (Glendale, 1940) and the same author's *The Journey of Fray Marcos de Niza* (Dallas, 1949). John L. Kessell focuses on the Pecos, New Mexico, area, 1540–1840, in *Kiva, Cross, and Crown* (1979; Albuquerque, 1987).

On Coronado, see the classic works by Herbert E. Bolton, *Coronado, Knight of Pueblos and Plains* (New York, 1949) and George P. Hammond, *Coronado's Seven Cities* (Albuquerque, 1940). Recent multidisciplinary scholarship is summarized in Richard Flint and Shirley Cushing Flint, eds., *The Coronado Expedition to Tierra Nueva: The 1540–1542 Route across the Southwest* (Niwot, 1997).

Oakah L. Jones, Jr., describes Spanish settlement in *Los Paisanos: Spanish Settlers on the Northern Frontier of New Spain* (Norman, 1979). See also Evelio Echevarria and Jose Otero, eds., *Hispanic Colorado: Four Centuries, History and Heritage* (Fort Collins, 1976). For Oñate, see George P. Hammond, *Don Juan de Oñate and the Founding of New Mexico* (Santa Fe, 1927); Marc Simmons, *The Last Conquistador: Don Juan de Oñate and the Settling of the Far Southwest* (Norman, 1991); and "Oñate and All of That, 1598–1998," *Journal of the West* 37 (July 1998): 5–6, also by Simmons.

Indian relations and excursions northward can be studied in Phil Carson, *Across the Northern Frontier: Spanish Explorations in Colorado* (Boulder, 1998); in Ralph H. Vigil, Frances W. Kaye, and John R. Wunder, eds., *Spain and the Plains: Myths and Realities of Spanish Exploration and Settlement on the Great Plains* (Niwot, 1994); and in a series of works by Alfred Barnaby Thomas, including *The Plains Indians and New Mexico, 1751–1778* (Albuquerque, 1940), *Forgotten Frontiers: A Study of the Spanish Indian Policy of Don Juan Bautista de Anza, Governor of New Mexico, 1777–1787* (Norman, 1932), and *After Coronado:*

Spanish Exploration Northeast of New Mexico, 1696–1727 (Norman, 1935). Ruth Marie Colville traces the 1694 expedition of Don Diego de Vargas into the San Luis Valley in *La Vereda: A Trail through Time* ([Alamosa], 1996). In addition, see Ron Kessler, *Old Spanish Trail North Branch and its Travelers* (Santa Fe, 1998).

French interest in the area is described in William E. Dunn, "Spanish Reaction against the French Advance toward New Mexico," *Mississippi Valley Historical Review* 2 (December 1915): 348–62. On Bourgmont, see Henri Folmer, "De Bourgmont's Expedition to the Padoucas in 1724: The First French Approach to Colorado," *The Colorado Magazine* 14 (July 1937): 121–28 and Frank Norall, *Bourgmont: Explorer of the Missouri, 1698–1725* (Lincoln, 1988). For the Mallet expedition, see Folmer, "The Mallet Expedition of 1739 through Nebraska, Kansas and Colorado to Santa Fe," *The Colorado Magazine* 16 (September 1939): 161–73 and Donald J. Blakeslee, *Along Ancient Trails: The Mallet Expedition of 1739* (Niwot, 1995).

Exploration and Indian relations northwest of Santa Fe can be traced in Eleanor Richie, "General Mano Mocha of the Utes and Spanish Policy in Indian Relations," *The Colorado Magazine* 9 (July 1932): 150–57; Joseph J. Hill, "Spanish and Mexican Exploration and Trade Northwest from New Mexico into the Great Basin, 1765–1853," *Utah Historical Quarterly* 3 (January 1930): 3–23; and Alfred Barnaby Thomas, "San Carlos: A Comanche Pueblo on the Arkansas River, 1787," *The Colorado Magazine* 6 (May 1929): 79–91. On the Comanches, see Stanley Noyes, *Los Comanches: The Horse People, 1751–1845* (Albuquerque, 1993).

For Rivera, see G. Clell Jacobs, "The Phantom Pathfinder: Juan Maria Antonio de Rivera and His Expedition," *Utah Historical Quarterly* 60 (summer 1992): 200–223. Joseph P. Sanchez includes translations of two Rivera diaries in *Explorers, Traders, and Slavers: Forging the Old Spanish Trail, 1678–1850* (Salt Lake City, 1997). On Dominguez and Escalante, see Fray Angelico Chavez, trans., and Ted J. Warner, ed., *The Dominguez-Escalante Journal: Their Expedition through Colorado, Utah, Arizona and New Mexico in 1776* (1976; reprint, with a foreword by Robert Himmerich y Valencia, Salt Lake City, 1995).

Chapter Three: Exploring Louisiana

For a general introduction to Colorado Indians, see Sally Crum, *People of the Red Earth: American Indians of Colorado* (Santa Fe, 1996) and J. Donald Hughes, *American Indians in Colorado* (1977; 2d ed., Boulder, 1987). Roger L. Nichols provides an overall perspective in *Indians in the United States and Canada: A Comparative History* (Lincoln, 1998).

On the Utes, see Virginia McConnell Simmons, *The Ute Indians of Utah, Colorado, and New Mexico* (Boulder, 2000); Wilson Rockwell, *The Utes: A Forgotten People* (Denver, 1956); Marvin K. Opler, "The Southern Ute of Colorado," in *Acculturation in Seven American Indian Tribes*, ed. Ralph Linton (New York, 1940); and Helen Sloan Daniels, ed., *The Ute Indians of Southwestern Colorado* (Durango, 1941). Omer C. Stewart, *Ethnohistorical Bibliography of the Ute Indians of Colorado* (Boulder, 1971) is a good research tool.

For the Eastern Slope tribes, see Donald J. Berthrong, *The Southern Cheyennes* (Norman, 1963); E. Adamson Hoebel, *The Cheyennes: Indians of the Great Plains* (New York,

1960); George Bird Grinnell, *The Fighting Cheyennes* (1915; reprint, with an introduction by Stanley Vestal, Norman, 1956); and Virginia Cole Trenholm, *The Arapahoes: Our People* (Norman 1970). On the American bison or buffalo, see Harold P. Danz, *Of Bison and Man: From the Annals of a Bison Yesterday to a Refreshing Outcome from Human Involvement with America's Most Valiant of Beasts* (Niwot, 1997); David A. Dary, *The Buffalo Book: The Full Saga of the American Animal* (Chicago, 1974); and Tom McHugh, *The Time of the Buffalo* (New York, 1972).

On the Louisiana Purchase, see Marshall Sprague, *So Vast, So Beautiful a Land: Louisiana and the Purchase* (Boston, 1974). William H. Goetzmann, *Army Exploration in the American West, 1803–1863* (1959; reprint, with a new introduction by the author, Austin, 1991) provides a fine introduction to the exploration of the area. See also the same author's *Exploration and Empire* (New York, 1966) and *New Lands, New Men: America and the Second Great Age of Discovery* (New York, 1986). Donald Jackson analyzes Jefferson's interest in western exploration in *Thomas Jefferson and the Stony Mountains: Exploring the West from Monticello* (Urbana, 1981).

For a full-length biography of Pike, see W. Eugene Hollon, *The Lost Pathfinder: Zebulon Montgomery Pike* (Norman, 1949). See also Harvey L. Carter, *Zebulon Montgomery Pike, Pathfinder and Patriot* (Colorado Springs, 1956) and Carrol Joe Carter, *Pike in Colorado* (Fort Collins, 1978). For Pike's own account of the expedition, see Donald Jackson, ed., *The Journals of Zebulon Montgomery Pike, with Letters and Related Documents* (2 vols., Norman, 1966).

The Long expedition can be studied in vols. 14–17 of Reuben Gold Thwaites, ed., *Early Western Travels* (Cleveland, 1905) containing Edwin James's *Account of an Expedition from Pittsburgh to the Rocky Mountains, Performed in the Years 1819 and '20* ... and in Harlin M. Fuller and LeRoy R. Hafen, eds., *The Journal of Captain John R. Bell, Official Journalist for the Stephen H. Long Expedition to the Rocky Mountains, 1820* (Glendale, 1957), which is vol. 6 of Hafen's The Far West and the Rockies Historical Series, 1820–1875. Maxine Benson, ed., *From Pittsburgh to the Rocky Mountains: Major Stephen Long's Expedition, 1819–1820* (Golden, 1988), a one-volume abridgement of the *Account*, includes a bibliography of recent literature. See also two articles in the *Mississippi Valley Historical Review*: Cardinal Goodwin, "A Larger View of the Yellowstone Expedition, 1819–1820," 4 (December 1917): 299–313 and Ralph C. Morris, "The Notion of a Great American Desert East of the Rockies," 13 (September 1926): 190–200.

On Stephen H. Long, see Richard G. Wood, *Stephen Harriman Long, 1784–1864: Army Engineer, Explorer, Inventor* (Glendale, 1966) and Roger L. Nichols and Patrick L. Halley, *Stephen Long and American Frontier Exploration* (1980; reprint, with a new preface by Nichols, Norman, 1995). Recent studies focusing on Edwin James include Carlo Rotella, "Travels in a Subjective West: The Letters of Edwin James and Major Stephen Long's Scientific Expedition of 1819–1820," *Montana* 41 (autumn 1991): 20–35 and Phil Carson, "Through a Glass, Sharply: Edwin James and the First Recorded Ascent of Pikes Peak, July 13–15, 1820," *Essays in Colorado History*, no. 14 (1994): 1–35.

For details on the scientific contributions of the Long expedition, see Howard Ensign Evans, *The Natural History of the Long Expedition to the Rocky Mountains, 1819–1820* (New York, 1997); George J. Goodman and Cheryl A. Lawson, *Retracing Major Stephen H. Long's 1820 Expedition: The Itinerary and Botany* (Norman, 1995); and

Richard G. Beidleman, "The 1820 Long Expedition," *American Zoologist* 26 (1986): 307–13.

Chapter Four: The Fur Frontier

David Dary provides a general overview of the Santa Fe Trail in *The Santa Fe Trail: Its History, Legends, and Lore* (New York, 2000). For a guide to trail literature, see Jack D. Rittenhouse, *The Santa Fe Trail: A Historical Bibliography* (Albuquerque, 1971). On women's experiences, see Marc Simmons, "Women on the Santa Fe Trail: Diaries, Journals, Memoirs: An Annotated Bibliography," *New Mexico Historical Review* 61 (July 1986): 233–43. One of the best accounts is Stella M. Drumm, ed., *Down the Santa Fe Trail and into Mexico: The Diary of Susan Shelby Magoffin, 1846–1847* (1926; reprint, with a foreword by Howard R. Lamar, New Haven, 1962).

Many aspects of trail life are covered in papers presented at the 1986 Santa Fe Trail Symposium and published in *Essays in Colorado History,* no. 6 (1987) and later as *The Santa Fe Trail: New Perspectives* (Niwot, 1992). The Santa Fe Trail Association (www.santafetrail.org), founded at the 1986 conference, includes scholarly research and trail information in its quarterly publication *Wagon Tracks.* See also the special Santa Fe Trail issue of *Kansas History* 19 (winter 1996–97) and Marc Simmons, *The Old Trail to Santa Fe: Collected Essays* (Albuquerque, 1996). Sam'l P. Arnold combines history, literature, and authentic frontier recipes in the delightful *Eating Up the Santa Fe Trail* (Niwot, 1990).

The classic account of the Santa Fe trade is Josiah Gregg, *Commerce of the Prairies* (1844); see the edition by Max L. Moorhead (Norman, 1954). See also Paul Horgan, *Josiah Gregg and His Vision of the Early West* (New York, 1979). Seymour V. Connor and Jimmy M. Skaggs analyze the trade in *Broadcloth and Britches: The Santa Fe Trade* (College Station, Tex., 1977). In addition, see the following works by Mark L. Gardner: "The Mexican Road: Trade, Travel, and Confrontation on the Santa Fe Trail," *Journal of the West* 28 (April 1989): 3–87; *Brothers on the Santa Fe and Chihuahua Trails: Edward James Glasgow and William Henry Glasgow, 1846–1848* (Niwot, 1993); and *Wagons for the Santa Fe Trade: Wheeled Vehicles and Their Makers, 1822–1880* (Albuquerque, 2000).

On the fur trade generally, see the classic study by Hiram M. Chittenden, *The American Fur Trade of the Far West* (3 vols., New York, 1902); Paul C. Phillips, *The Fur Trade* (2 vols., Norman, 1961); Robert Glass Cleland, *This Reckless Breed of Men: The Trappers and Fur Traders of the Southwest* (New York, 1950); David J. Weber, *The Taos Trappers: The Fur Trade in the Far Southwest, 1540–1846* (Norman, 1971); David J. Wishart, *The Fur Trade of the American West, 1807–1840: A Geographical Synthesis* (Lincoln, 1979); and John Phillip Langellier, ed., "Fur Trade in the West," *Journal of the West* 26 (October 1987): 3–75. On the rendezvous, see Fred R. Gowans, *Rocky Mountain Rendezvous: A History of the Fur Trade Rendezvous, 1825–1840* (Provo, 1976).

On the Mountain Men, see Robert M. Utley, *A Life Wild and Perilous: Mountain Men and the Paths to the Pacific* (New York, 1997); LeRoy R. Hafen, ed., *The Mountain Men and the Fur Trade of the Far West* (10 vols., Glendale, 1965–72); William R. Swagerty, "Marriage and Settlement Patterns of Rocky Mountain Trappers and Traders," *Western Historical Quarterly* 11 (April 1980): 15–80; and Harvey Lewis Carter and Marcia Carpenter

Spencer, "Stereotypes of the Mountain Man," *Western Historical Quarterly* 6 (January 1975): 17–32. Carl P. Russell describes the equipment used in the fur trade in *Firearms, Traps, and Tools of the Mountain Men* (New York, 1967). The *Museum of the Fur Trade Quarterly*, published since 1965, contains specialized articles.

For the Bent enterprises, see David Lavender, *Bent's Fort* (New York, 1954); Douglas C. Comer, *Ritual Ground: Bent's Old Fort, World Formation, and the Annexation of the Southwest* (Berkeley and Los Angeles, 1996); Janet Lecompte, "Bent, St. Vrain and Company among the Comanche and Kiowa," *The Colorado Magazine* 49 (fall 1972): 273–93; Jackson W. Moore, *Bent's Old Fort: An Archeological Study* (Denver, 1973); and the special Bent's Fort issue of *The Colorado Magazine* (fall 1977).

The Glenn-Fowler operations are described in the journal of one of the leaders: Elliott Coues, ed., *The Journal of Jacob Fowler, Narrating an Adventure from Arkansas through the Indian Territory, Oklahoma, Kansas, Colorado, and New Mexico, to the Sources of the Rio Grande del Norte, 1821–22* (New York, 1898). On Antoine Robidoux and Fort Uncompahgre, see Joseph J. Hill, "Antoine Robidoux, Kingpin of the Colorado River Fur Trade, 1824–1844," *The Colorado Magazine* 7 (July 1930): 125–32; Ken Reyher, *Antoine Robidoux and Fort Uncompahgre: The Story of a Western Colorado Fur Trader* (Ouray, 1998); and Margie Cooke Porteus, "The New Fort Uncompahgre," *Persimmon Hill* 25 (winter 1997): 60–66, on a 1990s reconstruction of the fort. For other companies, fur men, and forts, see Don Berry, *A Majority of Scoundrels: An Informal History of the Rocky Mountain Fur Company* (New York, 1961) and the following articles by LeRoy R. Hafen in *The Colorado Magazine:* "Fort Jackson and the Early Fur Trade on the South Platte," 5 (February 1928): 9–17; "Old Fort Lupton and Its Founder," 6 (November 1929): 220–26; "Fort Davy Crockett, Its Fur Men and Visitors," 29 (January 1952): 17–33; "Fort St. Vrain," 29 (October 1952): 241–55; and "Fort Vasquez," 41 (summer 1964): 198–212.

Chapter Five: The Frontier in Transition

The standard biography of John Charles Frémont is by Allan Nevins, *Frémont: Pathmarker of the West* (New York, 1939). Andrew F. Rolle combines psychology and history in the more recent *John Charles Frémont: Character as Destiny* (Norman, 1991). Jessie Benton Frémont played a vital but behind-the-scenes role in her husband's career; for insights into her contributions, see Pamela Herr, *Jessie Benton Frémont: A Biography* (New York, 1987) and Herr and Mary Lee Spence, eds., *The Letters of Jessie Benton Frémont* (Urbana, 1993).

For the early Frémont expeditions, see Donald Jackson and Mary Lee Spence, eds., *The Expeditions of John Charles Frémont, Vol. 1: Travels from 1838 to 1844* (Urbana, 1970) and *Vol. 2: The Bear Flag Revolt and the Court Martial* (Urbana, 1973) and supplement, *Proceedings of the Court Martial* (Urbana, 1973). David Roberts focuses on the relationship between Frémont and Kit Carson in *A Newer World: Kit Carson, John C. Frémont, and the Claiming of the American West* (New York, 2000). On Carson, see Harvey L. Carter, *"Dear Old Kit": The Historical Christopher Carson* (Norman, 1968); Carter and Thelma S. Guild, *Kit Carson: A Pattern for Heroes* (Lincoln, 1984); R. C. Gordon-McCutchan, ed., *Kit Carson: Indian Fighter or Indian Killer?* (Niwot, 1996); and Thomas W. Dunlay, *Kit Carson and the Indians* (Lincoln, 2000). For Fitzpatrick, see LeRoy R. Hafen and W. J. Ghent, *Broken Hand: The Life Story of Thomas Fitzpatrick, Chief of the Mountain Men* (1931; rev. ed. published as *Broken Hand: The Life of Thomas Fitzpatrick: Mountain Man, Guide, and Indian Agent,* Denver, 1973).

On the Mormons, see John F. Yurtinus, "Colorado, Mormons, and the Mexican War: A History of the Mississippi Saints and Sick Detachments of the Mormon Battalion," *Essays in Colorado History*, no. 1 (1983): 107–45 and Norma Baldwin Ricketts, *The Mormon Battalion: U.S. Army of the West, 1846–1848* (Logan, 1996).

Janet Lecompte describes life in the early settlements along the Arkansas River in *Pueblo, Hardscrabble, Greenhorn: The Upper Arkansas, 1832–1856* (1978; reprint published as *Pueblo, Hardscrabble, Greenhorn: Society on the High Plains, 1832–1856*, with an introduction by Ann H. Zwinger, Norman, 1999). See also Morris F. Taylor, *A Sketch of Early Days on the Purgatory* (Trinidad, 1959) and Deborah Mora-Espinosa on one of the women at El Pueblo, "Teresita Sandoval: Woman in Between," in Vincent C. De Baca, ed., *La Gente: Hispano History and Life in Colorado*, Colorado History, no. 2 (Denver, 1998): 3–20.

Frémont's fourth expedition is described in William Brandon, *The Men and the Mountain: Frémont's Fourth Expedition* (New York, 1955); Robert V. Hine, *Edward Kern and American Expansion* (New Haven, 1962); LeRoy R. and Ann W. Hafen, eds., *Frémont's Fourth Expedition: A Documentary Account of the Disaster of 1848–1849 ...* (vol. 11, The Far West and the Rockies Historical Series, 1820–1875; Glendale, 1960); and Mary Lee Spence, ed., *The Expeditions of John Charles Frémont, Vol. 3: Travels from 1848 to 1854* (Urbana, 1984). Patricia Joy Richmond meticulously traces Frémont's route in *Trail to Disaster: The Route of John C. Frémont's Fourth Expedition from Big Timbers, Colorado, through the San Luis Valley, to Taos, New Mexico,* Monographs in Colorado History, no. 4 (Denver, 1989). In addition, see Alpheus Hoyt Favour, *Old Bill Williams, Mountain Man* (1936; reprint, with an introduction by William Brandon, Norman, 1962) and Frank C. Spencer, "The Scene of Frémont's Disaster in the San Juan Mountains, 1848," *The Colorado Magazine* 6 (July 1929): 141–46.

On Gunnison, see two works by Nolie Mumey, *John Williams Gunnison (1812–1853): The Last of the Western Explorers* (Denver, 1955) and "John Williams Gunnison: Centenary of His Survey and Tragic Death (1853–1953)," *The Colorado Magazine* 31 (January 1954): 19–32, and Leland Hargrave Creer, "The Explorations of Gunnison and Beckwith in Colorado and Utah, 1853," *The Colorado Magazine* 6 (September 1929): 184–92. For a biography of Richard H. Kern, a member of Frémont's fourth expedition who met his death with Gunnison's party, see David J. Weber, *Richard H. Kern, Expeditionary Artist in the Far Southwest, 1848–1853* (Albuquerque, 1985).

Indian relations are described in LeRoy R. Hafen and Francis M. Young, *Fort Laramie and the Pageant of the West, 1834–1890* (Glendale, 1938) and in two articles by Hafen: "Thomas Fitzpatrick and the First Indian Agency in Colorado," *The Colorado Magazine* 6 (March 1929): 53–62 and "The Fort Pueblo Massacre and the Punitive Expedition against the Utes," *The Colorado Magazine* 4 (March 1927): 49–58.

On the San Luis Valley generally, see Virginia McConnell Simmons, *The San Luis Valley: Land of the Six-Armed Cross* (1979; 2d ed., Niwot, 1999) and Olibama Tushar, *The People of "El Valle": A History of the Spanish Colonials in the San Luis Valley* (1975; 3d ed., Pueblo, 1997). See also Tom Wolfe, *Colorado's Sangre de Cristo Mountains* (Niwot, 1995). The *San Luis Valley Historian*, published by the San Luis Valley Historical Society since 1969, contains a wealth of documentation on specific subjects.

Social, cultural, and religious aspects are treated in Frances Leon Swadesh, *Los Primeros Pobaladores: Hispanic Americans of the Ute Frontier* (Notre Dame, 1974); Robert Adams, *The Architecture and Art of Early Hispanic Colorado* (Boulder, 1974); Arthur L. Campa, *Hispanic Culture in the Southwest* (Norman, 1979); Aurelio M. Espinosa, *The Folklore of Spain in the American Southwest: Traditional Spanish Folk Literature in Northern New Mexico and Southern Colorado*, ed. J. Manuel Espinosa (Norman, 1985); and Randi Jones Walker, *Protestantism in the Sangre de Cristos, 1850–1920* (Albuquerque, 1991). Issue 3 (1988) of *Colorado Heritage* was devoted to Colorado's Hispanic traditions.

For an overview of the Mexican period, see David J. Weber, *The Mexican Frontier, 1821–1846: The American Southwest under Mexico* (Albuquerque, 1982). Land grants are covered in Victor Westphall, *Mercedes Reales: Hispanic Land Grants of the Upper Rio Grande Region* (Albuquerque, 1983); John R. Van Ness, ed., "Spanish Land Grants in New Mexico and Colorado," *Journal of the West* 19 (July 1980): 3–99; Malcolm Ebright, ed., "Spanish and Mexican Land Grants and the Law," *Journal of the West* 27 (July 1988): 3–84; Ebright, *Land Grants and Lawsuits in Northern New Mexico* (Albuquerque, 1994); LeRoy R. Hafen, "Mexican Land Grants in Colorado," *The Colorado Magazine* 4 (May 1927): 81–93; Harold H. Dunham, "Coloradans and the Maxwell Grant," *The Colorado Magazine* 32 (April 1955): 131–45; and Purnee A. McCourt, "The Conejos Land Grant of Southern Colorado," *The Colorado Magazine* 52 (winter 1975): 34–51. Related biographical studies include Morris F. Taylor, *O. P. McMains and the Maxwell Land Grant Conflict* (Tucson, 1979) and Lawrence R. Murphy, *Lucien Bonaparte Maxwell, Napoleon of the Southwest* (Norman, 1983).

Military life is covered in Morris F. Taylor, "Fort Massachusetts," *The Colorado Magazine* 45 (spring 1968): 120–42 and Duane Vandenbusche, "Life at a Frontier Post: Fort Garland," *The Colorado Magazine* 43 (spring 1966): 132–48. A woman's view of life at Fort Garland can be found in Sandra L. Myres, ed., *Cavalry Wife: The Diary of Eveline M. Alexander, 1866–1867* (College Station, Tex., 1977).

Chapter Six: Gold Rush

General works on the westward migration include John D. Unruh, Jr., *The Plains Across: The Overland Emigrants and the Trans-Mississippi West, 1840–1860* (Urbana, 1979); John Mack Faragher, *Women and Men on the Overland Trail* (New Haven, 1979); and Lillian Schlissel, *Women's Diaries of the Westward Journey* (1982; expanded ed., New York, 1992). The *Overland Journal*, published since 1983 by the Oregon-California Trails Association (www.octa-trails.org) includes recent scholarship; see especially Merrill J. Mattes, "The South Platte Trail: Colorado Cutoff of the Oregon-California Trail," 10 (fall 1992): 2–16.

Any study of the Colorado gold rush must now begin with Elliott West, *The Contested Plains: Indians, Goldseekers, and the Rush to Colorado* (Lawrence, 1998). See also West's *The Way to the West: Essays on the Central Plains* (Albuquerque, 1995) and "Golden Dreams: Colorado, California, and the Reimagining of America," *Montana* 49 (autumn 1999): 2–11.

Other accounts include Agnes Wright Spring, "Rush to the Rockies, 1859," *The Colorado Magazine* 36 (April 1959): 83–120; Calvin W. Gower, "Gold Fever in Kansas Territory: Migration to the Pike's Peak Gold Fields, 1858–1860," *Kansas Historical Quarterly* 39 (spring 1973): 58–74; and the following works by James F. Willard: "The Gold

Rush and After," chapter 5 in *Colorado: Short Studies of Its Past and Present* (Boulder, 1927); "Spreading the News of the Early Discoveries of Gold in Colorado," *The Colorado Magazine* 6 (May 1929): 98–104; and "Sidelights on the Pike's Peak Gold Rush, 1858–59," *The Colorado Magazine* 12 (January 1935): 3–13.

For firsthand views, see Julia Archibald Holmes, "To Pikes Peak and New Mexico, 1858," in Kenneth L. Holmes, ed., *Diaries and Letters from the Western Trails, 1854–1860*, vol. 7 of *Covered Wagon Women* (Glendale, 1987); Ovando J. Hollister, *The Mines of Colorado* (Springfield, Mass., 1867); S. W. Burt and E .L. Berthoud, *The Rocky Mountain Gold Regions* (Denver, 1861); and three volumes in the *Southwest Historical Series* (Glendale, 1941–42) edited by LeRoy R. Hafen: *Pike's Peak Gold Rush Guidebooks of 1859* (vol. 9); *Colorado Gold Rush: Contemporary Letters and Reports, 1858–1859* (vol. 10); and *Overland Routes to the Gold Fields, 1859, from Contemporary Diaries* (vol. 11).

On Governor Denver, see George C. Barns, *Denver, the Man: The Life, Letters, and Public Papers of the Lawyer, Soldier, and Statesman* (Wilmington, Ohio, 1949) and Edward Magruder Cook, *Justified by Honor: Highlights in the Life of General James William Denver* (Falls Church, Va., 1988). For the Larimers, father and son, see William H. H. Larimer, *Reminiscences of General William Larimer and of His Son William. H. H. Larimer, Two of the Founders of Denver City* (Lancaster, Pa., 1918) and Joan Ostrom Beasley, "Unrealized Dreams: General William Larimer, Jr.," *Colorado Heritage* (summer 1996): 2–20.

Other biographical studies related to the events of the Gold Rush include Marita Hayes, "D. C. Oakes, Early Colorado Booster," *The Colorado Magazine* 31 (July 1954): 216–26; Caroline Bancroft, "The Elusive Figure of John H. Gregory, Discoverer of the First Gold Lode in Colorado," *The Colorado Magazine* 20 (July 1943): 121–35; and Liston E. Leyendecker, "Young Man Gone West: George M. Pullman's Letters from the Colorado Goldfields," *Chicago History* 7 (Winter 1978–79): 208–25. Leyendecker's full-scale account of Pullman's life is *Palace Car Prince: A Biography of George Mortimer Pullman* (Niwot, 1992).

The Colorado mining frontier can be related to the general history of western American mining in William S. Greever, *The Bonanza West: The Story of the Western Mining Rushes, 1848–1900* (Norman, 1963) and the shorter but more suggestive study by Rodman W. Paul, *Mining Frontiers of the Far West, 1848–1880* (New York, 1963). See also Paul's *The Far West and the Great Plains in Transition, 1859–1900* (New York, 1988) and Duane A. Smith, *Rocky Mountain West: Colorado, Wyoming, and Montana, 1859–1915* (Albuquerque, 1992).

Each of the three journalists who reported on the goldfields left a personal account of his visit: Villard in *The Past and Present of the Pike's Peak Gold Region* (1860; reprint, with an introduction and notes by LeRoy R. Hafen, Princeton, 1932); Richardson in *Beyond the Mississippi* (Hartford, 1867); and Greeley in *An Overland Journey from New York to San Francisco in the Summer of 1859* (1860; reprint, with an introduction by Jo Ann Manfra, Lincoln, 1999).

Chapter Seven: Miners and Merchants

T. A. Rickard's *A History of American Mining* (New York, 1932) and *The Romance of Mining* (Toronto, 1944) are useful general studies. For terminology and mining procedures, see Otis E. Young, Jr., *Western Mining* (Norman, 1970) and *Black Powder and Hand Steel: Miners and Machines on the Old Western Frontier* (Norman, 1976).

The Colorado experiences are detailed in Francis S. Williams, "The Influence of California upon the Placer Mining Methods of Colorado," *The Colorado Magazine* 26 (April 1949): 127–43; "Overland to Pikes Peak with a Quartz Mill: Letters of Samuel Mallory," *The Colorado Magazine* 8 (May 1931): 108–15; and Rodman W. Paul, "Colorado as a Pioneer of Science in the Mining West," *Mississippi Valley Historical Review* 47 (June 1960): 34–50. Terry Cox focuses on Central City in *Inside the Mountains: A History of Mining around Central City, Colorado* (Boulder, 1989). Joseph E. King analyzes the financial aspects in *A Mine to Make a Mine: Financing the Colorado Mining Industry, 1859–1902* (College Station, Tex., 1977). Duane A. Smith provides an illustrated view in *Colorado Mining: A Photographic History* (Albuquerque, 1977) and surveys Colorado mining historiography in "The Untapped Ore of History," *Colorado Heritage* (Issue 1,1985): 41–47. In *Mining America: The Industry and the Environment, 1800–1980* (Lawrence, 1987), Smith focuses on the attitudes of mining toward environmental concerns. See also Smith's article, "'This Reckless and Disastrous Practice': The Impact of Mining on Forests in the Rocky Mountains, 1859–1880," *Journal of the West* 38 (October 1999): 15–24.

On coinage, minting, and banking, see Nolie Mumey, *Clark, Gruber, and Company, 1860–1865: A Pioneer Denver Mint* (Denver 1950); LeRoy R. Hafen, "Currency, Coinage, and Banking in Pioneer Colorado," *The Colorado Magazine* 10 (May 1933): 81–90; Eugene H. Adams, Lyle W. Dorsett, and Robert S. Pulcipher, *The Pioneer Western Bank—First of Denver: 1860–1980* (Denver, 1984); and Thomas J. Noel, *Growing through History with Colorado: The Colorado National Banks, the First 125 Years, 1862–1987* (Denver, 1987).

Transportation and communication problems are described in Oscar Osburn Winther, *The Transportation Frontier: Trans-Mississippi West, 1865–1890* (New York, 1964). See also Arthur Ridgway, "The Mission of Colorado Toll Roads," *The Colorado Magazine* 9 (September 1932): 161–69; three articles by LeRoy R. Hafen in the same journal: "Supplies and Market Prices in Pioneer Denver," 4 (August 1927): 136–42; "Early Mail Service to Colorado, 1858–60," 2 (January 1925): 23–32; and "Pioneer Struggles for a Colorado Road across the Rockies," 3 (March 1926): 1–10; Morris F. Taylor, *First Mail West: Stagecoach Lines on the Santa Fe Trail* (1971; reprint, with an introduction by Mark L. Gardner, Albuquerque, 2000), on mail service on the Santa Fe Trail between 1850 and 1880; W. Turrentine Jackson, *Wells Fargo in Colorado Territory* (Denver, 1982); Doris Monahan, *Destination, Denver City: The South Platte Trail* (Athens, Ohio, 1985); Thomas C. Jepsen, "The Telegraph Comes to Colorado: A New Technology and Its Consequences" *Essays in Colorado History*, no. 7 (1987): 1–25; and Robert C. Black III, *Railroad Pathfinder: The Life and Times of Edward L. Berthoud* (Evergreen, 1988).

Chapter Eight: Culture Comes to the Gold Towns

Impressions of early architecture, as well as many other facets of pioneer Colorado's social scene, are captured in the text and invaluable illustrations of Muriel Sibell Wolle's *Stampede to Timberline: The Ghost Towns and Mining Camps of Colorado* (1949; rev. ed., Chicago, 1974) and *Timberline Tailings: Tales of Colorado's Ghost Towns and Mining Camps* (Chicago, 1977). For the overall view, see Duane A. Smith, *Rocky Mountain Mining Camps: The Urban Frontier* (1967; reprint, with a new preface, Niwot, 1992). Accounts by two

1860s visitors, now available in modern editions, are Bayard Taylor, *Colorado: A Summer Trip* (1867; reprint, edited by William W. Savage, Jr., and James H. Lazalier, Niwot, 1989) and Samuel Bowles, *The Parks and Mountains of Colorado: A Summer Vacation in the Switzerland of America, 1868* (1869; reprint, with an introduction by James H. Pickering, Norman, 1991).

Works on Central City include Caroline Bancroft, *Gulch of Gold: A History of Central City* (Denver, 1958) and H. William Axford, *Gilpin County Gold: Peter McFarlane, 1848–1929, Mining Entrepreneur in Central City, Colorado* (Chicago, 1976). For Summit County, see Mary Ellen Gilliland, *Summit: A Gold Rush History of Summit County, Colorado* (Silverthorne, Colo., 1980). Elliott West focuses on children in "Heathens and Angels: Childhood in the Rocky Mountain Mining Towns," *Western Historical Quarterly* 14 (April 1983): 145–64; in "Beyond Baby Doe: Child Rearing on the Mining Frontier," in Susan Armitage and Elizabeth Jameson, eds., *The Women's West* (Norman, 1987); and in *Growing Up with the Country: Childhood on the Far Western Frontier* (Albuquerque, 1989).

Alice Cochran provides an overview of the religious scene in *Miners, Merchants, and Missionaries: The Roles of Missionaries and Pioneer Churches in the Colorado Gold Rush and Its Aftermath, 1858–1870* (Metuchen, N.J., 1980). See also Louisa Ward Arps, ed., *Faith on the Frontier: Religion in Colorado before August 1876* (Denver, 1976).

On Catholicism, see Thomas J. Noel, *Colorado Catholicism and the Archdiocese of Denver, 1857–1989* (Niwot, 1989). For Bishop Machebeuf, see Lynn Bridgers, *Death's Deceiver: The Life of Joseph P. Machebeuf* (Albuquerque, 1997) and Thomas F. O'Conner, "Bishop Machebeuf," *The Colorado Magazine* 12 (July 1935): 130–39. On Jean Baptiste Lamy, see Thomas J. Steele, S.J., ed. and trans., *Archbishop Lamy: In His Own Words* (Albuquerque, 2000).

The Jewish experience can be studied in Allen duPont Breck, *The Centennial History of the Jews of Colorado, 1859–1959* (Denver, 1960) and in Phil Goodstein, *Exploring Jewish Colorado* (Denver, 1992).

Ferenc Morton Szasz focuses on the "mainline" Protestant ministers (Methodist, Baptist, Presbyterian, Congregational, and Episcopal) in *The Protestant Clergy in the Great Plains and Mountain West, 1865–1915* (Albuquerque, 1988). For specific denominations, see J. Alton Templin, Allen duPont Breck, and Martin Rist, eds., *The Methodist, Evangelical, and United Brethren Churches in the Rockies, 1850–1976* (Denver, 1977); Virginia Greene Millikin et al., *The Bible and the Gold Rush: A Century of Congregationalism in Colorado, 1863–1963* (Denver, 1962); Linda K. Kirby, *Heritage of Heroes: Trinity United Methodist Church, 1859–1988* (Denver, 1988); and on Presbyterianism, Norman J. Bender, "Crusade of the Blue Banner in Colorado," *The Colorado Magazine* 47 (spring 1970): 91–118 and *Winning the West for Christ: Sheldon Jackson and Presbyterianism on the Rocky Mountain Frontier, 1869–1880* (Albuquerque, 1996). See Mark Fiester, *Look for Me in Heaven* (Boulder, 1980), for a biography of the pioneering Methodist circuit rider John Dyer.

Ann W. Hafen and LeRoy R. Hafen, "The Beginnings of Denver University," *The Colorado Magazine* 24 (March 1947): 58–66 gives details on the school's early days. See also Allen duPont Breck, *From the Rockies to the World: A Companion to the History of the University of Denver, 1864–1997* (Denver, 1997). For broader implications, see Michael McGiffert, *The Higher Learning in Colorado: An Historical Study, 1860–1940* (Denver, 1964).

The history of Denver's first newspaper and much of the history of the city and region as well are imaginatively related in Robert L. Perkin, *The First Hundred Years: An Informal History of Denver and the Rocky Mountain News* (New York, 1959). See also

David F. Halaas, "Frontier Journalism in Colorado," *The Colorado Magazine* 44 (summer 1967): 185–203 and *Boom-Town Newspapers: Journalism on the Rocky Mountain Mining Frontier, 1859–1881* (Albuquerque, 1981) and Sherilyn Cox Bennion, *Equal to the Occasion: Woman Editors of the Nineteenth-Century West* (Reno and Las Vegas, 1990). Gunther Barth compares and contrasts the development of San Francisco and Denver in *Instant Cities: Urbanization and the Rise of San Francisco and Denver* (New York, 1975).

On medicine, see Robert H. Shikes, *Rocky Mountain Medicine: Doctors, Drugs, and Disease in Early Colorado* (Boulder, 1986) and Mary De Mund, *Women Physicians of Colorado* (Denver, 1976).

Several studies explore the role of the frontier saloon. See Elliott West, *The Saloon on the Rocky Mountain Mining Frontier* (Lincoln, 1979) and the following works by Thomas J. Noel: "The Multifunctional Frontier Saloon: Denver, 1858–1876," *The Colorado Magazine* 52 (spring 1975): 114–36; "The Immigrant Saloon in Denver," *The Colorado Magazine* 54 (summer 1977): 201–19; *Denver's Larimer Street: Main Street, Skid Row, and Urban Renaissance* (Denver, 1981); *The City and the Saloon: Denver, 1858–1916* (Lincoln, 1982); and *Colorado: A Liquid History and Tavern Guide to the Highest State* (Golden, 1999). Elliott West describes activities of temperance advocates in Colorado to 1900 in "Of Lager Beer and Sonorous Songs," *The Colorado Magazine* 48 (spring 1971): 108–28.

On Gore, see Jack Roberts, *The Amazing Adventures of Lord Gore: A True Saga from the Old West* (Silverton, 1977). Melvin Schoberlin describes entertainment on the mining frontier in *From Candles to Footlights: A Biography of the Pike's Peak Theatre, 1859–1876* (Denver, 1941). See also Lynn I. Perrigo, "The First Two Decades of Central City Theatricals," *The Colorado Magazine* 11 (July 1934): 141–52; Alice Cochran, "Jack Langrishe and the Theater of the Mining Frontier," *The Colorado Magazine* 46 (fall 1969): 324–37; Virginia McConnell, "A Gauge of Popular Taste in Early Colorado," *The Colorado Magazine* 46 (fall 1969): 338–50; and Harlan Jennings, "'The Singers Are Not on Speaking Terms': Grand Opera in Denver, 1864–1881," *Colorado Heritage* (spring 1999): 2–19.

Duane A. Smith looks at early baseball in "Mighty Casey Matches the Mountains: The Origins of Baseball in Colorado," *Colorado Heritage* (spring 1995): 4–18. See also Smith and Mark S. Foster, *They Came to Play: A Photographic History of Colorado Baseball* (Niwot, 1997); Foster and Irvin Moss, *Home Run in the Rockies: The History of Baseball in Colorado* (Denver, 1994); and James Whiteside, *Colorado: A Sports History* (Niwot, 1999).

Details on the 1863 fire and on subsequent Denver conflagrations are given in Dick Kreck, *Denver in Flames: Forging a New Mile High City* (Golden, 2000). For the other great disaster of the period, see Albert B. Sanford, "The 'Big Flood' in Cherry Creek, 1864," *The Colorado Magazine* 4 (May 1927): 100–105. Sanford's mother provides a revealing glimpse of life in early Colorado in Donald F. Danker, ed., *Mollie: The Journal of Mollie Dorsey Sanford in Nebraska and Colorado Territories, 1857–1866* (Lincoln, 1959).

Chapter Nine: Legal Beginnings

The mining districts have been described by many authors, but the most useful summaries are chapter 7, "The Mining Districts," in Percy Fritz, *Colorado: The Centennial State* (New York, 1941) and Thomas Maitland Marshall "The Miners' Laws of Colorado," *American Historical Review* 25 (April 1920): 426–39. See also Henry A. Dubbs, "The Unfolding of Law in the Mountain Region," *The Colorado Magazine* 3 (October 1926): 113–32 and Marshall, *Early Records of Gilpin County, Colorado, 1859–1861* (Boulder, 1920). Other articles in *The Colorado Magazine* describing early government and politics are Francis S. Williams, "Trials and Judgments of the People's Courts of Denver," 27 (October 1950): 294–302; two articles by George L. Anderson, "The El Paso Claim Club, 1859–1862," 13 (March 1936): 41–53 and "The Canon City or Arkansas Valley Claim Club, 1860–1862," 16 (November 1939): 201–10; "The Middle Park Claim Club, 1861," 10 (September 1933): 189–92; and Milo Fellows, "The First Congressional Election in Colorado (1858)," 6 (March 1929): 46–47. The constitution of Jefferson Territory is printed in *The Colorado Magazine* 12 (November 1935): 215–20.

Chapter Ten: Battlegrounds

Colorado's first two territorial governors are the subjects of modern biographies: Thomas L. Karnes, *William Gilpin, Western Nationalist* (Austin, 1970) and Harry E. Kelsey, Jr., *Frontier Capitalist: The Life of John Evans* (Denver, 1969). See also LeRoy R. Hafen, "Colorado's First Legislative Assembly," *The Colorado Magazine* 20 (March 1943): 41–50 and Jason H. Silverman, "Making Brick out of Straw: Delegate Hiram P. Bennet," *The Colorado Magazine* 53 (fall 1976): 309–27. For Bennet's memoirs, see Liston Leyendecker, ed., *Hiram Pitt Bennet: Frontier Lawyer, Politician*, Monographs in Colorado History, no. 2 (Denver, 1988).

Daniel Ellis Conner (1837–1920) describes Confederate activity in southern Colorado in *A Confederate in the Colorado Gold Fields*, ed. Donald J. Berthrong and Odessa Davenport (Norman, 1970), especially 126–57. See also Morris F. Taylor, "Confederate Guerrillas in Southern Colorado," *The Colorado Magazine* 46 (fall 1969): 304–23 and Duane A. Smith, "The Confederate Cause in the Colorado Territory, 1861–1865," *Civil War History* 7 (March 1961): 71–80.

For Colorado and the Civil War, see, generally, Alvin M. Josephy, Jr., *The Civil War in the American West* (New York, 1991); LeRoy H. Fischer, ed., "Civil War Battles in the West," *Journal of the West* 19 (October 1980): 3–75; and Ray C. Colton, *The Civil War in the Western Territories: Arizona, Colorado, New Mexico, and Utah* (Norman, 1959). Duane A. Smith focuses on events in Colorado in *The Birth of Colorado: A Civil War Perspective* (Norman, 1989). Albert B. Sanford describes Camp Weld in "Camp Weld, Colorado," *The Colorado Magazine* 11 (March 1934): 46–50.

Details on the battle at Glorieta Pass are provided in Don E. Alberts, *The Battle of Glorieta: Union Victory in the West* (College Station, Tex., 1998) and in Thomas S. Edrington and John Taylor, *The Battle of Glorieta Pass: A Gettysburg in the West, March 26–28, 1862* (Albuquerque, 1998). See also William Clarke Whitford, *Colorado Volunteers in the Civil War: The New Mexico Campaign in 1862* (1906; reprint, Glorieta, N. Mex., 1971); Ovando J. Hollister, *Boldly They Rode: A History of the First Colorado Regiment of Volunteers* (1863; reprint, Lakewood, 1949); and Robert Lee Kirby, *The Confederate Invasion of New Mexico and Arizona, 1861–1862* (Los Angeles, 1958). *Rebels on the Rio Grande: The Civil War Journal of A. B. Peticolas*, ed. Don E. Alberts (Albuquerque, 1984) provides a firsthand account of the events in New Mexico.

Robert M. Utley, *The Indian Frontier of the American West, 1846–1890* (Albuquerque, 1984) furnishes a modern overview of the subject. William E. Unrau analyzes the Fort Wise treaty and the complex problems surrounding it in "A Prelude to War," *The Colorado Magazine* 41 (fall 1964): 299–313. Harry E. Kelsey, Jr., focuses on the role of the agent in "Background to Sand Creek," *The Colorado Magazine* 45 (fall 1968): 279–300. See also Lillian B. Shields, "Relations with the Cheyennes and Arapahoes in Colorado to 1861," *The Colorado Magazine* 4 (August 1927): 145–54 and "The Struggle for Eastern Colorado" in Edmund J. Danziger, Jr., *Indians and Bureaucrats: Administering the Reservation Policy during the Civil War* (Urbana, 1974).

For a history of the military units involved in the fighting during the era, see John H. Nankivell, *History of the Military Organizations of the State of Colorado, 1860–1935* (Denver, 1935). One of these is the topic of Blanche V. Adams, "The Second Colorado Cavalry in the Civil War," *The Colorado Magazine* 8 (May 1931): 95–106. Raymond G. Carey details the history of the hundred-dayers in "The 'Bloodless Third' Regiment, Colorado Volunteer Cavalry," *The Colorado Magazine* 38 (October 1961): 275–300. Darlis A. Miller examines the economic aspects of the army in the Southwest, including southern Colorado, in *Soldiers and Settlers: Military Supply in the Southwest, 1861–1885* (Albuquerque, 1989).

The events at Sand Creek, memorialized in 2000 with the establishment of the Sand Creek Massacre National Historic Site, have attracted the attention of many authors. Good introductions to the topic are Stan Hoig, *The Sand Creek Massacre* (Norman, 1961) and Janet Lecompte, "Sand Creek," *The Colorado Magazine* 41 (fall 1964): 314–35. Michael A. Sievers provides an excellent analysis of the literature in "Sands of Sand Creek Historiography," *The Colorado Magazine* 49 (spring 1972): 116–42, while Raymond G. Carey summarizes the problems of interpreting the conflicting evidence in "The Puzzle of Sand Creek," *The Colorado Magazine* 41 (fall 1964): 279–98.

A contemporary account by a participant is Lynn I. Perrigo, ed., "Major Hal Sayr's Diary of the Sand Creek Campaign," *The Colorado Magazine* 15 (March 1938): 41–57. For modern evaluations of the events, see chapter 11, "Massacre at Sand Creek," in Robert L. Perkin, *The First Hundred Years: An Informal History of Denver and the* Rocky Mountain News (Denver, 1959); chapter 9, "Massacre at Sand Creek," in Donald J. Berthrong, *The Southern Cheyennes* (Norman, 1963); and chapter 14, "The Sand Creek Massacre," in George Bird Grinnell, *The Fighting Cheyennes* (1915; reprint, with an introduction by Stanley Vestal, Norman, 1956). Much of Grinnell's information came from George Bent, the half-Cheyenne son of William Bent, who was in the encampment at the time; for details, see David Fridtjof Halaas, "'All the Camp Was Weeping': George Bent and the Sand Creek Massacre," *Colorado Heritage* (summer 1995): 1–17. Michael Straight's historical novel *A Very Small Remnant* (New York, 1963) and Bruce Cutler's *The Massacre at Sand Creek: Narrative Voices* (Norman, 1995) combine history and literature to provide additional insights. These writers all condemn the whites' actions. For contrast, see Reginald S. Craig, *The Fighting Parson: The Biography of Colonel John M. Chivington* (Los Angeles, 1959) and Robert Scott, *Blood at Sand Creek: The Massacre Recalled* (Caldwell, Idaho, 1994).

On Wynkoop, see Thomas D. Isern, "The Controversial Career of Edward W. Wynkoop," *The Colorado Magazine* 56 (winter/spring 1979): 1–18 and Christopher B. Gerboth, ed., *The Tall Chief: The Unpublished Autobiography of Edward W. Wynkoop,*

1856–1866, Monographs in Colorado History, no. 9 (Denver, 1993). For Soule, see Stan Hoig, "Silas Soule, Partizan of the Frontier," *Montana* 26 (January 1976): 70–77. David Svaldi analyzes the writings of major figures such as William N. Byers, John Evans, and John Chivington in *Sand Creek and the Rhetoric of Extermination: A Case Study in Indian-White Relations* (Lanham, Md., 1989), portions of which were published as "The *Rocky Mountain News* and the Indians," *Journal of the West* 27 (July 1988): 85–93.

The Cheyenne view of the South Platte River raids after Sand Creek can be studied in detail in Jean Afton, David Fridtjof Halaas, and Andrew E. Masich, with Richard N. Ellis, *Cheyenne Dog Soldiers: A Ledgerbook History of Coups and Combat* (Niwot, 1997). See also Halaas and Masich, "'You Could Hear the Drums for Miles': A Cheyenne Ledgerbook History," *Colorado Heritage* (autumn 1996): 2–15, accompanied by a selection of drawings (17–37) and "A Brief Chronology of Battles and Skirmishes, 1864–65" (38–44).

The best account of the Battle of Beecher Island is John H. Monnett, *The Battle of Beecher Island and the Indian War of 1867–1869* (Niwot, 1992). See also David Dixon, *Hero of Beecher Island: The Life and Military Career of George A. Forsyth* (Lincoln, 1994); Harry H. Anderson, ed., "Stand at the Arikaree," *The Colorado Magazine* 41 (fall 1964): 336–42; and on Sigmund Shlesinger, Merrill J. Mattes, ed., "The Beecher Island Battlefield Diary of Sigmund Shlesinger," *The Colorado Magazine* 29 (July 1952): 161–69 and John H. Monnett, "A Scout's Perceptions of Indians at the Battle of Beecher Island: An Essay on Ethnocentrism and the Reminiscences of Sigmund Shlesinger," *Montana* 43 (autumn 1993): 32–43.

For Summit Springs, see Jack D. Filipiak, "The Battle of Summit Springs," *The Colorado Magazine* 41 (fall 1964): 343–54; Richard Weingardt, *Sound the Charge* (Englewood, 1978), which includes source material on the conflict; Don Russell, *The Lives and Legends of Buffalo Bill* (Norman, 1960), 129–48; and James T. King, *War Eagle: A Life of General Eugene A. Carr* (Lincoln, 1965), 94–119.

Chapter Eleven: Smelters and Railroads

For a comprehensive treatment of smelting, see James E. Fell, Jr., *Ores to Metals: The Rocky Mountain Smelting Industry* (Lincoln, 1979). Frank Fossett, *Colorado* (New York, 1879) contains much contemporary information about mining and smelting. Charles Henderson, *Mining in Colorado* (Washington, D.C., 1926) is packed with statistics and mining data. See also Jesse D. Hale, "The First Successful Smelter in Colorado," *The Colorado Magazine* 13 (September 1936): 161–67; Fell, "Nathaniel P. Hill: A Scientist-Entrepreneur in Colorado," *Arizona and the West* 15 (winter 1973): 315–32; and Eleanor Fry, *Smelters of Pueblo* (Pueblo, 2000).

John Willard Horner recounts the history of Georgetown in *Silver Town* (Caldwell, Idaho, 1950). See also Liston E. Leyendecker, *Georgetown: Colorado's Silver Queen, 1859–1876* (Fort Collins, 1977) and *Guide to the Georgetown–Silver Plume Historic District* (1986; 3d ed., Evergreen, 1995). Leyendecker discusses a noted legal dispute in the Georgetown–Silver Plume area in *The Pelican-Dives Feud: A Study in Frustration and Terror,* Monographs in Colorado History, no. 1 (1985). For the story of a famous army officer's experiences with a mine southwest of Silver Plume, see Duane A. Smith, "'Where a Bird Could Hardly Obtain a Footing': George Armstrong Custer and the Stevens Mine," *Colorado Heritage* (spring 1997): 25–37.

For other areas, see Duane A. Smith's *Silver Saga: The Story of Caribou, Colorado* (Boulder, 1974) and Mark Fiester, *Blasted, Beloved Breckenridge* (Boulder, 1973). Smith provides a comparative view of Colorado and California mining in "Decade of Frustration: Colorado and California Silver Mining in the 1860s," *Southern California Quarterly* 56 (summer 1974): 135–58.

On the mining men generally, see two works by Richard H. Peterson, *The Bonanza Kings: The Social Origins and Business Behavior of Western Mining Entrepreneurs, 1870–1900* (Lincoln, 1977) and *Bonanza Rich: Lifestyles of the Western Mining Entrepreneurs* (Moscow, Idaho, 1991), and Clark Spence, *Mining Engineers and the American West* (New Haven, 1970). Steven F. Mehls analyzes the relationship between "bonanza king" David Moffat and mining engineer Eben Smith in "Success on the Mining Frontier: David H. Moffat and Eben Smith: A Case Study," *Essays in Colorado History*, no. 1 (1983): 91–105.

The literature about early Colorado railroads is extensive. Good reference sources are Tivis E. Wilkins, *Colorado Railroads: Chronological Development* (Boulder, 1974) and Donald B. Robertson, *Encyclopedia of Western Railroad History*, vol. 2, *The Mountain States: Colorado, Idaho, Montana, Wyoming* (Caldwell, Idaho, 1991). An introduction is Elmer Orville Davis, *The First Five Years of the Railroad Era in Colorado* (Golden, 1948), while Robert M. Ormes, *Railroads and the Rockies: A Record of Lines in and near Colorado* (Denver, 1963) is a helpful guide. Two articles by S. D. Mock in *The Colorado Magazine* provide useful details: "Colorado and the Surveys for a Pacific Railroad," 17 (March 1940): 54–63 and "The Financing of Early Colorado Railroads," 18 (November 1941): 201–9. Much railroad history can be found in the volumes of the *Colorado Rail Annual*, published by the Colorado Railroad Museum in Golden since 1963.

For histories of individual lines, see M. C. Poor, *Denver, South Park and Pacific* (Denver, 1949); David Digerness, *The Mineral Belt* (2 vols., Silverton, 1977–78), also on the South Park; James Marshall, *Santa Fe: The Railroad that Built an Empire* (New York, 1945); Keith L. Bryant, Jr., *History of the Atchison, Topeka and Santa Fe Railway* (New York, 1974); Robert G. Athearn, *Rebel of the Rockies: A History of the Denver and Rio Grande Western Railroad* (New Haven, 1962); Robert A. LeMassena, *Rio Grande … to the Pacific!* (Denver 1974); O. Meredith Wilson, *The Denver and Rio Grande Project, 1870–1901* (Salt Lake City, 1982); Athearn, *Union Pacific Country* (Chicago, 1971); and Maury Klein, *Union Pacific: The Birth of a Railroad, 1862–1893* (Garden City, 1987). Thomas J. Noel discusses the first railroad to reach Denver in "All Hail the Denver Pacific: Denver's First Railroad," *The Colorado Magazine* 50 (spring 1973): 91–116. For stage and railroad transportation in southern Colorado, see Morris F. Taylor, "The Barlow and Sanderson Stage Lines in Colorado, 1872–1884," *The Colorado Magazine* 50 (spring 1973): 142–62.

The Rio Grande's history may be supplemented with the history of one of its "towns," delightfully narrated by Marshall Sprague in *Newport in the Rockies: The Life and Good Times of Colorado Springs* (1961; 4th rev. ed., Athens, Ohio, 1987). Morris F. Taylor discusses another Rio Grande town in "El Moro: Failure of a Company Town," *The Colorado Magazine* 48 (spring 1971): 129–45.

Chapter Twelve: Utopias in the Desert

The most useful survey of colony towns in Colorado is the Introduction to James F. Willard and Colin B. Goodykoontz, eds., *Experiments in Colorado Colonization, 1869–1872*

(Boulder, 1926). Willard also edited *The Union Colony at Greeley, Colorado, 1869–1871* (Boulder, 1918). Annie (Mrs. A. M.) Green writes about Union Colony life in *Sixteen Days on the Great American Desert* (1887), a portion of which is included in Ruth B. Moynihan, Susan Armitage, and Christiane Fischer Dichamp, eds., *So Much to Be Done: Women Settlers on the Mining and Ranching Frontier* (Lincoln, 1990).

Additional studies include Guy L. Peterson, *Fort Collins: The Post—The Town* (Fort Collins, 1972); Barbara Allbrandt Fleming, *Fort Collins: A Pictorial History* (Norfolk, Va., 1985); John Dugan, *Greeley and Weld County: A Pictorial History* (Norfolk, Va., 1986); Kathryn Young, "Pioneer Days in Sterling," *The Colorado Magazine* 4 (March 1927): 58–63; Nicholas G. Morgan, "Mormon Colonization in the San Luis Valley," *The Colorado Magazine* 27 (October 1950): 269–93; Dorothy Roberts, "The Jewish Colony at Cotopaxi," *The Colorado Magazine* 18 (July 1941): 124–31; and Ralph E. Blodgett, "The Colorado Territorial Board of Immigration," *The Colorado Magazine* 46 (summer 1969): 245–56. Later life in the Wet Mountain Valley is delightfully recounted in William A. Weber, ed., *Theodore D. A. Cockerell: Letters from West Cliff, Colorado, 1887–1889* (Boulder, 1976). For more on the English-born Cockerell, who became a distinguished University of Colorado professor, see Weber, ed., *The American Cockerell: A Naturalist's Life, 1866–1948* (Boulder, 2000).

Chapter Thirteen: Carpetbagger's Kingdom

Earl S. Pomeroy, *The Territories and the United States, 1861–1890: Studies in Colonial Administration* (Philadelphia, 1947) and Howard R. Lamar, *The Far Southwest: 1846–1912: A Territorial History* (1966; rev. ed., Albuquerque, 2000) analyze the relationships between western territories and the federal government. See also John Porter Bloom, ed., *The American Territorial System* (Athens, Ohio, 1973) and for Colorado, Douglas C. McMurtrie, "The Public Printing of the First Territorial Legislature of Colorado," *The Colorado Magazine* 13 (March 1936): 72–78 and George W. Collins, "Colorado's Territorial Secretaries," *The Colorado Magazine* 43 (summer 1966): 185–208. Legal aspects are covered in two works by Gordon M. Bakken, "The Development of Law in Colorado, 1861–1912," *The Colorado Magazine* 53 (winter 1976): 63–78 and *The Development of Law on the Rocky Mountain Frontier: Civil Law and Society, 1850–1912* (Westport, Conn., 1983), and John D. W. Guice, *The Rocky Mountain Bench: The Territorial Supreme Courts of Colorado, Montana, and Wyoming, 1861–1890* (New Haven, 1972).

For a general view of reconstruction, see Eugene H. Berwanger, *The West and Reconstruction* (Urbana, 1981). See also the same author's "Reconstruction on the Frontier: The Equal Rights Struggle in Colorado, 1865–1867," *Pacific Historical Review* 44 (August 1975): 313–29, reprinted in Monroe Lee Billington and Roger D. Hardaway, eds., *African Americans on the Western Frontier* (Niwot, 1998).

Other studies of equal rights include Harmon Mothershead, "Negro Rights in Colorado Territory (1859–1867)," *The Colorado Magazine* 40 (July 1963): 212–23; Eugene H. Berwanger, "William J. Hardin: Colorado Spokesman for Racial Justice, 1863–1873," *The Colorado Magazine* 52 (winter 1975): 52–65; William M. King, "Black Children, White Law: Black Efforts to Secure Public Education in Central City, Colorado, 1864–1869,"

Essays in Colorado History, no. [3] (1984): 55–79; and Jesse T. Moore, Jr., "Seeking a New Life: Blacks in Post–Civil War Colorado," *Journal of Negro History* 78 (summer 1993): 166–87. Activities of black cavalry and infantry troops in Colorado and the West after the Civil War are detailed in a series of articles in the spring 1996 issue of *Colorado Heritage.*

The statehood struggle is covered in Elmer Ellis, "Colorado's First Fight for Statehood, 1865–1868," *The Colorado Magazine* 8 (January 1931): 23–30 and Duane A. Smith, "Colorado's Struggle for Statehood," *Journal of the West* 15 (January 1976): 29–37.

On Teller, see Elmer Ellis, *Henry Moore Teller: Defender of the West* (Caldwell, Idaho, 1941) and Christian J. Buys, "Henry M. Teller: Colorado's 'Silver Senator,'" *Colorado Heritage* (summer 1998): 29–36. Other useful biographical studies include William Hanchett, "'His Turbulent Excellency,' Alexander Cummings, Governor of Colorado Territory, 1865–1867," *The Colorado Magazine* 34 (April 1957): 81–104; Thomas F. Dawson, "Major Thompson, Chief Ouray, and the Utes," *The Colorado Magazine* 7 (May 1930): 113–22; and Albert B. Sanford, "John L. Routt, First State Governor of Colorado," *The Colorado Magazine* 3 (August 1926): 81–86.

Chapter Fourteen: The Centennial State

The debates of the constitutional convention were not officially recorded or published, but the basic order of business is revealed in *Proceedings of the Constitutional Convention* (Denver, 1907). The issues are discussed in Colin B. Goodykoontz, "Some Controversial Questions before the Colorado Constitutional Convention of 1876," *The Colorado Magazine* 17 (January 1940): 1–17. See also Henry J. Hersey, "The Colorado Constitution," *The Colorado Magazine* 3 (August 1926): 65–76 and Elmer Herbert Meyer, "The Constitution of Colorado," *Iowa Journal of History and Politics* 2 (April 1904): 256–74. Gordon M. Bakken, *Rocky Mountain Constitution Making, 1850–1912* (New York, 1987) provides a general perspective.

For the 1876 election, see Robert E. Smith, "Thomas M. Patterson, Colorado Statehood, and the Presidential Election of 1876," *The Colorado Magazine* 53 (spring 1976): 153–62. Patterson's career as lawyer, politician, and newspaperman is covered in Smith and Sybil Downing, *Tom Patterson: Colorado Crusader for Change* (Niwot, 1995).

Billie Barnes Jensen discusses woman suffrage during the 1870s in "Colorado Woman Suffrage Campaigns of the 1870s," *Journal of the West* 12 (April 1973): 254–71. Evelyn Kaye narrates the life of Isabella Bird in *Amazing Traveler, Isabella Bird: The Biography of a Victorian Adventurer* (1994; 2d ed., Boulder, 1999). For Bird's classic account of her 1873 western journey, published in London in 1879, see Ernest S. Bernard, ed., *Isabella Lucy Bird's "A Lady's Life in the Rocky Mountains": An Annotated Text* (Norman, 1999). Hester McClung also traveled through some of the same area in 1873; see Susan Armitage, "The Letters of Hester McClung: Another Lady's Life in the Rocky Mountains," *Essays in Colorado History,* no. 5 (1987): 79–138.

For the Colorado scene in 1876, see Duane A. Smith, "Colorado Mining in 1876," *Journal of the West* 15 (January 1976): 38–53; Maxine Benson, "Colorado Celebrates the Centennial, 1876," *The Colorado Magazine* 53 (spring 1976): 129–52; and Michael J. Brodhead, "A Naturalist in the Colorado Rockies, 1876," *The Colorado Magazine* 52 (summer 1975): 185–99. Benson analyzes the life of a Colorado woman naturalist who gained fame at the Philadelphia Centennial Exposition in *Martha Maxwell, Rocky Mountain Naturalist* (Lincoln, 1986).

The best modern history of Denver is Stephen J. Leonard and Thomas J. Noel, *Denver: Mining Camp to Metropolis* (Niwot, 1990). See also Lyle W. Dorsett, *The Queen City: A History of Denver* (1977; 2d ed., with Michael McCarthy, Boulder, 1986); Thomas J. Noel, *Denver: Rocky Mountain Gold* (Tulsa, 1980); and "Denver Boosters and Their 'Great Braggart City,'" *Colorado Heritage* (autumn 1995): 2–29, also by Noel. Still valuable are Jerome C. Smiley's massive *History of Denver* (Denver, 1901), available in a reprint edition (Evansville, Ind., 1971) with an index by Robert L. Perkin, and *History of the City of Denver, Arapahoe County, and Colorado* (Chicago, 1880). The City and County of Denver web site (www.denvergov.org) includes both current information and a section on Denver history.

Accounts of specific ethnic groups include Stephen J. Leonard, "The Irish, English, and Germans in Denver, 1860–1890," *The Colorado Magazine* 54 (spring 1977): 126–53; Christine Ann DeRose, "Inside 'Little Italy': Italian Immigrants in Denver," *The Colorado Magazine* 54 (summer 1977): 277–93; and Xi Wang, "The Chinese in Denver: A Demographical Perspective, 1870–1885," *Essays in Colorado History*, no. 12 (1991): 37–58. See also Stanley L. Cuba, "Polish Impressions of Early Colorado: Letters, Diaries, and Reminiscences of Polish Visitors and Immigrants, 1873–1891," *Essays in Colorado History*, no. 5 (1987): 1–52 and "Polish Impressions of Colorado: Letters, Diaries, and Reminiscences of Polish Visitors and Immigrants, 1894–1934," *Essays in Colorado History*, no. 7 (1987): 49–109.

Other aspects are treated in Robert M. Tank, "Mobility and Occupational Structure on the Late-Nineteenth-Century Urban Frontier: The Case of Denver, Colorado," *Pacific Historical Review* 47 (May 1978): 189–216 and Lyle W. Dorsett, "Equality of Opportunity on the Urban Frontier: Access to Credit in Denver, Colorado Territory, 1858–1876," *Journal of the West* 18 (July 1979): 75–81. See also S. D. Mock, "Effects of the 'Boom' Decade, 1870–1880, upon Colorado Population," *The Colorado Magazine* 11 (January 1934): 27–34.

On the University of Colorado, see Frederick S. Allen et al., *The University of Colorado, 1876–1976* (New York, 1976) and Stephen Carroll, "Territorial Attempts to Establish a University of Colorado at Boulder," *Red River Valley Historical Review* 1 (winter 1974): 351–67. Silvia Pettem focuses on the extraordinary private life of the university's first woman professor in *Separate Lives: The Story of Mary Rippon* (Longmont, 1999).

For information on other early institutions of higher learning, see James E. Hansen II, *Democracy's College in the Centennial State: A History of Colorado State University* (Fort Collins, 1977) and J. Juan Reid, *Colorado College: The First Century, 1874–1974* (Colorado Springs, 1979).

Chapter Fifteen: Carbonate Camps

On Leadville history generally, see Don L. and Jean Harvey Griswold, *The Carbonate Camp Called Leadville* (Denver, 1951); Edward Blair, *Leadville: Colorado's Magic City* (Boulder, 1980); and Stephen M. Voynick, *Leadville: A Miner's Epic* (Missoula, 1984). The

Griswolds' *History of Leadville and Lake County, Colorado: From Mountain Solitude to Metropolis* (2 vols., Denver and Niwot, 1996) covers the years between 1879 and 1901 in detail; see also James E. Fell, Jr., "The Carbonate Camp: A Brief History and Selected Bibliography of Leadville," *Colorado History*, no. 1 (1997): 70–86, adapted from his introduction to this massive, two-thousand-plus-page work.

History of the Arkansas Valley, Colorado (Chicago, 1881) and Frank Hall's *History of the State of Colorado* (4 vols., Chicago, 1889–95) offer a varied assortment of information on the camp, its life, and its people. For a modern overview of the region, see Virginia McConnell Simmons, *The Upper Arkansas: A Mountain River Valley* (Boulder, 1990).

Carlyle Channing Davis, *Olden Times in Colorado* (Los Angeles, 1916) is a personal, informative memoir by an early Leadville newspaper editor. Author and artist Mary Hallock Foote gives additional insights in *A Victorian Gentlewoman in the Far West*, ed. Rodman Paul (San Marino, 1972).

Other aspects of early Leadville are detailed in Donald Fremont Popham, "The Early Activities of the Guggenheims in Colorado," *The Colorado Magazine* 27 (October 1950): 263–69 and Christian Buys, "Of Frozen Hydrants and 'Drunkin Sons of Bitches': Early Leadville's Volunteer Firemen," *Colorado Heritage* (summer 1997): 2–15. See also Buys's *Historic Leadville in Rare Photographs and Drawings* (Ouray, 1977). Dorothy M. Degitz tells the story of one Leadville building in "History of the Tabor Opera House at Leadville," *The Colorado Magazine* 13 (May 1936): 81–89. For more on the built environment, see Lawrence Von Bamford, *Leadville Architecture: A Legacy of Silver, 1860–1899* (Estes Park, 1996) and C. Eric Stoehr, *Bonanza Victorian: Architecture and Society in Colorado Mining Towns* (Albuquerque, 1975).

Horace Tabor's financial and political affairs are treated in Duane A. Smith, *Horace Tabor: His Life and the Legend* (1973; reprint, with a new introduction, Niwot, 1989). Other works on the Tabors include Augusta Tabor, "Cabin Life in Colorado," *The Colorado Magazine* 4 (March 1927): 71–75; Betty Moynihan, *Augusta Tabor, A Pioneering Woman* (Evergreen, 1988); John Burke, *The Legend of Baby Doe* (1974; reprint, with an introduction by Duane A. Smith, Lincoln, 1989); and Smith, "'So fleet the works of man': 'The Ballad of Baby Doe' and Mining," *Mining History Journal* (1998): 53–62.

Stanley Dempsey and James E. Fell, Jr., recount the history of the area north of Leadville in *Mining the Summit: Colorado's Ten Mile District, 1860–1960* (Norman, 1986). Duane A. Smith discusses Leadville and other Colorado mining rushes between 1859 and 1893 in relation to the "safety-valve" theory in "Colorado's Urban-Mining Safety Valve," *The Colorado Magazine* 48 (fall 1971): 299–318.

Transportation problems are discussed in Elmer R. Burkey, "The Georgetown-Leadville Stage," *The Colorado Magazine* 14 (September 1937): 177–87; two articles by Robert G. Athearn, "Origins of the Royal Gorge Railroad War," *The Colorado Magazine* 36 (January 1959): 37–57 and "Captivity of the Denver and Rio Grande," *The Colorado Magazine* 37 (January 1960): 39–58; Albert B. Sanford, "The Old South Park Railroad," *The Colorado Magazine* 5 (October 1928): 173–78; and Richard Carroll, "The Founding of Salida, Colorado," *The Colorado Magazine* 11 (July 1934): 121–33. See also David J. Ham, "Salida, Colorado, 1880–1886: The Transition from End-of-Track Construction Camp to Established Community," *Essays in Colorado History*, no. 1 (1983): 53–69.

For the Clear Creek Valley, see Duane A. Smith and Hank Wieler, *Secure the Shadow: Lachlan McLean, Colorado Mining Photographer* (Golden, 1980), which includes images of

Central City, Idaho Springs, and Georgetown, and the older but still valuable *History of Clear Creek and Boulder Valleys, Colorado* (Chicago, 1880). On the Georgetown Loop, see P. R. "Bob" Griswold, Richard H. Kindig, and Cynthia Trombly, *Georgetown and the Loop* (Denver, 1988) and Dianna Litvak, "Colorado's Railroad to Nowhere: Building and Rebuilding the Georgetown Loop," *Colorado Heritage* (spring 1999): 34–47.

Other towns are described in Don and Jean Griswold, *Colorado's Century of "Cities"* (Denver, 1958). For Gunnison and the surrounding area, see Duane Vandenbusche, *Early Days in the Gunnison Country* (Gunnison, 1974); C. E. Hagie, "Gunnison in Early Days," *The Colorado Magazine* 8 (July 1931): 121–29; George A. Root, "Gunnison in the Early 'Eighties," *The Colorado Magazine* 9 (November 1932): 201–13; Carl L. Haase, "Gothic, Colorado: City of Silver Wires," *The Colorado Magazine* 51 (fall 1974): 294–316; S. E. Poet, "The Story of Tin Cup, Colorado," *The Colorado Magazine* 9 (January 1932): 30–38; and Lawrence Von Bamford and Kenneth R. Tremblay, Jr., "St. Elmo, Colorado: The Little Mining Camp That Tried," *Colorado Heritage* (spring 2000): 2–18. For Aspen, see Malcolm J. Rohrbough, *Aspen: The History of a Silver-Mining Town, 1879–1893* (New York, 1986), and for Creede, Nolie Mumey, *Creede: History of a Colorado Silver Mining Town* (Denver, 1949).

Max Evans chronicles the history of a ranch in the mountains near Creede in *This Chosen Place: Finding Shangri-La on the 4UR* (Niwot, 1997). For the experience of one family, the Browns, in southern Colorado during the early 1880s, see Byrd Gibbens, ed., *This Is a Strange Country: Letters of a Westering Family, 1880–1906* (Albuquerque, 1988) and Gibbens, Lillian Schlissel, and Elizabeth Hampsten, *Far From Home: Families of the Westward Journey* (New York, 1989).

Chapter Sixteen: Open Range Days

The basic studies of the Colorado cattle industry are Ora Brooks Peake, *The Colorado Range Cattle Industry* (Glendale, 1937); chapter 5, "The Range Livestock Industry," in Alvin T. Steinel, *History of Agriculture in Colorado* (Fort Collins, 1926); and Maurice Frink, W. Turrentine Jackson, and Agnes Wright Spring, *When Grass Was King: Contributions to the Western Range Cattle Industry Study* (Boulder, 1956). These may be supplemented with the more general works by Edward Everett Dale, *The Range Cattle Industry* (Norman, 1930); Walter Prescott Webb, *The Great Plains* (New York, 1931); and Terry G. Jordan, *North American Cattle-Ranching Frontiers: Origins, Diffusion, and Differentiation* (Albuquerque, 1993). On cattle trailing, see Jimmy M. Skaggs, *The Cattle-Trailing Industry: Between Supply and Demand, 1866–1890* (Lawrence, 1973).

For an introduction to the world of the cowboy, see David Dary, *Cowboy Culture: A Saga of Five Centuries* (New York, 1981); William W. Savage, *The Cowboy Hero: His Image in American History and Culture* (Norman, 1979); Don D. Walker, *Clio's Cowboys: Studies in the Historiography of the Cattle Trade* (Lincoln, 1981); Don Rickey, Jr., *$10 Horse, $40 Saddle: Cowboy Clothing, Arms, Tools, and Horse Gear of the 1880s* (Fort Collins, 1976); Issue 1, 1981, of *Colorado Heritage*; and Keith Schrum, "Of Myth and Men: The Trail of the Black Cowboy," *Colorado Heritage* (autumn 1998): 2–17.

Biographical studies of men involved in the cattle enterprises include Mark S. Foster, *Henry M. Porter, Rocky Mountain Empire Builder* (Niwot, 1991); P. G. Scott, "John W.

Prowers, Bent County Pioneer," *The Colorado Magazine* 7 (September 1930): 183–87; Edgar C. McMechen, "John Hittson, Cattle King," *The Colorado Magazine* 11 (September 1934): 164–70; Vernon Maddux, *John Hittson: Cattle King on the Texas and Colorado Frontier* (Niwot, 1994); and Rufus Phillips, "Early Cowboy Life in the Arkansas Valley," *The Colorado Magazine* 7 (September 1930): 165–79. For an insight into ranching in southeastern Colorado, see Richard Louden, ed., "Some Memories from My Life, as Written by Elfido Lopez, Sr.," in Vincent C. De Baca, ed., *La Gente: Hispano History and Life in Colorado,* Colorado History, no. 2 (Denver, 1998): 21–44. Clarice E. Richards describes turn-of-the-century ranching in Elbert County in *A Tenderfoot Bride: Tales from an Old Ranch* (1920; reprint, with an introduction by Maxine Benson, Lincoln, 1988).

Related studies are Albert W. Thompson, "The Great Prairie Cattle Company, Ltd.," *The Colorado Magazine* 22 (March 1945): 76–83; Clifford P. Westermeier, "The Legal Status of the Colorado Cattleman, 1867–1887," parts 1 and 2, *The Colorado Magazine* 25 (May and July 1948): 109–18, 157–66; Edward G. Hayes, "ZA Roundup," *The Colorado Magazine* 41 (summer 1964): 213–24; Sue Flanagan, "Charles Goodnight in Colorado," *The Colorado Magazine* 43 (winter 1966): 1–21; Morris F. Taylor, "Ranching on the Outboundaries of the Las Animas Grant in Colorado, 1884–1899," *Arizona and the West* 16 (summer 1974): 125–40 and "The Maxwell Cattle Company, 1881–1888," *New Mexico Historical Review* 49 (October 1974): 289–324; and William R. White, "Illegal Fencing on the Colorado Range," *The Colorado Magazine* 52 (spring 1975): 93–113. John Rolfe Burroughs describes range contests in northwestern Colorado in *Where the Old West Stayed Young* (New York, 1962). Morris Taylor focuses on life in an important southern Colorado cow town in *Trinidad, Colorado Territory* (Trinidad, 1966). See also Sister Blandina Segale's impressions of Trinidad in the 1870s in *At the End of the Santa Fe Trail* (1932; reprint, with a foreword by Marc Simmons and an afterword by Anne M. Butler, Albuquerque, 1999).

Chapter Seventeen: Beyond the Continental Divide

On the history and mystique of the Western Slope, see Duane A. Smith and Duane Vandenbusche, *A Land Alone: Colorado's Western Slope* (Boulder, 1981) and Smith, "A Land unto Itself: The Western Slope," *The Colorado Magazine* 55 (spring/summer 1978): 181–204. In addition, see Vandenbusche, *The Gunnison Country* (Gunnison, 1980); Donald A. MacKendrick, "Thunder West of the Divide: James W. Bucklin, Western Colorado Utopian Reformer," *Essays in Colorado History,* no.[3] (1984): 35–53; Walter R. Borneman, "The Race for the Gunnison Country," *American West* 21 (January/February 1984): 70–77; and the *Journal of the Western Slope,* published since 1986 at Mesa State College, Grand Junction.

On Grand Junction, see James H. Rankin, "The Founding and Early Years of Grand Junction," *The Colorado Magazine* 6 (March 1929): 39–45 and Kathleen Underwood, *Town Building on the Colorado Frontier* (Albuquerque, 1987). To the east, Angela K. Parkison relates the early history of Glenwood Springs in *Hope and Hot Water: Glenwood Springs from 1878 to 1891* (Glenwood Springs, 2000). For Delta County, southeast of Grand Junction, see Olivia Spalding Ferguson, "A Sketch of Delta County History," *The Colorado Magazine* 5 (October 1928): 161–64.

Studies focusing on the region west of the Divide and north of the Colorado River include John Rolfe Burroughs, *Steamboat in the Rockies* (Fort Collins, 1974); Julie Jones-

Eddy, *Homesteading Women: An Oral History of Colorado, 1890–1950* (New York, 1992), on Moffat and Rio Blanco counties; and Grace McClure, *The Basset Women* (Athens, Ohio, 1985), on the Brown's Park area of northwestern Colorado. On Grand County, see Robert C. Black III, *Island in the Rockies: The History of Grand County, Colorado, to 1930* (1969; 2d ed. published as *Island in the Rockies: The Pioneer Era of Grand County, Colorado*, Granby, 1977) and *Fraser Haps and Mishaps: The Diary of Mary E. Cozens*, ed. Alice Reich and Thomas J. Steele, S.J. (Denver, 1990).

For the San Juan area generally, see Robert L. Brown, *An Empire of Silver* (Caldwell, Idaho, 1965); Rob Blair, ed., *The Western San Juan Mountains: Their Geology, Ecology, and Human History* (Niwot, 1996); P. David Smith, *Images of the San Juans: Historical Selections from the Ruth and Marvin Gregory Photograph Collection* (Ouray, 1997); and Mike Foster, ed., *Summits to Reach: An Annotated Edition of Franklin Rhoda's "Report on the Topography of the San Juan Country"* (Boulder, 1984), an account of an 1874 Hayden Survey party. See also Foster, *Strange Genius: The Life of Ferdinand Vandeveer Hayden* (Boulder, 1994) and Lloyd M. Pierson, ed., "Rollin J. Reeves and the Boundary between Utah and Colorado," *Utah Historical Quarterly* 66 (spring 1996): 100–117.

Studies of San Juan mines and miners include Duane A. Smith: "Silver Coquette— The San Juans, 1869–1875," *Brand Book 1969* (Denver, 1970): 221–52, "The San Juaner: A Computerized Portrait," *The Colorado Magazine* 52 (spring 1975): 137–52, and *Song of the Hammer and Drill: The Colorado San Juans, 1860–1914* (1982; reprint, with a new preface by the author, Boulder, 2000); P. David Smith, *Mountains of Silver: The Story of Colorado's Red Mountain Mining District* (Boulder, 1994); and Robert J. Torrez, "The San Juan Gold Rush of 1860 and Its Effect on the Development of Northern New Mexico," *New Mexico Historical Review* 63 (July 1988): 257–72.

On the development of San Juan mining camps and towns, see Duane A. Smith, *Rocky Mountain Boom Town: A History of Durango* (Albuquerque, 1980), *Durango Diary: A Collection of Durango Herald Columns* (Durango, 1996), "'Ever Optimistic': Animas Forks, Colorado," *Journal of the West* 36 (October 1997): 61–73, and *Silverton: A Quick History* (Fort Collins, 1997); Allen Nossaman, *Many More Mountains*: vol. 1, *Silverton's Roots* (Denver, 1989), vol. 2, *Ruts into Silverton* (Denver, 1993), and vol. 3, *Rails into Silverton* (Denver, 1998); and Doris H. Gregory, *History of Ouray*, vol. 1, *A Heritage of Mining and Everlasting Beauty* (Ouray, 1995) and vol. 2, *Historical Homes, Buildings, and People* (Ouray, 1997).

Other aspects of life in the San Juans are detailed in Duane A. Smith, "Two Literary Miners: The West of Novelist Frank Nason and Poet Alfred King," *Colorado Heritage* (Issue 1, 1982): 65–77; Harriet Backus, *Tomboy Bride* (Boulder, 1969), on the Telluride area and Leadville; Carl A. Hanson, "Letters from the Rockies: John Cotton Dana in Southwestern Colorado, 1880–81," *Colorado History*, no. 1 (1997): 31–56; and Stephen J. Leonard, "Avenging Mary Rose: The Lynchings of Margaret and Michael Cuddigan in Ouray, Colorado, 1884," *Colorado Heritage* (summer 1999): 34–47. Telluride native David Lavender's novel *Red Mountain* (1963; reprint, with an introduction by Duane A. Smith, Ouray, 2000) catches the spirit of a vanished age.

Works on transportation problems and solutions in southwestern Colorado include Frances and Dorothy Wood, *I Hauled These Mountains in Here* (Caldwell, Idaho, 1977) on the life of pioneer freighter Dave Wood, and three studies by Michael Kaplan on Otto Mears: "Otto Mears and the Silverton Northern Railroad," *The Colorado Magazine* 48 (summer 1971): 235–54; "The Toll Road Building Career of Otto Mears, 1881–1887,"

The Colorado Magazine 52 (spring 1975): 153–70; and Otto Mears, Paradoxical Pathfinder (Silverton, 1982). Robert E. Sloan and Carl A. Skowronski relate the story of the Silverton, Silverton Northern, and Silverton, Gladstone, and Northerly lines in The Rainbow Route (Denver, 1975). On the Rio Grande Southern, see Mallory Hope Ferrell, Silver San Juan: The Rio Grande Southern Railroad (Boulder, 1973). For the line between Durango and Silverton, now operated as a prime tourist attraction, see Duane A. Smith, Durango and Silverton Narrow Gauge: A Quick History (Ouray, 1998).

On the Utes, see Robert W. Delaney, "The Southern Utes a Century Ago," Utah Historical Quarterly 39 (spring 1971): 114–28; The Southern Ute People (Phoenix, 1974); The Ute Mountain Utes (Albuquerque, 1989); and with James Jefferson and Gregory Thompson, The Southern Utes: A Tribal History (Ignacio, 1972). For Ouray, see P. David Smith, Ouray, Chief of the Utes (Ouray, 1986). Stephen J. Leonard discusses the 1863 treaty in "John Nicolay in Colorado: A Summer Sojourn and the 1863 Ute Treaty," Essays in Colorado History, no. 11 (1990): 25–54.

The standard narrative of the 1879 Meeker Massacre is Marshall Sprague, Massacre: The Tragedy at White River (Boston, 1957). On Meeker's reform efforts, see Mark W. T. Harvey, "Misguided Reformer: Nathan Meeker among the Ute," Colorado Heritage (Issue 1, 1982): 36–44 and James Whiteside, "Interacting with the Sacred: American Indian Sports in Colorado," Colorado Heritage (summer 1998): 37–45, which includes a discussion of Meeker's altercation with the Utes over horse racing. Mark E. Miller provides a modern account of the Milk Creek conflict in Hollow Victory: The White River Expedition of 1879 and the Battle of Milk Creek (Niwot, 1997). See also Forbes Parkhill, "The Meeker Massacre and Thornburgh Battle: Fact and Fiction," Brand Book 1945 (Denver, 1946): 91–110 and Elmer R. Burkey, "The Thornburgh Battle with the Utes on Milk Creek," The Colorado Magazine 13 (May 1936): 90–110. On the removal of the Utes, see Walker D. Wyman, "A Preface to the Settlement of Grand Junction: The Uncompahgre Utes 'Goes West,'" The Colorado Magazine 10 (January 1933): 22–27 and Jo Lea Wetherilt Behrens, "'The Utes Must Go'—with Dignity: Alfred B. Meacham's Role on Colorado's Ute Commission, 1880–1881," Essays in Colorado History, no. 14 (1994): 37–71.

Author and reformer Helen Hunt Jackson, who lived in Colorado Springs during the 1870s, was deeply influenced by the events in western Colorado. For details, see Virginia McConnell, "'H.H.,' Colorado, and the Indian Problem," Journal of the West 12 (April 1973): 272–80. For more on Jackson, see the following works by Valerie Sherer Mathes: "Helen Hunt Jackson: A Legacy of Indian Reform," Essays in Colorado History, no. 4 (1986): 25–58; Helen Hunt Jackson and Her Indian Reform Legacy (Austin, 1990); and The Indian Reform Letters of Helen Hunt Jackson, 1879–1885 (Norman, 1998). Some of Jackson's Colorado essays are reprinted in Joseph T. Gordon and Judith A. Pickle, eds., Helen Hunt Jackson's Colorado (Colorado Springs, 1989) and Mark I. West., ed., Westward to a High Mountain: The Colorado Writings of Helen Hunt Jackson (Denver, 1994).

Chapter Eighteen: Ditchdiggers and Sodbusters

The most useful short account of Colorado's agricultural history is Robert G. Dunbar, "History of Agriculture," in LeRoy R. Hafen, ed., Colorado and Its People: A Narrative and Topical History of the Centennial State (4 vols., New York, 1948), 2:121–57.

See also the previously cited Alvin T. Steinel, *History of Agriculture in Colorado* (Fort Collins, 1926).

Studies of settlement on the plains include Millard Fillmore Vance, "Pioneering at Akron, Colorado," *The Colorado Magazine* 8 (September 1931): 173–77; Morris F. Taylor, "The Town Boom in Las Animas and Baca Counties," *The Colorado Magazine* 55 (spring/summer 1978): 111–32; Ava Betz, *A Prowers County History* (Lamar, 1986); Paul D. Friedman, *Valley of Lost Souls: A History of the Pinon Canyon Region of Southeastern Colorado*, Monographs in Colorado History, no. 3 (Denver, 1988); Kenneth R. Weber, "Otero County: A Demographic History of a Colorado High Plains County, 1889–1987," *Social Science Journal* 26 (no. 3, 1989): 265–75; and Frances Bollacker Keck, *Conquistadors to the 21st Century: A History of Otero and Crowley Counties, Colorado* (La Junta, 1999).

For western water law and policy generally, see Robert G. Dunbar, *Forging New Rights in Western Waters* (Lincoln, 1983); Donald Worster, *Rivers of Empire: Water, Aridity, and the Growth of the American West* (New York, 1986); and two works by Donald J. Pisani: *To Reclaim a Divided West: Water, Law, and Public Policy, 1848–1902* (Albuquerque, 1992) and *Water, Land, and Law in the West: The Limits of Public Policy, 1850–1920* (Lawrence, 1996). See also Dunbar, "The Origins of the Colorado System of Water-Right Control," *The Colorado Magazine* 27 (October 1950): 241–62 and John D. Leshy, "The Prior Appropriation Doctrine of Water Law in the West: An Emperor with Few Clothes," *Journal of the West* 29 (July 1990): 5–13.

Early irrigation efforts are treated in Joseph O. Van Hook, "Development of Irrigation in the Arkansas Valley," *The Colorado Magazine* 10 (January 1933): 3–11; in two works by James E. Sherow: "Utopia, Reality, and Irrigation: The Plight of the Fort Lyon Canal Company in the Arkansas River Valley," *Western Historical Quarterly* 20 (May 1989): 162–84 and "Marketplace Agricultural Reform: T. C. Henry and the Irrigation Crusade in Colorado, 1883–1914," *Journal of the West* 31 (October 1992): 51–58; and in Kate Lee Kienast, "Oasis in the 'Great American Desert': Early Irrigation Ditch Systems in the Denver Area," *Colorado Heritage* (spring 1998): 20–31. Clark C. Spence describes "rainmaking" in *The Rainmakers: American "Pluviculture" to World War II* (Lincoln, 1980).

Chapter Nineteen: New Frontiers

On the Colorado Midland Railway, see Morris Cafky, *Colorado Midland* (Denver, 1965) and Edward M. "Mel" McFarland, *Midland Route: A Colorado Midland Guide and Data Book* (Boulder, 1980). For more on the railroad enterprises of the era, see John Burton Phillips, "A Colorado Railroad Pool," in *University of Colorado Studies* 5 (April 1908): 137–48; the same author's "Freight Rates and Manufactures in Colorado," *University of Colorado Studies* 7 (December 1909): 5–62; William S. Jackson, "Railroad Conflicts in Colorado in the 'Eighties," *The Colorado Magazine* 23 (January 1946): 7–25; and James R. "Jim" Jones, *Denver and New Orleans: In the Shadow of the Rockies* (Denver, 1997). Eugene C. Tidball describes General William Tecumseh Sherman's 1883 railroad tour of Colorado and the West in "General Sherman's Last March," *Colorado History*, no. 1 (1997): 1–29.

Industrial developments are treated in Ellsworth C. Mitick, "A History of Mining Machinery Manufacture in Colorado," *The Colorado Magazine* 24 (November 1947): 225–41;

The Colorado Magazine 25 (March 1948): 75–94; and *The Colorado Magazine* 25 (May 1948): 136–42; Albert E. Seep, "History of the Mine and Smelter Supply Company," *The Colorado Magazine* 23 (May 1946): 128–34; and Robert L. Spude, "Cyanide and the Flood of Gold: Some Colorado Beginnings of the Cyanide Process of Gold Extraction," *Essays in Colorado History*, no. 12 (1991): 1–35.

Biographical studies include John H. Davis, *The Guggenheims: An American Epic* (New York, 1978); Richard H. Peterson, "Thomas F. Walsh and Western Business Elitism: The Lifestyle of a Colorado Mining Magnate, 1896–1910," *Red River Valley Historical Review* 6 (fall 1981): 53–63; Jay E. Niebur and James E. Fell, Jr., *Arthur Redman Wilfley: Miner, Inventor, and Entrepreneur* (Denver, 1982); and H. Lee Scamehorn, *Albert Eugene Reynolds: Colorado's Mining King* (Norman, 1995).

Other developments of the times are detailed in Howard T. Vaille, "Early Years of the Telephone in Colorado," *The Colorado Magazine* 5 (August 1928): 121–33; Elmer S. Crowley, "The Opening of the Tabor Grand Opera House, 1881," *The Colorado Magazine* 18 (March 1941): 41–48; John W. and Doris G. Buchanan, *A Story of the Windsor* (Boulder, 1944); Herbert J. Hackenburg, Jr., *Muttering Machines to Laser Beams: A History of Mountain Bell* (Denver, 1986); Ellen Kingman Fisher, *One Hundred Years of Energy: Public Service Company of Colorado and Its Predecessors, 1869–1969* (New York, 1989); Christine Whitacre, *The Denver Club, 1880–1995* (Denver, 1998); and Don Robertson, Morris Cafky, and E. J. "Ed" Haley, *Denver's Street Railways*, vol. 1, *1871–1900: Not an Automobile in Sight* (Denver, 1999).

Works on legal and political aspects of the period include William M. King, *Going to Meet a Man: Denver's Last Legal Public Execution, 27 July 1886* (Niwot, 1990); Elliott West, "Dirty Tricks in Denver," *The Colorado Magazine* 52 (summer 1975): 225–43, on the 1889 Denver mayoral election; and Alan J. Kania and Diane Hartman, *The Bench and the Bar: A Centennial View of Denver's Legal History* (Denver, 1993), published to commemorate the establishment of the Denver Bar Association in 1891.

For an insight into some of the less savory facets of life, see Phil Goodstein, *The Seamy Side of Denver: Tall Tales of the Mile High City* (Denver, 1993); Clark Secrest, *Hell's Belles: Denver's Brides of the Multitudes, with Attention to Various Gamblers, Scoundrels, and Mountebanks, and a Biography of Sam Howe, Frontier Lawman* (Aurora, 1996); Joanne West Dodds, *What's a Nice Girl Like You Doing in a Place Like This?: Prostitution in Southern Colorado, 1860 to 1911* (Pueblo, 1996); Henry O. Whiteside, *Menace in the West: Colorado and the American Experience with Drugs, 1873–1963* (Denver, 1997); and Robert K. DeArment, "Bat Masterson and the Boxing Club War of Denver," *Colorado Heritage* (autumn 2000): 28–36, part of a special issue devoted to Colorado lawlessness during the latter part of the nineteenth century.

Studies of prominent reformers and philanthropists include Marjorie Hornbein, "Frances Jacobs: Denver's Mother of Charities," *Western States Jewish Historical Quarterly* 15 (January 1983): 131–45; James A. Denton, *Rocky Mountain Radical: Myron W. Reed, Christian Socialist* (Albuquerque, 1997); and William Joseph Convery, *Pride of the Rockies: The Life of Colorado's Premiere Irish Patron, John Kernan Mullen* (Boulder, 2000). Thomas J. Noel, with Stephen J. Leonard and Kevin E. Rucker, *Colorado Givers: A History of Philanthropic Heroes* (Niwot, 1998), includes profiles of Jacobs, Reed, and Mullen. See also Peggy Pascoe, *Relations of Rescue: The Search for Female Moral Authority in the American West, 1874–1939* (New York, 1990), which contains a discussion of Denver's Colorado Cottage Home, and Sherilyn Brandenstein, "The Colorado Cottage Home," *The Colorado Magazine* 53 (summer 1976): 229–42.

Emily: The Diary of a Hard-Worked Woman, ed. Janet Lecompte (Lincoln, 1987), provides an unusual glimpse into the life of Emily French, a poor Colorado working woman, throughout the year 1890. For more on women's lives during the period, see Joyce D. Goodfriend, "The Struggle for Survival: Widows in Denver, 1880–1912," in Arlene Scadron, ed., *On Their Own: Widows and Widowhood in the American Southwest, 1848–1939* (Urbana, 1988) and Elizabeth Herr, "Women, Marital Status, and Work Opportunities in 1880 Colorado," *Journal of Economic History* 55 (June 1995): 339–66.

For the construction of the Capitol, see Rex C. Myers, "Railroads, Stone Quarries, and the Colorado State Capitol," *Journal of the West* 39 (spring 2000): 37–45. On the surrounding neighborhood, see Phil Goodstein, *Denver's Capitol Hill: One Hundred Years of Life in a Vibrant Urban Neighborhood* (Denver 1988) and *The Ghosts of Denver: Capitol Hill* (Denver 1996). See also Jack A. Murphy, *Geology Tour of Denver's Capitol Hill Stone Buildings* (Denver, 1997) and Leigh A. Grinstead, *Molly Brown's Capitol Hill Neighborhood* (Denver, 1997) in the Historic Denver Guides series.

Accounts of other Denver neighborhoods include Ruth Wiberg, *Rediscovering Northwest Denver: Its History, Its People, Its Landmarks* (Denver, 1976); Thomas J. Noel, *Richthofen's Montclair: A Pioneer Denver Suburb* (Denver, 1976); William Allen West and Don D. Etter, *Curtis Park: A Denver Neighborhood* (Boulder, 1980); Phil Goodstein, *South Denver Saga* (Denver 1991); Millie Van Wyke, *The Town of South Denver: Its People, Neighborhoods, and Events since 1858* (Boulder, 1991); Robert Autobee, *If You Stick with Barnum: A History of a Denver Neighborhood,* Monographs in Colorado History, no. 8 (Denver, 1992); *Side by Side: A History of Denver's Witter Cofield Historic District* (Denver, 1995); and Alice Millett Bakemeier, *Hilltop Heritage: A History and Guide to a Denver Neighborhood* (Denver, 1997) and *Country Club Heritage: A History and Guide to a Denver Neighborhood* (Denver, 2000).

Information on Denver neighborhood architecture and historic districts can be found also in the following Historic Denver Guides: Diane Wilk, *The Wyman Historic District* (Denver, 1995) and *The Potter-Highlands Historic District* (Denver 1997); Nancy L. Widmann, *The East 7th Avenue Historic District* (Denver 1997) and *The Baker Historic District* (Denver 1999); Thomas J. Noel and William J. Hansen, *The Montclair Neighborhood* (Denver, 1999); and Annette L. Student, *Historic Cheesman Park Neighborhood* (1999).

Richard Hogan focuses on Denver, Central City, Greeley, Golden, Pueblo, and Canon City in *Class and Community in Frontier Colorado* (Lawrence, 1990). On Colorado Springs, see Marshall Sprague, *One Hundred Plus: A Centennial Story of Colorado Springs* (Colorado Springs, 1971); Nancy E. Loe, *Life in the Altitudes: An Illustrated History of Colorado Springs* (Woodland Hills, Calif., 1983); and Thomas J. Noel and Cathleen M. Norman, *A Pikes Peak Partnership: The Penroses and the Tutts* (Boulder, 2000).

On Cripple Creek and its neighbors, see Marshall Sprague, *Money Mountain: The Story of Cripple Creek Gold* (Boston, 1953); Robert Taylor, *Cripple Creek* (Bloomington, 1966); Edgar C. McMechen, "The Founding of Cripple Creek," *The Colorado Magazine* 12 (January 1935): 28–35; S. E. Poet, "Victor, Colorado—The City of Mines," *The Colorado Magazine* 10 (May 1933): 106–14; and Leo J. Keena, "Cripple Creek in 1900," *The Colorado Magazine* 30 (October 1953): 269–75. Elizabeth Jameson focuses on the social, political, ethnic, and family relationships of Cripple Creek workers in *All that Glitters: Class, Conflict, and Community in Cripple Creek* (Urbana, 1998). Frank Waters's *Midas of the Rockies* (Denver, 1949) is a biography of Winfield S. Stratton.

Mabel Barbee Lee offers a personal view in *Cripple Creek Days* (Garden City, 1958) and *Back in Cripple Creek* (Garden City, 1968). For a delightful look at the less glamorous aspects of mining and mining camp life, see Anne Ellis, *The Life of an Ordinary Woman* (1929; reprint, with a foreword by Elliott West, Lincoln, 1980).

Chapter Twenty: Politics and Populists

The political history of the era is described in Frank Hall, *History of the State of Colorado* (4 vols., Chicago, 1889–95), especially vol. 3, and in Elmer Ellis, *Henry Moore Teller: Defender of the West* (Caldwell, Idaho, 1941). See also Richard C. Welty, "The Greenback Party in Colorado," *The Colorado Magazine* 28 (October 1951): 301–11; Jane E. and Lee G. Norris, *Written in Water: The Life of Benjamin Harrison Eaton* (Athens, Ohio, 1990); and many of the titles listed for the following chapter.

Robert W. Larson provides a regional assessment in *Populism in the Mountain West* (Albuquerque, 1986). James E. Wright describes the social, economic, and political factors that contributed to the development of Colorado Populism in *The Politics of Populism: Dissent in Colorado* (New Haven, 1974). On Populist leaders, see G. Michael McCarthy, "Colorado's Populist Leadership," *The Colorado Magazine* 48 (winter 1971): 30–42 and "Who Were the Populists," *Journal of the West* 15 (January 1976): 54–62.

Chapter Twenty-One: The Silver Crusade

For the Populists and Governor Waite, see John R. Morris, *Davis H. Waite: The Ideology of a Western Populist* (Washington, D.C., 1982); Marjorie Hornbein, "Davis Waite, Silver, and Populism," *Essays in Colorado History*, no. 1 (1983): 71–90; and Leon W. Fuller, "Governor Waite and His Silver Panacea," *The Colorado Magazine* 10 (March 1933): 41–47. Charles Hartzell, *A Short and Truthful History of Colorado during the Turbulent Reign of "Davis the First"* (Denver, 1894), is an example of anti-Populist sentiment. Robert V. Hunt, Jr., analyzes the activities of the anti-Catholic American Protective Association in "The Heyday of the Denver APA, 1892–1894," *Journal of the West* 35 (October 1996): 74–81. On relief efforts during the depression, see Louisa Ward Arps, *Denver in Slices* (1959; 2d. ed. Athens, Ohio, 1983).

On hard-rock mining and miners, see, generally, Richard E. Lingenfelter, *The Hardrock Miners: A History of the Mining-Labor Movement in the American West, 1863–1893* (Berkeley, 1974); Ronald C. Brown, *Hard-Rock Miners: The Intermountain West, 1860–1920* (College Station, Tex., 1979); and Mark Wyman, *Hard-Rock Epic: Western Miners and the Industrial Revolution, 1860–1910* (Berkeley, 1979).

David Brundage focuses on labor radicalism in Denver in "After the Land League: The Persistence of Irish-American Labor Radicalism in Denver, 1897–1905," *Journal of American Ethnic History* 11 (spring 1992): 3–26 and *The Making of Western Labor Radicalism: Denver's Organized Workers, 1878–1905* (Urbana, 1994).

For the Cripple Creek strike, see Stewart H. Holbrook, *The Rocky Mountain Revolution* (New York, 1956); George G. Suggs, Jr., "Catalyst for Industrial Change: The WFM, 1893–1903," *The Colorado Magazine* 45 (fall 1968): 322–39; Oliver M. Dickerson, "The

Labor Movement," in LeRoy R. Hafen, ed., *Colorado and Its People: A Narrative and Topical History of the Centennial State* (4 vols., New York, 1948), 2:311–31; and Emil W. Pfeiffer, "The Kingdom of Bull Hill," *The Colorado Magazine* 12 (September 1935): 168–72. In addition, see Edmund E. Radlowski, "Law and Order at Cripple Creek, 1890–1900," *Journal of the West* 9 (July 1970): 346–55 and H. Lee Scamehorn, "In the Shadow of Cripple Creek: Florence from 1885 to 1910," *The Colorado Magazine* 55 (spring/summer 1978): 205–29.

On the Leadville strike of 1896, see William Philpott, *The Lessons of Leadville, Or, Why the Western Federation of Miners Turned Left*, Monographs in Colorado History, no. 10 (Denver, 1994) and Merrill Hough, "Leadville and the Western Federation of Miners," *The Colorado Magazine* 49 (winter 1972): 19–34.

Woman suffrage is treated in Beverly Beeton, *Women Vote in the West: The Woman Suffrage Movement, 1869–1896* (New York, 1986); Carolyn Stefanco, "Networking on the Frontier: The Colorado Women's Suffrage Movement, 1876–1893," in Susan Armitage and Elizabeth Jameson, eds., *The Women's West* (Norman, 1987); Billie Barnes Jensen, "Let the Women Vote," *The Colorado Magazine* 41 (winter 1964): 13–25; and John R. Morris, "The Women and Governor Waite," *The Colorado Magazine* 44 (winter 1967): 11–19. Jensen looks at the other side of the coin in "'In the Weird and Wooly West': Anti-Suffrage Women, Gender Issues, and Woman Suffrage in the West," *Journal of the West* 32 (July 1993): 41–51. The spring 1993 special issue of *Colorado Heritage* on woman suffrage includes Marcia T. Goldstein and Rebecca A. Hunt, "From Suffrage to Centennial: A Research Guide to Colorado and National Women's Suffrage Sources," 40–48. Joyce D. Goodfriend and Dona K. Flory detail opportunities for research on Colorado women in "Women in Colorado before the First World War," *The Colorado Magazine* 53 (summer 1976): 201–28.

Biographies of noteworthy Colorado women are included in Elinor Bluemel, *One Hundred Years of Colorado Women* (Denver, 1973) and Jeanne Varnell, *Women of Consequence: The Colorado Women's Hall of Fame* (Boulder, 1999). For more information on the Hall of Fame, founded in 1985, see www.cogreatwomen.org.

Chapter Twenty-Two: The Good Old Days

For a pictorial view of the era, see William C. and Elizabeth B. Jones, *Buckwalter: The Colorado Scenes of a Pioneer Photojournalist, 1890–1920* (Boulder, 1989). H. H. Buckwalter also took moving pictures of many Colorado events; for more on early Colorado moviemaking, see David Emrich, *Hollywood, Colorado: The Selig Polyscope Company and the Colorado Motion Picture Company* (Lakewood, 1997) and "The Hand of the Law: A Theoretical Plot," *Colorado Heritage* (autumn 1998): 30–39, about a 1913 movie shot in Canon City. Duane A. Smith compares and contrasts life in Durango, Colorado, and Sandwich, Illinois, in *A Tale of Two Towns: A Mining and a Farming Community in the 1890s* (Niwot, 1997). Clark Secrest, ed., "'Learn to Labor and to Wait': The 1899 Diary of Anna Kennicott with the Glass Plate Photography of Eugenia Kennicott," *Colorado Heritage* (summer 1999): 2–33, offers a glimpse of daily life in Westcliffe and Canon City. The winter 1991 issue of *Colorado Heritage* furnishes an introduction to the decade 1900–1910.

Aspects of the medical scene are covered in Douglas R. McKay, *Asylum of the Gilded Pill: The Story of Cragmor Sanitarium* (Denver, 1983); Helen Clapesattle, *Dr. Webb of Colorado*

Springs (Boulder, 1984); and Jeanne Abrams, *Blazing the Tuberculosis Trail: The Religio-Ethnic Role of Four Sanatoria in Early Denver,* Monographs in Colorado History, no. 6 (1990). Patricia Paton, *A Medical Gentleman: James J. Waring, M.D.* (Denver, 1993), is a biography of a one-time Cragmor patient who became a leading Colorado doctor in the treatment of tuberculosis. Other facets of medicine are detailed in Rickey Hendricks, "Feminism and Maternalism in Early Hospitals for Children: San Francisco and Denver, 1875–1915," *Journal of the West* 32 (July 1993): 61–69 and in Hendricks and Mark S. Foster, *For a Child's Sake: History of the Children's Hospital, Denver, Colorado, 1910–1990* (Niwot, 1994).

On the emigrants from the Netherlands, see Dorothy Roberts, "A Dutch Colony in Colorado," *The Colorado Magazine* 17 (November 1940): 229–36; on Nucla, Ellen Z. Peterson, "Origin of the Town of Nucla," *The Colorado Magazine* 26 (October 1949): 252–58 and *The Spell of the Tabeguache* (Denver, 1957). For Fort Amity, see Clark C. Spence, *The Salvation Army Farm Colonies* (Tucson, 1985) and Roberts, "Fort Amity: The Salvation Army Colony in Colorado," *The Colorado Magazine* 17 (September 1940): 168–74.

Karen Waddell analyzes the Dearfield experience in "Dearfield . . . A Dream Deferred," *Colorado Heritage* (Issue 2, 1988): 2–12. For the general perspective, see W. Sherman Savage, *Blacks in the West* (Westport, Conn., 1976); William Loren Katz, *The Black West* (1971; 3d ed., Seattle, 1987); and two works by Quintard Taylor: "From Esteban to Rodney King: Five Centuries of African American History in the West," *Montana* 46 (winter 1996): 2–23 and *In Search of the Racial Frontier: African Americans in the American West, 1528–1990* (New York, 1998). In addition, see Roger D. Hardaway, *A Narrative Bibliography of the African-American Frontier: Blacks in the Rocky Mountain West, 1535–1912* (Lewiston, N.Y., 1995).

The autumn 1999 issue of *Colorado Heritage* is devoted to the early years of the automobile era in Colorado; see especially Lyle Miller, "Earliest Automobiling in Colorado, 1899–1904," 22–38. In addition, see "The Hi-Ho, Lucky U, Bugs Bunny, and Sleepy Hollow: A History of Colorado Motels," *Colorado Heritage* (autumn 1997): 2–21, also by Miller; LeRoy R. Hafen, "The Coming of the Automobile and Improved Roads to Colorado," *The Colorado Magazine* 8 (January 1931): 1–16; and Thomas J. Noel, "Paving the Way to Colorado: The Evolution of Auto Tourism in Denver," *Journal of the West* 26 (July 1987): 42–49.

The literature on Mesa Verde is extensive. Gustaf Nordenskiöld's classic work is *The Cliff Dwellers of the Mesa Verde, Southwestern Colorado: Their Pottery and Implements,* trans. D. Lloyd Morgan (1893; reprint, Glorieta, N. Mex., 1979). See also Duane A. Smith, "Removing Our Relics: Durango Versus Gustaf Nordenskiöld over Mesa Verde Ruins," *Colorado Heritage* (Issue 3, 1989): 2–11. For the Wetherills, see Frank McNitt, *Richard Wetherill, Anasazi* (1957; rev. ed., Albuquerque, 1966); Benjamin Alfred Wetherill, *The Wetherills of the Mesa Verde: Autobiography of Benjamin Alfred Wetherill,* ed. Maureen S. Fletcher (Rutherford, N.J., 1977); and David Harrell, "'We contacted Smithsonian': The Wetherills at Mesa Verde," *New Mexico Historical Review* 62 (July 1987): 229–48.

William Henry Jackson described his 1874 expedition to Mesa Verde in "First Official Visit to the Cliff Dwellings," *The Colorado Magazine* 1 (May 1924): 151–59 and in *Time Exposure: The Autobiography of William Henry Jackson* (1940; reprint, with an introduction by Ferenc M. Szasz, Albuquerque, 1986). On Jackson, see also Peter B. Hales, *William Henry Jackson and the Transformation of the American Landscape* (Philadelphia, 1988); Douglas Waitley, *William Henry Jackson: Framing the Frontier* (Missoula, 1998); and

Lloyd W. Gundy, ed., *William Henry Jackson: An Intimate Portrait: The Elwood P. Bonney Journal*, Colorado History, no. 4 (Denver, 2000).

Duane A. Smith relates the history of Mesa Verde National Park in *Mesa Verde National Park: Shadows of the Centuries* (Lawrence, 1988). In addition, see Bruce J. Noble, Jr., "A Legacy of Distrust: The Ute Mountain Utes and the Boundaries of Mesa Verde National Park," *Colorado Heritage* (summer 1995): 32–42 and Joseph Owen Weixelman, "Jesse Nusbaum and the Re-Creation of Mesa Verde National Park," *Colorado Heritage* (spring 2000): 19–32. For more on the role women played in establishing the park, see Virginia McClurg, "The Making of Mesa Verde into a National Park," *The Colorado Magazine* 7 (November 1930): 216–19 and "Mesa Verde: The Issue of a Woman's Park," in Polly Welts Kaufman, *National Parks and the Woman's Voice: A History* (Albuquerque, 1996).

On Enos Mills and Rocky Mountain National Park, see Alexander Drummond, *Enos Mills: Citizen of Nature* (Niwot, 1995); Carl Abbott, "The Active Force: Enos A. Mills and the National Park Movement," *The Colorado Magazine* 56 (winter/spring 1979): 56–73; and C. W. Buchholtz, *Rocky Mountain National Park: A History* (Boulder, 1983). James H. Pickering describes Mills's contributions in introductions to reprint editions of four of his books: *Wild Life on the Rockies* (1909; Lincoln, 1988); *The Spell of the Rockies* (1911; Lincoln, 1989); *In Beaver World* (1913; Lincoln, 1990); and *The Rocky Mountain Wonderland* (1915; Lincoln, 1991). See also Pickering's *This Blue Hollow: Estes Park, the Early Years, 1859–1915* (Niwot, 1999), *Frederick Chapin's Colorado: The Peaks about Estes Park and Other Writings* (Niwot, 1995), and *Mr. Stanley of Estes Park* (Kingfield, Maine, 2000). Karl Hess, Jr., discusses contemporary ecological issues in *Rocky Times in Rocky Mountain National Park: An Unnatural History* (Niwot, 1993).

Alan J. Kania narrates the interrelated story of John Otto and the Colorado National Monument in *John Otto of Colorado National Monument* (Boulder, 1984) and *John Otto: Trials and Trails* (Niwot, 1996).

The Mineral Palace is described in Frank Hall, *History of the State of Colorado* (4 vols., Chicago, 1889–95), 3:480–83; the Ice Palace in Carlyle Channing Davis, *Olden Times in Colorado* (Los Angeles, 1916), 337–51 and Darlene Godat Weir, *Leadville's Ice Palace: A Colossus in the Colorado Rockies* (Lakewood, 1994). Other aspects of the era are covered in Levette J. Davidson, "The Festival of Mountain and Plain," parts 1 and 2, *The Colorado Magazine* 25 (July and September 1948): 145–57, 203–12; Andrew W. Gillette, "The Bicycle Era in Colorado," *The Colorado Magazine* 10 (November 1933): 213–17; "Hard Rock Drilling Contests in Colorado: As Told by Victor I. Noxon to Forest Crossen," *The Colorado Magazine* 11 (May 1934): 81–85; "Overland Park," which is chapter 9 of Arps, *Denver in Slices* (1959; 2d ed., Athens, Ohio, 1983); Mary Galey, *The Grand Assembly: The Story of Life at the Colorado Chautauqua* (Boulder, 1981); and Larry G. Bowman, "'The Players Redeemed Themselves': Major League Baseball Visits Colorado: 1888," *Colorado Heritage* (spring 1999): 20–33.

Activities of women's clubs are treated in Gail M. Beaton, "The Widening Sphere of Women's Lives: The Literary Study and Philanthropic Work of Six Women's Clubs in Denver, 1881–1945," *Essays in Colorado History*, no. 13 (1992): 1–68; Lynda F. Dickson, "Lifting as We Climb: African-American Women's Clubs of Denver, 1890–1925," *Essays in Colorado History*, no. 13 (1992): 69–98, reprinted in Elizabeth Jameson and Susan Armitage, eds., *Writing the Range: Race, Class, and Culture in the Women's West* (Norman,

1997); Eva Hodges and Clé Cervi, "Founded by Accident: The Denver Woman's Press Club," *Colorado Heritage* (autumn 1997): 22–43; and Cervi and Nancy M. Peterson, eds., *The Women Who Made the Headlines: Denver Woman's Press Club: The First Hundred Years* (Lakewood, 1998).

On colleges and universities, see Thomas Russell Garth, *The Life of Henry Augustus Buchtel* (Denver, 1937); Harold L. Stansell, S.J., *Regis: On the Crest of the West* (Denver, 1977); Wallace B. Turner, *Colorado Women's College, 1888–1982: The Story of a Dream* (Marceline, Mo., 1982); Robert W. Larson, *Shaping Educational Change: The First Century of the University of Northern Colorado at Greeley* (Boulder, 1989); J. Manuel Espinosa, "The Neapolitan Jesuits on the Colorado Frontier, 1868–1919," *The Colorado Magazine* 15 (March 1938): 64–73; and Norman J. Bender, "The Elusive Quest for the 'Princeton of the West,'" *The Colorado Magazine* 52 (fall 1975): 299–316. Kathleen Underwood analyzes the lives of teachers who graduated from the Colorado State Normal School in the 1890s in "The Pace of Their Own Lives: Teacher Training and the Life Course of Western Women," *Pacific Historical Review* 55 (November 1986): 513–60.

Gene Fowler's famous *Timber Line* (New York, 1933) continues to delight readers as a study of the era's journalism. For more on Tammen, Bonfils, and the *Post,* see William Hosokawa, *Thunder in the Rockies: The Incredible Denver Post* (New York, 1976); Mort Stern, "Harry Tammen and His *Great Divide*: Early Magazine Journalism in Colorado," *Essays in Colorado History*, no. 10 (1989): 1–49; William H. Hornby, *Voice of Empire: A Centennial Sketch of the Denver Post* (Denver, 1992); and Jay Sanford, "African-American Baseballists and the Denver Post Tournament," *Colorado Heritage* (spring 1995): 20–43. Kathleen P. Chamberlain recounts the career of Dave Day in "David F. Day and the *Solid Muldoon*: Boosterism and Humor on Colorado's Mining Frontier," *Journal of the West* 34 (October 1995): 61–68.

Chapter Twenty-Three: The Era of Industrial Warfare

For details on the Colorado and Southern, see Richard C. Overton, "The Colorado and Southern Railway: Its Heritage and Its History," parts 1 and 2, *The Colorado Magazine* 26 (April and July 1949); 81–98, 196–219. Sam Speas provides a personal view of the C&S in *Goin' Railroading: Two Generations of Colorado Stories,* as told to Margaret Coel (1985; rev. ed., Niwot, 1998). On the Moffat Road, see Edward T. Bollinger and Frederick Bauer, *The Moffat Road* (Denver, 1962) and P. R. "Bob" Griswold, *David Moffat's Denver, Northwestern and Pacific: "The Moffat Road"* (Denver, 1995); for the building of the Moffat Tunnel, see the suggested readings for Chapter 27.

For an overview of the role of organized labor, see Harold V. Knight, *Working in Colorado: A Brief History of the Colorado Labor Movement* (Boulder, 1971). James Whiteside discusses regulation and reform in "Protecting the Life and Limb of Our Workmen: Coal Mining Regulation in Colorado, 1883–1920," *Essays in Colorado History*, no. 4 (1986): 1–24 and in *Regulating Danger: The Struggle for Mine Safety in the Rocky Mountain Coal Industry* (Lincoln, 1990). David L. Lonsdale describes one of labor's battles in "The Fight for an Eight-Hour Day," *The Colorado Magazine* 43 (fall 1966): 339–53.

The materials for a study of the Cripple Creek strike tend toward "special pleading" and must be used with care, but see the following: Benjamin M. Rastall, *The Labor His-*

tory of the Cripple Creek District (Madison, 1908), a contemporary publication viewing events from a close range; Emma F. Langdon, *The Cripple Creek Strike* (Denver, 1904), a pro-union tract; and Stewart H. Holbrook, *The Rocky Mountain Revolution* (New York, 1956), a biography of Harry Orchard that sets the background for Orchard's acts of violence. On "Big Bill" Haywood, see Peter Carlson, *Roughneck: The Life and Times of Big Bill Haywood* (New York, 1983) and Thomas J. Noel, "William D. Haywood, 'The Most Hated and Feared Figure in America,'" *Colorado Heritage* (Issue 2, 1984): 2–12. Michael Neuschatz focuses on the organizing efforts of the WFM in Cripple Creek, Telluride, and other areas in *The Golden Sword: The Coming of Capitalism to the Colorado Mining Frontier* (New York, 1986).

On the labor disturbances of the Peabody administration, see the following articles, all by George G. Suggs, Jr.: "Strike-Breaking in Colorado: Governor James H. Peabody and the Telluride Strike, 1903–1904," *Journal of the West* 5 (October 1966): 454–76; "Prelude to Industrial Warfare: The Colorado City Strike," *The Colorado Magazine* 44 (summer 1967): 241–62; "Religion and Labor in the Rocky Mountain West: Bishop Nicholas C. Matz and the Western Federation of Miners," *Labor History* 11 (spring 1970): 190–206; and "The Colorado Coal Miners' Strike, 1903–1904: A Prelude to Ludlow?" *Journal of the West* 12 (January 1973): 36–52. Suggs's book-length study of these events was published under the title *Colorado's War on Militant Unionism* (Detroit, 1972).

On company towns generally, see James B. Allen, *The Company Town in the American West* (Norman, 1966). Rick J. Clyne focuses on Colorado in *Coal People: Life in Southern Colorado's Company Towns, 1890–1930*, Colorado History, no. 3 (Denver, 1999). In addition, see Eric Margolis, "Western Coal Mining as a Way of Life: An Oral History of the Colorado Coal Miners to 1914," *Journal of the West* 24 (July 1985): 4–115 and "'Life Is Life': One Family's Struggle in the Southern Colorado Coalfields," *Colorado Heritage* (summer 2000): 30–47, and Denise Pan, "Peace and Conflict in an Industrial Family: Colorado Fuel & Iron's Cameron and Walsen Camps, 1913–28," *Mining History Journal* (1996): 67–75.

For the history of the CF&I, see H. Lee Scamehorn, *Pioneer Steelmaker in the West: The Colorado Fuel and Iron Company, 1872–1903* (Boulder, 1976) and *Mill and Mine: The CF&I in the Twentieth Century* (Lincoln, 1992). On Osgood, see Scamehorn, "John C. Osgood and the Western Steel Industry," *Arizona and the West* 15 (summer 1973): 133–48. Dolores Plested tells the story of the small, independent Bear Canon Coal Company in *Life and Death of a Coal Mine* (Denver, 1987). M. James Kedro provides information on two major ethnic groups involved in mining in "Czechs and Slovaks in Colorado, 1860–1920," *The Colorado Magazine* 54 (spring 1977): 93–125.

Union organizer Mother Jones is the subject of several works, including Priscilla Long, *Mother Jones, Woman Organizer* (Cambridge, 1976) and Linda Atkinson, *Mother Jones: The Most Dangerous Woman in America* (New York, 1978). For her views, see Philip S. Foner, ed., *Mother Jones Speaks: Collected Writings and Speeches* (New York, 1983).

A good general account of the 1913–14 strike is George S. McGovern and Leonard F. Guttridge, *The Great Coalfield War* (Boston, 1972). In addition, see Priscilla Long, "The Women of the Colorado Fuel and Iron Strike, 1913–14," in Ruth Milkman, ed., *Women, Work, and Protest: A Century of U.S. Women's Labor History* (Boston, 1985) and M. Edmund Vallejo, "Recollections of the Colorado Coal Strike, 1913–1914," in Vincent C. De Baca, ed., *La Gente: Hispano History and Life in Colorado*, Colorado History, no. 2 (Denver, 1998):

85–104. A work generally sympathetic to the union is Barron B. Beshoar, *Out of the Depths* (Denver, 1942). Zeese Papanikolas discusses a major figure in *Buried Unsung: Louis Tikas and the Ludlow Massacre* (Salt Lake City, 1982). A contemporary publication on the battle at Ludlow by a UMW official, Walter Fink, *The Ludlow Massacre* (Denver, 1914), indicates something of the tone of events. For Upton Sinclair's fictional view, see *The Coal War: A Sequel to "King Coal,"* introduction by John Graham (Boulder, 1976). Howard Gitelman discusses the influence of Ludlow in *Legacy of the Ludlow Massacre: A Chapter in American Industrial Relations* (Philadelphia, 1988).

Chapter Twenty-Four: Water and Sugar

The early years of federal reclamation work are described in George Wharton James, *Reclaiming the Arid West: The Story of the United States Reclamation Service* (New York, 1917). See also J. B. Smallwood, ed., "Water in the West," *Journal of the West* 22 (April 1983): 3–68 and Ed Marston, ed., *Western Water Made Simple* (Washington, D.C., 1987). The story of the first federal project in Colorado is related in Barton W. Marsh, *The Uncompahgre Valley and the Gunnison Tunnel* (Lincoln, 1909) and in Richard G. Beidleman, "The Gunnison River Diversion Project," parts 1 and 2, *The Colorado Magazine* 36 (July and October 1959): 187–201, 266–85. See also Donald A. MacKendrick, "Before the Newlands Act: State-sponsored Reclamation Projects in Colorado, 1888–1903," *The Colorado Magazine* 52 (winter 1975): 1–21. James E. Sherow discusses *Kansas v. Colorado* in "The Contest for the 'Nile of America': *Kansas v. Colorado* (1907)," *Great Plains Quarterly* 10 (winter 1990): 48–61 and in *Watering the Valley: Development along the High Plains Arkansas River, 1870–1950* (Lawrence, 1990).

On the sugar industry, see Geraldine B. Bean, *Charles Boettcher: A Study in Pioneer Western Enterprise* (Boulder, 1976); William J. May, Jr., "The Colorado Sugar Manufacturing Company: Grand Junction Plant," *The Colorado Magazine* 55 (winter 1978): 15–45; and Dena S. Markoff, "The Sugar Industry in the Arkansas River Valley: National Beet Sugar Company," *The Colorado Magazine* 55 (winter 1978): 69–92 and "A Bittersweet Saga: The Arkansas Valley Beet Sugar Industry, 1900–1979," *The Colorado Magazine* 56 (summer/fall 1979): 161–78. James E. Hansen II discusses extension programs in *Beyond the Ivory Tower: A History of Colorado State University Cooperative Extension* (Fort Collins, 1991).

On the plains, see Dabney Otis Collins, *Land of Tall Skies: A Pageant of the Colorado High Plains* (Colorado Springs, 1977); Perry Eberhart, *Ghosts of the Colorado Plains* (Athens, Ohio, 1986); and three works by Nell Brown Propst: *Forgotten People: A History of the South Platte Trail* (Boulder, 1979), *Those Strenuous Dames of the Colorado Prairie* (Boulder, 1982), and *Uncommon Men and the Colorado Prairie* (Caldwell, Idaho, 1992). Katherine Harris discusses homesteading in "Homesteading in Northeastern Colorado, 1873–1920: Sex Roles and Women's Experience," in Susan Armitage and Elizabeth Jameson, eds., *The Women's West* (Norman, 1987) and in *Long Vistas: Women and Families on Colorado Homesteads* (Niwot, 1993). For a general perspective, see Glenda Riley, *The Female Frontier: A Comparative View of Women on the Prairie and the Plains* (Lawrence, 1988).

Works on the Germans from Russia include Kenneth W. Rock, "'Unsere Leute': The Germans from Russia in Colorado," *The Colorado Magazine* 54 (spring 1977): 154–83 and Sidney Heitman, ed., *Germans from Russia in Colorado* (Fort Collins, 1978).

Clara Hilderman Ehrlich recalls life in a German-Russian family on the plains in *My Prairie Childhood*, ed. Sidney Heitman (Fort Collins, 1977), also published in part as "My Childhood on the Prairie," *The Colorado Magazine* 51 (spring 1974): 115–40. For a realistic fictional view, see Hope Williams Sykes, *Second Hoeing* (1935; reprint, with an introduction by Timothy Kloberdanz, Lincoln, 1982).

Chapter Twenty-Five: The Progressive Era

The winter 1992 issue of *Colorado Heritage* focuses on the years between 1910 and 1920. General works include Gerald Nash, *The American West in the Twentieth Century* (Englewood Cliffs, N.J., 1973); Nash and Richard W. Etulain, eds., *The Twentieth-Century West: Historical Interpretations* (Albuquerque, 1989); and Etulain and Michael P. Malone, *The American West: A Twentieth-Century History* (Lincoln, 1989). See also Robert G. Athearn, *The Mythic West in Twentieth-Century America* (Lawrence, 1986) and Ferenc Szasz, *Religion in the Modern American West* (Tucson, 2000), a volume in the Modern American West series.

For conditions in Denver at the beginning of the twentieth century, see Roland L. DeLorme, "Turn-of-the-Century Denver: An Invitation to Reform," *The Colorado Magazine* 45 (winter 1968): 1–15. Ellen Kingman Fisher focuses on the city's gas and electric industry in "Power's Dynamo Unloosed: Henry L. Doherty and the Denver Gas and Electric Company," *Essays in Colorado History*, no. 14 (1994): 73–96. Carl Abbott, "Boom State and Boom City: Stages in Denver's Growth," *The Colorado Magazine* 50 (summer 1973): 207–30, is a sophisticated analysis ranging from the gold rush to the present. Marjorie Hornbein discusses home rule in "Denver's Struggle for Home Rule," *The Colorado Magazine* 48 (fall 1971): 337–54. On prohibition, see James E. Hansen II, "Moonshine and Murder: Prohibition in Denver," *The Colorado Magazine* 50 (winter 1973): 1–23 and Elliott West, "Cleansing the Queen City: Prohibition and Urban Reform in Denver," *Arizona and the West* 14 (winter 1972): 232–46.

On Speer and his administration, see Edgar C. McMechen, *Robert W. Speer: A City Builder* (Denver, 1919). The city auditorium and the Democratic Convention of 1908 are described in "Denver's Democratic Invasion," *The Colorado Magazine* 41 (summer 1964): 185–97 and Phil Goodstein, "Convention City: When the Democrats Came to Denver," *Colorado Heritage* (Issue 4, 1984): 2–8. The history of the capitol and civic center complex is given in Virginia McConnell, "'For These High Purposes,'" *The Colorado Magazine* 44 (summer 1967): 204–23 and William Wilson, "A Diadem for the City Beautiful: The Development of Denver's Civic Center," *Journal of the West* 22 (April 1983): 73–83. Wilson discusses Denver and four other cities in *The City Beautiful Movement* (Baltimore, 1989). On Denver's park system, see Seth B. Bradley, "The Origin of the Denver Mountain Parks System," *The Colorado Magazine* 9 (January 1932): 26–29. For an account of the opposition to Speer and his defeat, see J. Paul Mitchell, "Municipal Reform in Denver: The Defeat of Mayor Speer," *The Colorado Magazine* 45 (winter 1968): 42–60. See also Mitchell's "Boss Speer and the City Functional: Boosters and Businessmen versus Commission Government in Denver," *Pacific Northwest Quarterly* 63 (October 1972): 155–64.

On Judge Lindsey's work, see Ben B. Lindsey and Rube Borough, *The Dangerous Life* (New York, 1931). A modern biography is Charles Larsen, *The Good Fight: The Life and*

Times of Ben B. Lindsey (Chicago, 1972). See also D'Ann Campbell, "Judge Ben Lindsey and the Juvenile Court Movement, 1901–1904," *Arizona and the West* 18 (spring 1976): 5–20. One of Lindsey's staunch supporters and friends was Margaret Tobin "Unsinkable Molly" Brown; for details, see Kristen Iversen, *Molly Brown: Unraveling the Myth* (Boulder, 1999). Elinor Bluemel describes Emily Griffith and her school in *Opportunity School and Emily Griffith, Its Founder* (Denver, 1970).

Works on elections of the period include Stephen J. Kneeshaw and John M. Linngren, "Republican Comeback, 1902," *The Colorado Magazine* 48 (winter 1971): 15–29, on reasons for the success of the Republican party in 1902; Marjorie Hornbein, "Three Governors in a Day," *The Colorado Magazine* 45 (summer 1968): 243–60, on the gubernatorial election of 1904 and its aftermath; and David Sarasohn, "The Election of 1916: Realigning the Rockies," *Western Historical Quarterly* 11 (July 1980): 285–305.

Biographical information on Charles S. Thomas can be found in Sewell Thomas, *Silhouettes of Charles S. Thomas: Colorado Governor and United States Senator* (Caldwell, Idaho, 1959) and Stephen J. Leonard, "Swimming against the Current: A Biography of Charles S. Thomas, Senator and Governor," *Colorado Heritage* (autumn, 1994): 29–34. On Governor Buchtel, see Thomas Russell Garth, *The Life of Henry Augustus Buchtel* (Denver, 1937). Shafroth and his administration are detailed in E. K. MacColl, "John Franklin Shafroth: Reform Governor of Colorado, 1909–1913," *The Colorado Magazine* 29 (January 1952): 37–52.

For details on the progressive Republican split of 1912, see Charles J. Bayard, "The Colorado Progressive Republican Split of 1912," *The Colorado Magazine* 45 (winter 1968): 61–78 and C. Warren Vander Hill, "Colorado Progressives and the Bull Moose Campaign," *The Colorado Magazine* 43 (spring 1966): 93–113. Bayard explores Philip Stewart's relationship with Roosevelt in "Theodore Roosevelt and Colorado Politics: The Roosevelt-Stewart Alliance," *The Colorado Magazine* 42 (fall 1965): 311–26. For more on the Stewart-Roosevelt friendship and on Roosevelt's Colorado visits, see Duane A. Smith, "'The Bulliest Time': Theodore Roosevelt and Colorado," *Journal of the West* 34 (April 1995): 8–15.

For details of Edward P. Costigan's life and career, see Colin B. Goodykoontz, *Papers of Edward P. Costigan Relating to the Progressive Movement in Colorado, 1902–1917* (Boulder, 1941). On the national level, see Robert Earl Smith, "Colorado's Progressive Senators and Representatives," *The Colorado Magazine* 45 (winter 1968): 27–41 and "The Anti-imperialist Crusade of Thomas M. Patterson," *The Colorado Magazine* 51 (winter 1974): 28–42. Duane A. Smith discusses judicial recall in "Colorado and Judicial Recall," *American Journal of Legal History* 7 (July 1963): 197–209.

Chapter Twenty-Six: State and Nation

For accounts of the discovery and mining of rare metals, see Lee Emerson Deets, "Paradox Valley—An Historical Interpretation of Its Structure and Changes," *The Colorado Magazine* 11 (September 1934): 186–98; T. M. McKee, "Early Discovery of Uranium Ore in Colorado," *The Colorado Magazine* 32 (July 1955):191–203; Kathleen Bruyn, *Uranium Country* (Boulder, 1955); Percy Stanley Fritz, "Tungsten and the Road to War," *University of Colorado Studies,* Series C (Boulder, 1941): 195–205; Otis King, *Gray Gold*

(Denver, 1959); and Edward R. Landa, "Radium at Jamestown, 1918–1919," *Essays in Colorado History*, no. 7 (1987): 27–47. Duane Vandenbusche and Rex Myers, *Marble, Colorado: City of Stone* (Denver, 1970) is an account of a different mineral. Activities of Colorado troops in the conflict with Spain are detailed in Frank Harper, "Fighting Far from Home: The First Colorado Regiment in the Spanish-American War," *Colorado Heritage* (Issue 1, 1988): 2–32 and *Just Outside of Manila: Letters from Members of the First Colorado Regiment in the Spanish-American and Philippine-American Wars*, Monographs in Colorado History, no. 7 (Denver, 1991).

Developments on the home front during the World War I period are treated in Lyle W. Dorsett, "The Ordeal of Colorado's Germans during World War I," *The Colorado Magazine* 51 (fall 1974): 277–93; Stephen J. Leonard, "The 1918 Influenza Epidemic in Denver and Colorado," *Essays in Colorado History*, no. 9 (1989): 1–24; and Ellen Kingman Fisher, *Junior League of Denver: Leaders in Community Service, 1918–1993* (Denver, 1993).

On the conservation movement, see G. Michael McCarthy, *Hour of Trial: The Conservation Conflict in Colorado and the West, 1891–1907* (Norman, 1977) and two articles by the same author: "Colorado Progressives and Conservation," *Mid-America* 57 (October 1975): 213–26 and "Insurgency in Colorado: Elias Ammons and the Anticonservation Impulse," *The Colorado Magazine* 54 (winter 1977): 26–43.

Chapter Twenty-Seven: The Twenties

On the Ku Klux Klan, see Robert A. Goldberg, "Beneath the Hood and Robe: A Socioeconomic Analysis of Ku Klux Klan Membership in Denver, Colorado, 1921–1925," *Western Historical Quarterly* 11 (April 1980): 180–98 and *Hooded Empire: The Ku Klux Klan in Colorado* (Urbana, 1981); John Creighton, "The Small-town Klan in Colorado," *Essays in Colorado History*, no. 2 (1983): 175–97; and James H. Davis, "Colorado under the Klan," *The Colorado Magazine* 42 (spring 1965): 93–108. For a recent reassessment, see Shawn Lay, ed., *The Invisible Empire in the West: Toward a New Historical Appraisal of the Ku Klux Klan of the 1920s* (Urbana, 1992), which includes a chapter on Denver by Robert Goldberg.

The red scare is described in Philip L. Cook, "Red Scare in Denver," *The Colorado Magazine* 43 (fall 1966): 309–26. For the tramway strike, see Stephen J. Leonard, "Bloody August: The Denver Tramway Strike of 1920," *Colorado Heritage* (summer 1995): 18–31.

Studies of agriculture include Irwin Thomle, "Rise of the Vegetable Industry in the San Luis Valley," *The Colorado Magazine* 26 (April 1949): 112–25 and Mary Rait, "Development of the Peach Industry in the Colorado River Valley," *The Colorado Magazine* 22 (November 1945): 247–58.

On the Colorado River Compact, see Norris Hundley, Jr., *Water and the West: The Colorado River Compact and the Politics of Water in the American West* (Berkeley, 1975) and Jennifer King, "The State of Wyoming's Participation in the Colorado River Compact," *Annals of Wyoming* 69 (spring 1997): 11–21. For Delph Carpenter, see Ralph Carr, "Delph Carpenter and River Compacts between Western States," *The Colorado Magazine* 21 (January 1944): 5–14 and two articles by Daniel Tyler: "Delph E. Carpenter, Father of Interstate Water Compacts: The Evolution of an Innovative Concept," *Colorado History*, no. 1 (1997): 87–105, and "The Silver Fox of the Rockies: Delphus

Emory Carpenter and the Colorado River Compact," *New Mexico Historical Review* 73 (January 1998): 25–43.

Aspects of the political scene are treated in John C. Livingston, "Governor William Sweet: Persistent Progressivism vs. Pragmatic Politics," *The Colorado Magazine* 54 (winter 1977): 1–25 and Leonard Schlup, "Colorado Crusader and Western Conservative: Lawrence C. Phipps and the Congressional Campaign of 1926," *Essays in Colorado History*, no. 9 (1989): 25–36. The activities of the City Club of Denver, founded in 1922 to focus on civic issues and municipal improvement, are discussed in Barbara Gibson, *The City Club of Denver, 1922–1997* (Denver, 1999).

Jess H. Lombard remembers Cripple Creek in the 1920s in "Three Years in the Cripple Creek Mines," *Essays in Colorado History*, no. 2 (1983): 235–50. On coal mining, see Marjorie Hornbein, "Josephine Roche: Social Worker and Coal Operator," *The Colorado Magazine* 53 (summer 1976): 243–60 and Phyllis Smith, *Once a Coal Miner: The Story of Colorado's Northern Coal Field* (Boulder, 1989).

On the 1921 flood, see Guy E. Macy, "The Pueblo Flood of 1921," *The Colorado Magazine* 17 (November 1940): 201–11. Joanne West Dodds provides a general overview of Pueblo history in *Pueblo: A Pictorial History* (Norfolk, Va., 1982) and *They All Came to Pueblo: A Social History* (Virginia Beach, Va., 1994). In addition, see Morris Cafky and John A. Haney, *Pueblo's Steel Town Trolleys* (Golden, 1999). The history of the Moffat Tunnel is treated in Ernest Morris, "A Glimpse of Moffat Tunnel History," *The Colorado Magazine* 4 (March 1927): 63–66 and in Edgar C. McMechen, *The Moffat Tunnel of Colorado* (2 vols., Denver, 1927).

For early aviation, see Roger D. Launius and Jessie L. Embry, "Cheyenne versus Denver: City Rivalry and the Quest for Transcontinental Air Routes," *Annals of Wyoming* 68 (summer 1996): 8–23 and Frank Harper, "Colorado's Forgotten Airbase: The Original Lowry Field, 1924–1938," *Colorado Heritage* (autumn 1994): 2–11. Jeff Miller focuses on the first Denver city airport in *Stapleton International Airport* (Boulder, 1983).

Chapter Twenty-Eight: Depression Decade

For the overall view, see Richard Lowitt, *The New Deal and the West* (Bloomington, 1984); Lowitt, ed., "The Great Depression in the West," *Journal of the West* 24 (October 1985): 3–94; and James T. Patterson, "The New Deal in the West," *Pacific Historical Review* 38 (August 1969): 317–27. John A. Brennan unravels the complexities of the silver issue in *Silver and the First New Deal* (Reno, 1969).

On Colorado, see Stephen J. Leonard, *Trials and Triumphs: A Colorado Portrait of the Great Depression, with FSA Photographs* (Niwot, 1993), and three works by James F. Wickens: "The New Deal in Colorado," *Pacific Historical Review* 38 (August 1969): 275–91; "Tightening the Colorado Purse Strings," *The Colorado Magazine* 46 (fall 1969): 271–86; and *Colorado in the Great Depression* (New York, 1979). Bernard Mergen describes the workings of the Unemployed Citizens' League of Denver in "Denver and the War on Unemployment," *The Colorado Magazine* 47 (fall 1970): 326–37. Elinor M. McGinn discusses the 1934 Democratic primary contest between incumbent governor Ed Johnson and Josephine Roche in "'A Bonnet in the Ring': Josephine Roche Runs for Governor," *Colorado Heritage* (summer 1997): 31–47.

Accounts of life on the plains during the Dust Bowl years can be found in John R. Wunder, Frances W. Kaye, and Vernon Carstensen, eds., *Americans View Their Dust Bowl Experience* (Niwot, 1999) and in Stephen S. Hart and Thomas J. Noel, "'You Got That Dust Pneumonie': Dust Bowls and Droughts in Colorado," *Colorado Heritage* (autumn 1997): 43–47. See also Vern Barry, "Caravan West: Family Survival during Hard Times on the Colorado Plains," *American West* 21 (July/August 1984): 47–50.

Works on Depression-era agriculture include Brian Q. Cannon, *Remaking the Agrarian Dream: New Deal Rural Resettlement in the Mountain West* (Albuquerque, 1996), which features accounts of farms in the San Luis Valley and on the Western Slope, and Leslie Hewes, *The Suitcase Farming Frontier: A Study in the Historical Geography of the Central Great Plains* (Lincoln, 1973), on suitcase farming in eastern Colorado and western Kansas. For the activities of one farmer in this area, see H. Craig Miner, *Harvesting the High Plains: John Kriss and the Business of Wheat Farming, 1920–1950* (Lawrence, 1998).

On the Taylor Grazing Act, see Joe A. Stout, Jr., "Cattlemen, Conservationists, and the Taylor Grazing Act," *New Mexico Historical Review* 45 (October 1970): 311–32 and the memoir of the first director of the Division of Grazing, Farrington R. Carpenter, *Confessions of a Maverick: An Autobiography* (Denver, 1984).

For accounts of transmountain diversion projects, see Donald Bernard Cole, "Transmountain Water Diversion in Colorado," parts 1 and 2, *The Colorado Magazine* 25 (March and May 1948): 49–65, 118–35. On the Big Thompson, see Daniel Tyler, *The Last Water Hole in the West: The Colorado–Big Thompson Project and the Northern Colorado Water Conservancy District* (Niwot, 1992); Oliver Knight, "Correcting Nature's Error: The Colorado–Big Thompson Project," *Agricultural History* 30 (October 1956): 157–69; and Fred N. Norcross, "Genesis of the Colorado–Big Thompson Project," *The Colorado Magazine* 30 (January 1953): 29–37. James E. Sherow, "The Chimerical Vision: Michael Creed Hinderlider and Progressive Engineering in Colorado," *Essays in Colorado History*, no. 9 (1989): 37–59, details the career of Colorado's state engineer, 1923–1954.

Chapter Twenty-Nine: Life in Colorado Between Two Wars

The history of welfare in Colorado is best summarized in Efay Nelson Grigg, "Social Legislation and the Welfare Program," which is chapter 12, vol. 2, of LeRoy R. Hafen, *Colorado and Its People: A Narrative and Topical History of the Centennial State* (4 vols., New York, 1948). There is also much information in the various publications of the Colorado League of Women Voters; these generally are concerned with contemporary problems, but collectively they form excellent introductions to a variety of special topics. An analysis of the pension amendment's early effects is Don C. Sowers, "Old Age Pensions in Colorado," University of Colorado *Bulletin* 37 (October 1938).

On education, see Duane A. Smith, *Sacred Trust: The Birth and Development of Fort Lewis College* (Niwot, 1991) and Ralph E. Ellsworth, ed., *A Voice from Colorado's Past for the Present* (Boulder, 1985), a collection of essays by George Norlin, who served as president of the University of Colorado between 1919 and 1939.

The winter 1993 issue of *Colorado Heritage* focuses on the decade between 1920 and 1930; the winter 1994 number covers the years between 1930 and 1940. Edgar M. Wahlberg, a liberal minister, provides a perspective on the times in *Voices in the Darkness:*

A Memoir (Boulder, 1983). For a young man's view, see David Lavender, *One Man's West* (New York, 1943). Myrtle D. Metz tells about her life in Crawford on the Western Slope in *Of Haviland and Honey: A Colorado Girlhood, 1924 to 1947* (Boulder, 1992); Keith A. Cook recalls his youth in western Kansas and eastern Colorado, 1928–1946, in "A Whiskey Train and a Doughnut Day: Coming of Age on the Eastern Colorado Plains," *Colorado Heritage* (spring 1998): 2–19. For a different look at Colorado, see Thomas Hornsby Ferril, *New and Selected Poems* (New York, 1927).

The growth of tourism during these years is particularly well described in Earl Pomeroy, *In Search of the Golden West: The Tourist in Western America* (New York, 1957). In addition, see Hal K. Rothman, *Devil's Bargains: Tourism in the Twentieth-Century American West* (Lawrence, 1998). For the Sand Dunes, see Frank C. Spencer, "Colorado's Desert of Shifting Sand," *The Colorado Magazine* 1 (September 1924): 241–51. On the Black Canyon, see Mark T. Warner, "Black Canyon of the Gunnison National Monument," *The Colorado Magazine* 11 (May 1934): 86–97 and Richard G. Beidleman, "The Black Canyon of the Gunnison National Monument," *The Colorado Magazine* 40 (July 1963): 161–78. Ferenc Szasz discusses other monuments in "Wheeler and Holy Cross: Colorado's 'Lost' National Monuments," *Journal of Forest History* 21 (July 1977): 133–44.

On the Central City opera, see Charles A. Johnson, *Opera in the Rockies: The History of the Central City Opera House Association, 1932–1992* (n.p., 1992); Allen Young, *Opera in Central City* (Denver, 1993); and Thomas J. Noel, ed., *The Glory That Was Gold* (n.p., 1992), which contains biographies of persons honored with opera house Memorial Chairs. For a brief glimpse of opera co-founder Anne Evans, see Thomas J. Steele, S.J., "Anne Evans's Christmas Pilgrimage," *Colorado History*, no. 1 (1997): 57–67.

Chapter Thirty: Decades of Boom, Years of Bust

The regional setting is provided in two works by Gerald Nash: *The American West Transformed: The Impact of the Second World War* (Bloomington, 1985) and *World War II and the West: Reshaping the Economy* (Lincoln, 1990), and in Arthur R. Gomez, *Quest for the Golden Circle: The Four Corners and the Metropolitan West, 1945–1970* (Albuquerque, 1994). See also Robert G. Athearn, *High Country Empire* (New York, 1960).

On the home front in Colorado, see "World War II," vol. 1, chapter 31, in LeRoy R. Hafen, ed., *Colorado and Its People: A Narrative and Topical History of the Centennial State* (4 vols., New York, 1948), which describes changes and events in the state during the era; Michael H. Levy and Patrick M. Scanlan, *Pursuit of Excellence: A History of Lowry Air Force Base, 1937–1987* (Denver, 1987); Stephen J. Leonard, "Denver at War: The Home Front in World War II," *Colorado Heritage* (Issue 4, 1987): 30–39; Joan Reese, "Two Enemies to Fight: Blacks Battle for Equality in Two World Wars," *Colorado Heritage* (Issue 1, 1990): 2–17; Christine Pfaff, "Bullets for the Yanks: Colorado's World War II Ammunition Factory," *Colorado Heritage* (summer 1992): 33–45; and Tom Lytle, "Shipbuilding on a 'Mountaintop': World War II's Rocky Mountain Fleet," *Colorado Heritage* (summer 1998): 14–24.

For Camp Hale and the Tenth Mountain Division, see Rene Coquoz, *The Invisible Men on Skis* (Boulder, 1970); Jack A. Benson, "Skiing at Camp Hale: Mountain Troops during World War II," *Western Historical Quarterly* 15 (April 1984): 161–74; Flint Whitlock and Bob Bishop, *Soldiers on Skis: A Pictorial Memoir of the 10th Mountain Division* (Boulder, 1992); and Tom Wolf, *Ice Crusaders: A Memoir of Cold War and Cold Sport* (Boulder, 1999).

On the Japanese in the United States during World War II, see Roger Daniels, *Concentration Camps U.S.A.: Japanese Americans and World War II* (New York, 1972). Studies of the camp at Amache in southeastern Colorado include M. Paul Holsinger, "Amache," *The Colorado Magazine* 41 (winter 1964): 50–60 and Melyn Johnson, "At Home in Amache: A Japanese-American Relocation Camp in Colorado," *Colorado Heritage* (Issue 1, 1989): 2–10, followed by "Uprooted: A Portfolio of Japanese-Americans in World War II," 12–27.

For European prisoners of war in Colorado, see Allen W. Paschal, "The Enemy in Colorado: German Prisoners of War, 1943–46," *The Colorado Magazine* 56 (summer/fall 1979): 119–42; Janet E. Worrall, "Prisoners on the Home Front: Community Reactions to German and Italian POWs in Northern Colorado, 1943–1946," *Colorado Heritage* (Issue 1, 1990): 32–47; and Daniel A. Jepson, "Camp Carson, Colorado: European Prisoners of War in the American West during World War II," *Midwest Review* 13 (1991): 32–53. Helmut Hörner describes his experiences at Camp Greeley and other U.S. POW camps in *A German Odyssey: The Journal of a German Prisoner of War,* trans. and ed. Allen Kent Powell (Golden, 1991).

For the uranium boom, see Michael B. Husband, "'History's Greatest Metal Hunt': The Uranium Boom on the Colorado Plateau," *Journal of the West* 21 (October 1982): 17–23; Raye C. Ringholz, *Uranium Frenzy: Boom and Bust on the Colorado Plateau* (New York, 1989); and Kevin J. Fernlund, "Mining the Atom: The Cold War Comes to the Colorado Plateau, 1948–1958," *New Mexico Historical Review* 69 (October 1994): 345–56. On molybdenum and the Climax mine, see Stephen M. Voynick, *Climax: The History of Colorado's Climax Molybdenum Mine* (Missoula, 1996) and Jim Ludwig, *The Climax Mine: An Old Man Remembers the Way It Was* (Buena Vista, 1999). Aspects of the "boom and bust" 1980s are covered in Steven Wilmsen, *Silverado: Neil Bush and the Savings and Loan Scandal* (Washington, D.C., 1991).

Chapter Thirty-One: Colorado and the Nation

On Colorado politics and governance generally, see Thomas E. Cronin and Robert D. Loevy, *Colorado Politics and Government: Governing the Centennial State* (Lincoln, 1993); Robert S. Lorch, *Colorado' s Government: Structure, Politics, Administration, and Policy* (6th ed., Niwot, 1997); and Roger Alan Walton, *Colorado: A Practical Guide to Its Government and Politics* (1973; rev. ed., Fort Collins, 1983). See also *The Colorado Constitution: Is It Adequate for the Next Century? Report of the Citizens' Assembly on the State Constitution, August 27–29, 1976* (Morrison, 1976). Current information can be found on the Colorado state government web site: www.state.co.us.

Works on the Colorado legislature include John A. Straayer, *The Colorado General Assembly* (1990; 2d ed., Boulder, 2000) and Joe Shoemaker, *Budgeting Is the Answer: A Story of a Unique Committee, the Joint Budget Committee (JBC) of Colorado* (Denver, 1977). Biographies of legislative leaders can be found in *Presidents and Speakers of the Colorado General Assembly: A Biographical Portrait from 1876* (Denver, 1980) and the "Colorado" section of

Nancy Weatherly Sharp and James Roger Sharp, eds., *American Legislative Leaders in the West, 1911–1994* (Westport, Conn., 1997).

On the Colorado governorship, see Richard D. Lamm and Duane A. Smith, *Pioneers and Politicians: 10 Colorado Governors in Profile* (Boulder, 1984). For Lamm's views, see *The Angry West: A Vulnerable Land and Its Future*, with Michael McCarthy (Boston, 1982); *Megatraumas: America at the Year 2000* (Boston, 1985); and *The Immigration Time Bomb: The Fragmenting of America*, with Gary Imhoff (New York, 1985). Governor John A. Love is profiled in Donald L. Walker, Jr., "Governor John A. Love: The Story of Colorado's Thirty-Sixth Governor," University of Colorado at Denver, *Historical Studies Journal* 17 (spring 2000).

Accounts of other Colorado politicians include Michael McCarthy, "He Fought for His West: Colorado Congressman Wayne Aspinall," *Colorado Heritage* (Issue 1, 1988): 33–44 and Herman J. Viola, *Ben Nighthorse Campbell: An American Warrior* (New York, 1993). Patricia Schroeder discusses her experiences as Colorado's first woman representative in *Champion of the Great American Family* (New York, 1989) and *24 Years of House Work . . . and the Place Is Still a Mess: My Life in Politics* (Kansas City, 1998). On Colorado native and University of Colorado football star Byron R. White, who served on the United States Supreme Court between 1962 and 1993, see Dennis Hutchinson, *The Man Who Once Was Whizzer White: A Portrait of Justice Byron R. White* (New York, 1998).

President Dwight D. Eisenhower (1953–1961) spent many vacations in Colorado, the home of his wife, Mamie. For details, see Maxine Benson, "Dwight D. Eisenhower and the West," *Journal of the West* 34 (April 1995): 58–65. In 1955 Eisenhower suffered a heart attack after playing golf at the suburban Denver Cherry Hills Country Club; Clarence G. Lasby analyzes the political implications of his illness in *Eisenhower's Heart Attack: How Ike Beat Heart Disease and Held on to the Presidency* (Lawrence, 1997). See also "The Picture that Reassured the World," *Colorado Heritage* (winter 1996): 31–35, on a famous photograph of the recuperating president waving from the roof of Fitzsimons Army Hospital.

Gerald D. Nash discusses the influential role of the federal government in western development in *The Federal Landscape: An Economic History of the Twentieth-Century West* (Tucson, 1999). For the Air Force Academy, see George V. Fagan, *The Air Force Academy: An Illustrated History* (Boulder, 1988) and Robert Bruegmann, ed., *Modernism at Mid-century: The Architecture of the United States Air Force Academy* (Chicago, 1994). See also "The Capps Homestead," *Colorado Heritage* (winter 1996): 38–39, on the history of the Air Force Academy site. The activities of Martin Marietta (now the Lockheed Martin Corporation) and Ball Brothers (Ball Aerospace and Technologies Corporation) are related in Rick W. Sturdevant and David N. Spires, "Mile-High Ventures: Highlights from Colorado Aerospace History, 1923–1997," *Journal of the West* 36 (July 1997): 67–77. Andrew Gulliford recounts the oil-shale saga in "The Tiger Empties the Tank: The Oil-Shale Boom-and-Bust in Colorado," *Journal of the West* 28 (October 1989): 19–25 and in *Boomtown Blues: Colorado Oil Shale, 1885–1985* (Niwot, 1989).

On the underground nuclear blasts, see Christian J. Buys, "Isaiah's Prophecy: Project Plowshare in Colorado," *Colorado Heritage* (Issue 1, 1989): 28–39. For the history of Rocky Flats, see John J. Kennedy, Jr., "Annihilation Beckons: A Brief History of Colorado's Nuclear Bomb-Trigger Factory," *Colorado Heritage* (spring 1994): 1–37, and two works by Len Ackland: *Making a Real Killing: Rocky Flats and the Nuclear West* (Albuquerque, 1999), and "Rocky Flats: Expect a Fire, But Produce," *Montana* 50 (summer 2000): 36–49. Bruce Hevly and John M. Findlay, eds., *The Atomic West* (Seattle, 1998) and Kevin J. Fernlund, ed., *The Cold War in the American West, 1945–1989* (Albuquerque, 1998) furnish the overall perspective.

Chapter Thirty-Two: Urban Colorado

Carl Abbott, *The Metropolitan Frontier: Cities in the Modern American West* (Tucson, 1993) provides an overview of the urban West since 1940. For Denver, see Stephen J. Leonard and Thomas J. Noel, *Denver: Mining Camp to Metropolis* (Niwot, 1990) and the other Denver histories cited in Chapter 14. Phil Goodstein offers an alternative view in *Big Money in the Big City*, vol. 1 of *Denver in Our Time: A People's History of the Modern Mile High City* (Denver, 1999). Pictorial histories include Sandra Dallas, *Yesterday's Denver* (Miami, 1974); William C. Jones and Kenton Forrest, *Denver: A Pictorial History from Frontier Camp to Queen City of the Plains* (1973; 3d ed., Golden, 1993); Morey Engle, *Denver Comes of Age: The Postwar Photography of Morey Engle* (Boulder, 1994); and Thomas J. Noel, *Mile High City: An Illustrated History of Denver* (Denver, 1997).

George V. Kelley profiles Denver mayors Benjamin Stapleton, Quigg Newton, Will Nicholson, Richard Batterton, Tom Currigan, and Bill McNichols in *The Old Gray Mayors of Denver* (Boulder, 1974). See also Stephen J. Leonard, "Denver's Postwar Awakening: Quigg Newton, Mayor, 1947–1955," *Colorado Heritage* (spring 1997): 13–24 and Rodney E. Hero and Kathleen M. Beatty, "The Elections of Federico Peña as Mayor of Denver: Analysis and Implications," *Social Science Quarterly* 70 (June 1989): 300–310.

Lee Olson analyzes crusading Denver editor and Democratic activist Eugene Cervi in "The Annoying Gene Cervi: A Terror of Colorado Journalism," *Colorado Heritage* (spring 2000): 33–38. Gene Amole, another longtime Denver newspaperman, offers a personal view of his city in his *Rocky Mountain News* columns, collected in *Morning* (Denver, 1983); *Amole Again* (Denver, 1985); and *Amole, One More Time* (Boulder, 1998).

Accounts of Denver suburbs include three works published by the Arvada Historical Society: *Waters of Gold: A History of Arvada, Colorado, during the Period 1850–1870* (Arvada, 1973); *More Than Gold: A History of Arvada, Colorado, during the Period 1870–1904* (Arvada, 1976); and *Arvada, Just between You and Me: A History of Arvada, Colorado, during the Period 1904–1941* (Arvada, 1985); Steven F. Mehls, Carol J. Drake, and James E. Fell, Jr., *Aurora: Gateway to the Rockies* (Evergreen, 1985); Robert J. McQuarie and C. W. Buchholtz, *Littleton, Colorado: Settlement to Centennial* (Littleton, 1990); and Patricia K. Wilcox, ed., *Lakewood, Colorado: An Illustrated Biography* (Lakewood, 1994).

On Boulder and its environs, see Phyllis Smith, *A Look at Boulder from Settlement to City* (Boulder, 1981); Thomas J. Noel and Dan W. Corson, *Boulder County: An Illustrated History* (Carlsbad, Calif., 1999); and "A Promise Kept: The Denver-Boulder Toll Road," in the 1950s special issue of *Colorado Heritage* (winter 1996): 13–15.

Aspects of rural life in the western states are discussed in R. Douglas Hurt, ed., *The Rural West since World War II* (Lawrence, 1998). For a look at rural Colorado during the 1970s, see Nancy Wood, *The Grass Roots People: An American Requiem* (New York, 1978). Two San Luis Valley ranches near Saguache are profiled in Sam Bingham, *The Last Ranch: A Colorado Community and the Coming Desert* (New York, 1996) and Stephen M. Voynick,

Riding the Higher Range: The Story of Colorado's Coleman Ranch and Coleman Natural Beef (Boulder, 1998). Joan M. Jensen recounts her experiences in a San Luis Valley commune in the early 1970s in *Promise to the Land: Essays on Rural Women* (Albuquerque, 1991). On the Drop City commune near Trinidad, see "'No Right to Be Poor': Colorado's Drop City," *Colorado Heritage* (winter 1998): 14–21.

On the Ute Indians after their removal to reservations, see Richard K. Young, *The Ute Indians of Colorado in the Twentieth Century* (Norman, 1997) and Katherine M. B. Osburn, *Southern Ute Women: Autonomy and Assimilation on the Reservation, 1887–1934* (Albuquerque, 1998). Nancy Wood portrays contemporary Ute culture in *When Buffalo Free the Mountains: The Survival of America's Ute Indians* (Garden City, 1980). Jim Carrier profiles a Ute family on the Ute Mountain Ute reservation and a contemporary ranching family in the Gunnison Valley in *West of the Divide: Voices from a Ranch and a Reservation* (Golden, 1992).

Works on Hispanic Americans generally include Carey McWilliams, *North from Mexico: The Spanish-speaking People of the United States* (1948; new edition updated by Matt S. Meier, New York, 1990); Meier and Feliciano Ribera, *Mexican Americans, American Mexicans: From Conquistadors to Chicanos* (1972; rev. ed., New York, 1993); David J. Gutierrez, "Significant to Whom?: Mexican Americans and the History of the American West," *Western Historical Quarterly* 24 (November 1993): 519–39; Richard Griswold del Castillo and Arnoldo de Leon, *North to Aztlan: A History of Mexican Americans in the United States* (New York, 1996); and David Maciel and Isidro D. Ortiz, eds., *Chicanas/Chicanos at the Crossroads: Social, Economic, and Political Change* (Tucson, 1996). Ernesto Vigil focuses on Rodolfo "Corky" Gonzales and the Crusade for Justice in "Rodolfo Gonzales and the Advent of the Crusade for Justice," in Vincent C. De Baca, ed., *La Gente: Hispano History and Life in Colorado,* Colorado History, no. 2 (Denver, 1998): 155–201 and *The Crusade for Justice: Chicano Militancy and the Government's War on Dissent* (Madison, 1999).

Chapter Thirty-Three: The Old and the New

Howard R. Lamar contrasts Colorado in 1876 and 1976 in "Colorado: The Centennial State in the Bicentennial Year," *The Colorado Magazine* 53 (spring 1976): 109–28, while Duane A. Smith examines the differences and similarities between 1896 and 1996 in Colorado and Wyoming in "'Always begin right here where you are': The Changing Faces of the Central Rocky Mountains," *Journal of the West* 37 (July 1998): 55–65. Both dramatic change and timeless continuity are evident in the paired photographs taken a century apart by William Henry Jackson and John Fielder and reproduced in *Colorado 1870–2000* (Englewood, 1999), with accompanying essays by Ed Marston, Roderick Nash, Eric Paddock, and Fielder.

Accounts of nature's wrath include "The Night the South Platte Got Even," *Colorado Heritage* (winter 1997): 24–28, on the 1965 flood; David McComb, *Big Thompson: Profile of a Natural Disaster* (Boulder, 1980), on the 1976 flood; and Andrew Gulliford, "Fire on the Mountain: Tragic Death and Memorialization of the Storm King Fourteen," *Montana* 47 (summer 1997): 44–57 and John N. Maclean, *Fire on the Mountain: The True Story of the South Canyon Fire* (New York, 1999), on the 1994 forest fire near Glenwood Springs.

Studies of skiing in Colorado include Abbott Fay, *A History of Skiing in Colorado* (Ouray, 2000); Jack A. Benson, "Before Skiing Was Fun," *Western Historical Quarterly* 8 (October 1977): 431–41; and Annie Gilbert Coleman, "The Unbearable Whiteness of Skiing," *Pacific Historical Review* 65 (November 1996): 583–614. On Winter Park, see *Winter Park: Colorado's Favorite for Fifty Years, 1940–1990* ([Denver], 1989) and on Vail, Peter W. Seibert, with William Oscar Johnson, *Vail: Triumph of a Dream* (Boulder, 2000) and Dick Hauserman, *The Inventors of Vail* (Edwards, Colo., 2000).

General works on Aspen include Peggy Clifford, *To Aspen and Back* (New York, 1980) and Kathleen Krieger Daily and Gaylord T. Guenin, *Aspen: The Quiet Years* (Aspen, 1994). Annie Gilbert Coleman discusses life between the end of the mining boom and the coming of the ski industry in "'A Hell of a Time All the Time': Farmers, Ranchers, and the Roaring Fork Valley during the 'Quiet Years,'" *Montana* 47 (spring 1997): 32–45. Jon T. Coleman explores myth and reality in nearby Ashcroft in "The Men in McArthur's Bar: The Cultural Significance of the Margins," *Western Historical Quarterly* 31 (spring 2000): 47–68.

Coloradans and visitors alike also climb mountains. Histories of mountaineering include William M. Bueler, *Roof of the Rockies: A History of Colorado Mountaineering* (1974; 2d ed., Evergreen, 1986); Hugh E. Kingery, assisted by Elinor Eppich Kingery, *The Colorado Mountain Club: The First Seventy-Five Years of a Highly Individual Corporation, 1912–1987* (Evergreen, 1988); and Janet Robertson, *The Magnificent Mountain Women: Adventures in the Colorado Rockies* (Lincoln, 1990).

The Broncos' triumphs and disasters are described in Woodrow Paige, *Orange Madness* (New York, 1978) and Russell Martin, *The Color Orange: A Superbowl Season with the Denver Broncos* (New York, 1987). On pre-Rockies baseball, see Mark S. Foster, *The Denver Bears: From Sandlots to Sellouts* (Boulder, 1983).

For an introduction to historic preservation, see Elaine Freed, *Preserving the Great Plains and Rocky Mountains* (Albuquerque, 1992). Robert L. Spude describes preservation efforts in Buckskin Joe in "Looking Back at 'The Rush to the Rockies': Preserving Four 1860s Gold Camps," *Journal of the West* 35 (October 1996): 7–17. Victor J. Danilov includes information on more than six hundred museums, historic sites, and related facilities in *Colorado Museums and Historic Sites* (Boulder, 2000). Founded in 1970, Historic Denver, Inc., has made impressive contributions to preservation in the city, including the publication of Richard Brettell, *Historic Denver: The Architects and the Architecture, 1858–1893* (Denver, 1973); Thomas J. Noel and Barbara Norgren, *Denver: The City Beautiful and Its Architects, 1893–1941* (Denver, 1987); and the Historic Denver Guides to buildings and neighborhoods (1995–).

Thomas J. Noel provides an overview of Colorado's architectural development in *Buildings of Colorado* (New York, 1997), a volume in the Buildings of the United States series commissioned by the Society of Architectural Historians. Other works on architects and architecture include James E. Hansen II, ed., *Challenge to Build: A History of Public Works and APWA in Colorado* (Fort Collins, 1987); Francine Haber, Kenneth R. Fuller, and David N. Wetzel, *Robert S. Roeschlaub, Architect of the Emerging West, 1843–1923* (Denver, 1988); Jan Jennings, "Frank J. Grodavent, Western Army Architect," *Essays in Colorado History*, no. 11 (1990): 1–23; and Dan W. Corson, "Architect J.J.B. Benedict and His Magnificent Unbuilt Buildings," *Colorado Heritage* (summer 1997): 16–30.

Environmental concerns came to the forefront with the battle over the 1976 Olympics. For details, see Mark S. Foster, "Colorado's Defeat of the 1976 Winter

Olympics," *The Colorado Magazine* 53 (spring 1976): 163–86 and "Little Lies: The Colorado 1976 Winter Olympics," *Colorado Heritage* (winter 1998): 22–33.

Other struggles were fought over the Animas–La Plata and the Two Forks Dam projects. For details, see Sandra K. Davis, "Water Politics in Colorado: Change, or Business as Usual?" in *Politics in the Postwar American West,* ed. Richard Lowitt (Norman, 1995).

Thomas Hornsby Ferril's poem "Stories of Three Summers, Colorado, 1776 * 1876 * 1976," can be found in Robert C. Baron, Stephen J. Leonard, and Thomas J. Noel, eds., *Thomas Hornsby Ferril and the American West* (Golden, 1996), which includes a number of other Ferril poems as well as biographical and critical essays.

Chapter Thirty-Four: "We Can't Remember Who We Were Tomorrow"

The winter 2000 issue of *Colorado Heritage* is devoted to the decade of the 1990s. In *DIA and Other Scams,* vol. 2 of *Denver in Our Time: A People's History of the Modern Mile High City* (Denver, 2000), Phil Goodstein focuses on the period from Federico Peña's 1983 election as mayor to 2000. Goodstein and attorney Walter L. Gerash narrate the story of a notorious 1991 Denver bank robbery and its aftermath in *Murders in the Bank Vault: The Father's Day Massacre and the Trial of James King* (Denver, 1997).

Several books chronicle the Colorado Rockies first year, including Alan Gottlieb, *In the Shadow of the Rockies: An Outsider's Look Inside a New Major League Baseball Team* (Niwot, 1994); Bob Kravitz, *Mile High Madness: A Year with the Colorado Rockies* (New York, 1994); and *Colorado Rockies: The Inaugural Season* (Golden, 1993). See also the works on Colorado baseball history cited in Chapter 8.

Recent studies that deal with western environmental issues include Ed Marston, ed., *Reopening the Western Frontier* (Washington, D.C., 1989); Donald Worster, *Under Western Skies: Nature and History in the American West* (New York, 1992); and John B. Wright, *Rocky Mountain Divide: Selling and Saving the West* (Austin, 1993).

The "New West"—its characteristics, its resources, its people—is also the subject of much current discussion and debate. A good starting point is the *Atlas of the New West: Portrait of a Changing Region,* ed. William E. Riebsame et al. (New York, 1997), a project of the Center of the American West at the University of Colorado, Boulder. More information is available at the center's web site: www.centerwest.org. See also *"Atlas of the New West: A Forum," Pacific Historical Review* 67 (August 1998): 379–420; Michael L. Johnson, *New Westers: The West in Contemporary American Culture* (Lawrence, 1996); and Richard Aquila, ed., *Wanted Dead or Alive: The American West in Popular Culture* (Urbana, 1996). Peter R. Decker offers a personal view of Ouray County's transformation from isolated ranching and mining backwater to New West mecca in *Old Fences, New Neighbors* (Tucson, 1998).

Chapter Thirty-Five: Colorado in the New Millennium

The sources available for the study of contemporary Colorado, both in print and on the web, are voluminous and await only the appearance of the imaginative researcher. Basic to any study are the files of the *Rocky Mountain News* (www.rockymountainnews.com) and the *Denver Post* (www.denverpost. com), as well as issues of specialized publications such as the Denver weekly *Westword* (www.westword.com). *Post* columnist Ed Quillen views current events and issues from outside the metropolitan area in *Deep in the Heart of the Rockies: Selected Columns from the* Denver Post, *1985–1998*, with a foreword by Richard Lamm (Westcliffe, Colo., 1998).

In recent years a number of magazines have appeared that both promote and reflect life in present-day Colorado. See, for example, *Colorado Homes & Lifestyles Magazine* (1980–); *Colorado Expression* (1992–); *5280, Denver's Mile-High Magazine* (1994–); *Coloradobiz* (1999–), continuing the earlier *Colorado Business Magazine*; *Steamboat Magazine* (1978/79–); and *Aspen Magazine* (1988–).

For an introduction to the issues surrounding growth and urban sprawl, see Michael E. Long, "Colorado's Front Range," *National Geographic*, November 1996, 86–103, and two series in the *Denver Post*: "Snapshot of Colorado," beginning April 12, 1998, and "Growth in the '90s," February 7, 1999. Information on the 2000 census is available at www.census.gov.

Legalized gambling brought enormous changes to Central City, Black Hawk, and Cripple Creek in the 1990s. See Patricia A. Stokowski, *Riches and Regrets: Betting on Gambling in Two Colorado Mountain Towns* (Niwot, 1996); Katherine Jensen and Audie Blevins, *The Last Gamble: Betting on the Future in Four Rocky Mountain Mining Towns* (Tucson, 1998); Eric L. Clements and Duane A. Smith, "Uneasy Money: The High-Stakes Consequence of Low-Stakes Gambling for Black Hawk, Central City, and Cripple Creek, Colorado," *Mining History Journal* (1997): 55–65; and Ariana Harner, "The Second Time Around: Legal Gambling Returns to Colorado," *Colorado Heritage* (winter 2000): 35–37.

The web site of the Colorado Tourism Office, created by the legislature to promote Colorado as a tourist and travel destination, is www.colorado.com. Bruce Caughey and Dean Winstanley, *The Colorado Guide* (1989; 4th ed., Golden, 1997) includes details on outdoor activities, local events and festivals, scenic drives, parks and wilderness areas, and historic sites and museums. On the state park system, see Martin G. Kleinsorge, *Exploring Colorado State Parks* (1992; 2d ed., Niwot, 1997). Information on national parks and monuments can be found on the National Park Service web site, www.nps.gov.

Paul Stephen Dempsey, Andrew R. Goetz, and Joseph S. Szyliowicz, *Denver International Airport: Lessons Learned* (New York, 1997) provides an in-depth look at DIA. See also David N. Wetzel, "The Road to DIA," *Colorado Heritage* (winter 2000): 30–34.

On Interstate 70 through Glenwood Canyon, see Conrad F. Schader, *Glenwood Canyon: From Origin to Interstate* (Golden, 1996) and Ariana Harner, "The Delicate Salvation of Glenwood Canyon," *Colorado Heritage* (winter 2000): 23–29.

For information on sports in the 1990s, see James Whiteside, *Colorado: A Sports History* (Niwot, 1999), especially chapter 10 on the Avalanche and the history of hockey in Colorado. See also Patrick Fraker, "A Long Time Coming: Colorado's Rockies and Avalanche," *Colorado Heritage* (winter 2000): 13–22.

Mark S. Foster discusses Coors Field and its predecessors in "Mile High Greenfields: Denver's Notable Ballparks," *Colorado Heritage* (spring 1995): 35–43. See also Diane Bakke and Jackie Davis, *Places around the Bases: A Historic Tour of the Coors Field Neighborhood* (Englewood, 1995) and Kenton H. Forrest, *The Railroads of Coors Field: A Brief History of Railroading in the Vicinity of Coors Field* (Golden, 1995).

Colorado's Governors, Senators, and Congressional Representatives

GOVERNORS OF COLORADO TERRITORY

William Gilpin (R). 1861–1862
John Evans (R) 1862–1865
Alexander Cummings (R) . . . 1865–1867
A. Cameron Hunt (R) 1867–1869

Edward McCook (R) 1869–1873
Samuel H. Elbert (R) 1873–1874
Edward McCook (R) 1874–1875
John L. Routt (R). 1875–1876

GOVERNORS OF COLORADO

John L. Routt (R). 1876–1879
Frederick W. Pitkin (R) 1879–1883
James B. Grant (D) 1883–1885
Benjamin H. Eaton (R). 1885–1887
Alva Adams (D) 1887–1889
Job A. Cooper (R) 1889–1891
John L. Routt (R). 1891–1893
Davis H. Waite (Populist). . . . 1893–1895
Albert W. McIntire (R) 1895–1897
Alva Adams (D) 1897–1899
Charles S. Thomas (D). 1899–1901
James B. Orman (D). 1901–1903
James H. Peabody (R) 1903–1905
Alva Adams (D) 1905–
James H. Peabody (R) 1905–
Jesse F. McDonald (R) 1905–1907
Henry A. Buchtel (R) 1907–1909
John F. Shafroth (D). 1909–1913
Elias M. Ammons (D) 1913–1915
George A. Carlson (R) 1915–1917

Julius C. Gunter (D) 1917–1919
Oliver H. Shoup (R). 1919–1923
William E. Sweet (D). 1923–1925
Clarence J. Morley (R) 1925–1927
William H. Adams (D) 1927–1933
Edwin C. Johnson (D) 1933–1937
Ray H. Talbot (D). 1937–
Teller Ammons (D) 1937–1939
Ralph L. Carr (R). 1939–1943
John Vivian (R) 1943–1947
William Knous (D) 1947–1950
Walter Johnson (D) 1950–1951
Dan Thornton (R) 1951–1955
Edwin Johnson (D) 1955–1957
Stephen McNichols (D) 1957–1963
John Love (R) 1963–1973
John Vanderhoof (R) 1973–1975
Richard Lamm (D). 1975–1987
Roy Romer (D) 1987–1999
Bill Owens (R). 1999–

UNITED STATES SENATORS FROM COLORADO

Henry M. Teller (R) 1876–1882
Jerome B. Chaffee (R) 1876–1879
Nathaniel P. Hill (R) 1879–1885
George M. Chilcott (R) 1882–
Horace A. W. Tabor (R) 1883–
Thomas M. Bowen (R) 1883–1889
Henry M. Teller (R/D) 1885–1909
Edward O. Wolcott (R) 1889–1901
Thomas M. Patterson (D). . . . 1901–1907
Simon Guggenheim (R) 1907–1913
Charles J. Hughes, Jr. (D). . . . 1909–1911
Charles S. Thomas (D) 1913–1921
John F. Shafroth (D) 1913–1919
Lawrence C. Phipps (R) 1919–1931
Samuel D. Nicholson (R) 1921–1923
Alva B. Adams (D) 1923–1925
Rice W. Means (R) 1925–1927
Charles W. Waterman (R) . . . 1927–1932

Edward P. Costigan (D) 1931–1937
Walter Walker (D) 1932–
Karl C. Schuyler (R) 1932–1933
Alva B. Adams (D) 1933–1942
Edwin C. Johnson (D) 1937–1955
Eugene Millikin (R) 1942–1957
Gordon Allott (R) 1955–1973
John Carroll (D) 1957–1963
Peter Dominick (R) 1963–1975
Floyd Haskell (D) 1973–1979
Gary Hart (D) 1975–1987
William Armstrong (R) 1979–1991
Tim Wirth (D) 1987–1993
Hank Brown (R) 1991–1997
Ben Nighthorse Campbell
   (D/R) 1993–
Wayne Allard (R) 1997–

UNITED STATES REPRESENTATIVES FROM COLORADO

James B. Belford (R) 1876–1877
Thomas M. Patterson (D). . . . 1877–1879
James B. Belford (R) 1879–1885
George G. Symes (R) 1885–1889
Hosea Townsend (R) 1889–1893
John C. Bell (P/D) 1893–1903
Lafe Pence (P) 1893–1895
John F. Shafroth (R/D) 1895–1904
Herschel H. Hogg (R) 1903–1907
Franklin E. Brooks (R) 1903–1907
Robert W. Bonygne (R) 1904–1909
George W. Cook (R) 1907–1909
Warren A. Haggot (R) 1907–1909
Edward T. Taylor (D) 1909–1941
Atterson W. Rucker (D) 1909–1913
John A. Martin (D) 1909–1913
Edward Keating (D) 1913–1919
George J. Kindel (D) 1913–1915
H. H. Seldomridge (D) 1913–1915
Benjamin C. Hilliard (D) 1915–1919
Charles B. Timberlake (R) . . . 1915–1933

William N. Vaile (R) 1919–1927
Guy U. Hardy (R) 1919–1933
S. Harrison White (D) 1927–1928
William R. Eaton (R) 1928–1933
Lawrence Lewis (D) 1933–1943
John A. Martin (D) 1933–1939
Fred Cummings (D) 1933–1941
William E. Burney (D) 1940–1941
J. Edgar Chenoweth (R) 1941–1949
                                    1951–1965
William S. Hill (R) 1941–1959
Robert Rockwell (R) 1941–1949
Dean Gillespie (R) 1944–1947
John Carroll (D) 1947–1951
John Marsalis (D) 1949–1951
Wayne Aspinall (D) 1949–1973
Byron Rogers (D) 1951–1971
Byron Johnson (D) 1959–1961
Peter Dominick (R) 1961–1963
Donald Brotzman (R) 1963–1965
                                    1967–1975

Roy McVicker (D) 1965–1967
Frank Evans (D) 1965–1979
James McKevitt (R) 1971–1973
Patricia Schroeder (D) 1973–1997
James Johnson (R) 1973–1981
William Armstrong (R) 1973–1979
Tim Wirth (D) 1975–1987
Ray Kogovsek (D) 1979–1985
Ken Kramer (R) 1979–1987
Hank Brown (R). 1981–1991
Dan Schaefer (R) 1983–1999

Mike Strang (R) 1985–1987
David Skaggs (D) 1987–1999
Ben Nighthorse Campbell (D) 1987–1993
Joel Hefley (R) 1987–
Wayne Allard (R) 1991–1997
Scott McInnis (R) 1993–
Dianna DeGette (D) 1997–
Robert Schaffer (R) 1997–
Thomas Tancredo (R) 1999–
Mark Udall (D) 1999–

Picture Credits

Page 7, Mesa Verde National Park; 16, 22, courtesy, Colorado Historical Society (CHS); 27, *Account of an Expedition from Pittsburgh to the Rocky Mountains* (1822), CHS; 32, *The Santa Fe Trail*, U.S. Department of the Interior, National Park Service, 1963; 38, *Journal of Lt. J. W. Abert, from Bent's Fort to St. Louis in 1845* (Washington, D.C., 1846), CHS; 46, CHS; 49, Richard H. Kern, "Pike's Peak, 1848, 'Mon Songe'," 1853, watercolor and graphite on paper, museum number 1975.16.1, Amon Carter Museum, Fort Worth, Texas; 50, *Reports of Expeditions and Surveys . . . 1853-1854,* vol. 2, CHS; 52, LeRoy R. and Ann W. Hafen, *Our State: Colorado* (Denver, 1966), CHS; 62, Kansas State Historical Society, Topeka; 64, William N. Byers and John H. Kellom, *Handbook to the Gold Fields of Nebraska and Kansas* (Chicago, 1859); 66, The Denver Public Library, Western History Department (DPLW); 74, 76, 81, CHS; 86, First Federal Savings and Loan Association of Denver; 87, DPLW; 91, *Frank Leslie's Illustrated Newspaper,* May 17, 1879, p. 169, CHS; 106, 108, CHS; 113, *Harper's Weekly,* May 30, 1874, p. 457, CHS; 119, CHS; 127, 131, DPLW; 135, CHS; 140, A. A. Hayes, *New Colorado and the Santa Fe Trail* (New York, 1880), p. 55, DPLW; 150, CHS; 156 (Leadville), Leadville Civic Center Association; 156 (Red Mountain), CHS; 164, 168, 171, CHS; 177, U.S. Geological Survey; 178, C. M. Engel Collection; 179, U.S. Geological Survey; 185, Center of Southwest Studies, Durango; 188, *Immigrant's Guide to the Great San Luis Park* (Denver, 1884), CHS; 193, 198, 200, 204, 214, 221, CHS; 223, *Denver Republican,* November 5, 1893, p. 1, CHS; 229, City of Greeley Museums, Permanent Collection; 232, 233, 240, 248, 257, 260, 265, 266, CHS; 278, Special Collections, The Colorado College Library; 287, DPLW; 292, 294, CHS; 305, DPLW; 308, 311, 317, 325, CHS; 326, Special Collections, The Colorado College Library; 328, Center of Southwest Studies, Durango; 335, Mesa Verde National Park; 337, Rob DeNier; 340, CHS; 342, *Durango Herald;* 349, CHS; 351, U.S. Forest Service; 352, CHS; 362, Archives, University of Colorado at Boulder Libraries (World Citizens Scrapbook); 364, Jerry Hanes; 368, Colorado Aerial Photo; 371, Jerry Hanes; 374, Durango Herald; 376, Duane A. Smith; 381, Durango Herald; 385, courtesy, Sarah Law; 387, Dr. Larry Cohen, DVM; 389, Durango Herald.

Index